Contents

INTRODUCTION

The purpose of this manual is to help marketing lecturers to make full use of the first edition of the textbook *Principles of Marketing*. The difficulty in designing such a manual is that it cannot be all things to all people. Having looked closely at several instructors' manuals for other texts, and indeed having tried to use them in practice, we decided that we had to tread a very fine line between being too bland and obvious on the one hand, and being far too detailed and prescriptive on the other! We hope that we have created a manual that will:

- Stimulate lecturers in planning their own lectures, seminars and assessment activities
- give sufficiently detailed answers to the book's case studies to allow the tutor to provide a fulfilling debrief in class
- give sufficiently detailed answers to the book's case studies to allow different tutors to run the same case study to a consistent quality level with different seminar groups
- give material that is sufficiently concisely presented to be a useful guideline to those lecturers who are pressed for time
- provide additional materials that can be used to construct more varied seminar activities
- provide ideas for assignment work, covering group and individual work, and written and verbally presented work.

This manual is divided into two parts. The first part relates directly to material within the main textbook. It offers:

- Suggested lecture outlines, incorporating the 100 OHP transparencies supplied with the text. Each outline contains:
  ⇒ Major points to be covered in the lecture, with page number references from the main text
  ⇒ suggested OHP transparencies.
  There is a lecture outline for each chapter, except chapter 26 which stands alone as an overview of the book and as an interesting and detailed insight into the real world of marketing.
- Outline answers to the end of chapter *Questions for Review* with page numbers to refer the reader back to the relevant sections of the main text.
- Commentary relating to the end of chapter *Questions for Discussion* either outlining the broad content of an expected answer or giving tutors general guidelines on what students ought to be researching, as appropriate.
- Detailed answers to the text's case studies, and some supplementary questions and answers.
- A discussion question and outline answer to it for each of the *Marketing in Action* vignettes.
- Suggested assignments, some of which relate to *Questions for Review* or *Discussion*, some of which are unique to this manual. There is a mixture of practical assignments that could be used as group work and more conceptual essay style assignments for individual work.

In using some of the above material for seminars, a number of points should be noted:

- Some of the shorter or more straightforward cases can be done from scratch within a one hour session, particularly if students working are working in small groups each of which can be allocated just one or two questions to concentrate on
- all the cases, of course, can be prepared in advance of a seminar by the students
- supplementary questions, where provided, can be used to add an unpredictable element into a seminar or to liven up a slow-moving or flagging seminar session
- tutors have the option to make up a seminar session consisting of a selection of *Questions for Review* or *Discussion*, or mini-cases based on the *Marketing in Action* vignettes
- as with any case study type of material, the answers given herein represent our interpretation of the world. We do not claim to include absolutely every possibility, nor do we claim to be always 'right'! We would welcome any feedback or alternative angles on the cases from you.

The second part of this manual includes 10 additional case studies, which can be used either as seminar material or for assignment or examination purposes. These cases have been written in the same style as those in the main textbook, and thus students should be reasonably confident in tackling them. Model answers have not been given for security purposes in case they are to be used as assignments. The additional cases do have indicative questions attached and they relate to the various sections of the main textbook as follows:

- Section 1: ConvaTec (UK): Leaders in Stoma Care
- Section 2: A Market Full of Beans; SNCF Seeks Relationships
- Section 3: Directory Publishing
- Section 4: Price Volatility
- Section 5: Category Management; Royal Mail by Rail; Fine Foods Deserve Fine Marketing
- Sections 6 and 7: Power Generation; China's Flying High into the Future.

An updating service on these and all the cases and marketing in action vignettes in the text is expected to be introduced later in 1997.

By providing lecture outlines for 25 different chapters, we have, of course given you far more material than can be covered in the average one semester module with 13 or 15 teaching weeks. We would like, therefore, to suggest the following programme of lectures and supporting reading to cover one semester:

Week	Topic & chapter(s)
1	*Introduction:* chapter 1
2	*The Marketing Environment:* chapter 2
3	*Consumer Behaviour:* chapter 3
4	*Organisational Behaviour:* chapter 4
5	*Segmentation:* chapter 5
6	*Market research:* chapter 6
7	*Product:* mainly drawing on chapter 7, with elements of 8 added
8	*Price:* mainly drawing on chapter 10, with elements of 11 added
9	*Place:* chapter 12
10	*Promotion I:* chapter 15
11	*Promotion II:* draws on the basic elements of chapters 16-20, depending on the lecturer's preference.
12	*Marketing strategy:* mainly drawing on chapter 21 with elements of 22.
13	*Review or Marketing Application:* some might use this session to draw the module to a close with a broad review. Others might prefer to do this through focusing on a specific application, such as International marketing, retailing, small business, or services marketing.

In terms of seminar material, a case can be selected from the chapter(s) relevant to each lecture. Within this manual, each case has specified learning objectives to guide lecturer choice. Otherwise, as mentioned earlier, the lecturer is free to create seminars from the other material offered.

Finally, we sincerely hope that you enjoy using the textbook and this manual as much as we have enjoyed compiling them. We also hope that we have succeeded in providing a wide variety of interesting and relevant material that will help you to show students how crucial and yet how much fun marketing can be. Now, with *Principles of Marketing* by your side, it's over to you ...

Fran Brassington & Steve Pettitt
December 23rd 1996.

LECTURE PLANS AND SEMINAR MATERIAL

Chapter 1
MARKETING DYNAMICS

LECTURE PLAN

A lecture based on this chapter should help the student to:
1. Define what marketing is;
2. trace the development of marketing as a way of doing business;
3. appreciate the importance and contribution of marketing as both a business function and an interface between the organisation and its customers;
4. understand the scope of tasks undertaken in marketing; and
5. understand the structure of the rest of the course.

The key sections of this lecture should be:

Defining marketing (pp 4-11):
- Contrasting definitions of marketing
- what marketing means and does
- marketing as an exchange process including OHP 1, figure 1.1 (p 7) Exchange Transactions:
  ⇒ Both parties value what the other offers
  ⇒ value measured in a variety of ways
  ⇒ benefit measured in a variety of ways
  ⇒ the objective is mutual satisfaction.
- Relationship and social marketing.

The history of marketing (pp 11-17):
- Production orientation
- product orientation
- selling orientation
- marketing orientation.

This section could be condensed to a brief outline of the marketing orientation and students encouraged to read up the rest in the textbook for themselves.

The importance of marketing in today's environment (pp 17-22):
- The complexity of the organisation's operating environment, including OHP 2, figure 1.3 (p 18) The Organisation's Environment:
  ⇒ *Current and potential customers:* the importance of finding them, understanding what they want, delivering it, and monitoring satisfaction and perceptions.
  ⇒ *Competitors:* the importance of understanding and anticipating their strategies.
  ⇒ *Intermediaries:* their role in getting products to customers and adding value.
  ⇒ *Suppliers:* their role in ensuring that products can be produced to the right quality at the right time.
  ⇒ *The marketing environment:* briefly mention the impact of uncontrollable environmental factors, as this is to be covered more fully in chapter 2.
- The need for the organisation to develop and manage relationships with those groups, including OHP 3, figure 1.4 (p 21) Marketing as an Interface:
  ⇒ How the needs and demands of each group affect various internal functions other than marketing
  ⇒ thus the importance of regular and accurate information flows in and out of the organisation
  ⇒ the role of marketing as a means of managing and channelling those communication flows.

Marketing responsibilities (pp 22-29):
- Identifying customer needs and how the marketing function does this
- satisfying customer needs and the use of the marketing mix to achieve customer satisfaction, including OHP 4, figure 1.5 (p 24) The Marketing Mix:
  $\Rightarrow$ The role of each P in satisfying the customer
  $\Rightarrow$ the range of tasks and management concerns within each P
  $\Rightarrow$ the importance of creating a coherent, integrated and consistent marketing mix
  $\Rightarrow$ the concept of creating differential advantage from the marketing mix.

A brief overview of the rest of the course:
A broad outline of the course structure and week by week topics.

QUESTIONS FOR REVIEW

1.1 What essential concepts should a definition of marketing include? (pp 4-12)

- Management process
- identifying/anticipating customer needs
- delivering what customers need, efficiently and profitably
- exchanges leading to a mutually beneficial relationship.

1.2 What is meant by the description of marketing as 'an exchange process'? (pp 6-7)

Each party to the transaction has something that the other one wants. Usually, the seller is offering goods or services and the buyer is offering money.

1.3 Why are central and eastern European countries only just starting to develop a marketing orientation? (pp 12-13)

Until the late 1980s, these countries did not have free market economies. Since they were centrally planned economies, this meant that organisations were told by central government what to produce, how much to sell it for, and often to whom. The focus was thus on efficient production rather than on identifying and satisfying customer needs.

1.4 Distinguish between the four main business orientations. (pp 13-17)

1. *Production:* focus on producing more; selling high volumes; controlling costs and production efficiency.
2. *Product:* focus on improving quality; assumes that customers want a better quality version of the same product.
3. *Selling:* focus on aggressive sales and promotion to sell whatever the organisation wants to make; seller's needs come first.
4. *Marketing:* focus on defining customer needs and then developing offerings that deliver what the customer wants; customer needs come first.

1.5 What are the main groups within the organisational environment that can influence how the organisation operates? (pp 17-19)

- Competitors
- suppliers
- intermediaries
- customers/potential customers.

1.6   What factors contribute towards the wider marketing environment? (p 19)
- Sociocultural factors
- technological factors
- economic and competitive factors
- political and regulatory constraints.

1.7   How do business functions other than marketing contribute towards satisfying customer needs and wants? (pp 19-20)

1. *Finance:* e.g. cost control to help maximise price flexibility; credit control to help develop financing packages that suit customers.
2. *Purchasing:* e.g. ensuring that materials/components are purchased to the right specification to meet the customer's needs; cost effective materials/components sourcing to help maximise price flexibility; cultivating suppliers to encourage maximum co-operation and joint problem solving.
3. *Production:* e.g. ensuring that the right quantity of goods are produced at the right time and to the right quality for the customer; ensuring reliable and consistent quality levels.
4. *R&D/engineering:* e.g. developing products that best solve customers' problems; refining products so that they better solve customers' problems.
5. *HRM:* e.g. ensuring that the organisation has the right mix of skills and the right people to serve the customers' needs.

1.8   What is the marketing philosophy? (pp 20-22)

The marketing philosophy is a way of doing business that places the customer at the centre of everything and acknowledges that the whole organisation should be orientated towards developing positive relationships with customers and meeting their current and future needs.

1.9   What are (a) the 4Ps of the marketing mix and (b) the 7Ps of the services marketing mix?

a) pp 23-26
- Product
- price
- place
- promotion.

b) pp 23-27
- Product
- price
- place
- promotion
- people
- physical evidence
- processes.

1.10   What is competitive edge and why is it so important? (p 27)

Developing a competitive edge means using one or more elements of the marketing mix to offer something attractive to the customer that competitors do not. It is important because without there being something unique, customers have no positive reason to buy your product rather than someone else's.

QUESTIONS FOR DISCUSSION

1.1   Which is the most important element of the marketing mix and why?

No one element of the marketing mix is more important than any of the others. One element may be emphasised more than the others, but even then, the marketing mix is an integrated whole within which the individual elements support and reinforce each other and work together to create a consistent and complete package that appeals to the customer.

1.2   Choose a product that you have purchased recently and show how the elements of the marketing mix came together to create the overall offering.

E.g. Nescafé Instant Coffee:
- *Product:* distinctive rich taste; consistent quality and reliability; easy to make; recognisable packaging reflecting quality and taste; various sized packs available to suit different customer needs and usage rates.
- *Price:* cheaper than many ground coffees, but more expensive than many other brands of instant coffee; enhances image of quality and distinctiveness.
- *Place:* sold in virtually all grocery outlets so that it is conveniently available for both planned and impulse purchases; also sold through hot drinks vending machines and in cafes etc.
- *Promotion:* mass media advertising - television and press, for example - to remind and to reinforce quality and taste image; occasional sales promotions to encourage trial/brand switching or increase short term usage.

1.3   Choose three different products within the same market and explain how each one is trying to gain a competitive edge over the others.

Within the answer, students should systematically analyse the implementation of the marketing mix elements for each of the three products, also showing an appreciation of the target customer and the competitive environment. The student should be able to identify the critical points of difference i.e. those that matter to the customer between the products.

1.4   Why is the question "What business are we in?" so important? How might (a) a fast food retailer, (b) a national airline, (c) a car manufacturer and (d) a hairdresser answer that question if they were properly marketing orientated?

It is important because it focuses the organisation's attention on the customer's problem that it is trying to solve rather than on the product as such. This is more likely to lead to a creative and flexible approach to designing a marketing mix, more likely to lead to a marketing offering that the customer appreciates, and less likely to lead to the organisation being left behind by more innovative competitors.
a) *A fast food outlet* might be in the business of satisfying hunger quickly, cheaply and conveniently.
b) *A national airline* might be in the business of moving passengers from A to a variety of destinations safely, comfortably and smoothly.
c) *A car manufacturer* might be in the business of giving people the freedom and flexibility to transport themselves and/or their families for work, educational or leisure purposes.
d) *A hairdresser* might be in the business of helping people to feel pampered, more attractive, and more confident.

1.5   How might the application of the marketing concept differ between a small organisation and a very large multinational?

Students should be comparing the two types of organisation on criteria such as:
- Resources available

- ability to access market information
- size of customer base
- closeness to individual customers
- breadth and depth of managerial expertise.

The overall conclusion may be that although the actual implementation of the marketing concept may be different the core philosophy and culture of it remains exactly the same.

CASE STUDY 1.1 Liptonice (p 34)

Teaching Objectives

1. To underline the importance of a marketing orientation and understanding the customer's needs;
2. to ensure that students understand the concept of the marketing mix and how its elements integrate;
3. to reinforce the importance of creating differential advantage.

1   What market is Liptonice in and what are its competitors?

The initial response to this is likely to be 'soft drinks', but students should be encouraged to explore the wider structure of this market, discussing the marketing significance of the possible sub-divisions within it. They might raise:
- Fizzy *vs.* still drinks
- adult orientated *vs.* child orientated
- packaging types - bottles, cartons, cans
- purchasing situations - supermarkets, newsagents, cafes.

Likely competitors might be:
- In the child/teenage orientated group - Tango, Coke, Pepsi, 7Up, Sprite, Fruitopia, alcopops etc
- in the adult orientated group - Coke, Pepsi, Schizan, Snapple, Fruitopia, Aqua Libra type products, alcopops.

Supplementary question
Why is it important to be precise in defining what market we are in?

It is important because it:
- Helps to define the competition
- helps to differentiate between direct and indirect competition and substitution
- helps us to understand the customer's real needs.

2   Why was this product less successful than hoped in the UK market?

- Concept of cold fizzy tea alien to UK culture
- taste not right - even if people did overcome their prejudices to try it, they just didn't like it
- too different from cola etc?
- not sufficiently clearly differentiated/positioned?

Supplementary question
Why do you think this product worked better in continental Europe?

- Different culture - less hostility to product concept?
- Possibly different competitive structure?
- Clearer positioning?

What aspects of marketing strategy/management did the producers of Liptonice do well?

- Strong marketing support for product launch
- ensuring wide distribution
- sampling seen as important to generate trial
- monitoring performance - picking up problems early & prepared to invest in revamp/relaunch.

3   **On the basis of the evidence presented in this case, do you think that Liptonice could survive in the UK market?**

Against survival:
- Potential distribution problems after loss of Britvic
- if supermarket withdrawal rumour is true, then that is a major blow
- basic cultural problem not yet overcome
- strong competition.

Supplementary question
What are the problems of withdrawing a brand like this? At what point do you think the withdrawal decision might have to be made?

- Disappointing the customers that do like the brand
- damaging your image with retailers - will they remember this when you ask them to stock your next new product?
- Justifying the withdrawal decision in the light of all the investment and effort that has gone into the brand
- knowing when to withdraw:
    ⇒ When losses reach a certain level?
    ⇒ When key retailers pull out?
    ⇒ When market share figures hit a defined low point?
    ⇒ When sales volumes fall below a certain threshold?
    ⇒ When market research tells you that attitudes towards the product are too far gone to salvage?

If the product is to survive the producer might consider:
- Securing distribution channels
- de-emphasise tea content?
- Make it not fizzy?
- Major repositioning e.g. as sports/health drink or New Age type adult drink or funky 'cool' tango type teenybopper product?

4   **Analyse how soft drink producers use the elements of the marketing mix to create differential advantage.**

This question is to get students talking generally and freely about the marketing mix and interaction between elements and to remind them subtly of what differential advantage is and why it matters.
Product:
- Brand imagery
- packaging
- taste, flavour etc.
Price:
- Premium *vs.* 'value'
- emphasis on product image tends to make consumers less price sensitive.
Place:
- All use extensive distribution i.e. as many outlets as possible of all types

- other than producing retailer own brand drinks, it is thus difficult to differentiate on place.

Promotion:

- Mainly advertising and sales promotions e.g. Tango's off the wall approach, but otherwise largely boring.
- Liptonice tried television advertising with Angus Deayton being dry and cynically witty about the peculiarity of fizzy cold tea, but presumably the audience took it too literally!
- Personal selling important in getting the product into the retail trade in the first place.

CASE STUDY 1.2 Plasser & Theurer Make Tracks (p 35)

Teaching Objectives

1. To encourage students to explore what makes an organisation marketing orientated;
2. to ensure that students understand the marketing concept and how it can be implemented through the elements of the marketing mix in an industrial situation;
3. to underline that marketing concepts are equally applicable and just as important in organisational markets as in consumer markets.

1   To what extent and why do you think this company is marketing orientated?

- The company works closely with its customers to ensure that it produces what the customer wants
- it thus understands customer needs
- it tries to develop relationships with its customers
- it invests in R&D/technology to develop products that solve the customer's problems cost effectively
- it invests in customer service, both through its sales force and its after sales support.

2   How does the marketing mix for a company in this kind of organisational market differ from what you might find in a mass market, fast moving consumer goods (fmcg) situation?

Product:
- High tech
- low purchase volumes
- infrequent purchases
- developed with direct co-operation of individual customer.

Price:
- High price
- negotiable price package
- negotiable payment terms.

Place:
- Direct transaction between manufacturer and customer; no intermediaries involved
- goods delivered direct to where customer wants them.

Promotion:
- Much more emphasis on personal selling and two-way ongoing dialogue between buyer and seller.

Both this product and an fmcg product might, however, have common objectives from their very different marketing mixes: customer satisfaction, and a desire for repeat business.

Supplementary question
What particular problems do you think the length of time between a particular customer's purchases might cause Plasser & Theurer and which elements of their marketing mix are designed to overcome these problems?

- Customer's interest in the company cools
- customer 'forgets' what the company offers
- the company loses sight of the customer's needs as they change over time.

These can be overcome through reminder advertising in the trade press; ongoing social visits to customers from sales representatives, and ongoing research to ensure that changing customer needs are tracked.

3   What lessons can other companies in organisational markets learn from the marketing success of Plasser & Theurer?

- The need to be customer centred
- the need to invest in developing products that solve the customer's problem
- the need to create a unique selling point/differential advantage i.e. to offer something that the competition do not
- the need to make customer support freely available
- the need to recognise that post-purchase marketing activities and support are as important as what happens in the build up to a sale
- the importance of cultivating co-operative relationships.

Marketing in Action Fisherman's Friends (p 6)

Discussion question
How might the marketing mix for a cough sweet differ from that of a confectionery product?

- *Price:* could be more expensive if it has pseudo-medicinal claims representing extra product benefits.
- *Product:* could taste stronger and slightly nastier to give psychological reinforcement to its medicinal properties; packaging could be more serious in tone - less fun than confectionery, stressing medicinal benefits and active ingredients.
- *Place:* could be sold in a wider range of outlets e.g. pharmacies as well as usual confectionery outlets, and in different positions within outlets e.g. the medicines section of the supermarket rather than on the confectionery shelves.
- *Promotion:* again, this will stress different product benefits - soothing and relaxing rather than pleasurable and tasty. Advertising activity might peak during the winter months when most people get coughs and colds.

Marketing in Action Slovenia's Struggle (p 15)

Discussion question
What are the problems of developing a marketing orientation within a relatively young, emerging market economy?

- Lack of infrastructure to help deliver marketing promises
- need for capital investment in organisations
- the need to improve product design and quality to meet threat of foreign competition
- managers inexperienced in operating within a marketing orientated environment
- potential problems in getting hold of market research data
- consumers inexperienced in interpreting more sophisticated marketing packages.

Marketing in Action Virgin Direct (p 28)

Discussion question
How does Virgin Direct use the elements of the marketing mix to meet its customers' needs and wants?

- *Product:* a range of fairly standard financial products in the insurance, pensions and investment fields that will appeal to the 'ordinary' person looking simply for future financial security on relatively limited means.
- *Price:* with the PEPs, emphasis on lower management and administration fees.
- *Place:* sold direct over the phone. No potential embarrassment or threat to the customer from having to deal face to face with a pushy sales representative. Very convenient to the customer, too.
- *Promotion:* no nonsense, no jargon 'honest' advertising, prominently featuring Richard Branson's name because he is perceived as trustworthy by the target market. It reassures the nervous or uncertain potential customer, and is certainly aimed at those with little or no experience of financial management.

SUGGESTED ASSIGNMENTS

- To what extent and why do you believe that a marketing orientation is essential for today's organisations?
- Questions for Discussion 1.3.

Chapter 2
THE EUROPEAN MARKETING ENVIRONMENT

LECTURE PLAN

A lecture based on this chapter should help the student to:
1. Understand the importance of the external environment to marketing decision making;
2. assess the role and importance of scanning the environment as a means of early identification of opportunities and threats;
3. appreciate the evolving and diverse nature of the European marketing environment;
4. define the broad categories of factors that affect the marketing environment; and
5. understand the influences at work within each of those categories and their implications for marketing.

The key sections of this lecture should be:

Introduction - the broad nature of the marketing environment (pp 38-41):
- Broad definition of the marketing environment, including OHP 5, figure 2.1 (p 39) Elements of the External Environment:
  - ⇒ The impact of each element on the organisation's approach to business and its flexibility
  - ⇒ their impact on the shape of the marketing mix
  - ⇒ their ability to present threats and opportunities
  - ⇒ their uncontrollable and sometimes unpredictable nature.
- The importance of understanding the environment
- definition of environmental scanning
- the practical problems of scanning.

The sociocultural environment (pp 41-55):
- Demographic structures and change
- sociocultural factors, including OHP 6, figure 2.2 (p 49) The Impact of Societal Attitudes On Marketing Strategy:

$\Rightarrow$ How the various issues outlined have changed organisational culture

$\Rightarrow$ how they have changed products

$\Rightarrow$ how they have changed the content of marketing communication

$\Rightarrow$ how they have created new market segments.

- Additional influences from organised consumer groups and pressure groups.

The technological environment (pp 55-60):

- The role of technology in product development
- the role of technology in production
- the role of technology in administration and distribution
- the role of technology in customer research and support.

The economic and competitive environment (pp 60-70):

- Defining the macroeconomic environment
- the impact of macroeconomic factors on marketing decisions
- defining the microeconomic environment
- the impact of different market structures on marketing decisions.

The legal and regulatory environment (pp 70-78):

This section is based on OHP 7, figure 2.6 (p 71) The European Regulatory Framework:

- The forces within this environment and their impact on marketing activities
- the influence of local, national and EU governmental bodies
- the ability of lobby groups and pressure groups to influence the regulatory environment
- the pros and cons of industry self-regulation *vs.* legislation.

QUESTIONS FOR REVIEW

2.1   What does the acronym STEP stand for? (pp 38-39)

STEP refers to the marketing environment:

- Sociocultural environment
- technological environment
- economic/competitive environment
- political/legal environment.

2.2   What is environmental scanning, why is it important, and what are the potential problems of implementing it? (pp 40-41)

Environmental scanning is the ongoing collection and evaluation of information from the marketing environment. It is an important activity if the organisation is to anticipate change, spot emerging opportunities early enough to capitalise on them proactively, or spot potential problems early enough to remedy them before they cause damage. There may be potential problems of information overload, handling and sorting information, or failure to appreciate the significance of information.

2.3   What kind of information does the study of demographics cover? (pp 41-46)

Demographics covers measurable information about populations and individuals, including:

- Age
- gender
- family status
- geographic spread
- income
- occupation
- education level

- race.

2.4   Why might consumer demands for variation and variety in the products they buy cause problems for marketers? (pp 46-48)

- Fragments the market - too many small groups of customers
- potentially destroys economies of scale - the organisation has to create individual offerings for each group
- creates short-lived demand - consumers get bored and want something new, so the marketer has to be constantly innovative.

2.5   To what extent have consumer concerns about environmental issues affected organisations' approaches to marketing? (p 48)

Consumer concerns have led to demand for:
- Products not tested on animals
- more natural ingredients in products
- ingredients from renewable resources and/or processed with minimal environmental impact
- organic/non factory farmed produce
- health orientated foods and drinks with minimal artificial additives
- recyclable/refillable packaging
- minimal packaging
- more durability/less disposability.

2.6   Why are consumer groups and other pressure groups a major influence in an organisation's marketing environment? (pp 51-55)

They have the ability to act as opinion leaders since through the mass media and their own communications efforts they can sway public opinion and attitudes. This could lead, at one extreme, to bad PR for an organisation and consumer boycotts of its product, or at the other extreme, to an evolving longer term shift in consumer tastes and preferences. Either way, the organisation cannot afford to ignore what is being said and done by such groups. It may need to prepare its defence or to start adapting its marketing approaches to better accommodate changing attitudes.

2.7   Summarise the main implications of the SEM for organisations doing business within the EU. (pp 73-75)

- Freedom to buy and sell without restriction throughout the EU thus opening up a much larger potential market and the potential for Europe-wide niche segments
- eventual harmonisation of product standards, marketing regulations, taxation, codes of practice etc so that all competitors are operating to the same rules and so that it is easier to standardise marketing activities across geographic borders.

2.8   In what ways can technology contribute to the marketing environment? (pp 55-60)

Technology can contribute to:
- Research and development efforts
- improved materials and components
- improved, faster and more reliable production processes
- better quality products
- more efficient and cost effective administration and distribution systems
- new ways of communicating with customers and developing relationships with them.

2.9   Differentiate between the macro- and microeconomic environments. (pp 60-70)

The macroeconomic environment gives the broadest picture, including national and international economies and trading blocs. Major influences within this include taxation, government spending policies, regional development policies, and interest rates, for example. The microeconomic environment focuses more on the kind of market structure that an organisation finds itself competing in. The organisation's ability to make decisions and influence both buyer and competitor behaviour within the market place might be determined by whether the market is a monopoly or oligopoly, or whether it is characterised by monopolistic or perfect competition.

2.10   What are the four main types of market structure? (pp 65-70)

1. Monopoly
2. oligopoly
3. monopolistic competition
4. perfect competition.

QUESTIONS FOR DISCUSSION

2.1   What sources of published demographic data are available in your own University or College library?

Students should demonstrate that they have spent some time in the library and have located a wide range of available sources, for example market research reports, government statistics, on-line data bases etc. The tutor should have a list of key sources prepared in advance to fill in any gaps! The discussion may broaden into the usefulness of the data found to a marketer and its limitations.

2.2   Find and discuss examples of products that are particularly vulnerable to changing consumer tastes.

The choice of product here does not necessarily matter, as long as the student can build a convincing argument, clearly based on the factors making up the sociocultural environment in particular, that shows an appreciation of the relationship between consumers, marketers and their products.

2.3   To what extent, and why, do you think marketers should be seen to lead the way in addressing 'ethical' issues rather than waiting until consumer concern reaches a level where the organisation is prompted to react?

This is a free discussion that allows students to consider the wider responsibilities of marketers and their relationship with the society within which they have to operate. Students should be encouraged to introduce a wide range of ethical issues into the discussion, for example marketing to children and other vulnerable groups; marketers and animal welfare and other environmental concerns; the use of 'shock' advertising; the promotion of greed and excessive behaviour; the sale and promotion of potentially dangerous products e.g. alcohol, tobacco, pharmaceuticals, fireworks etc.

2.4   What are the differences between the ASA and the ITC? Find and discuss recent examples of adjudications by these two bodies (or equivalent regulatory bodies in your own country). Do you agree with their judgement?

This encourages students to investigate the structure of the regulatory environment for advertising within their own country. Discussion of recent adjudications helps students to understand how these bodies reach their decisions, and what criteria of 'good practice' they are applying. It also opens up further debate on marketing ethics and the extent to which there should be boundaries constraining what marketers can do.

2.5   Using figure 2.1 as a framework, choose a product and list under each of the STEP factors the relevant influences that have helped to make that product what it is.

The student should demonstrate a clear understanding of what the STEP factors are and the kinds of influences each one includes. In the context of the chosen product, the student will show how these influences are linked and what impact they have had on the marketing mix.

CASE STUDY 2.1 Sanpro (p 82)

Teaching Objectives

1. To ensure that students understand the nature of the STEP factors within the marketing environment;
2. to demonstrate how the STEP factors interact for a particular type of product;
3. to begin to explore how the environment affects marketing decisions.

1   Outline the ways in which the STEP factors affect this market.

Sociocultural:
- Traditional embarrassment about the product makes communication difficult and offence easy
- but busier female lifestyles and the demand for shopping convenience mean that the products need to be more widely available and more reliable
- health awareness has changed (a) customer information needs and (b) the balance of the market split between tampons and towels.

Technological:
- Development of superabsorbents leading to better, more reliable products.

Economic/competitive:
- Customers are not necessarily price sensitive, as most care more about quality and reliability
- the market is largely oligopolistic, with two or three suppliers between them setting the pace of change, although the supermarkets might disturb the status quo.

Political/legal:
- Packaging might have to carry certain information re absorbency, use and health risks
- manufacturers might have to conform to restrictions re advertising content and media used
- flushable products will have to be compatible with sewage disposal systems.

Supplementary question
One sociocultural issue not specifically mentioned in the case is that girls are coming into this market at a younger age. What problems face the manufacturers in trying to make contact with them and generate brand loyalty?

- Sensitivity, both of the girls themselves and of their parents
- finding the right media - possibly through teen magazines or even through health education in schools
- encouraging product trial - free samples?
- Education and reassurance - not only through advertising and on-pack information, but perhaps also through free detailed information packs as a mail-in offer, or help lines. This also helps relationship building, leading to brand loyalty.

2   Why do supermarket own label products pose a threat in this market?

- Their quality is similar to that of branded products as they are manufactured by companies respected within the market
- their price is more competitive, given their quality
- consumers are now more trusting of supermarket own brands generally

- they are conveniently available to the consumer and additionally, the retailer can control the amount of display space and prominence they are given in store.

3   Why do you think sales promotions are particularly effective for these products?

- They add interest to what might be viewed as almost a commodity purchase
- they attract attention and might encourage a buyer to switch brands
- they reward loyal customers and perhaps prevent them from switching brands
- on-pack or point of sale promotions are a discreet form of marketing communication.

Supplementary question
Why are Smith & Nephew and Tambrands spending so much on marketing support (£5m and £10m respectively)?

- As a means of defence against each other and against the impact of supermarket own brands on market share
- as a means of maintaining customer awareness and trust in the brands; reassuring them so that they are less tempted to try something different.

Supplementary question
What are the problems of using advertising as a means of marketing communication for these products?

- In some media, the message content has to be constrained to the point where it can be difficult to make meaningful statements about the product or even show it.
- A significant proportion of the target audience does not want to be faced with advertising for these products, especially in 'family' media.

4   In terms of the marketing environment, how does this product differ from (a) toilet paper and (b) condoms?

a) Toilet paper:
Sociocultural:
- Toilet paper has nothing like the same embarrassment factor attached to it, probably because the whole family uses it every day
- it is seen as a normal part of the weekly shopping, and even as an essential part of bathroom decor!
Technological:
- This product has also benefited in advances in materials technology improving product absorbency and softness etc.
Economic/competitive:
- Also a fairly oligopolistic market with a few major brands leading a lot of smaller ones
- retailer own brands also beginning to make an impact.
Political/legal:
- In the UK toilet paper can be freely and fairly explicitly advertised
- also needs to conform to disposal criteria.

b) Condoms:
Sociocultural:
- Similar embarrassment factor but attitudes relaxing because of health worries
- no longer seen as purely a male responsibility/purchase
- product more widely available e.g. in supermarkets for customer's convenience.
Technological:
- This product has benefited in advances in materials technology, improving reliability, sensitivity, fit etc.

Economic/competitive:
- Also a fairly oligopolistic market with a few major brands leading a lot of smaller ones
- retailer own brands also beginning to make an impact.

Political/legal:
- In the UK, similarly restricted in what can be said and in what media, but less constrained than in the pre-AIDS era
- needs to conform to product standards.

CASE STUDY 2.2 Kabo (p 83)

Teaching Objectives

1. To ensure that students understand the nature of the STEP factors within the marketing environment;
2. to demonstrate how the nature of STEP factors can change over time and between different markets;
3. to begin to explore how the environment affects marketing decisions, particularly in an international marketing situation.

1   In what ways did Kabo's marketing environment change in the transition to a free market economy?

Sociocultural:
- More discerning customers now comparing competitive products
- more price sensitive customers
- effective loss of USSR market.

Technological:
- No track record in R&D to capitalise on.

Economic/competitive:
- Higher raw material costs
- higher fuel costs
- upward pressure on wages
- unreliable revenue flow
- high interest rates
- loss of subsidies
- potentially unrestricted competition, of both domestic and foreign origin.

Political/legal:
- Loss of state support/protection
- loss of guaranteed prices.

2   Why did Kabo's initial venture into the US, French and Chinese markets fail?

- Lack of international marketing expertise generally
- lack of logistical skills
- inability to get quality and packaging right
- probable lack of knowledge of what customer really wanted, and thus ...
- ... lack of market segmentation and targeting.

3   If Kabo was thinking of moving into the UK (or other western European) market with its canned fish, what are the key aspects of the marketing environment that it should investigate before entry?

Sociocultural:
- Customer tastes and preferences e.g. do they want fish canned in oil? brine? mayonnaise? what is the preferred pack size?
- How might customers want to use the product? as a main dish? as a cooking ingredient? as a sandwich filling?
- Do customers have particular attitudes towards product additives or the environmental credentials of the brand?
- Where do customers want to buy the product?

Technological:
- Can we meet the quality/consistency expectations of the market?
- Does our approach to packaging for the wholesale/retail trade fit in with any automated handling systems it might have to go through?

Economic/competitive:
- What sort of pricing level is appropriate for the market, given likely customer affluence and competitor pricing?
- What sort of prices do the retail/wholesale trade expect?
- Who are the competitors and what differential advantages do they have?

Political/legal:
- Does the product conform with all regulations re additives, product claims, hygiene, labelling etc?
- Can we comply with import regulations?

4   From your general knowledge of the market, what do you think might be the biggest barriers to such an entry?

- Competition from established brands
- marketing skills of established manufacturers who will defend their share
- knowing precisely what consumers want and finding a gap in the market
- overcoming consumer apathy towards a new brand or their suspicion of it
- funding sufficient marketing effort to make an impact and finding the right marketing approach
- generating sufficient volume to keep trade price competitive
- convincing major retailers to list the product - perhaps offering to make an own brand might help to gain initial market presence?

Marketing in Action Bread (p 50)

Discussion question
What problems and opportunities does the broadening of tastes in bread present to the major supermarket chains?

Problems:
- Monitoring trends and fads and ensuring that the right varieties are available
- the proliferation of varieties putting pressure on limited store space and in-store bakery capacity and skills
- educating customers (and staff) about what is what and encouraging trial.

Opportunities:
- Encouraging consumers to increase bread consumption and amount spent on bread
- enhances store's image of wide choice and up-market orientation
- it makes an attractive display
- it can be premium priced.

Marketing in Action Environmentally Friendly Tyres (p 54)

Discussion question
Why are companies like Pirelli and Continental being driven towards developing 'green' tyres?

- Tyres are notoriously difficult to dispose of
- bad publicity generated through green pressure groups
- organisational desire to be seen as socially responsible
- represents an attractive product benefit to buyers
- represents a more cost effective position.

Marketing in Action Austria plc Joins the EU (p 64)

Discussion question
What commercial benefits do you think existing members might have expected to gain from Austria's admission to the EU?

- A new geographic market to target
- easier access to Austrian goods
- potential for joint ventures with Austrian companies
- access to another border with eastern Europe.

Marketing in Action Airline Deregulation (p 74)

Discussion question
What factors within the marketing environment have led to the formation of 'peanut airlines'?

- Increasing popularity of air travel
- increasing mobility e.g. people taking short breaks within Europe
- demand for cheaper air travel as the big airlines push upmarket and increase service quality and price
- thus the opening of a market segment demanding low price, minimal quality, functional travel
- increasing deregulation of routes and access to slots.

SUGGESTED ASSIGNMENTS

- In what ways can an understanding of the marketing environment influence organisations' approaches to marketing?
- Questions for Discussion 2.5 could be adapted as an assignment thus: choose a product and using the STEP factors as a framework, analyse the relevant environmental influences that have helped to make that product what it is.

Chapter 3
CONSUMER BEHAVIOUR

LECTURE PLAN

A lecture based on this chapter should help the student to:
1. Understand the decision-making processes that consumers go through as they make a purchase;
2. appreciate how those processes differ between different buying situations;
3. understand the influences which affect decision making, whether environmental, psychological or sociocultural; and
4. appreciate the implications of those processes and influences for marketing strategies.

The key sections of this lecture should be:

Introduction (pp 87-88):
The scope of the lecture, including OHP 8, figure 3.1 (p 88) The Consumer Buying Decision-making Process and its Influencing Factors:
- This figure provides an overview of what the lecture will cover
- the decision-making process is not isolated
- it is influenced by the marketing environment and the marketing activities of organisations
- it is influenced by individual and group influences on the consumer.

The decision-making process (pp 88-96):
- *Problem recognition:* internal and external triggers.
- *Information search:* sources of information, both controlled and not controlled by the marketer; depth of information sought.
- *Information evaluation:* criteria for evaluation, rational *vs.* irrational; speed and formality of evaluation; how the marketer can help.
- *Decision:* ease of decision; need to reiterate previous stages; rationalising a decision; how the marketer can help.
- *Post-purchase evaluation:* cognitive dissonance; how the marketer can help.

Buying situations (pp 96-98):
- The three different kinds of buying situation
- their impact on the speed of the decision-making process
- their impact on its complexity
- their impact on its degree of formality.

This section could be omitted and students encouraged to read it up in the textbook for themselves.

The marketing environment (pp 98-100):
- A brief overview of how the STEP factors might influence both the consumer's and the marketer's actions within the decision-making process.

Individual influences on the decision-making process (pp 100-109):
- Personality
- perception
- learning
- motivation
- attitudes.

Group influences on the decision-making process (pp 109-119):
- Social class
- culture, including OHP 9, figure 3.4 (p 111) Influences on Culture:
  - ⇒ What makes up 'culture'
  - ⇒ the variety of cultures within the European market
  - ⇒ how culture affects the consumer's choices and actions
  - ⇒ the interaction between marketing and culture.
- Reference groups
- the family, including OHP 10, figure 3.5 (p 117) A Family Life-cycle Model for the 1990s:
  - ⇒ How the structure of the family has changed generally
  - ⇒ how the influence of the family has changed
  - ⇒ how family structure impacts on buying decisions.

QUESTIONS FOR REVIEW

3.1   What are the main stages of the consumer buying decision-making process? (pp 88-96)

- Problem recognition
- information search
- information evaluation
- decision
- post-purchase evaluation.

3.2   Differentiate between the internal and external stimuli that might trigger the buying process. (pp 88-89)

Internal stimuli come from within the consumer. This may through an emotion or feeling, for example hunger, boredom or depression. It could also arise from a more conscious assessment of their situation, for example, checking the fridge and the larder to see what's needed just before going to the supermarket. An event, for example a flat tyre, or a phone call from friends inviting themselves to dinner tonight, or a burst pipe could also pressure the consumer into a purchasing situation. External stimuli, generally provided by marketers, are independent of the consumer and lead to a realisation that a purchase is needed. Advertisers, for example could bring a problem to the consumer's attention, convince them that they have this problem and that a particular product could solve it. Up until then , the consumer was blissfully unaware that there was a problem!

3.3   What are the potential sources of information that a consumer might use in the buying process? (pp 89-91)

- Advertising and other marketing communications
- point of sale leaflets, brochures and information
- sales assistants or sales representatives
- directories, specialist magazines and consumer guides
- word of mouth recommendations from friends, family or colleagues
- past experience of similar or related purchases.

3.4   Why is post-purchase evaluation important for (a) the consumer and (b) the marketer? (pp 94-96)

a)   For the consumer:
- Reassurance about choices made
- learning from experience.

b)   For the marketer:
- Helps to assess how well the marketer's promises were fulfilled
- helps to identify strengths and weaknesses in the marketing mix
- could help to generate customer loyalty.

3.5   Summarise some of the ways in which marketers can 'help' the consumer at each stage in the decision-making process. (pp 88-96)

- *Problem recognition:* e.g. advertising demonstrating a problem, its effects, and how the product or service can solve it.
- *Information search:* where appropriate, ensure that the consumer can easily access detailed information through leaflets and brochures, advertising and point of sale materials. Ensure too that sales staff are well versed in the product, its benefits and its differential advantages.
- *Information evaluation:* ensure that the information sources used above make product benefits and their implications for the consumer very clear. The consumer needs a meaningful, relevant and sound reason to buy this particular product instead of a competing one.
- *Decision:* ensure that the product is readily available in the kinds of outlets where the consumer will want to find it. Also ensure that sales staff are trained to close a sale, where appropriate, or that

on-pack information is appealing and persuasive. Packaging might also have to stand out from the crowd, and show a clear difference from the competition.
- *Post-purchase evaluation:* for fmcg products, reinforcement advertising can reassure the consumer that a wise choice has been made. For bigger purchases, follow-up personal customer care calls can also reassure and be used to dispel any lingering doubt.

3.6   What are the three different types of buying situation and what kinds of products might be included in each of them? (pp 96-98)

- *Routine problem solving:* probably fmcg products, which are frequently purchases, relatively low priced goods with little financial or emotional risk inherent in a 'wrong' choice. Likely to be a habitual or impulse purchase with little conscious deliberation.
- *Limited problem solving:* less frequently purchased, moderately expensive goods, representing a medium amount of risk. It might include products such as small electrical goods, holidays, clothing etc for which a 'wrong' decision is a clear disappointment, but not necessarily a total disaster.
- *Extended problem solving:* very infrequently purchased goods, such as cars or houses, representing a great deal of financial investment on the consumer's part, and thus a high risk. A 'wrong' decision is a serious set-back, and not necessarily easy to remedy.

3.7   How and why might the duration of the decision-making process and the extent of information search differ between the three different types of buying situations? (pp 96-98)

- *Routine problem solving:* this involves low risk habitual purchasing with little conscious information searching or evaluation, and thus is likely to be of very short duration.
- *Limited problem solving:* this involves a moderate amount of expenditure and risk, and thus the consumer might invest some time in consciously seeking and evaluating information from a range of sources. The amount of time and effort spent is likely to be limited, however, depending on the perceived risk and importance of the choice to the individual consumer.
- *Extended problem solving:* these decisions are likely to take longer than any others, and to involve a very wide range of information searching and evaluation, because of the inherent risk. It could take weeks or even months to decide, for example, which house or car to buy.

3.8   How do perception and learning affect consumer decision-making, and how can the marketer influence these processes? (pp 102-104)

Perception affects the way in which the consumer analyses and interprets information, and thus will affect the consumer at the information evaluation and decision stages in particular. The marketer can influence this by ensuring that available information points out the product benefits and their relevance to the consumer, and perhaps also trying to communicate with consumers when they are relaxed and receptive to information. Learning helps to build consumers' experience and could affect their future choices. Repetitive and very visual advertising can help to teach brand names and product benefits to consumers. Using positive (and sometimes negative) emotions can also aid learning, as consumers become more personally involved in the message.

3.9   What is an attitude and why are attitudes so difficult to change? (pp 107-109)

An attitude is the stance that an individual takes on a subject which predisposes them to respond in a particular way to that subject. Attitudes are difficult to change because:
- They can be very deeply held
- they can involve emotional rather than purely rational responses
- consumers do their best to interpret any message in such a way as to reinforce the attitude rather than overturn it
- the consumer might feel that changing an attitude represents loss of face.

3.10 **Summarise the stages of Maslow's Hierarchy of Needs and their marketing implications.**
(pp 104-107)

- *Physiological needs:* hunger and thirst, for example. Largely applicable to impulse snack purchases which thus need to be widely available?
- *Safety needs:* centred on protection of one's self and one's family. Largely reflected in the marketing of financial services; home security products; insurance and health care products. Marketing approaches raise the fear of the consequences of inadequate protection and then allay that fear through the product or service sold.
- *Belongingness and love needs:* centred on the emotional security generated from those closest to the consumer. Used by marketers in advertising, either showing how a product can reduce the risk of rejection or ridicule, or how the product will make your friends and family love you more.
- *Esteem needs:* seeking status, respect and good opinion within wider society. Most likely to apply to products that claim to enhance status or to denote an elite and discerning buyer.
- *Self-actualisation needs:* achieving complete fulfilment through reaching one's ultimate personal goals. Difficult for the marketer to generalise about these as they are so personal, but the marketer can try to demonstrate how a product can lead towards self-actualisation.

QUESTIONS FOR DISCUSSION

3.1 **Outline the main sources of information that might be used in purchasing (a) a new car and (b) a packet of biscuits.**

Students might include the following information sources in considering either of these purchases:
- Past experience
- advertising
- sales literature/packaging information
- general point of sale information
- sales staff
- the media
- word of mouth recommendation.

Students should be able to show how the use of each of these sources varies between the two buying situations and why, linking it clearly to the likely duration and formality of the consumer's decision-making process.

3.2 **Think of a purchase that you have made recently. What products or brands made up your evoked set of alternatives, and what choice criteria did you use to differentiate between them to lead to your eventual purchase?**

Students should show an appreciation of the wide range of factors that potentially influence choice, and clearly relate them to their own buying behaviour, for example:
- Personal past experience
- personality, motivation, attitudes etc
- friends, family and groups
- marketing influences.

Answers should relate strongly to figure 3.1 (p 88).

3.3 **To what extent do you think that social class is a helpful concept in improving the marketer's understanding of consumer behaviour?**

This is a free and wide discussion question, encouraging students to consider the meaning and relevance of 'class' and how it might link with other meaningful variables that help the marketer. This might include the correlation between class and income, reference groups, attitudes, and perceptions, for example. They might conclude that class in itself, however it is defined, is of limited use to the marketer, but taken in conjunction with other variables, it can help to develop a more detailed customer profile.

3.4 **Define the three main types of reference groups. Within each type, think of examples that relate to you as a consumer, and analyse how this might affect your own buying behaviour.**

1. *Membership groups (p 113):* those groups to which the consumer already belongs, based, for example, on work or social groupings.
2. *Aspirant groups (p 115):* those groups to which the consumer would like to belong, but as yet does not. These aspirations may be realistic or totally unrealistic. Again, they might centre on work or social ambitions and aspirations.
3. *Dissociative groups (p 115):* those groups to which the consumer does not want to belong or would not want others to associate them with.

Students' examples should be relevant to the group concerned, showing a clear understanding of the differences between the groups and the practical implications to both marketers and consumers.

3.5 **How might the roles undertaken by various members of a two-parent family vary between the buying decisions for (a) a house, (b) something for tonight's dinner, and (c) a birthday present for a 10-year-old child? How would your answer change if it was a one-parent family?**

Students should place their answers to this primarily within the context of the family as a decision-making unit and the broad roles defined in figure 3.6 (p 117). Their answers should show an appreciation of what those roles mean, and how their importance varies with the type of buying situation, depending on the degree of financial risk involved, or the level of psychological involvement by the family in the purchase. Students should also appreciate that different family members will take on different roles in different buying situations and that multiple roles are also possible, for example situation (b) might only involve mother in all roles! The comparison with the one-parent family encourages consideration of the different economic and psychological pressures on such a family unit.

CASE STUDY 3.1 Madame Tussaud's Rock Circus (p 122)

Teaching Objectives

1. To ensure that students understand the concept of the consumer buying decision-making process and the stages involved;
2. to ensure that students understand the concept of buying situations and the implications for the marketer;
3. to emphasise how individual and group behavioural factors can influence the decision-making process;
4. to show how the marketer's actions can also influence the decision-making process.

1 **Outline how the buyer decision-making process might work for a leisure attraction such as Rock Circus.**

As an example:

Problem recognition: a foreign family, for whom English is not the native language, is on holiday in London with teenaged children. The weather forecast is not good and they are wondering what to do tomorrow.

Information search: the family might:
- Look through the guidebooks
- pick up some leaflets from the hotel reception

- ask hotel staff for advice
- ask a tourist information office for advice
- talk to other hotel guests about what they have seen and done
- remember some advertising they saw on the London Underground
- remember some venues they have seen in passing during the previous few days
- remember the things they did when they were last in London.

Information evaluation: aspects of this might centre on:
- Rational factors: proximity to the hotel; any travelling problems; whether an attraction is dependent on good weather; opening hours; cost of getting the whole family in; amount of time likely to be needed to 'do it properly' etc
- More psychological factors: ability of an attraction to offer something for all members of the family; family members' particular likes and dislikes ('oh no mum, not another BORING museum. I wanna go to Planet Hollywood'); perceived entertainment level offered; likely language problems; whether an attraction is on a tourist's 'must see ...' list; persuasive ability of the sources cited in information search above etc.

Decision: the family as a decision-making unit (figure 3.6 p 117) could have a tough job in reaching a decision, as there could well be conflicting views. The decision depends on which of the above factors come across most strongly, and who is cast into the role of decision maker. Some options could be:
- The parents take an executive decision, having duly considered the children's views
- a broad consensus is reached, with everyone feeling that they have made some concession to the rest
- one family member is given the privilege of making the decision, perhaps because (a) it is their turn to decide (b) it is their birthday treat or (c) this was the price the family agreed to pay in return for that person's agreement to go to that 'boring museum' yesterday.

Post-purchase evaluation: in reflecting on the day's excursion, family members are likely to consider:
- Did I actually enjoy it?
- Did it seem to keep all family members happy?
- Was it sufficiently entertaining or educational?
- Were my doubts realised or was it better than I had expected?
- Was it a thoroughly memorable experience?
- Was it good value for money?
- Was it too crowded/busy?
- Did we spend too long queueing?
- Was I satisfied with the peripheral things i.e. the cafe, the gift shop, the toilets etc?
- Was I satisfied with the service received from staff?
- Would I go again?
- Would I recommend this attraction to anyone else?

2   **Why did Rock Circus change its marketing communications messages in 1993 and why was this important to the buyer's decision-making process?**

Reasons for change:
- Current image not conveying interactive exhibition element
- 'History of Rock' emphasis implying stuffy museum image
- not enough emphasis, therefore, on fun, entertainment and multisensory experience.

The change in marketing communications strategy was important for buyers because:
- It broadened the communications media and techniques used
- it gave the attraction a more lively image
- it better represented what the attraction had to offer
- it emphasised the interactive and experiential features of the attraction
- it better differentiated the attraction from its competitors.

3   **What kind of buying situation is this, and what are the implications for the marketer?**

Given the family scenario outlined in the outline answer to question 1 above, this is likely to be a limited problem solving kind of buying situation. It could be seen as a moderate risk, both financially (once the cost of getting the whole family into the attraction is taken into account) and psychologically (this could be a whole day of our holiday ruined), and some time and effort is put into assessing alternatives and negotiating the final choice. In some cases, however, it could almost be an impulse purchase if, for example, the family was passing the attraction and decided to go in on the spur of the moment. The implications for the marketer are to ensure that:

- information about the attraction is widely disseminated - see for example the suggested answer to question 1 above
- the information is sufficiently detailed to assist the consumer's decision-making process and clearly communicates the attraction's benefits for all members of the family
- the attraction is clearly differentiated so that it stands up well against comparison with competing attractions
- the consumer is convinced that the attraction represents a good use of both time and money and is unmissable.

4   **In terms of individual and sociocultural influences, how would you broadly explain the customer profile presented here?**

- Rock music is primarily a youth interest, hence 67 per cent of visitors are aged between 16 and 34.
- 12-15s are possible still a little too young to appreciate this, and are more likely to be influenced by parents into going to more 'suitable' attractions!
- The 45+ group are highly likely to be there under sufferance, entertaining younger members of their family.
- The format of the attraction might also have its major appeal to the young.
- Its tight focus is likely to appeal to those with a genuine interest in rock music, or those looking for a 'cool', stimulating day out that they can boast about to their friends.
- It is not a sufficiently well established attraction to be on the standard tour operator circuit, hence only 30 per cent of visitors arrive in larger groups. Apart from this, it may be too specialised an attraction for the general tour operators.
- Rock music as presented here is largely a US/Western European phenomenon, thus the emphasis on European visitors who are more likely to relate to the stars' names featured and to have an emotional response to the rock scene.

CASE STUDY 3.2 Premium Lagers (p 123)

Teaching Objectives

1. To ensure that students understand the concept of consumer motivation and how it can be applied;
2. to explore the impact of individual and group factors on brand choice;
3. to show how consumer behaviour can affect marketers' product development and launch choices.

1   **Where does premium lager fit on Maslow's hierarchy of needs and why?**

It could fit into:
- *Belongingness and love needs:* fulfilling the need to be seen to belong to a group, drinking what one's social peers or what one's aspirant groups drink. The drinker might feel that the choice of lager creates a stronger bond with the group and increases his/her acceptability to that group.

Or perhaps more likely into:
- *Esteem needs:* a premium lager might be a means of making a clear statement about the drinker's status or discernment. Look at me: I can afford a better quality lager; the ordinary stuff isn't good enough for me; I know what I'm drinking; I'm trendy, I'm cool. The drinker might also want to be

seen as an opinion leader, the one to whom the close social group look to introduce them to new and different products. He/she, however, might then need to move onto something different or more premium as soon as his/her social group starts to adopt the latest trendy brand.

2   Why do you think that the premium lager market is primarily aimed at males aged between 20 and 40?

- Young men represent the largest segment of the lager market generally
- young men are more image or status conscious in terms of what they drink and are particularly conscious of their standing within a peer group
- for young men, choice of drink is an integral part of a fashion/lifestyle statement expressed through brand choices
- there is a move towards drinking less, but buying better quality, more expensive drinks.

3   What individual and group influences are likely to affect someone's choice of lager brand?

Individual:
- *Personality:* outgoing and individualistic or conservative and wanting to blend in with the crowd?
- *Perception:* interpretation of advertising and other marketing messages and the consumer's understanding of how each product might enhance their self-image or status.
- *Motivation:* again, the consumer's perception of how this product will improve the fulfilment of belongingness or esteem needs (see also the answer to question 1 above).
- *Attitude:* attitudes towards various brands and beliefs about the kind of people who buy them; attitudes to product attributes, for example country of origin, strength or ingredients.

Group:
- *Social class:* premium lager might be seen as 'less vulgar' than ordinary lager?
- *Reference groups:* the choices made by one's close social or other membership group, and whether the consumer wants to match them or be seen to be different; the consumer's perceptions of what an aspirant group might choose. The consumer might also identify brands with an image that appeals to a dissociative group, and avoid being seen with that brand.
- *Culture/subculture:* this could influence what brands or countries of origin are perceived to be fashionable, and whether lager is felt to be an acceptable choice at all within a particular group.

4   Given the huge range of lagers available, why do you think there is still room for premium ciders and products such as Smirnoff Mule?

- Most premium lagers, as 'fashion accessories' have a short life span. Consumers are perhaps open to something a bit different.
- Consumers could simply become bored with the taste of lager.
- Consumers could simply become bored with the image of lager.
- Consumers could simply become bored or confused with the proliferation of lager brands.
- Lager might be viewed as largely a male orientated product. Cider and spirits based premium products could have a more universal appeal.
- Premium products based on ciders and spirits are still sufficiently new to have a high novelty factor and to be appealing to innovators and opinion leaders. The real test of whether there is long term room for them in the market will come when that novelty has worn off, and they become more mainstream and have to compete with the next wave of fashionable competition.

Marketing in Action The 90s Woman (p 99)

Discussion question
Why do you think women might have rejected the advertising images of the power dressing career woman of the late 1980s/early 1990s?

- Unrealistic compared with most women's lives, yet not the kind of fantasy that many women can identify with
- presents just another stereotype
- too ruthless and hard edged - seen as unfeminine?
- too ambitious?
- denies the reality and stresses of juggling home and work that many women face
- focuses on flirtatious romance rather than the real complexities of relationships?

Marketing in Action Savoury Snacks (p 101)

Discussion question
What seem to be the main influences on a consumer's choice of savoury snack brand?

- Their age
- their experience of the market, thus their level of loyalty or boredom threshold
- their desire for quality, a taste experience, or credibility, and thus brand imagery
- their health considerations, thus the development of low fat, low salt brand variants
- perhaps for children, the parental influence over their consumption of 'junk' food.

Marketing in Action Reaching the Youth Market (p 113)

Discussion question
To what extent do you think 'yob' advertising is a legitimate marketing approach? What are its disadvantages?

This should provoke some ethical discussion about the boundaries of taste and decency. Issues that might arise for and against this kind of advertising include:
For:
- It appeals directly to a certain type of target audience
- it could be seen as more honest than much other advertising
- it could be seen as mould-breaking.
Against:
- It is too offensive to too many people
- it degrades the advertiser, the product and the customer, offering no positive product benefits
- it encourages anti-social attitudes and behaviour.

Marketing in Action Pester Power (p 118)

Discussion question
What do you think might characterise each of the five types of child mentioned in terms of their pester power?

1. *Fussy and fixed on favourites:* brand loyal - substitutes will not do. Mum is given precise instructions about what to buy.
2. *Strong-willed influencers:* once the child has seen something it wants, it will enter into a battle of wills with mum until it gets its way. Mum is more likely to concede in order to stop the child screaming or whining (see the last paragraph of the marketing in action vignette in the main text).
3. *Gimmick gurus:* latch onto anything new or different; likely to pester for character licensed products or those featuring promotional free gifts or offers.
4. *Junk food fiends:* pester for anything that looks as if it will not be good for them, such as sweets and crisps for immediate consumption, and burgers, chips and pizzas for the freezer.
5. *Well adjusted 'eat what you're given':* probably not serious pests; no particularly strong food fads or preferences; realistic about what they can persuade mum to do and don't push their luck too far.

SUGGESTED ASSIGNMENTS

- Questions for Review 3.7 might be adapted as an assignment thus: for each of the types of buying situation defined on pp 96-98, choose an appropriate product and compare and contrast how the duration of the consumer decision-making process and the extent of the information search might differ and why.
- What are reference groups and in what ways can they influence a consumer's buying decisions and behaviour?

Chapter 4
ORGANISATIONAL BUYING BEHAVIOUR

LECTURE PLAN

A lecture based on this chapter should help the student to:
1. Understand the nature and structure of organisational buying;
2. appreciate the differences between organisational and consumer buying;
3. analyse the reasons why purchasing varies across different buying situations, and
4. link organisational buying with the development of marketing strategy.
The key sections of this lecture should be:

Defining organisational marketing (pp 127-129):
- What is organisational marketing
- the range of transactions it includes
- the differences between organisational and consumer marketing, including OHP 11, table 4.1 (p 129) Differences Between Organisational and Consumer Marketing:
    ⇒ The purpose of the purchase
    ⇒ the risk attached to the purchase
    ⇒ the degree of customisation and negotiation involved
    ⇒ the formality of the decision-making process
    ⇒ the speed of the decision-making process
    ⇒ the relative ease of switching suppliers.

Types of organisational customers (pp 129-132):
- Commercial enterprises
- governmental bodies
- institutions.
This section could be omitted and students encouraged to read it up in the textbook for themselves.

Characteristics of organisational markets (pp 132-142):
- *The nature of demand:* derived, joint and inelastic demand.
- *Structure of demand:* industrial and geographic concentration.
- *Buying process complexity:* the need for clear policies and guidelines in purchasing; the need for professionalism; the need for group involvement; purchase significance; the need to adhere to any relevant purchasing laws or regulations.
- *Buyer-seller relationships:* the need for strong ongoing relationships.

The decision-making process (pp 142-148):

An overview of the decision-making process, including OHP 12, figure 4.5 (p 143) Models of Organisational Buying Decision-making:

- The general character of the stages and what they involve
- *Precipitation:* internal and external triggers; the impact of business threats and opportunities.
- *Product specification:* the importance of precisely specifying what is needed; the involvement of various business functions in agreeing the specification.
- *Supplier selection:* the problems of supplier search and selection; established *vs.* new suppliers; single *vs.* multiple sourcing.
- *Commitment:* the importance of monitoring and evaluation; and of relationship building.
- A comparison with a consumer decision-making model.

The structure of the DMU (pp 152-153):

- Definition of the buying centre.
- Roles within the DMU, including OHP 13, table 4.5 (p 152) Comparison of DMUs in Consumer and Organisational Markets:
  ⇒ How they differ in terms of defined roles
  ⇒ how they differ in terms of formality and complexity
  ⇒ how the individual's roles might change from purchasing episode to purchasing episode.

Material from pp 148-151 can also be incorporated into this section.

Influences on the decision-making process (pp 154-157):

- *Economic influences:* prices, specifications, quality consistency, supply reliability and continuity, customer service provision.
- *Non-economic influences:* prestige, career security, social needs, other personal needs.

Relationship marketing (pp 157-161):

- The importance of relationships in organisational markets
- approaches to supplier handling
- prioritising relationships in terms of their relative importance
- the relationship life-cycle stages.

QUESTIONS FOR REVIEW

4.1   What are the different categories of organisational customer, and how do they differ from each other? (pp 129-132)

- *Commercial enterprises:* profit-making businesses e.g. manufacturers, service providers, retailers etc, which purchase in order to produce and/or resell goods and services for profit.
- *Government bodies:* bodies linked with local, national or EU government spending public money in order to provide services or goods for the general public, for example health services, defence, bridges, motorways, libraries etc.
- *Institutions:* non-profit organisations e.g. churches, charities and educational institutions etc, operating with or without public money, but purchasing autonomously to provide goods and services for the benefit of a clearly defined clientele which may or may not contribute to the cost.

4.2   What is derived demand and how might it affect organisational purchasing? (pp 132-133)

Derived demand means that demand for raw materials, components, semi-finished goods, or business services in organisational markets depends on forecast demand in a consumer market. Thus, as shown in figure 4.4, dye or fibre manufacturers need to predict what colours and fabrics are going to be fashionable in two years' time so that the weavers can create the right cloths and clothing manufacturers can have the right garments available when consumers want them. The implication for purchasing is that all organisations within the manufacturing and supply chain are buying with the ultimate end customer in mind, even if they are not dealing directly with that customer.

4.3   Why does organisational buying vary across different types of organisation, sometimes even within the same industry? (pp 137-142)

It varies because of:
- Differing purchasing policies and procedures implemented
- differing levels of professionalism exercised within purchasing functions
- differing types of production system imposing different levels of rigourousness on suppliers
- differently composed buying centres
- differing levels of significance attached to different purchases
- different types of buyer-seller relationship.

4.4   What are the main differences between organisational and consumer buying behaviour? (pp 127-129)

- Purpose of purchase
- quantity purchased
- frequency of purchase
- formality of purchasing process including the structure and involvement of DMU
- decision-making criteria
- degree of customisation
- degree of negotiation
- ability to switch suppliers
- degree of risk involved in the purchase.

4.5   Outline the main stages in the organisational buying decision-making process. (pp 142-148)

- *Precipitation:* internal or external triggers prompt the realisation that there is a purchasing need.
- *Product specification:* the purchasing organisation defines precisely what is needed and what the choice criteria are going to be.
- *Supplier selection:* the purchasing organisation develops a shortlist of qualified suppliers, assesses their suitability for the current purchase and perhaps as a potential long term relationship partner, then chooses the most appropriate one.
- *Commitment:* the order has been placed and fulfilled and then the supplier's performance and ability to meet its commitments is monitored, appraised and assessed.

4.6   What factors influence the complexity and the amount of time spent on the decision-making process? (pp 142-148)

- Urgency of purchase
- complexity and specification of the purchase
- degree of customisation
- degree of perceived risk
- existing supplier relationships
- type of purchase - new task, modified rebuy, routine rebuy
- structure of the decision-making unit.

4.7   What is a buying centre? (pp 152-153)

A buying centre is a group of individuals, perhaps from differing functional areas and levels within the organisation who collectively take responsibility for contributing towards, and making, a purchase decision.

4.8   How might people in different functional roles (for example R&D or marketing) participate in organisational buying? (pp 148-151)

- *Purchasing:* negotiating with suppliers and handling ongoing commercial relationships with them; liaison with suppliers; helping to locate and assess potential suppliers; may act as buyer within the DMU.
- *Production/operations:* precipitation and specification of purchases; perhaps also act as influencer and user.
- *Engineering:* specification and design; influencer within the DMU.
- *R&D:* might work on specifications and act as influencer or gatekeeper.
- *Finance:* influencer and possible decider.
- *Marketing:* influencer; possible role in specifying needs.

4.9   Define the main economic and non-economic influences on organisational decision-making. (pp 154-157)

Economic:
- Price
- product specification
- quality consistency
- supply reliability and continuity
- customer service.

Non-economic:
- Prestige
- career security
- friendship/social needs
- personal profiles and characteristics.

4.10   Why is it that in some buyer-seller relationships strong bonds and co-operation develop? (pp 158-159)

- *Economic benefits:* both derive benefit from the relationship; synergy is derived from working with each other rather than developing an adversarial relationship; both have invested in each other in terms of time, effort and perhaps even financial investment.
- *Social benefits:* trust, mutual knowledge and shared experience create a feeling of security. Mutual dependence as a result of joint development and investment might also encourage the maintenance of strong bonds.

QUESTIONS FOR DISCUSSION

4.1   From the supplier's point of view, how might the marketing approaches aimed at a customer making a new task purchase differ from those aimed at a routine rebuy customer?

Students may mention differences arising from:
- Customer's knowledge of product area
- customer's past experience of this kind of purchase
- level of risk perceived by the buyer in this purchase

- value and frequency of purchase
- supplier's knowledge of the buyer and its needs
- customer's knowledge of the supplier
- degree of reassurance needed by the buyer
- customer's choice criteria
- structure of customer's decision-making unit.

Students should show how these differences might translate into marketing action particularly in terms of communication strategies.

4.2   How are supplier handling strategies changing as organisations seek to improve their competitiveness?

Students should raise issues of the move towards more collaboration between buyers and sellers and the trend towards developing long term relationships. Advantages of collaboration, as outlined in table 4.6 (p 159) should be considered and explained.

4.3   What are the stages in the buyer-seller relationship life cycle, and how is each characterised? What difference might the stages make to the seller's marketing approaches? (pp 160-161)

- *Awareness:* initial contact, which can be initiated by either party. Seller might concentrate on getting to know key personnel within the buying organisation and establishing the buyer's capabilities and needs. Seller has to establish its credibility and ensure that the buyer understands and appreciates what the supplier can do.
- *Exploration:* gaining experience of each other, perhaps through test orders. In this case the supplier has to ensure that it makes promises based on the buyer's needs and priorities, and that those promises are fulfilled in practice. Buyer and seller might also discuss the potential for future joint development strategies.
- *Expansion:* more orders, the development of trust, commitment and mutual adaptation. Seller will be de-emphasising price and negotiating on benefits, long-term cost savings, and mutual advantages.
- *Commitment:* a comfortable and stable relationship, with perhaps a high level of mutual dependency. Marketing effort is still about detailed relationship maintenance and building to mutual advantage.
- *Dissolution:* something breaks the stability, perhaps complacency on the part of the supplier, or changes in the business environment, or the emergence of more vibrant competitors, and the relationship falls apart. The supplier can either focus its marketing attention on salvaging and rebuilding the relationship or on seeking and developing new business elsewhere.

4.4   You are the purchasing manager of a large organisation with an enormous annual spend. Most of your contracts are awarded by tender. What would your attitude be to the following offers from potential suppliers, and to what extent would they influence your decision-making: (a) a bottle of whisky at Christmas? (b) an invitation to lunch to discuss your requirements? (c) an offer of the free use of the supplier's Managing Director's Spanish villa for two weeks? (d) £1500?

This question should stimulate debate about ethics and professional practice in purchasing, encouraging students to think about the problems in drawing up definite guidelines on 'right and wrong' and declared interests. Discussion about the pros and cons of developing personal relationships between individuals within buying and selling organisations and the difficulty of maintaining an objective view might also arise.

4.5   What do you think are the advantages and disadvantages of long-term, close buyer-seller relationships?

Students may raise issues such as the following:
Advantages:
- Collaborative R&D; exchange of expertise and knowledge
- mutual flexibility
- mutual problem solving
- integrated systems; streamlined flow between buyer and seller
- long term improvements in quality and cost effectiveness.

Disadvantages:
- Over-dependence on each other
- staleness - no fresh stimulus to either
- standards slip through complacency
- over familiarity - loss of objectiveness in assessing supplier performance
- supplier adapts to better fit this buyer's needs and fails to develop wider interests or customer portfolio.

CASE STUDY 4.1 Taurus (p 163)

Teaching Objectives

1. To explore the kinds of issues that influence organisational purchasing decision-making;
2. to ensure that students understand the concept of the buying centre/DMU;
3. to gain a practical and analytical insight into what can go wrong in organisational decision-making.

1   Outline the problems leading up to the demise of Taurus 1. Could they have been predicted?

The major problems arise from two broad groups of factors:
Specification issues:
- The difficulty of agreeing a specification where previous experience of this kind of purchase is limited
- no model was agreed by the various parties of what they really wanted; there was no agreement on system procedures
- they were working on adapting the paper system, rather than examining the process from scratch from the user's perspective
- the project was allowed to grow to unmanageable levels.

Group buying issues:
- There was a shortage of technical expertise and advice
- different buyers were involved with different perspectives that were not reconciled
- there were problems in agreeing the decision rules and priorities in the buying unit
- the inability of any one organisation to act as the lead decision maker
- there was no conflict resolution strategy.

As a result of these two groups of issues, development time was extended and complexity increased.

Most of these problems of new task purchasing with group specification development really should have been highly predictable and could perhaps have been avoided or resolved if a more rigid and well defined decision-making framework had been developed at the start.

2   Given the eventual outcome of Taurus 1, what changes were needed to give Taurus 2 a better chance of successful launch?

A number of changes could be suggested:
- The need for a champion - Peter Rawlins.
- The need for one party (perhaps the Stock Exchange) to take a lead role.

- The simplification of the specification by working on existing commercial databases. The project, however, still tried to meet the full range of interests and seek group consensus and reconcile the needs of the private investor with those of the large financial institutions. They still did not aim to fully evaluate more limited systems elsewhere in order to start to change behaviour, better inform decision makers and develop better technical know-how.

3   **In a new major project such as Taurus, what consideration should be given to the composition and decision-making style of the buying committee?**

The major considerations are:
- The need for a full range of expertise to be represented on the committee, from system designers through to users.
- The committee might need an inner core group of key decision makers, supported by an outer group that informs, influences and provides input as needed. The outer group is not responsible for project management and ultimate decision-making responsibility. This could lead to a more streamlined yet flexible DMU.
- There is a clear need to gain consensus from all parties to an agreed specification as well as developing a clear view of the technical feasibility of options.
- The DMU should define and face up to conflicting user needs and priorities which are essential to the system specification.
- A recognised and agreed leader may alleviate some of the difficulties in finding agreement.
- The composition of the DMU might have to change as the project unfolds, from specifiers through to negotiators and implementors.

4   **In what ways do you think that implementation of the purchasing decision-making process in a manufacturing firm investing in new production machinery might differ from that of the Stock Exchange investing in a computer system?**

The main differences reflect the nature of the DMU. In comparison with the Stock Exchange, the manufacturer's DMU:
- Involves various specialists from within the organisation, and a single overall objective should predominate in the decision-making process. The Stock Exchange had to deal with a range of different objectives from different organisations.
- Should involve more clearly defined roles than in the Taurus case, including specifiers (production engineers etc), users (production managers, operatives), influencers (consultants, component suppliers, R&D), buyers (purchasing staff) and deciders (finance directors, senior managers).
- Can always refer conflicts and disagreements to more senior management within the organisation. It is also possible that established seniority among members of the DMU will impose a more natural discipline and a hierarchy of power, influence and decision-making ability within the DMU.
- May be able to draw on established experience and relationships with existing suppliers.

CASE STUDY 4.2 Philips Cultivates Suppliers (p 164)

Teaching Objectives

1. To explore the kinds of issues that encourage the creation and maintenance of close buyer-seller relationships in organisational markets;
2. to appreciate the links between quality and purchasing decisions;
3. to emphasise the importance of supplier monitoring and evaluation and its impact on supplier management.

1   **Why should Philips go to all this trouble to develop relationships with suppliers? Why doesn't it just choose suppliers on the basis of the lowest price?**

- Philips needs quality/reliability/consistency from its suppliers. Lowest price suppliers might not necessarily invest in any of that.
- It is of no use to Philips if a supplier cuts its costs too far and risks going out of business.
- Alternative suppliers might be hard to find for high tech or complex components.
- Philips might be looking to develop supplier loyalty - it wouldn't want its best suppliers moving over to the competition or giving the competition better terms of business.
- Philips is in the kind of technical markets where co-operative R&D efforts could be beneficial. These can only emerge where there is ongoing trust and a good relationship between a buyer and seller that know each other very well.

2   **What do you think each of the five principles of 'Philips Quality' actually means in practice? How are they consistent with the marketing concept and what impact might they have on the marketing mix?**

1. This could refer to product quality, administration quality or logistical quality, for example. It helps to create a differential advantage that is hard to imitate, and it helps to deliver the right product at the right time at the right place at the right price.
2. Products and marketing packages need to be designed to solve the customer's 'problem'. The company needs to be very responsive to the customer's needs both pre- and post-sale. This is at the heart of the marketing concept.
3. This might mean being innovative and ahead of the competition. It is consistent with the concept of differential advantage. It might even mean Philips defining and solving problems that customers didn't even know they had?
4. Internally, this generates commitment to customers and to products at all levels of the organisation and in all functional areas. Externally, it might mean that customers feel that they are being treated as individuals rather than as a faceless source of profit!
5. This leads to innovation in products, new ideas and longer term cost effectiveness. Jointly developed components, for instance might be more durable, more reliable, or perform their function more effectively.

All of these have a positive impact on all areas of the marketing mix, especially on products and on delivering customer satisfaction. Putting them into practice might lead to higher costs and prices in the short-term, but this could be justified by more responsive customer service etc. In the longer term, however, it might lead to lower costs as there will be less wastage and fewer customer complaints, and more satisfied customers might lead to higher sales volumes and thus better economies of scale.

3   **Suggest what criteria Philips might use to decide what category a particular supplier falls into.**

Some obvious suggestions might be:
- How crucial is this component to our product?
- Is it likely to become more or less crucial to us in the future?
- How easy is it to replace a supplier?
- How high tech/complex/precision is this component?
- How innovative is this supplier?
- What expertise do they have to offer?
- How willing are they to adapt/co-operate?
- How culturally compatible are they with us?

4   **What is the purpose of supplier evaluation? What do you think Philips might do if they found that a particular supplier had under performed in terms of costs and quality?**

38

The purpose is to check whether actual performance matches expected performance, and to review whether remedial action or further relationship building needs to take place. It might also act as a trigger to review changes in the external environment, so that Philips can check whether this supplier is still the best or most appropriate. The kinds of areas that might be reviewed are:

- Quality/meeting specifications
- delivery times/quantities
- cost profile
- R&D progress
- adaptability/flexibility
- problem solving.

Potential actions could be:

- Sack them!
- Give them a warning that things need to improve. This might mean cutting down the number or size of orders to this supplier and setting a deadline for improvement.
- Philips could 'lend' the supplier a troubleshooting team to help them diagnose and solve their problems.
- Philips might be prepared to invest in helping the supplier to update equipment/systems to better meet required standards.
- Philips might want to review its own supplier selection and negotiation process - were the performance targets too ambitious? Too rigourous? Beyond the supplier's skills and capabilities in the first place? Is it possible to relax targets to the point where the supplier CAN match them?

Supplementary question

What are the pros and cons of each of these courses of action?

- *Sack the supplier:* Philips would need to be sure that another supplier can take over the order, or that others are easily available. This is best, therefore, for less crucial suppliers (the commercial suppliers group, in Philips' terminology). With a supplier-partner, that Philips has spent many years building up or that supplies critical components, this would be an extremely drastic course of action not taken lightly. Philips would have to be sure that the problem is too fundamental to put right. Generally, sacking a supplier ensures that the buyer is completely free of the problem, as long as they can be sure that a new supplier can be found and would be definitely better ...
- *The warning shot:* the supplier is left in no doubt that the buyer is displeased, but has the chance to solve the problem if the will and the means exist. This is most useful for suppliers, such as the preferred suppliers, that the buyer really would like to hang on to, but which could be dropped as a last resort. It gives the buyer a breathing space to make alternative supply arrangements and test out other suppliers, just in case the worst happens, but the buyer does face a period of uncertainty as to whether the supplier will improve or not. If orders to that supplier have been reduced, then the buyer still has to make interim arrangements to make up the shortfall from another supplier.
- *Lend advice:* this is a positive response, appropriate for preferred suppliers or supplier-partners. The buyer is seen to be working with the supplier co-operatively to solve a problem and help them improve for their mutual benefit. It can be viewed as a confirmation of commitment to co-operation. Clearly, however, it does involve some cost to the buyer, and some suppliers might resent the 'invasion' of outsiders telling them what to do. The buyer also has to ensure that in the short term, quality supplies can be maintained, perhaps from an alternative supplier, until this supplier can guarantee its performance standards again.
- *Invest:* much of what was said immediately above also applies here. If the buyer is actually investing cash in new machinery or quality systems or whatever, the implications for commitment are even stronger. The risk is that it strengthens mutual dependency, and if the supplier continues to falter, despite the investment, the buyer is left with an ongoing dilemma not only regarding the supply problem, but also regarding recovery of the investment made.
- *Revise standards:* an honest evaluation of the buyer's expectations is no bad thing, but care must be taken to define exactly how and why certain performance criteria are to be relaxed. Serious re-negotiation of standards might be most likely with a supplier-partner involved in a critical, high

tech component, and where both buyer and supplier are still learning and developing their expertise and knowledge, for example.

Marketing in Action Buying Machine Tools (p 135)

Discussion question
Summarise the stages in MBM's purchasing process. Why does it need to be so comprehensive and formalised?

Stages in the process:
1. Define objectives of purchase
2. develop specification and criteria for purchase
3. draw up list of potential suppliers and request quotations
4. screen responses and draw up shortlist of three
5. negotiate package with each potential supplier
6. request test piece from each
7. assess outcomes and select supplier.

The process is comprehensive and formal because of the complexity of the purchase and because it represents long term capital investment. The potential losses from making the 'wrong' decision, resulting in an inappropriate machine, an unreliable machine, or poor after-sales service, could be extremely high, in terms of both cash and lost customers.

Marketing in Action Automotive Component Suppliers (p 139)

Discussion question
What are the risks of single sourcing a component (a) for Toyota as the buyer and (b) to the supplier concerned?

a) For Toyota:
- Supply failure
- over-dependence on that supplier
- thus potentially open to price rises as there is no overt competitive pressure on the supplier
- eventual needs might outstrip supplier's production capacity.

b) For the supplier:
- Over-dependence on that one customer
- if customer is taking a large percentage of the supplier's output, it is difficult for the supplier to diversify and develop a broader portfolio
- customer might want to 'interfere' in the supplier's way of doing things
- customer might use dependence to put undue pressure on price, quality etc.

Marketing in Action Pendolino - On Time, On Track (p 145)

Discussion question
What issues is the potential buyer of the Pendolino likely to take into account when making a purchasing decision?

- Technical specification
- comparison with competing locomotives/rolling stock
- compatibility with local railway system
- degree and cost of customisation required
- delivery schedules
- promised after-sales service and support
- possible joint venture for construction?

- Political pressures to buy more locally?
- Cost effectiveness and reliability in operation.

Marketing in Action Buyer - Supplier Co-operation (p 159)

Discussion question
Why do you think Jeyes switched from in-house production of bottles to supply from LMG?

- Allows Jeyes to concentrate attention and resources on core business
- LMG are experts in the field
- thus might be more cost effective
- thus might be more innovative
- investment in relevant machinery and product development is LMG's problem
- LMG might achieve economies of scale through also taking on other customers.

SUGGESTED ASSIGNMENTS

- Questions for Discussion 4.2 might be adapted as an assignment thus: how and why are supplier handling strategies changing as organisations seek to improve their competitiveness? Cite examples.
- Choose a product that could be sold in either an organisational or a consumer market (a PC, for example). To what extent, how and why might the buying decision-making process differ between the two types of customer? What are the implications for the marketer?

Chapter 5
SEGMENTING MARKETS

LECTURE PLAN

A lecture based on this chapter should help the student to:
1. Understand the potential benefits of breaking markets down into smaller, more manageable parts or segments;
2. explain the ways in which market segments are defined in both organisational and consumer markets;
3. understand the effects on the marketing mix of pursuing specific segments; and
4. appreciate the role of segmentation in strategic marketing thinking.

The key sections of this lecture should be:

Introduction (pp 168-169):
- The concept of segmentation
- why it is important.

Segmenting organisational markets (pp 169-172):
- *Macro segmentation bases:* organisational characteristics; application.
- *Micro segmentation bases:* product; applications; technology; purchasing policies; DMUs; decision-making processes; buyer - seller relationships.

Segmenting consumer markets (pp 172-184):
- Geographic segmentation
- demographic segmentation
- geodemographic segmentation
- psychographic segmentation
- behaviour segmentation, including OHP 14, figure 5.1 (p 182) Consumer Product Usage Categories:
  ⇒ The importance of protecting heavy users
  ⇒ the desirability of turning medium users into heavy users
  ⇒ the reasons why consumers might be light users and the problems of investing in this group
  ⇒ the different marketing messages suitable for each group
- and also including OHP 15, figure 5.2 (p 184) The AIDA Response Hierarchy Model:
  ⇒ Definition of the different stages
  ⇒ how the marketing task varies between them.
- Multivariable segmentation.

Targeting (pp 184-189):
- Definition and importance of clear targeting
- alternative strategies, including OHP 16, figure 5.3 (p 185) Segmentation Targeting Strategies:
  ⇒ Define each type of strategy
  ⇒ appropriate use of each
  ⇒ advantages and disadvantages of each.

Benefits and risks of segmentation (pp 189-190):
- To the customer
- for the marketing mix and marketing strategy
- for competitive position.

Criteria for successful segmentation (pp 191-192):
- Distinctiveness
- tangibility
- accessibility
- defendability.

QUESTIONS FOR REVIEW

5.1   What is the difference between macro and micro segmentation in organisational markets? (pp 170-172)

Macro segmentation focuses on organisational characteristics (size, location, product usage rate, for example) and the broad industry application for which they are purchasing. Micro segmentation looks more closely at the internal characteristics of the organisation, in terms of its purchasing policies and procedures, decision-making structures, approach to business relationships, management philosophy, as well as its needs and wants from the goods and services purchased.

5.2   What variables might be included in micro segmentation? (pp 171-172)

- The product areas covered by the purchaser
- the detailed applications for which a purchase is being made
- the buyer's technology level
- the buyer's purchasing policies
- the buyer's decision-making unit structure
- the buyer's decision-making processes and procedures
- the buyer's buyer-seller relationships.

5.3 **What is geographic segmentation and how is it used in consumer and organisational markets?** (p 170; pp 172-173)

Geographic segmentation means dividing customers into groups according to their location. In consumer markets it could be useful for small businesses looking for an appropriate catchment area. It could also be useful for subdividing large geographic regions as a starting point before more detailed segmentation within regions. In organisational markets certain industries might be geographically concentrated, with implications for a supplier's own logistics and distribution strategies. As with consumer markets, however, more detailed segmentation is likely to be superimposed on any geographic divisions.

5.4 **What are the main demographic variables used in consumer markets?** (pp 173-175)

- Age
- gender
- ethnic group
- income and occupation
- socioeconomic class
- family structure.

5.5 **What is geodemographic segmentation and how can it help the marketer?** (pp 175-177)

Geodemographic segmentation creates groups of customers based partly on their location and partly on their demographic profile. Some commercially available geodemographic classification systems also include lifestyle data to give an even more detailed profile. Such systems are useful for:
- Planning market research studies
- assessing potential retail locations
- planning direct mail campaigns
- planning the distribution of free product samples or leaflets door to door.

5.6 **What, according to Plummer, are the four main components of psychographic, or lifestyle, segmentation?** (pp 177-178)

1. Activities
2. interests
3. opinions
4. demographics.

5.7 **Why is psychographic segmentation so difficult and so risky to do?** (p 180)

- Lifestyles are complex
- many intangible variables are involved
- it is difficult to define which variables are relevant
- it is difficult to measure consumers on some of these variables
- it can thus be difficult to track how the membership of a psychographic segment is evolving.

5.8 **In what major way does behavioural segmentation differ from the other methods? Outline the variables that can be used in behavioural segmentation.** (pp 180-184)

Behavioural segmentation differs because instead of focusing purely on the characteristics of the customer, it looks at the relationship between the customer and the product. Variables include:
- End use of the product
- benefits sought from the product
- usage rate

- attitude towards the product
- buyer readiness stage (awareness; interest, desire, action - see figure 5.2 p 184)

5.9   What are the three approaches to targeting available to marketers? (pp 185-188)

1. Undifferentiated
2. differentiated
3. concentrated.

5.10   What factors might affect the marketer's choice of targeting strategy? (p 189)

- Size of organisation; capabilities; resources
- type of product involved
- product life cycle stage
- competitors' actions
- overall corporate objectives and strategies.

QUESTIONS FOR DISCUSSION

5.1   How might the market for personal computers, sold to organisational markets, be segmented?

Students should bring a range of possible organisational segmentation variables into the discussion, including organisational size, location, type of industry, number of machines to be purchased, proposed use of the machine(s), number and type of machines already owned by the customer etc. They should also demonstrate an appreciation of how these variables might be combined and applied to this specific type of purchase to give a rich and appropriate profile of the market.

5.2   Find examples of products that depend strongly on demographic segmentation, making sure that you find at least one example for each of the main demographic variables.

A wide range of products might be offered here. Students should be encouraged to justify their choices and to discuss how the demographic variables are also working with other types of segmentation base to target each product more closely. Products discussed might include:
- Magazines (sex, age, occupation, for example)
- clothing (basic segmentation by sex, age, and income, but with lifestyle elements added on)
- toiletries and cosmetics (again, basic segmentation by sex, age, family size/status and income, but with lifestyle elements added on)
- holidays (marital/family status? also some age segmentation).

5.3   Choose a consumer market and discuss how it might be segmented in terms of benefits sought.

Students should show:
- an understanding of what 'benefits sought' means (see p 181)
- insight into how it can be applied meaningfully to their chosen product
- and perhaps an appreciation of the difficulties of defining and measuring these segments, and the problems of incorporating the sought benefits into the marketing mix and communicating them.

5.4   For each targeting strategy, find examples of organisations that use it. Discuss why you think they have chosen this strategy and how they implement it.

Choice of organisation should be appropriate and well argued within the context of the question.

- *Undifferentiated:* it could be difficult to find a true example of this. Students could be encouraged to discuss the extent to which they think public sector bodies (for example, the police, hospitals, schools, libraries) pursue an undifferentiated strategy.
- *Differentiated:* the large car manufacturers - Ford, Renault, VW etc - are good examples of organisations pursuing this kind of strategy, with different marketing mixes for different groups of customers based on price, size of car, end use of car, psychological needs etc.
- *Concentrated:* these organisations are likely to be specialist or niche operators and could be found in any type of market. Luxury goods that target the top end of the market made by manufacturers, such as Gucci, Rolex, Rolls Royce motors, with no interest in the less affluent segments are obvious examples.

5.5   How can market segmentation influence decisions about the marketing mix?

As well as the general benefits of segmentation relating to competitive strategy and resource allocation, specific points about the marketing mix that might be raised include:
- *Price:* can be adapted depending on the perceived price sensitivity of the target segment. Selecting a non-sensitive segment could allow premium pricing.
- *Product:* can be designed to deliver exactly what benefits and product features the segment wants.
- *Place:* segments could be defined in terms of their 'place' preferences so that the product is made available where and when they want it, with the right level of pre- and post-sales support.
- *Promotion:* the nature of the segment helps to define the communication task. Does this segment need awareness generation? Emphasis on particular features or benefits? Explanation? Reassurance? Reminding? Incentive? The balance of the promotional mix and the choice of media will also be segment dependent.

CASE STUDY 5.1 Kings Hotel (A) (p 195)

Teaching Objectives

1. To ensure that students understand the concept of segmentation and its importance;
2. to explore how various segmentation bases might be applied in practice;
3. to analyse the link between segmentation and the marketing mix offering and its impact on marketing success.

1   How might the needs of the army segment differ from those of the independent traveller?

Segments could be based upon reason for travel and benefits sought during stay.
The army hotel guest:
- Is part of a captive market, in that the visit may not be voluntary, and therefore the guest may not be so discerning!
- may not have discretion over choice of hotel
- pays a price agreed centrally
- as a result of military experience is probably more willing to accept variable standards without question
- is likely to be a Polish national and therefore more familiar with local rather than international standards
- requires functional rather than luxury facilities.
The independent traveller:
- Has considerable choice so may shop around on price or facilities
- is likely to visiting Krakow on pleasure or business, and therefore is likely to be looking for a relaxing and comfortable ambience to enhance the trip
- may be looking for a convenient location for parking and access
- may be looking for extra hotel services (bar, satellite television, room service etc)

- may need currency exchange, local information services, and English or German speaking staff, assuming the guest is not Polish
- needs an efficient reservation system and faster check out system.

2   Evaluate Kings Hotel's strengths and weaknesses in terms of what it currently (a) the army guest; (b) the independent tourist; (c) the business traveller.

a)   The army guest strengths
- Within an acceptable price range
- offers appropriately basic facilities
- rooms are segmented by army rank
- the management approach and low level of customer service is probably appropriate for this market.

The army guest weaknesses: there are no major weaknesses, as the current offering has been developed with this target segment in mind.

b)   The independent tourist strengths:
- Location close to historic district
- cheaper than alternatives
- links with tourist information office.

The independent tourist weaknesses:
- Limited effort to use price seriously to maximise occupancy
- poor facilities and atmosphere compared with normal international standards
- lack of in-hotel entertainment and services
- limited restaurant facilities, thus guests are likely to eat out.

c)   The business traveller strengths:
- Suitable for low budget customer
- central location.

The business traveller weaknesses:
- Poor facilities for the business traveller e.g. international telephones; fax; desk in room.
- no business support or conference centre or facilities
- cannot to offer flexible service to suit guest needs e.g. airport shuttle, baggage handling, room service.
- limited restaurant facilities
- limited parking.

3   How might the Hotel's marketing task differ if it targeted tourists travelling in organised groups as opposed to the independent traveller? Is the hotel wise to avoid block bookings from tour operators, as it does currently?

The tour operator group is potentially easier to reach than the independent traveller because of the smaller number of potential customers to contact. This could be achieved, for example, through LOT by direct sales, mailshots, and advertising in targeted media. The main challenge would be to find those groups prepared to trade quality and service for price. This means it is unlikely to appeal to groups of American or European tourists expecting higher standards, and thus issues such as catering, baggage handling and entertainment would need to be addressed. The Kings Hotel is poorly placed to increase in-hotel sales (restaurant, bar etc) to compensate for a low group room rate.

The independent traveller or 'walk-ins' can be difficult to reach before booking, and the hotel is not set up to meet the variety of service requirements demanded by this group. This means developing coverage with travel agents and airlines as well as with the tourist office to generate awareness among potential guests as well as gaining access to a reservation system. Increasing use of IT in this area will probably leave the Kings Hotel behind. The poster campaign and advertising in tourist magazines will be essential for capturing those independent travellers who do not book in advance. The hotel will need to continue to refurbish and upgrade facilities and services if it is going to address the needs of this sector seriously.

It is probably unwise for the hotel to avoid group bookings, especially during the off season and during the shoulder months. As seen in the previous section there is a close match between the budget group travel sector and the capabilities of the Kings Hotel.

4   If the army business was lost, what market segment do you think Kings Hotel is currently best equipped to target?

Without major refurbishment, the hotel appears to be at a competitive disadvantage in many segments. It may have to focus on the low price sector. This would probably mean groups, i.e. students, cut price tours and parties. These groups would not expect high standards of facilities or customer service. The problem would be gaining sufficiently high occupancy level to provide reasonable profits to fund a refurbishment programme. Even the low price segments demand a certain minimum of services. A programme of in-hotel service improvement may be necessary to encourage more in-hotel spend i.e. food, personal services, room video, currency exchange.

CASE STUDY 5.2 A Night at the Opera (p 196)

Teaching Objectives

1. To ensure that students understand the concept of segmentation and its importance;
2. to explore how 'benefits sought' might be used to define segments and develop marketing offerings;
3. to analyse the link between segmentation and the marketing mix offering and its impact on marketing success.

1   What benefits is the opera-goer buying?

1. A musical experience
2. the thrill of live performance of a familiar work
3. the opportunity to see famous singers live
4. a social night out
5. a treat e.g. birthday, anniversary etc
6. enhancing status
7. something to boast about later!

Supplementary question
Which of these benefits are more likely to be delivered by a major opera house such as Covent Garden, and which by something similar to this Carmen 'arena' production?

Both types of experience could deliver all of these benefits, to a greater or lesser extent. It could, however, be argued that the opera house particularly delivers (2), (6) and (7) while the arena production is more likely to emphasise (1), (3) and (4)

2   Given that opera has indeed widened its appeal over the 1990s, why do you think the *Carmen* audience was still so 'traditional'?

- Advertising media targeted at traditionals
- pricing too high to attract casual visitor, compared with alternative 'nights out'
- possibly many, more attractive alternative things to do
- difference between liking opera and actually going to see it
- live opera still has a stuffy image

- 'highlights' mentality among newcomers? "I like the big arias and choruses, but the bits in between are a bit boring!"

3   What marketing advice would you give opera promoters to help them improve the mass appeal of live performances?

- Different and more varied advertising media targeted at younger age group
- revised pricing policy - cheaper or better justified value for money? Subsidy though sponsorship?
- 'Highlights' concerts rather than full performances?
- Big name at top of the bill
- 'softer' image? Get away from 'evening dress' elite prejudices
- sell packages - including travel, ticket, hotel etc (a) to make it a more attractive leisure break and (b) to disguise the price of the ticket
- is the location appropriate? Perhaps London would pull in a wider audience.
- If younger audiences want contemporary works or radical stagings, then give it to them! *Carmen* is now regarded as mainstream repertoire, and this staging was fairly 'safe'.

4   Do you ever attend live concerts? If not, why not? If you do, how would you define the target market segment for those events?

This should be a free discussion to encourage creative thinking about:
- Benefits sought
- how the concert market might be segmented re age, frequency of concert attendance, type of music offered, location etc
- the difference between 'consuming' a band on CD and at a live concert
- the decision-making process - how do you decide what concerts to go to and what the influences are on that choice e.g. need for self gratification; group pressures
- competition between concerts and other leisure pursuits
- how concerts can be used as marketing opportunities re merchandising of sweat shirts, CDs, souvenir programmes etc
- the role concerts might play as a marketing tool for building a band's image and profile - 'the world tour' as a branded product in its own right e.g. Rolling Stones' Voodoo Lounge tour!

Marketing in Action Go for Bust (p 173)

Discussion question
What segmentation variables are mentioned in this marketing in action?

- Geographic (country)
- demographic (gender, obviously!; dress size)
- psychographic (seductiveness; fashionability; attitudes towards role of lingerie)
- behavioural (benefits sought; occasions).

Marketing in Action Cola Fatigue (p 175)

Discussion question
Why is 'age' insufficient as a segmentation variable on its own for dividing the soft drinks market?

- Produces too large, broad and ill-defined a segment
- not everyone within an age band wants the same thing from soft drinks, as the points below show
- consumers want a variety of soft drinks for different usage occasions
- lifestyle considerations affect soft drink choices
- some consumers look to soft drink brands to reflect their self-image or status within peer groups
- some consumers want fun, variety and novelty from the range of soft drinks they buy.

Marketing in Action Are You a Yak or a Ewe? (p 179)

Discussion question
Why should a credit card company be interested in customers' demographic and lifestyle profiles?

It helps the company to understand:
- A customer's income flows and debt patterns
- cash flow pressure points
- spending priorities and patterns
- credit card usage.

This could directly affect:
- Types of retailer or service organisation that the credit card company cultivates
- control and flexibility of credit limits
- timing, style and content of promotional offers made to groups of customers
- content of advertising and other communication designed to build corporate image and to recruit new customers.

Marketing in Action Blue Circle's Standardised Boiler (p 188)

Discussion question
What kind of targeting strategy does this case represent, and why?

It could be seen as a concentrated strategy, because Blue Circle have tried to create a boiler to suit a pan-European 'green' segment. There is also evidence, however, of a differentiated strategy:
- Product adaptable to suit different national regulations and conventions (geographic segments)
- product adaptable to suit different national preferences for the location of a boiler within the home (geographic segments)
- product name and image varies from country to country (geographic; benefits sought segments?) as well as other marketing mix elements.

SUGGESTED ASSIGNMENTS

- Discuss the role and importance of psychographic segmentation in consumer markets. What problems do marketers face in using this segmentation base?
- Questions for Discussion 5.4.

Chapter 6
MARKETING INFORMATION AND RESEARCH

LECTURE PLAN

A lecture based on this chapter should help the student to:
1. Recognise the importance of information to an organisation and the role information plays in effective marketing decision making;
2. outline the sources and roles of secondary and primary data, and the issues involved in their collection and analysis;
3. become familiar with the various steps involved in the marketing research process;
4. appreciate some of the ethical concerns surrounding marketing research; and

5. understand the role of a marketing information system and a decision support system, and develop an awareness of the various types of information available.

The key sections of this lecture should be:

Overview of market research (pp 199-209):
- Defining market research
- why market research is important
- the role of market research in consumer and organisational markets.
- Terminology: primary research; secondary research; qualitative research; quantitative research.
- Types of research: exploratory; descriptive; causal.

Secondary research (pp 209-214):
- Overview of sources
- risks and benefits of secondary data.

Primary research (pp 214-230):
- Overview of the main data collection methods, including OHP 17, table 6.1 (p 215) Comparative Performance of Interviews and Survey Techniques:
  ⇒ Definition of what each technique involves
  ⇒ type of research problem each is best for
  ⇒ type of information each is best for
  ⇒ relative costs
  ⇒ relative speed of implementation.
- Observational research
- experimentation.

Sampling (pp 221-224):
- The sampling process, stage by stage.
Because of time constraints, this section will probably have to be omitted, and students encouraged to read it for themselves.

Questionnaire design (pp 225-230):
- Questionnaire objectives
- types of questions and types of information
- layout and design.
Again, because of time constraints this section can be omitted. This topic is perhaps better dealt with as a practical seminar exercise.

The marketing research process and its ethics (pp 230-239):
Overview of the stages involved, including OHP 18, figure 6.4 (p 230) The Marketing Research Process:
- *Problem definition:* the importance of clear problem definition.
- *Research objectives:* precise definition of what the research is to achieve; role of exploratory research.
- *Planning the research:* preparing the brief; agreeing the research plan.
- *Data collection:* checking secondary sources; designing primary research data collection mechanisms.
- *Conducting the research:* implementing the research plan; problems that might arise.
- *Analysing and interpreting the information:* use of data processing packages; importance of qualitative interpretation.
- *Prepare and present the report:* importance of clear communication; deciding what to put in and what to omit.
- *Research evaluation:* importance of reviewing the process and learning from mistakes.

- The importance of an ethical approach to implementing this process.

Marketing information systems (pp 240-244):
- Defining the MIS, including OHP 19, figure 6.5 (p 241) The Marketing Information System:
  - ⇒ An overview of internal and external data sources
  - ⇒ the importance of having a structured data collection and sorting mechanism
  - ⇒ the importance of having data readily available at the right time to the right people
  - ⇒ the differences between the MIS and the DSS and the links between them.
- The role of the DSS in supporting the marketing decision-maker.
- The need to plan the inputs into the MIS to avoid information overload, including OHP 20, table 6.2 (p 242) Defining Information Requirements:
  - ⇒ Helps to define types of information needed
  - ⇒ helps to define sources of information
  - ⇒ helps to define the best way of storing and categorising data
  - ⇒ helps to define the best way of accessing and presenting data.

QUESTIONS FOR REVIEW

6.1   Why is marketing research an essential tool for the marketing manager? (pp 202-204)

Marketing research helps the marketing manager to:
- Define and locate market segments
- understand segments' needs and wants
- develop more appropriate marketing mixes
- monitor progress and diagnose the root causes of marketing problems
- monitor changing needs and attitudes etc.

6.2   What is the difference between primary and secondary research? (p 202)

Primary research is commissioned for a specific purpose. The information or data required do not already exist in any usable form. Secondary research involves collating data that already exist either within the organisation's own records or in published reports, government statistics etc.

6.3   What kinds of marketing problems might be addressed through (a) exploratory, (b) descriptive, and (c) causal research projects? (pp 205-206)

a) *Exploratory research* might be used to collect preliminary data to further clarify the nature of a marketing problem before designing a more extensive research project.
b) *Descriptive research* might be used to explain a particular issue or problem, for example, building customer profiles and measuring attitudes towards a product or brand.
c) *Causal or predictive research* might be used to test cause and effect relationships - does a price reduction increase sales? What effect does a sales promotion have on volume sales? Will a change in advertising approach significantly shift customer attitudes towards the product?

6.4   Differentiate between qualitative and quantitative research, highlighting their relative advantages and disadvantages. (pp 206-207)

Qualitative research explores issues or asks questions that cannot be analysed statistically easily (if at all). Its advantages are that:
- It can handle complex emotional issues
- it can provide rich insights into behavioural issues.

Its disadvantages are that:
- it can be difficult to design qualitative research
- it can be difficult to analyse

- it can be difficult to validate results.

Quantitative research collects data that can be quantified, and thus collated and analysed statistically. Its advantages are that:
- It can be validated
- it is a cost efficient and effective way of dealing with factual data
- it can be relatively easy to make generalisations from the results
- it can be undertaken through a variety of research methods.

Its disadvantages are that:
- It is not so good for exploring complex emotional issues
- the research design might over-simplify issues in the interests of data coding and analysis
- there is a risk that it will focus on 'what' and 'how much' instead of 'why'.

6.5   What are the criteria for evaluating secondary sources, and why are they important? (p 214)

- *Pertinence of the data:* are the data sufficiently detailed and relevant to shed light on the current problem? Can we generalise from these data? If the data are less pertinent than the researcher would like, then further primary research might have to be commissioned.
- *Who collects the data and why:* is the source reputable? Are the data thus likely to be reliable, accurate and valid? Was there any ulterior motive that might have influenced the research design or reporting? Again, this is important because if there is any doubt, then further research might be necessary to corroborate the results of the original study.
- *Method of collecting data:* was the method appropriate to the nature of the problem? Is it still appropriate for our current problem? Might a different method give significantly different results?
- *Evidence of careful work:* see item 2 above - Was there bias in the research design? Was the data collection carried out rigorously, ethically and thoroughly? Have these data been analysed methodically, appropriately and objectively? Any evidence of sloppiness might again cast doubt on the results and indicate that further work is needed.

6.6   What is observational research, and in what circumstances might it be more appropriate than interviews or surveys? (pp 219-220)

Observational research is a means of gathering data through trained researchers watching or recording individual or group behaviour. It is most appropriate for situations where:
- The researcher does not want the 'respondent' to be aware that they are participating in research (e.g. mystery shopping - see p 219)
- the researcher is interested in the natural responses and interactions between the 'respondent' and a product in use or a retail display, for example
- the researcher is interested in responses and reactions that a respondent would have difficulty explaining because they are largely unconscious or impulsive.

6.7   What are the main stages in the sampling process, and what does each involve? (pp 221-224)

- *Population definition:* defining the broad target group of interest to the researcher; may be based on segmentation variables.
- *Sampling frame development:* finding a means of accessing the population, perhaps from trade directories, telephone directories; electoral lists, brokered lists, internal customer records etc.
- *Sampling unit specification:* defining the actual individual from whom the researcher wants a response. In a consumer survey it might be important, for example to get a response from the house owner, or from the main wage earner or the main user of the family car. In an organisational market, the researcher might want to target someone with a particular job title or decision-making responsibility.

- *Sampling method selection:* define a subgroup from within the population which will be targeted from the research. This might involve random or non-random choices, depending on the size and structure of the population and the nature of the research problem.
- *Sample size determination:* deciding how large a sample is needed to make the research valid, yet without pushing the costs up too high.

6.8   How does quota sampling work, and what are its advantages? (pp 223-224)

Rather than a completely random sample from the whole population, quota sampling allows the researcher to define how the total number of respondents should be broken down, perhaps by age, marital status, income or any other significant variable. Its advantages are that:
- It allows the researcher to reflect the actual structure of a market
- it is quicker and cheaper to implement than a truly random sample
- it does not commit the researcher to following up a specific respondent, as long as the overall quota is met.

6.9   Define the stages of the marketing research process and outline what each one involves. (pp 230-239)

- *Problem definition:* recognising that research is needed and defining the broad nature of the problem.
- *Research objectives:* more detailed specification of what the client wants to achieve through the research. It may involve exploratory research to help clarify what is really needed.
- *Research planning:* preparing the research brief for the researchers and agreeing the detailed research plan, including budgets, timescales and expected outputs. The brief needs to include sufficient background for the researchers to be able to view the job in context, and a clear statement of the client's needs and expectations. There will be some negotiation and refinement of the task at this stage.
- *Data collection:* defining what data are needed in order to fulfil the research objectives, and defining where those data are to come from, and how they are to be collected.
- *Conducting the research:* implementing the data collection plan, ensuring that the job is done to the expected standards of thoroughness, rigour and objectivity. It is also important to ensure that the task is completed within the planned timescales and to budget.
- *Data analysis:* collating and interpreting all the data collected. Thus might means using appropriate statistical analysis packages and then interpreting the outputs or using expert interpretation of qualitative data.
- *Report presentation:* presenting data and analysis in the form that the client expects and in a form that can be easily understood, disseminated, and used as a decision-making aid.
- *Research evaluation:* a review of the research project to ensure that it met its objectives, and to analyse and assess how well and how cost effectively it was done. Both the client and the researcher can learn from mistakes.

6.10   Discuss the role and content of an MIS and how it might relate to a DSS. (pp 240-244)

The MIS:
- Helps to organise information in a user friendly centralised way
- helps the organisation to manage the flow of information
- feeds the information needs of decision makers
- contains a variety of internally and externally generated data from various sources
- can be developed into a DSS by linking databases with analytical aids such as spreadsheets or other statistical packages to allow the decision maker to manipulate data and explore the implications of various courses of action.

QUESTIONS FOR DISCUSSION

6.1 Without looking back at pp 210-14, how many of the ten different categories of sources of secondary data can you list? Check your list against pp 210-14, and then investigate what your library has to offer under each category.

The ten sources are:
1. Government data
2. European Commission data
3. trade data
4. chambers of commerce
5. directories and publications
6. market research agencies
7. press published data
8. financial institutions' data
9. electronic data sources
10. syndicated data services.

6.2 Evaluate the appropriateness of each of the different interview and survey based primary research methods for (a) investigating the buying criteria used by organisational purchasers, (b) defining the attitudes of a target market towards a brand of breakfast cereal, (c) profiling purchasers of small electrical goods, and (d) measuring levels of post-purchase satisfaction among customers. Clearly define any assumptions you make about each of the situations.

Methods covered should include personal interviews, group interviews, telephone interviews and mail surveys. For each of the research problems presented in the question, in assessing the appropriateness of each method, students should take into account factors such as:
- Size of population
- likely number of responses needed to give a representative view
- likely level of co-operation
- access to the population
- sensitivity of information required
- complexity of information required
- quantitative/qualitative nature of information required
- speed of data collection
- costs involved.
Table 6.1 (p 215) could also help.

6.3 Design a questionnaire. It should contain about 20 questions, and you should use as many of the different types of question as possible. Pay particular attention to the concerns discussed on pp 225-230 of the chapter. The objective is to investigate respondents' attitudes to music CDs and their purchasing habits. Pilot your questionnaire on 12 to 15 people (but preferably not people on the same course as you), analyse the results and then make any adjustments. Within your seminar group, be prepared to discuss the rationale behind your questionnaire, the outcome of the pilot, and any data analysis problems.

This is very much a practical, creative exercise to demonstrate to students the real problems of putting together a 'good' questionnaire. Some issues to look for in de-briefing them on this one:
- Types of question: each questionnaire should contain a mix of dichotomous closed questions, multiple choice closed questions, open questions, and rating scales.
- Range of information sought: the questionnaire is likely to have covered the following information needs:

⇒ Basic demographic information about the respondent
⇒ type and variety of hi-fi equipment owned
⇒ range of music formats available to the respondent and frequency of use of each
⇒ feelings about CD as a format, and degree of preference for it
⇒ reasons for purchasing CDs; frequency; types of outlet
⇒ price sensitivity of respondent.
- Howlers and groaners: look out for the following common mistakes:
⇒ Ambiguity
⇒ leading questions; bias
⇒ blunt questions on sensitive issues
⇒ questions that are too complex to answer, either through incomprehensible wording or trying to cover too much ground in one question
⇒ questions that are too closed, and thus beg for deeper clarification through a follow-up
⇒ closed questions that may not cover all the options fully
⇒ questions that do not actually get to what the researcher really wants to know
⇒ poor layout
⇒ poor question order.

6.4 Why is an ethical approach to marketing research important, and what are the main areas of concern?

Issues that might be raised include:
- The need for a respondent to trust researcher in order to encourage full and honest responses
- the need to maintain public's goodwill to encourage them to participate in research
- the need to ensure a continuous and objective flow of useful information
- the need to avoid accusations of exploiting vulnerable groups
- the need to avoid accusations of selling under the guise of market research (sugging)
- the need for the research industry to be seen as responsible and properly and appropriately self-regulated in order to avoid any threat of legislation to curb activities.

6.5 Why is a sound research brief important, what should it contain, and how does it influence each of the subsequent stages in the process?

The brief is important because it encapsulates what the client thinks the problem is. It acts as a starting point for the client and the researcher in discussing and negotiating precisely what actually needs to be done within the research project. It thus sets the tone for all the stages that follow. It should contain:
- The background to the problem
- details of the product/market concerned
- research objectives
- time and budgetary constraints
- reporting requirements.

Once the research plan resulting from the brief has been agreed, it influences subsequent stages thus:
- *Data sources:* linked very closely to the nature of the problem, the product/market, and the research objectives. Choice of sources and data collection methods might also be linked with time and cost constraints.
- *Conducting the research:* could be severely constrained by time and available budgets, in terms of the speed with which data must be generated, the quality and motivation of field research staff, and the ability to use CATI or CAPI methods.
- *Data analysis:* data interpretation in particular needs to be sympathetic to the research objectives and the client's needs. Any conclusions and recommendations have to be relevant to the problem and clearly put into the context of the product/market.
- *Reporting:* needs to be in the client's preferred format, and be directly relevant to the initial brief as set.

- *Evaluation:* the initial brief is an essential part of this. To what extent did the actual research project move away from the brief, and why? Was that a purposeful and controlled process? Could the brief have been better?

CASE STUDY 6.1 Kings Hotel (B) (p 247)

Teaching Objectives

1. To gain an insight into defining a research problem;
2. to develop an understanding of the link between problem definition and information needs;
3. to explore the appropriateness and practicalities of alternative research methods within a defined context.

1   What marketing problem is this research trying to help solve?

The marketing problem is to decide upon the most appropriate product development strategy to enhance services and facilities for the independent guest. This means identifying basic requirements and then using such information to prioritise development activities and to assess their likely impact on the overall competitive offering from the Kings Hotel.

2   What information do you think the hotel manager would actually need in order to investigate this problem?

The marketing research problem is to profile existing independent customers in terms of their needs and preferences for facilities and services in order to identify gaps in provision. Useful information would therefore be:
a) Profile of guests:
- Purpose of visit to Krakow
- frequency of visits
- length of visit
- nationality
- previous and next destination
- party size
- pre booking (when/where) or 'walk-in'?

Some of this data could be collected from the check in or reservation system rather than bothering the guest with numerous additional questions. Such profile data may be useful in linking benefits sought with usage characteristics.
b) Benefits sought from services and facilities:
This list could be very extensive. There would probably be a need to prioritise the areas of concern, and students could be invited to attempt this task. Some of the areas raised might be:
- Convenience
- good value for money
- comprehensive range of services to meet every need
- relaxation
- entertainment to enhance a holiday.

From this information, initial insights could be gathered on gaps in current provision. The management could then compare facilities with those offered by other hotels in the city and assess relative prices. The management will really have to assess how much extra guests would realistically pay for the additional services. Some services could be tested on an experimental basis, for example, an airport shuttle service or baggage handling, to see how well they are received.

3   To what extent and why do you feel that the research method employed is appropriate for gathering the information needed?

The research method revolves around self-administered questionnaires completed by actual customers. This creates certain constraints on the information available for marketing decision-making:

- It does not involve potential customers or those using other hotels. The guests of Kings Hotel have already made a positive decision to stay at the hotel and have accepted the trade off between the range of facilities, level of service and the price offered. The other groups have not been prepared to make that trade off, whether by conscious decision or not. This could bias the findings.
- The self-administered nature of the questionnaire might mean that the majority of guests do not bother. Only those with major complaints or strong feelings might reply. This could create a bias in the responses as well as affecting the response rate.
- A self-administered questionnaire can be useful for factual data, but does not have the ability to probe underlying expectations and attitudes concerning the hotel experience.
- A self-administered questionnaire cannot be too long or complicated otherwise people will not bother with it. Hotel guests in particular will not be eager to spend more time than necessary filling in details and questionnaires when checking in. They are likely to just want to get settled into their rooms as quickly as possible.
- The timing of the questionnaire is dubious. The profile of guests is likely to vary between the summer months and the shoulder months when the research is actually being carried out. Expectations and needs could differ significantly, yet the management of the hotel will not know precisely how and to what extent!

Supplementary question
What are the alternatives?

- Survey of trade opinion (travel agents etc)
- group discussions and semistructured interviews
- experimentation may also be of use, for example, developing some rooms with better facilities, mini bars
- a lot could be learned from comparative research, for example looking at similar establishments.

4   Criticise the questionnaire outlined in the case in terms of the choice of questions, their wording and their response mechanism.

There are many problems with the questionnaire as proposed that would undermine the quality and usefulness of the information provided.
Choice of questions:
- Does not provide a detailed demographic profile of the respondent
- does not distinguish between the lone traveller, the family party, or a group
- does not touch on the purpose of travel
- does not ask how or why the respondent chose this hotel
- does not really probe the respondent's expectation of what their stay here is going to be like.

Since the questionnaire is administered at check in, it cannot gain insight into the respondent's reaction to their actual stay. As it stands, this questionnaire is of little use to the management in gathering the information needed to develop new, better targeted products.
Wording of questionnaire:
- Q1 begs the answer 'yes'
- Q2 too precise - is this necessary? Respondents might be reluctant to give away their precise age and might be happier admitting to a certain age band instead.
- Sloppy use of multiple choice question, for example a literal interpretation of Q3 is likely to result in 100 per cent response 'car' (not only travellers arriving in their own cars, but also those taking taxis or hire cars from the airport or railway station!).
- Q4 is far too general and broad and is fairly meaningless without an indication of how often the respondent uses hotels and why.
- Q5 is too closed and does not actually tell the management anything meaningful.

- The wording of Q6 tends to restrict response. Rank ordering, or an open choice of criteria might be better.
- Generally there are no open ended questions to allow for freedom of expression and exploration of feelings.
- Certain words or phrases may be interpreted differently by different respondents, for example shop or larger car park.

Response mechanisms:
- No coding for data analysis
- no attempt to rank priorities (see Q6)
- no attempt to measure degree of strength of attitude or expectation.

CASE STUDY 6.2 Gathering Information on an Up and Coming Market (p 248)

Teaching Objectives

1. To emphasise the importance of market research information and to highlight the wide range of information likely to be needed;
2. to explore the problems of defining and implementing market research programmes in sensitive markets;
3. to raise ethical issues surrounding market research.

1   Briefly outline the types of market research information that might be useful to a condom manufacturer.

Quantitative research:
- Age of purchasers
- gender of purchasers
- socioeconomic grouping of purchasers
- frequency/quantity of purchases
- pack size purchased
- brand/variety purchased
- awareness of brands/variants available
- where purchased
- usage occasions (e.g. see section of case on casual encounters!).

Qualitative research:
- Why purchased - e.g. purely contraceptive purposes? disease prevention? under pressure from partner? 'just in case ...?'
- Attitudes towards who should buy - e.g. is it felt acceptable for women to purchase this product?
- Attitudes towards product - e.g. purely functional 'necessary evil'? a fun part of the relationship?
- Reasons for brand choice - e.g. whatever is conveniently available? cheapest? reputation for quality and safety? variety of choice within the brand family?
- Attitude towards/feelings about the purchasing process - e.g. embarrassment about purchasing in chemist or supermarket? preference for anonymity of vending machine? is it equally easy for both men and women to purchase the product?
- Price perceptions/sensitivities.
- Awareness of, and reactions to, advertising and promotional activity.

Supplementary question
What impact do you think the market research findings outlined in this case have had on the marketing of condoms generally?

They could have affected:
- Pricing strategies
- distribution strategies

- advertising media
- advertising approaches
- brand imagery and product development
- product positioning generally.

2   What are the problems of undertaking primary consumer research for a product like this? How can these problems be overcome?

Problems:
- Respondent embarrassment or likelihood of being offended
- inaccurate responses
- locating respondents fitting the required research profile
- tact in making initial contact with respondents - it's not the kind of product for which you can do open surveys in shopping centres!

Solutions:
- Use of focus groups rather than one to one questioning might lead to more relaxed respondents, but group members might lie to impress the rest or for fear of being thought abnormal! Still leaves the problem of creating the focus group in the first place.
- Mail questionnaires can be completed in relative privacy and with anonymity, but still leave problems of inaccuracy and locating/contacting sample.
- Researchers might advertise in magazines like *Cosmopolitan* that deal more liberally with sexual matters for people willing to participate in research, but this could produce a biased/skewed sample.
- Extremely careful and subtle wording of questions, but needs to strike a balance between being inoffensive and being unambiguous while still getting at the required information.
- Asking the same question twice but in different ways might help the researcher to cross-check a respondent's accuracy.

3   Thirty per cent of buyers still have some reservations about purchasing condoms. Suggest a programme of primary research that might tell the manufacturers why this is.

- Focus groups of buyers to talk about the purchasing process/experience. Problem is that the reluctant 30 per cent might not want to participate.
- Magazine published mail-in survey to get a wide cross section of responses (but see comments in Q2 above).
- Observational research at different types of outlet, but risk of offending, frightening or alienating customers if they think they are being watched!?
- Semi structured interviews with customers at point of sale, but same risk as above.

4   To what extent do you think it would be ethical for condom manufacturers to undertake a survey of 14-16 year olds?

Free class discussion of ethical pros and cons. This group is under the age of consent in the UK, but nevertheless some will be users and they are potential users for the future, thus the companies have a legitimate interest in their views. If it was to be done at all, it would have to be very carefully designed and supervised in implementation, almost certainly done in conjunction with teachers and parents. It could, however, be a bad move, if such companies were to be perceived as encouraging under age promiscuity. It could be possible to broaden the discussion re the ethics of researching young people's relationships with alcohol, drugs and tobacco.

Marketing in Action Research for Your Convenience (p 202)

Discussion question
What do you think might be the problems of carrying out market research into this kind of facility?

- Ill-defined target market - any member of the general public
- respondents' embarrassment about the product making them reluctant to participate
- getting useful information about attitudes and feelings
- drawing meaningful conclusions from questions about proposed usage - this is essentially a distress purchase!

Marketing in Action Big Brother Is Watching You (p 219)

Discussion question
To what extent do you think that research methods such as this are going too far?

This is a broad question designed to stimulate some debate about ethics and safeguards in observational research. Points that might be raised include:
- The extent to which this is an invasion of privacy
- the extent and the adequacy of the safeguards cited in the case
- alternative methods of gaining the same information
- the commercial value of the information gained
- if this is acceptable, what would constitute 'going too far'?

Marketing in Action Trouble Brewing (p 224)

Discussion question
In what ways might researching consumers and researching intermediaries be different for a brewer?

- There are far more consumers than intermediaries, thus ...
- it is easier to have closer interaction and ongoing exchange of information with intermediaries.
- The breweries are likely to use different data collection methods - mass surveys for consumers, in depth one to one interviews with key intermediaries.
- Consumer surveys are likely to be more costly because of broader extent.
- Information required from intermediaries is more likely to be factual whereas consumer information is likely to be about attitudes, feelings, and preferences.

Marketing in Action Business Travel (p 235)

Discussion question
How might an airline access potential respondents in order to conduct market research among non-users of its services?

- Purchase a list of airline users from an agency then filter out those who already use this airline?
- Contact people at random (for example by telephone or stop them in the street) and see if they qualify under the screening criteria? This is potentially very expensive and time consuming.
- Advertise for respondents? Risk of self-selecting sample, however; may not be truly representative of non-users as a whole.
- Hover around near other airlines' check-in desks at airports and accost their customers? Are airport authorities likely to allow this?
- If the focus is on business travellers, the airline could perhaps make contact with them through their employers (either from a purchased list or selected from trade directories etc).
- Join forces with a travel agent or airline ticket bucket shop and survey customers who buy tickets for other airlines. What would the travel agent's qualms be about doing this?
  $\Rightarrow$ Upsetting the other airlines
  $\Rightarrow$ irritating customers who just want a quick transaction
  $\Rightarrow$ risk of being seen as favouring that airline
  $\Rightarrow$ risk of customers feeling that the market research is being used as an underhand selling method.

- Questions for Discussion 6.3 would provide a suitable piece of assessed course work, perhaps undertaken in groups of 3 or 4 students. If it is to be group work, then perhaps the piloting of the questionnaire could be made more extensive, with each member of the group finding 12-15 respondents. The results could be presented in a written report, or as a formal verbal presentation to the tutor, or both.
- Imagine that you are a marketing manager evaluating the launch of a new toy targeted at 5-8 year olds. Outline what information you might need, where or who you would get it from, how you would collect the data, and what problems you might encounter in collecting it.

Chapter 7
ANATOMY OF A PRODUCT

LECTURE PLAN

A lecture based on this chapter should help the student to:
1. Define and classify products and the key terms associated with them;
2. understand the nature, benefits and implementation of branding;
3. appreciate the functional and psychological roles of packaging; and
4. understand the broad issues relating to product design and quality and their contribution to marketing.

The key sections of this lecture should be:

What is a product? (pp 253-256):
- Broad definition of product to include physical goods, services, ideas, people, places etc
- the structure of a product, including OHP 21, figure 7.1 (p 255) The Anatomy of a Product:
  ⇒ Define each layer and its components
  ⇒ develop an example, for instance a car or a box of chocolates
  ⇒ stress the importance of consistency between all the layers.
- Stress the importance of ensuring that all the elements of the product are fully integrated to create a single entity.

Classifying products (pp 256-262):
- Why it is useful to try to classify products.
- *Product-based classification:* durables; non-durables; services.
- *User-based classification (consumer):* convenience; shopping goods; speciality goods; unsought.
- *User-based classification (organisational):* capital goods; accessory goods; raw materials; semi-finished goods; components and parts; supplies and services.

Definition of product terms (pp 263-265):
- Product mix
- product line
- product item
- product line length
- product line depth
- product mix width.

These terms can perhaps best be defined through the use of an example, such as figure 7.2 (p 263).

Branding (pp 265-278):
- Defining 'brand'
- why branding is important, including OHP 22, figure 7.4 (p 269) The Benefits of Branding:
  ⇒ How branding helps the consumer to make choices
  ⇒ how branding helps the consumer to develop an ongoing relationship with a product
  ⇒ how branding helps the manufacturer's competitive strategy
  ⇒ how branding helps the retailer.
- *Types of brand:* manufacturer, retailer and wholesaler; why different types exist and what they achieve.
- *Branding strategy:* the importance of brand names; the degree of corporate branding applied; brand extension.

Packaging (pp 278-282):
- Why packaging is important
- the functions of packaging
- how packaging helps the marketing mix
- labelling issues.

Product design, quality and guarantees (pp 282-286):
- The role and importance of good design
- quality's impact, including OHP 23, figure 7.6 (p 284) Quality Dimensions:
  ⇒ Discuss each dimension
  ⇒ emphasise the importance of demonstrating quality to the customer
  ⇒ emphasise the importance of quality in the overall marketing mix
  ⇒ emphasise the importance of the 'right' quality i.e. too much is as bad as too little!
- The role of guarantees in marketing strategy.

QUESTIONS FOR REVIEW

7.1   What, other than physical goods, might be classed as products? (p 254)

- Services
- ideas
- personalities
- locations.

7.2   What is the augmented product, and why might it be important? (pp 255-256)

The augmented product consists of extra services or benefits which do not themselves from an intrinsic part of the product, but might be used by intermediaries or manufacturers to increase the attractiveness of the whole product offering. It is particularly important for the intermediaries as a means of creating differential advantage over their competitors. If all electrical retailers are selling the same brands of television sets at similar prices, then augmenting the product with free delivery, after-sales insurance and maintenance packages, or interest-free credit might allow one retailer to stand out from the rest.

7.3   Define durable and non-durable products, and summarise the likely marketing differences between them. (pp 256-257)

Durable products have a relatively long life span and are used many times before being replaced. Household electrical goods are an example of this. Non-durable products can only be used once or a few times before having to be replaced. Food products are an example of this. The differences are likely to be:

- Durables are likely to be higher priced than non-durables
- durables are less frequently purchased, therefore the marketer has to keep the consumer aware of the name and the product benefits over a long period
- durables are likely to involve a longer, more formal purchasing process, and thus the marketer needs to ensure that detailed information is available to the potential customer
- durables are likely to be found in specialist outlets whereas non-durables need extensive distribution in order to be conveniently available for the customer on demand.

7.4   What is a speciality product and how might its marketing mix and the kind of buying behaviour associated with it differ from those found with other products? (p259)

A speciality product is an infrequently purchased, expensive product. It differs in that it is likely to:

- Be sold through specialist outlets
- be perceived as expensive by the consumer
- be advertised on the basis of psychological benefits
- avoid price orientated promotions that might cheapen its image
- justify personal selling
- involve an extensive decision making process because of the 'high risk'.

7.5   What are the six different categories within the user-based product classification system for organisational products? (pp 260-262)

1. Capital goods
2. accessory goods
3. raw materials
4. semi-finished goods
5. components and parts
6. supplies and services.

7.6   Why do you think the EU felt it necessary to extend the range of things that can be registered as trade marks? (pp 267-268)

Because brand images are far more complex than just names. Distinctive brand character can be created through elements such as packaging shapes, colour, and graphic style, for instance. Consumers clearly associate brand values with these things, and therefore these elements need as much protection as names do.

7.7   What benefits does branding offer the consumer? (p 269)

Branding aids:

- Product recognition
- the communication of features and benefits
- product evaluation by the consumer
- positioning
- the reduction of purchasing risk
- the creation of a three dimensional character for a product for which the consumer can develop an affection.

7.8   Why do retailers develop own brand products? (pp 272-273)

Retailers might develop own brands in order to:

- Aid the development of customer loyalty

- differentiate themselves from other retailers
- make the retailer's image more tangible
- increase margins
- regain control over shelf space allocation
- reduce manufacturer power
- develop closer links with manufacturers.

7.9 What are the advantages and disadvantages of monolithic branding compared with discreet branding? (p 276)

Advantages of monolithic:
- It creates very powerful umbrella name with synergy between individual products; discreet needs each name building from nothing
- it allows economies of scale in communication; discreet products each need their own communications strategy and budget ·
- it eases new product launch and reduces risk of product failure as the brand concept is already in place; a discreet product needs new concepts and represents high risk.

Disadvantages of monolithic:
- Little room for flexibility or variety of product images compared with discreet
- new products under a monolithic umbrella might not be noticed by the consumer
- a crisis affecting the organisation or one product could affect sales of all products; discreet products are not linked to each other or to the organisation.

7.10 How can design contribute to the success of a new product? (pp 282-283)

Design can contribute by:
- Developing attractive packaging concepts
- making products more aesthetically attractive
- clearly differentiating the product from its competitors
- providing a rationale for a price premium
- improving the product's ergonomic qualities
- improving the arrangement of components and parts to:
  - $\Rightarrow$ Make the product easier to service
  - $\Rightarrow$ make the product more reliable
  - $\Rightarrow$ ease the production process
  - $\Rightarrow$ reduce costs.

QUESTIONS FOR DISCUSSION

7.1 Choose three different brands of shampoo which you think incorporate different core products. (a) Define the core product for each brand. (b) How does the tangible product for each brand reflect the core product?

The point of this question is to check that the students understand the difference between core and tangible product (refer them back to pp 254-256) and that they can apply these concepts to a real product.

a) The kinds of core product proposition they might raise include shampoo that:
- Has a tough medicinal quality e.g. cures dandruff
- has a cosmetic, beautifying quality
- has a scientific, 'nurturing' basis e.g. contains vitamins to strengthen hair or make it shine more.

b) Issues to be raised here include:
- Brand imagery
- packaging
- ingredients

- smell
- texture
- colour.

7.2   Adapt figure 7.1 to suit the specific example of a personal computer (a) for family use and (b) for the use of a small business. How do your two diagrams differ from each other, and why?

This question is designed to ensure that the students understand in principle the way in which products are structured and that they can appreciate how these concepts are applied in practice. The issues they might raise include:

- *Core product:* the definition is likely to differ for the two types of customer. The family buyer's core product might centre around the benefits of the computer as an entertainment or educational tool while the business might focus on increasing the organisation's cost effectiveness and efficiency in serving its customer's needs.
- *Tangible product:* the concerns of both types of customer might differ thus:
  ⇒ *Design:* family perhaps wants high tech look; business might be looking for something seriously businesslike design that doesn't take up too much office space
  ⇒ *Features:* both types of customer might well be looking for multi-media packages and a sufficiently powerful machine to run the desired types of application and software; the family might be more concerned about the quality of graphics and the soundcard for games purposed; software supplied will vary, with the family focusing on games and educational packages and the business focusing on more functional matters such as word-processing, accounting, spreadsheets and presentation support packages.
  ⇒ *Branding:* strong and respected brand name and image essential for both types of customer for reassurance.
  ⇒ *Quality and reliability:* important for both.
- *Augmented product:* both customers will be concerned about prompt delivery of a machine ready to plug in and use; existence of customer helplines; adequate guarantees; customer friendly financing packages. The business customer in particular might also be concerned with installation; help with staff training; servicing arrangements; software updates; software licensing agreements.
- *Potential product:* students might come up with ideas for future product differentiation.

7.3   Choose a manufacturer of consumer products and list all the brands they sell. How might these brands be grouped into product lines and why? (You might find figure 7.2 helpful.)

This exercise has two broad objectives

- To ensure that students understand the terminology relating to products - mix, line, item, length and depth
- to encourage students to think about product management issues and to explore how products within an organisation's portfolio could be grouped and why. The choice of organisation is not important, as long as the student can present a sensible rationale for the version of figure 7.2 presented.

7.4   List as many functions of packaging as you can.

- Protect the product
- preserve the product
- protect the consumer against product contamination or tampering

- facilitate handling within the logistics and distribution system
- identify the product and give information
- facilitate dosage/quantity measurement
- facilitate access to and use of the product
- enhance the brand image and differentiate it from competition
- enhance product display in the retail outlet
- provide a medium for promotion.

7.5 **Develop a weighted set of five or six criteria for 'good' labelling. Collect a number of competing brands of the same product and rate each of them against your criteria. Which brand comes out best? As a result of this exercise, would you adjust your weightings or change the criteria included?**

Possible criteria that might be raised are:
- Easy identification of the product
- clear instructions for use and applications
- clear warnings about health and safety dangers or constraints of product use
- clear indication of weight or volume
- detailed list of ingredients
- where appropriate, clear nutritional information
- where appropriate, clear instructions for product or packaging disposal/recycling.

Asking students to weight their criteria encourages them to prioritise criteria and to think about what is really important and essential. By relating these thoughts to a set of real brands, students can then begin to see how these criteria work in practice and re-assess their own thinking in the light of experience.

CASE STUDY 7.1 Cott Corporation, Cola and Copycatting (p 289)

Teaching Objectives

1. To develop an understanding of the nature of a retailer's own brand and its potential impact on a market;
2. to appreciate the problems of developing new brands for an oligopolistic market;
3. to explore the importance of brand imagery and character as a means of achieving differential advantage.

1 **Why did Cott choose to challenge Coca-Cola's and Pepsi's dominance through own-label products rather than through a mainstream manufacturer brand?**

Primarily, the dominance of Coke and Pepsi is such that a stand alone new brand from a relatively unknown name would:
- Have to spend an enormous amount of money to make any impact
- have difficulty persuading consumers to try it and trust it
- find it almost impossible to establish a brand image that could challenge Coke and Pepsi seriously
- have problems gaining widespread distribution.

The own-label approach thus guarantees Cott:
- An established retail brand name to trade on
- minimal marketing and advertising spend commitment
- widespread retail distribution
- prominent shelf space
- in-store sales and merchandising support.

2   **Given that both Coca-Cola and Pepsi are good quality, popular brands, why should a retailer such as Sainsbury's want an own-label cola?**

The retailer benefits are that the own-label:
- Provides more choice, especially for those customers who might be bored with Coke and Pepsi
- allows the retailer to cut down on the number of suppliers, if all existing brands do not continue to be stocked alongside the own-label
- gives the retailer more control over display space and promotional initiatives
- increases the retailer's bargaining power with Coke and Pepsi?
- Provides bigger and better profit margins and thus ...
- ... also gives the retailer more pricing discretion over the product. It can be used
- as a loss leader
- to reinforce a value for money image
- to generate revenue to subsidise other lower priced products
- to help the retailer to make its image and values more tangible to the customer.

3   **What contribution do you think the branding and packaging strategy adopted by Sainsbury's made to the success of the product launch? Was Coca-Cola right to object to the packaging's similarity to its own? Why?**

The strengths of the branding and packaging strategy adopted are that it:
- Clearly featured the Sainsbury's name
- featured the word 'classic' in the name to imply quality and a familiar taste
- developed a sufficiently individual character to prevent it from being seen as just a downmarket supermarket generic product
- traded on a generic cola colour scheme and graphic image.

Supplementary question
What other factors contributed to the launch success?

- High advertising spend
- lots of store space devoted to the product
- plenty of point of display promotion
- unbeatable trial prices
- a product that was actually felt to taste just as good as 'the real thing'.

Coca-Cola's objections could be seen as justified because:
- Customers could become confused
- it has taken Coke many years and massive investment to achieve the level of recognition that its packaging gets, and it does not want to lose its distinctiveness
- consumers might think that because the packaging is similar, that Coke manufacture the own-label product and that the two products are identical, other than on price.

Coca Cola's objections could be seen as unjustified because:
- Sainsbury's have done nothing 'illegal'
- consumers are not stupid!
- The red and white colour scheme could be regarded as a generic symbol of the cola market and thus as a legitimate choice to clearly signal a new product as being a cola.

4   **What are the risks arising from copycatting for (a) the retailer and (b) the manufacturer whose brand has been copycatted?**

a)   The risks of copycatting for the retailer are that:
- Consumers might not realise that there is a different product there!
- It makes the manufacturers more hostile towards them generally

- if the imitation goes too far, they are open to litigation
- they are not creating anything particularly new or different and thus ...
- ... they are having to compete head on with the manufacturer brand.
b) The risks of copycatting for the manufacturer are that:
- Consumers might confuse the two products
- if consumers do adopt the own-label version, the original brand might risk being de-listed
- consumers might feel that the two products are absolutely identical and made by the same manufacturer and thus ...
- ... it might lead to the dilution or depreciation of the brand's image and values
- it might also lead to the loss of clear differentiation, a big blow if the brand has taken a long time and a lot of investment to establish and refine
- it could put downward pressure on prices. This is not a focus that a manufacturer of premium brands would want consumers to develop!

Supplementary question
What can the brand manufacturer do to defend its products against copycatting?

- Take an aggressive stance towards exercising whatever legal rights it has to protect its products and to pursue offenders
- threaten to drop an offending retailer (a very high risk strategy indeed)!
- make the retailer an offer to produce an own-label product at extremely competitive rates as long as it's not a copycat product?
- Constantly innovate in terms of packaging, promotion and brand image development to stay one step ahead of the copycats
- make it clear on the packaging that 'we don't make own-label products' if that is the case.

Supplementary activity
Ask students to provide examples of own-label products and their major brand equivalents (or bring them in yourself). Discuss the points of similarity and difference between them and their likely impact on shopper attitudes and buying behaviour.

CASE STUDY 7.2 German Diesel Railcar (p 290)

Teaching Objectives

1. To ensure that students understand the different layers that make up a product and can apply them;
2. to explore issues of how products are designed to deliver the core need(s);
3. to look at issues of product design and branding within an organisational market, revising some of the behavioural issues covered in chapter 4.

Note: students may not be familiar with the technology concerned but the important issue is the application of the concepts considered in this chapter, building to some extent on the material covered in chapter 4 on organisational buying behaviour. The range of different designs has been included to show how different design concepts can be developed and different specifications offered to meet the same basic customer needs .

1   **What is the core product and what is the tangible product offered (a) to the Lander and (b) to the rail passengers?**

For the Lander, the core product is the ability to move passengers by rail in a comfortable but financially viable manner. The tangible product is primarily the design and technical specification of the railcar that enables the service to be provided. It might also include the infrastructure needed to enable the service to be offered, for example track, signalling and, of course, stations. For the rail passengers, the core product is again being able to reach the planned destination, safely, economically and reliably. The tangible product is again the railcar itself, the visible infrastructure and passenger handling facilities. It is debatable where the basic tangible product ends and the augmented product begins. Certain basic aspects of the tangible product would be considered essential such as:

- Adequate seating
- low noise levels
- comfort of ride
- warmth and cleanliness
- ease of access
- clear corporate branding.

Other factors would augment the basic product. These would include:

- Ease of ticketing
- integration of timetables with other services
- security and comfort whilst at stations
- buffet and other retail services available at stations
- ease of adjacent parking
- availability of service information.

These augmented aspects could be important in determining the customer decision to use rail rather than other transport modes and the price they are prepared to pay.

2   What are the main influences that have impacted on the design of the various railcars on offer?

The manufacturers have five main influences to reconcile in the design of the new railcars:

1. Meeting the needs of the Lander in terms of:
- Increasing efficiency and cutting operating costs
- delivering a railcar within a price band that meets Lander financial targets
- railcars that can match passenger loading expectations
- railcars with different carrying capacities to suit different applications
- enabling flexible use over dedicated track and tramway systems
- ensuring the technical ability to operate on poor lines.
2. Meeting the needs of DBAG in terms of:
- Their technical operating requirements for axle loading, maintenance and safety etc
- required degree of standardisation for ease of driver training, maintenance etc, as the German system is dominated by a small number of standard designs.
3. Meeting the needs of the ultimate user in terms of:
- Speed
- comfort
- seating capacity
- on-board facilities
- reliability.
4. Matching or bettering the offerings of competitors in terms of:
- Establishing a design that not only meets needs but offers advantages over competitors, for example the double decker railbus from DWA.
5. Meeting internal financial and marketing objectives in terms of:
- Developing the product within a budget that the organisation agrees
- forecasting the longer term prospects and profitability of any product design
- working towards a successful design that could become a generic name and set industry standards
- capitalising on, or investing in, necessary internal skills and assets
- where necessary, being prepared to combine technologies from different experts in transmission, chassis building etc.

3   What quality dimensions are likely to be most important to the Lander?

- *Performance:* the operating requirements have been clearly specified to act as a minimum requirement for manufacturers to meet. The designs at various stages of development appear to differ in terms of speed and engine capability as well as the weight limitations in order to operate over tramways as well as conventional track. The various performance dimensions would combine to generate the reduced operating costs required by the Lander. These dimensions could be regarded as essential to the Lander.

- *Durability:* in an area of leasing and planned replacement, there is likely to be an expectation that all manufacturers will meet the normal requirements of durability. It would, however, be difficult for a manufacturer to prove its product's durability at this stage, given the brief's prototype nature.
- *Design and style:* this dimension could be important in providing the required passenger carrying facilities and flexibility in terms of numbers and seating configurations. The appearance of the railcar is also important for communicating the image of a fast, reliable means of transportation.
- *Reliability and maintenance:* the Lander may not have a direct interest in this factor, as the train operating companies such as DBAG set the basic criteria. However unreliability due to technical problems would impact on customer service levels and high maintenance costs would work their way through to train operating costs.
- *Corporate name and reputation:* it is interesting to note that many of the designs offered are from well known European companies and alliances of well-known component specialists. This helps potential buyers to assess the likely pre- and post-sales service that is likely to be available and the future operating effectiveness of the alternative designs.

4   In what ways do you think the design process might differ for a consumer good compared with an organisational product such as the railcar?

Many of the characteristics of the design process are likely to be the same between consumer and organisational products:
- Careful briefing
- design to meet user needs
- creating an aesthetically pleasing design as well as an ergonomic and functional one.

In the case of the railcars, additional complexity is created by:
- Potentially conflicting requirements from the Lander, DBAG and passengers. This could cause conflict between aesthetics, economy and reliability. Whilst this conflict is also possible in the consumer goods sector, the conflicting interest may be less pronounced.
- An extended overall design process, in terms of both time and the number of parties involved, compared with a typical fmcg product. A number of different technologies are being combined from different companies, such as in the Eurailbus example. These all have to be planned, developed, co-ordinated and reconciled before the product can be built.
- The number of design options and product features that need to be reconciled compared with an fmcg product. A key success factor could be the ability to produce a design that best combines rail, bus and tram technology in a new formulation.
- The fact that each competing design has involved considerable investment, yet only a small number are likely to become sufficiently well accepted to achieve sufficent orders to generate economies of scale in production.

Marketing in Action Raw Material Pricing (p 261)

Discussion question
What factors, in addition to price, can lead to a decision to seek product substitution?

- Technological advantage
- environmental issues
- durability and usage
- reduced cost of manufacture or cost of finished product.
-

Marketing in Action Moving Brands into New Markets (p 271)

Discussion question
Compare the marketing infrastructure in Western Europe with Central/Eastern Europe for the launch of new fmcg brands.

Western Europe generally has:
- Established wholesale and retail distribution channels
- sophisticated logistics systems
- available marketing information both before and during launch
- wide range of media targeted at different segments, both niche and mass
- established packaging and design facilities and materials
- reasonably stable prices
- an established range of competitors.

Central/Eastern Europe generally has:
- Poorly established wholesale and distribution channels
- wide variations in product storage and handling capability
- a low level of marketing information in terms of both quantity and quality
- limited range and reliability of media
- design and packaging services still emerging
- price instability (devaluation, inflation, duties etc)
- a turbulent competitive environment.

Marketing in Action Own-label Manufacture (p 274)

Discussion question
What are the likely advantages and disadvantages to fmcg manufactures such as Mars and Heinz of moving into own-label manufacture?

Advantages:
- Use spare production capacity
- spread manufacturing overhead
- open new market segments based on price
- gain more shelf space
- can produce lower quality products do not impact upon main brand name
- strengthen relationships with retailers.

Disadvantages:
- Lower margins
- reduces retailers' preparedness to stock main brand
- competing with one's own mainstream brands.

Marketing in Action Ecolabelling (p 281)

Discussion question
What benefits and problems are likely to face manufacturers when implementing a Ecolabel scheme?

Benefits:
- Reassures customer of user friendliness of brand
- additional selling point through differentiation
- shows that the organisation is in touch with environmental trends in society.

Problems:
- No advantage if many suppliers in the market are offering it

- it may cause confusion to customers when assessing relative brand strengths if it fails to distinguish premium brands from rest
- additional or more stringent measures may be imposed
- additional costs in design may be incurred
- levy paid to Ecolabel Board.

SUGGESTED ASSIGNMENTS

- Choose a speciality product and a convenience product. To what extent and why do their marketing mixes and the kind of buying behaviour associated with them differ?
- Packaging serves the purely functional purpose of containing a quantity of product. Discuss.

Chapter 8
PRODUCT MANAGEMENT

LECTURE PLAN

A lecture based on this chapter should help the student to:
1. Understand the product life cycle concept, its influence on marketing strategies and its limitations;
2. appreciate the importance of product positioning and how it both affects and is affected by marketing strategies;
3. understand the scope and implications of the various decisions that management can take with regard to product ranges, including deletion;
4. define the role and responsibilities of the product or brand manager; and
5. outline the issues surrounding pan-European branding.

The key sections of this lecture should be:

The product life cycle (pp 294-303):
- Definition of the PLC, including OHP 24 figure 8.1 (p 294) The Product Life Cycle:
  ⇒ Overview of the stages
  ⇒ why the sales curve develops as it does
  ⇒ why the profit curve develops as it does
  ⇒ overview of how the product's marketing needs change through the stages.
- Problems of the PLC concept: length; self-fulfilling strategies; shape; definition of 'product'.

Market evolution (pp 303-308):
- The impact of customers themselves on the speed of development of a market, including OHP 25 figure 8.3 (p 304) Diffusion of Innovation: Adopter Categories:
  ⇒ Definition of each category
  ⇒ explanation of why the curve is so shaped
  ⇒ how each category's attitudes and behaviour might differ
  ⇒ how marketing approaches might differ.
- The impact of technology of market development
- the impact of competitive behaviour and market entry on market development.

Managing the product mix (pp 308-318):
- The concept of the product portfolio
- the concept of product positioning

- stages in defining and selecting a position
- the use of perceptual mapping, including OHP 26, figure 8.4 (p 311) Perceptual Map of the Toilet Tissue Market:
  - ⇒ The importance of defining the map in terms of attributes that are important to the buyer
  - ⇒ the importance of creating the map from well-researched consumer perceptions
  - ⇒ interpreting the map.
- How to reposition products
- extending and filling product ranges
- deleting products.

Customer specified products (pp 318-320):
- What they are
- their marketing implications
- their implications for buyer - seller relationships.

This section could be omitted, and students encouraged to read the material for themselves.

Product management and organisation (pp 320-321):
- Why product management is important
- what a product manager typically does
- how product management structures might differ.

Pan-European branding (pp 321-323):
- Definition of a Eurobrand
- why organisations might want to create them
- the marketing demands and problems of Eurobranding.

QUESTIONS FOR REVIEW

8.1   Define the four stages of the product life cycle. (pp 294-299)

1. *Introduction:* the new product launch period
2. *Growth:* establishing the product in the market; building repeat sales
3. *Maturity:* the period during which the product has achieved its maximum potential; a time for revamping the marketing mix?
4. *Decline:* consumer needs have moved on or the product itself has been superseded and thus sales start to decline.

8.2   What might be the main concerns for a marketing manager dealing with a mature product? (pp 297-298)

- Price competition
- maintaining distribution
- maintaining customer loyalty
- heavy reminder and reinforcement advertising
- extending the life cycle through reformulating the product or developing a fresh marketing approach.

8.3   To what extent is the PLC limited in its applicability as a management tool? (pp 300-303)

It is limited because of:
- The difficulty of predicting how long the life cycle should be
- the difficulty of assessing when the next stage in the life cycle has been reached
- the risk of turning it into a self-fulfilling prophecy

- the difficulty of assessing the shape of the PLC
- the problems of balancing and reconciling different levels of PLC (industry, product class, brand).

8.4   What are the alternative ways of allocating product management responsibility in organisational markets? (pp 320-321)

- By product
- by customer type
- by geographic territory.

8.5   Discuss the relationship between product adopter categories and the stages of the PLC. What are the implications for the marketer? (pp 303-306)

- *Innovators:* important in the introduction stage of the PLC to get the product established and to help build its credibility.
- *Early adopters:* emerge in the growth stage, as they follow the innovators' lead and begin to spread the product into a mass market.
- *Early majority:* important in the late growth stage as it moves towards maturity. Their entry signals the acceptance of the product by the mass market.
- *Late majority:* their entry signals the achievement of maturity. The bulk of potential customers are now active in the market, and the product is reaching its saturation level. This group helps to keep the product on the plateau of maturity.
- *Laggards:* this group is entering the market as the other start to leave it. Their entry is likely to coincide, therefore, with the end of maturity and the start of decline. They can, however, help to stave off steep decline.

8.6   Define product positioning, and summarise the reasons why it is important. (pp 308-311)

Product positioning means looking at how the product is perceived by the customer, in terms of attributes that matter to that customer, relative to the competition. It is important because it helps the marketer to:
- Develop products that better match customer needs and wants
- better define customer priorities
- find meaningful ways of differentiating a product
- develop successful competitive strategies.

8.7   Why might product repositioning be necessary, and in what ways can the organisation achieve it? (pp 312-315)

Repositioning might be necessary because:
- Customer needs and wants change
- new competition emerges
- existing competitors change their offerings
- technology changes.
It could be achieved through:
- Major product reformulation
- pricing
- marketing communication initiatives
- changing distribution channels.

8.8   Differentiate between product line extension and filling out the product range. In what circumstances might each be appropriate? (pp 315-317)

Product line extension involves moving beyond the current parameters of the brand by developing either more upmarket or more downmarket versions. It might be useful if the current line is fairly limited in scope, and the organisation wants to create a 'ladder' of products for the customer to move up as their needs (and affluence) change. Filling out the product range means creating new products to fill gaps that exist between existing products in the range. At its most basic, it means developing variants on existing products. This is a relatively low cost option as it might mean trading on existing marketing structures and it helps to keep customers involved and interested in the range.

8.9   Find examples of product line extension, both upmarket and downmarket. Try to analyse the marketing thinking behind the extensions.

This question aims to:
- Encourage students to think about market positioning in practice
- help students to understand the concept of product line extension
- analyse the reasons why extensions are undertaken.

8.10   Outline the alternative product deletion methods available, and the advantages and disadvantages of each. (pp 317-318)

Phase out: gradual fading away of the product with little or no marketing support:
- *Advantages:* revenue is not completely lost immediately; customers have time to adjust to the loss of the product; the organisation has time to develop and introduce a replacement.
- *Disadvantages:* the lingering product continues to absorb management time and resources; the lingering product might cast a shadow over a new product's image as it is phased in; customers and distributors might be slower to adopt a new product.

Run out: concentrating marketing effort on main markets only until sales dry up:
- *Advantages:* reasonable revenue is maintained as the product is milked; customers continue to have access to the product; the organisation has time to develop and introduce a replacement.
- *Disadvantages:* the lingering product continues to absorb management time and resources; the lingering product might cast a shadow over a new product's image as it is phased in; customers and distributors in these markets might be slower to adopt a new product.

Drop: immediate withdrawal of the product in all markets:
- *Advantages:* the organisation is free of the burden of the dying product; it frees resources to support new products; it leaves the market clear for a new product launch.
- *Disadvantages:* revenue from the product is lost immediately; customers could be taken by surprise and resent the product's loss; it is a drastic decision and it is difficult to know when is the best time to do it.

QUESTIONS FOR DISCUSSION

8.1   In what ways might customer-specified products complicate the product management task?

Issues raised might include:
- Determining the price
- controlling costs
- ensuring that the seller can meet the customer's needs on a case by case basis
- working with the customer to design a product package that solves their problem
- maintaining a core image for the broad product range despite the variations.

8.2   Why is product management essential?

It is essential in order to ensure that products:
- Achieve their revenue earning potential

- are allocated the resources they need for their development and maintenance through product, marketing, and corporate planning
- have their performance properly monitored and controlled
- are integrated into a coherent and appropriate marketing mix.

8.3 **Choose a consumer product area (be very specific - for example, choose shampoo rather than hair care products) and list as many brands available within it as you can. (a) What stage in the PLC has each product reached? (b) What stage has the product class or form reached? (c) Does any one organisation own several of your brands, and if so, how are these brands distributed across the different PLC stages?**

This question should:
- Test the student's ability to apply the PLC concept to a real situation and to justify categorising a product on the basis of market cues
- help students to differentiate between brand and product class PLCs and understand how and why they might differ
- provide a gentle foundation for the concept of the product portfolio through looking at how one company could have a number of products at different PLC stages and thinking about why this should be so.

8.4 **What circumstances might lead an organisation towards pan-European branding?**

Issues raised might include:
- Saturated domestic markets
- the existence of a pan-European segment or homogeneous demand
- seeking economies of scale
- seeking a strong European corporate image.

8.5 **Find an example of (a) a successful pan-European brand and (b) an unsuccessful pan-European brand. What do you think has contributed to the success/failure?**

This discussion question encourages students to investigate which familiar brands are or are not pan-European and the assess their success. Criteria that might be raised include:
- The nature of the target segment
- the ability to standardise this product in different geographic markets in terms of:
    ⇒ Product formulation
    ⇒ brand imagery
    ⇒ packaging
    ⇒ pricing
    ⇒ distribution strategy
    ⇒ communication strategies
- The competitive structure of the markets concerned.

CASE STUDY 8.1 Pubs in Peril (p 326)

Teaching Objectives

1. To ensure that the students understand the concept of the product life cycle and the broad characteristics of each stage;
2. to further explore the concept of product positioning and its links with the marketing mix;
3. to reinforce the relationship between the PLC, positioning and segmentation and their impact on the marketing mix.

1   **At what stage in the PLC are the following, and why? (a) Pubs generally, (b) the traditional 'local', and (c) the concept pub.**

a)   Pubs generally might be at the mature stage, possibly heading towards decline because:
- They have been around a long time and are an established part of the UK leisure scene, although facing competition from other types of activity
- they have developed a reasonably stable customer base over the years, but have reached saturation
- they are at risk, however, of losing customers through poor location and changing customer needs
- they are thus trying to emphasise differentiation and indulging in a form of product re-launch.

b)   The traditional 'local' is probably in decline because:
- People are making less frequent trips to the pub
- customers are more mobile and thus less likely to patronise just one local pub
- customers are also likely to have a more geographically spread circle of friends, hence they are likely to meet at centralised venues
- customers are looking for greater variety of experience and ambience, not just through pubs
- there is less sense of local community
- locals are in poor locations, as population centres shift.

c)   The concept pub is probably entering the growth stage because:
- It is still a relatively new product concept
- numbers and variations are proliferating still
- brand images are still being built and established
- major players are still entering the market
- although it is still fairly novel to the consumer, awareness and experience are spreading/diffusing.

2   **If you were to develop a two dimensional perceptual map of the pub market, how would you label the axes? Where would (a) a sports-themed concept pub, (b) a real ale traditional type pub, and (c) a family-orientated pub be positioned on your map, and why?**

Students should first be encouraged to develop a list of viable labels for the two axes. The list should include features, attributes or benefits of pubs that could be important to the customer and that could be used to create the product position. The type of labels that might come up includes:
- Wide/narrow variety of beers available
- wide/narrow variety of entertainment available
- wide/narrow variety of food available
- intimate/gregarious atmosphere
- lively/quiet ambience/atmosphere
- clearly focused/bland image
- wide/narrow range of other services e.g. food, function rooms
- convenient/distant location
- adult only/family orientation
- very good/very poor value for money night out

and probably many others - explore with the students what qualities make a decent pub in their view! Students' maps may come out very different in terms of chosen axes and where they have positioned each type of venue, but the important point is that they have thought out what criteria might be important in creating positioning and that they have developed a reasonable justification for what they have produced. Underline that if this was done for real, (a) they'd use more than two dimensions and (b) the construction of the map would be a result of detailed data analysis from extensive market research. This is a quick and dirty qualitative approach!

3   **How do you think Domecq's marketing mix will differ for each of its types of pub? To what extent do you think these differences might be driven by PLC theory or by segmentation considerations?**

Based on the information in the case an a little common sense, the broad marketing mixes for each type of venue could be:

a) Firkin:
- *Product:* focus on variety and quality of the beer, and as a student orientated pub, likely to be strong on atmosphere and entertainment.
- *Price:* student market, so could be price sensitive.
- *Place:* location close to university/college campuses.
- *Promotion:* needs to reach a localised student audience, thus on-campus advertising and themed promotional nights to encourage frequent visits.

b) John Bull:
- *Product:* clearly British in terms of both product and atmosphere, thus likely to recreate traditional British pub.
- *Price:* adapted to suit local conditions.
- *Place:* probably located in major cities or tourist destinations.
- *Promotion:* local media with strong focus on British heritage aspects of the experience?

c) Big Steak:
- *Product:* less focused on the range of drinks offered, and much more on the menu offered and restaurant aspects. Solid, predictable family fare.
- *Price:* needs to be fairly tightly controlled as it must offer value for money for the whole family, compared with alternative family eating out experiences.
- *Place:* likely to be located nearer cities or larger towns to generate a sufficiently large catchment area to make up for the fact that this is likely to be an infrequent purchase for any one customer? It must be accessible to mobile families.
- *Promotion:* television advertising to establish the image and desirability of the overall brand image and product benefits; local promotion to raise awareness of specific branches with perhaps promotional money off vouchers distributed door to door to encourage trial?

d) Football, Football:
- *Product:* focus on very strong themed image; a fun night out; less emphasis on quality or variety of drinks.
- *Price:* perhaps a less price sensitive market that wants the experience, the atmosphere and the good night out with the lads, and will pay for it?
- *Place:* located to cover a large catchment area; if this is to be a big night out, then customers may be prepared to travel to get to it.
- *Promotion:* again, needs to establish awareness, image and desirability of the venue, emphasising that it's 'not just a pub'?

e) Smiling Sam's:
- *Product:* it is a broad product, not just the drinks and the theme, but food and substantial leisure entertainment e.g. bowling too.
- *Price:* probably could get away with fairly premium pricing for the leisure pursuits, but perhaps the beer is cheaper as a loss leader to get customers in?
- *Place:* again, probably looking for big catchment areas close to major cities?
- *Promotion:* again, there is a need to establish awareness, image and desirability of the venue and comprehensiveness of entertainment offered.

These profiles are largely driven by segmentation, and are orientated towards customer needs. This expanding portfolio of pub types, however, is PLC driven, in the sense that the breweries are creating new concepts to take over as the traditional pub goes into decline, and re-formulating products (e.g. Firkins) to try to extend its maturity stage and milk it.

4   Is Greenall's right to try to use 'occasions' segmentation? Can a pub be all things to all people and survive?

The advantages of 'occasions' segmentation are that it:

- Makes maximum use of facilities at different times which otherwise would be lying idle or too quiet sometimes
- is a more cost effective use of facilities
- broadens the venue's appeal to a wider range of segments, and there might be synergies and overlaps between them.

The disadvantages are that it

- Could lead to bland image overall if it is trying to be a lot of things and ending up as nothing in particular, and thus ...
- ... could lose out to more focused establishments
- it may need to provide a broader range of products/services as well as ...
- more flexible and skilled staff to meet needs of all occasions catered for.

It is difficult to be all things to all people, as people look for wider leisure experiences, or seek tightly focused themes. It is possible to sympathise with Greenall's, however. In terms of services marketing, they have the classic dilemma of peaks and troughs in demand at different times and they are trying to even those out and maximise the use of expensive facilities. They have also got the problem of having fixed locations - pubs are located where they are located and have to make the best of it despite any changes in the profile of the area.

CASE STUDY 8.2 Fokker Takes Flight (p 327)

Teaching Objectives

1. To analyse the difficulties of applying the PLC to an organisational product;
2. to analyse how factors within the marketing environment, particularly the changing profile of customer demand, affect product range decisions;
3. to explore the concept and application of positioning in an organisational market.

1   How do you think the PLC for an aircraft model differs from that of a car, and why?

It is important to distinguish between the product class and individual models. Both cars and aircraft as product classes could be regarded as mature products, but in both cases, individual models have their own PLCs and are at different stages within them. In the aircraft market, for example, the jet aircraft PLC is probably on a mature plateau, as passenger traffic increases worldwide, but new technology and operating requirements are pushing some other aircraft types into decline. The life cycle comparison of the car model and an aircraft model has some other similarities and differences:

- The product development period can be longer for aircraft
- the life cycle for an aircraft model is likely to be much longer, although some classic car lines (for example, the Mini or the 2CV) have outlived a number of aircraft models
- there is unlikely to be a mass market for an aircraft, and the number of potential customers is much smaller, thus the purchasing decisions of any one key customer could have a profound effect on the shape and length of an aircraft's PLC
- both car and aircraft manufacturers could develop various strategies to extend the product life in the maturity stage
- both car and aircraft manufacturers need to achieve sufficient cumulative sales through the course of the PLC to recoup the high development costs.

2   What factors within the marketing environment have affected Fokker's product range decisions for jets?

Sociocultural:
- Growth in demand for, and acceptance of, regional air transportation as an alternative to road/rail.

Technological:

- The increased ability to use some common technology in different products, improving cost effectiveness and speed of new product development
- the development of more sophisticated navigation and landing systems.

Economic/competitive:

- Fokker has expanded into planes for the regional jet market rather than the long haul sector, where the large US companies such as McDonnell Douglas and Boeing are dominant. It is better able to compete with similar sized manufacturers in this market sector.
- The success of the Fokker 100 provided a foundation for further product development
- lack of other aircraft in the 70-seater niche
- demand for aircraft that are even more cost effective in operation
- opening up of global markets.

Political/legal: there is nothing particularly mentioned in the case, but students may suggest that:

- Some national airlines' purchasing decisions, in terms of favoured suppliers, are heavily influenced by politicians
- investment in regional air transportation might also be subject to political considerations
- the speed and nature of airline deregulation allowing new operators to enter the market
- Fokker will have to develop aircraft the conform to international and national safety and operating specifications.

3   The rationale for the Fokker 70 was an assumption that demand for regional jets from European airlines would grow. What factors are likely to influence that growth?

This growth is likely to be influenced by:

- Overall market growth in business and leisure markets in Europe
- the relative price of transport modes; the speed, reliability and efficiency of each alternative, for example congestion on roads; the development of high speed rail systems such as TGV
- increased handling capacity at smaller regional airports with short runways
- the market priority given by the major airlines to regional passenger traffic
- the spread of deregulation generating new operators to challenge established airlines
- perhaps the political will of governments and local authorities to support and invest in the necessary infrastructure
- the alliances formed between longhaul and regional operators that allow greater connectivity, and thus more appeal to passengers of regional flying.

4   How relevant do you think the concept of product positioning is in an organisational market such as this one? Against what criteria would an aircraft be positioned?

The same positioning principles apply in this market as in any other, using the main buying criteria and perceptions of the regional jet operators. Critical positioning factors are likely to be:

- The number of passengers that can be carried, as dictated by the fuselage length
- the ability to use a range of different runway lengths, determined by such factors as engine thrust and wing length
- operational cost effectiveness, assessed on capital cost, operating and maintenance costs, and durability
- sophistication in electronic systems and safety features to enable wider use.

Each model offers different performance and product specifications that could be used to position in a very general sense. However given the highly complex product specifications, the need for close interaction between buyer and seller, and the extended buying process the concept may only be applicable as an initial assessment of competing offerings.

Marketing in Action Male Fragrance (p 295)

Discussion question
What factors are likely have caused the slow development of the market for male fragrances?

The main factors revolve around:

- Male attitudes to fragrance as conflicting with perceptions of masculinity
- changing lifestyles and developing male willingness to become dress conscious
- the maturing mass market appeal of male aftershaves, which assists fragrance brand acceptance
- marketers' decisions to reposition products in terms of fashionability and stylishness
- the use of established and recognised brand names from other product segments.

Marketing in Action The Evolving PLC of the PC (p 307)

Discussion question

What factors do you think have affected the length and shape of the introduction and growth stages of the PC's PLC so far? What factors are likely to influence this PLC in the future?

Introduction:
- Relatively expensive
- not user friendly
- limited capability
- in organisational markets the investment in mainframes slowed down the willingness to change to PCs
- in small organisations manual systems were favoured and PCs were not considered cost effective
- no established usage benefits in consumer markets
- mainly a direct sales operation rather than mass distribution.

Growth:
- New software from IBM and Apple that became the industry standards
- the software market developed new and more sophisticated applications
- increased competition stimulated market interest
- prices fell making PCs more accessible
- change in emphasis towards selling benefits rather than the technology
- in line with growth, the wider availability of PCs through retail outlets.

The future: there are many possibilities as to how the market will continue to develop through the rest of the PLC. Particular issues are likely to be:
- The speed with which the PC will become a standard part of home technology
- new technology continuing to reduce relative prices
- the further development of multimedia PC capability
- the willingness of customers to upgrade their systems in line with developing technology
- the growth of more sophisticated software for games, education etc
- the maturity stage may be some time in arriving given the low level of household penetration of PCs across Europe.

Marketing in Action Repositioning for Good Health (p 312)

Discussion question

What considerations needed to be made before deciding to reposition Lucozade?

The main considerations were:
- Future market potential in the current market niche if no repositioning was undertaken
- the forecast purchasing frequency levels and sales volume expectations in different positions
- the growth of new market segments (health and fitness boom) and changing consumer attitudes towards dealing with illness
- whether the trade would accept change
- whether new and existing consumers would accept change
- whether premium price and quality image could be retained
- whether the repositioning could be communicated through promotion and packaging.

Marketing in Action Making Records (p 318)

Discussion question
Where are the Rolling Stones of the future going to come from? Can the record companies develop strategies to develop long term product winners?

This topic should generate a wide range of views in an area of which most students will have some experience or opinions. It is, of course, important to relate these experiences to the concepts introduced in the chapter. The key question is whether the space and time allowed to artists such as the Rolling Stones can be replicated. Given the state of competitiveness this is now much harder as it has become far more difficult to assess in advance future winners. Careful testing and consumer tracking is still possible. Each artist or group is essentially a brand that needs building, positioning and reformulating at various stages in its life. A record company will need to retain a portfolio of brands to include the popular artists that may be cash generators in order to support new artists, most of whom will fail to achieve long term success. It is perhaps easy to forget that many of the 60s artists, although still having a minority following, could not be regarded as cash winners.

SUGGESTED ASSIGNMENTS

- To what extent and why is the product life-cycle a useful strategic marketing tool?
- Is pan-European branding a logical and positive step forward for all manufacturers of consumer goods?

Chapter 9
NEW PRODUCT DEVELOPMENT

LECTURE PLAN

A lecture based on this chapter should help the student to:
1. Define the various types of product 'newness' and the marketing implications of each;
2. understand the reasons for new product development;
3. analyse the eight stages in the new product development process;
4. appreciate the reasons for new product failure; and
5. outline some current trends in R&D management.

The key sections of this lecture should be:

Introduction (pp 331-339):
- Definition of NPD
- defining 'new product' from the organisation's perspective
- defining 'new product' from the customer's perspective, including OHT 27, figure 9.1 (p 336) The Innovation Continuum:
  ⇒ Define different types of innovation
  ⇒ give examples of each
  ⇒ implications for marketing strategies.
- Why NPD is important
- proactive and reactive approaches to NPD.

The NPD process (pp 339-354):

This discussion is based on OHT 28, figure 9.2 (p 340) The New Product Development Process:

- *Idea generation:* importance of stream of new ideas; various sources of ideas; importance of creativity and lateral thinking.
- *Screening ideas:* the role of screening; how to screen.
- *Concept testing:* what it is; why it is done; how it is done.
- *Business analysis:* what it involves; its implications for a potential new product.
- *Product development:* creating a 'real' product and its marketing mix.
- *Test marketing:* what it is; why it is done; the risks and benefits of doing it.
- *Commercialisation:* different approaches to commercialisation; the risks and benefits of each.
- *Monitoring and evaluation:* the importance of reviewing the NPD process itself and of evaluating the performance of the product created from it.

New product failure (pp 354-356):

- Why products fail
- how the risks of failure can be minimised.

Trends in NPD management (pp 356-361):

- The practical constraints and problems of NPD
- outsourced R&D
- collaborative R&D
- organising for NPD in-house.

QUESTIONS FOR REVIEW

9.1   What is the difference between dynamically continuous innovation and discontinuous innovation? (pp 336-337)

Dynamically continuous innovation means that new products are developed that involve significant innovation, but in a familiar product. Discontinuous innovation involves a totally new product which bears no relationship to anything with which the customer is familiar.

9.2   What is the difference between reactive and proactive NPD? (pp 338-339)

Reactive NPD is undertaken in response to what competitors have done, essentially resulting in 'me too' products. Proactive NPD seeks to develop and commercialise completely new products and concepts before the competition.

9.3   What are the eight stages of the NPD process? (pp 339-354)

1. Idea generation
2. idea screening
3. concept testing
4. business analysis
5. product development
6. test marketing
7. commercialisation
8. monitoring and evaluation.

9.4   List as many potential general sources of new product ideas as you can. (pp 340-343)

- R&D department
- existing competitors
- potential competitors

- employees
- research into customers' needs
- analysis of customer complaints
- lead users
- licensing
- brainstorming and other types of 'organised creativity'
- agencies and consultants
- trade magazines and exhibitions.

9.5   What kind of criteria are likely to be taken into account during the idea screening stage? (pp 343-345)

- Fit with organisational and marketing goals
- fit with existing products and technology
- fit with existing distribution channels
- size of potential market
- potential market share
- nature of competition (direct and substitutes)
- profitability of potential market
- ability to deliver differential advantage.

9.6   What is concept testing and why is it a crucial stage in the NPD process? (pp 345-346)

Concept testing presents verbal statements, graphical images or storyboards, or models to a sample of the target market in order to gauge their reaction to it. It is important as it helps the researcher to:
- Test acceptance of the product concept
- assess the relative attractiveness of alternative ideas in the perceptions of the target market
- assess the strengths and weaknesses of alternative ideas
- gain an insight into what particular aspects of the idea appeal
- gain an insight into what would motivate customers to buy this product
- start to develop ideas for an appropriate marketing mix.

9.7   How are marketing, production and financial concerns brought together at the business analysis stage? (pp 346-347)

They are brought together in that marketing research will show what features and benefits have to be built into the product, and what the sales volumes and pricing are likely to be. Production, however, needs to assess whether these features and benefits can be delivered practically and cost effectively, whether the proposed sales volumes can actually be produced and whether they represent suitable economies of scale. Finance needs to analyse the production costs and forecasts and the sales and revenue forecasts to determine whether the product will be suitably profitable and cost efficient.

9.8   What might be the main causes of uncertainty at the business analysis stage? (pp 346-347)

- Competitive reaction
- assessing market size and potential
- forecasting sales volume
- forecasting production costs and how they will evolve with the learning curve and the effect of economies of scale
- calculating profitability.

9.9   What is the role of the product development stage for an fmcg product? (pp 347-348)

The role of this stage is to:
- Finalise the product itself in terms of formulation, design, quality, packaging etc
- develop brand identity
- develop the launch marketing mix
- undertake any last testing to fine tune the concept before test marketing or launch.

9.10   What is the difference between outsourced and collaborative R&D? (pp 356-359)

Outsourced R&D is contracted out externally to other organisations or consultants. Collaborative R&D involves a partnership with another organisation in order to share R&D skills and costs for mutual benefit.

QUESTIONS FOR DISCUSSION

9.1   Find an example of a new product for each of the types of newness categories discussed at pp 332 *et seq*. What particular marketing problems do you think the organisations launching each of those products might have had?

Students should be able to outline why each chosen product fits within the category with which it has been associated. The kinds of marketing problems discussed might range over issues of:
- Lack of customer acceptance of the product
- lack of product acceptance by distribution channels
- lack of clear differentiation from competition
- poor or unfocused brand imagery
- lack of convincing communication re product benefits
- lack of sales promotion to encourage trial
- low launch budgets
- inconsistent quality
- patchy availability.

9.2   What are the potential benefits and pitfalls of using a screening approach based on rating ideas against weighted criteria?

Benefits:
- Encourages debate about what criteria are really important
- imposes the same systematic approach on all alternative ideas on the same criteria
- encourages debate about how each idea should be rated on each criterion
- provides a useful guideline for decision making, helping to justify qualitative feelings.

Pitfalls:
- It is still difficult to differentiate between similar ideas
- the numbers lend the process a spurious certainty
- the choice of criteria is judgemental
- the rating of ideas against those criteria is also judgemental.

9.3   How might the product development stage differ for (a) an fmcg product and (b) an organisational product?

This outline answer below assumes that the organisational product concerned is something like a component that involves tight specifications. Students could, however, also be encouraged to look at this question from a less 'engineering biased' point of view, for example by looking at the product development stage for a new type of disposable paper hat for the catering industry.
- It may take a lot longer for an organisational product

- the organisational product is likely to involve a greater range of expertise and functional areas at this stage
- the organisational product is more likely to involve the customer directly and deeply in this stage
- the organisational product is likely to involve more fine tuning and rigourous testing of the actual physical product on a reiterative basis than an fmcg product
- both types of product need their marketing mixes developing at this stage, although their emphases will differ considerably.

9.4   To what extent do you think that test marketing is a good idea?

Students should be encouraged to debate the advantages and disadvantages of test marketing. They might bring in the following points:

Advantages:
- It is a real test in a real environment
- it offers a last opportunity for fine tuning the product
- it offers a last opportunity for testing and fine tuning the other elements of the marketing mix
- it allows the assessment and measurement of 'real' consumer and distributor behaviour
- it could prevent the organisation from making a costly mistake.

Disadvantages:
- The test area might not be typical
- it shows the competition exactly what is planned
- competition might try to influence the test market results
- it may go on too long, simply delaying the full launch, or for not long enough, giving an unbalanced assessment of the product's performance
- it incurs extra costs and wastes time. Simulations can do the same job better and more cheaply.

9.5   Find examples of two recently launched fmcg products, one of which was given a full national launch, and the other of which was rolled out gradually. Why do you think the particular approach chosen was appropriate for each product?

Students should be encouraged to debate the advantages and disadvantages of a national launch *vs.* a rolling launch, using their chosen products as examples. They might bring in the following points:
- Rolling out warns the competition
- multiple retailers might find a national launch administratively and logistically easier to handle
- a national launch makes a big impact
- a gradual roll out might be more affordable for a smaller organisation
- rolling out gives the organisation time to learn and refine in terms of both its marketing and production strategies as it builds sales volume
- rolling out a new product could be integrated with the gradual withdrawal of an old one.

CASE STUDY 9.1 Digital Compact Cassette *vs.* MiniDisc (p 363)

Teaching Objectives

1. To examine some of the reasons why new products perform less well than expected in the market;
2. to emphasise the importance of planning ahead and particularly of securing the full co-operation of members of the distribution channel;
3. to think about ways of refining marketing strategies in order to stimulate sales of a poorly performing new product.

1   Outline the reasons why MiniDisc and DCC are having greater problems making an impact on the market than the CD did originally.

- CD sound quality was markedly better than existing formats available at the time. MiniDisc and DCC are not perceived to offer such improvement
- consumers have invested heavily in CD and are reluctant to change formats yet again
- record companies are not releasing many titles on the new formats. When CD was introduced, record companies were quick to respond.
- Music retailers were slower to adopt the new formats than they had been with CD
- hi-fi retailers were similarly reluctant to stock the new 'hardware'
- perhaps consumers are also comparing the price of the new formats with current CD 'hardware' prices, which could seem a lot lower.

2   Could these problems have been predicted and avoided?

To some extent, these problems could perhaps have been predicted and avoided. A more forceful campaign of stressing each of the new formats' benefits, clearly differentiating them from CD would have given consumers a better 'reason to buy'. The need for a substantial range of 'software' to be widely available was obvious - consumers would not be investing in the 'hardware' for its own sake! Both Philips and Sony, therefore, could have liaised more closely with both the record companies and the music retailers to ensure that potential customers would be reassured that they would have lots of choice of things to play on the new format, and that the 'software' would be readily and conveniently available. This liaison would not be easy to achieve, however. Consumers want to see that 'software' is available before they will invest in a new format, yet the 'software' producers and retailers need to be sure that there is consumer demand out there. A lot more hard work, negotiation and persuasion was required to achieve a satisfactory simultaneous launch of both 'hardware' and 'software'.

Problems with the 'hardware' retailers should also have been predictable. Why were they reluctant to promote the new formats heavily? Perhaps again they were not given sufficient reason to be enthusiastic by the manufacturers; they were not well enough persuaded that these were 'better' products. Perhaps too they were not given enough support to allow them to:
- Talk knowledgeably about the product benefits to potential customers
- demonstrate the product in store
- offer consumers price or non-price incentives to buy
- stock the products on a trial basis to reduce risk?

3   Why do you think Philips cut the number of retailers stocking DCC?

- To maintain tighter control over distribution
- to allow Philips to develop closer relationships with retailers
- to allow Philips to concentrate its marketing support to the retail trade, so that each remaining retailer gets more. This has allowed Philips to:
  - ⇒ Increase point of sale promotion, and
  - ⇒ provide in-store demonstration units with demonstrators
  - ⇒ to support a repositioning towards a more specialist niche product, consistent with the proposed concentration of advertising in the specialist press?

4   Are these products failures?

Yes, in the sense that both manufacturers feel that their respective systems have had a 'slow start' and that they are not capturing any significant market share or selling in sufficient volumes to threaten CD seriously. They are far from dead, however!

Supplementary question
What has Philips done to try to reverse its product's fortunes, and do you think they have done the right things?

- *Product:* essentially the product is the same, but it is being repositioned through the other elements of the marketing mix.
- *Price:* cut by 50 per cent. Probably a sensible move to bring the product's price closer to that of a CD player. Providing that it is not also accompanied by a cut in the retailer's margin, it should make it easier for the retailer to sell the product benefits.
- *Place:* more concentrated distribution through specialist outlets, as mentioned in question 3 above. This could help to get the product established and accepted among hi-fi enthusiasts as opinion leaders? It certainly helps to increase the enthusiasm with which the product is sold.
- *Promotion:* as mentioned in question 3 above, promotional support has been concentrated in specialist press, at the point of sale, and within the distribution channel. This is entirely consistent with the 'place' strategy and the repositioning. It is the kind of product:
  ⇒ That needs strong personal selling and
  ⇒ for which the customer is likely to seek information and guidance in specialist magazines and in specialist outlets.

These moves seem to be consistent with each other, and seem to provide a realistic strategy to get the product better accepted and established in the market in the short term at least, even if it never reaches the mass market appeal of the CD. The key outstanding issue, however, is the range and availability of 'software', unless the DCC is to be heavily sold as primarily a recording device rather than a playback machine.

CASE STUDY 9.2 Soap Wars (p 364)

Teaching Objectives

1. To examine the risks of new product launch within an existing brand family;
2. to emphasise the need for a flexible launch strategy in case of unforeseen responses by the competition;
3. to discuss the problems of taking the decision to delete a new product that is in trouble.

1   Why do you think Lever launched the new product using the Persil name? What were the risks and benefits of doing this?

Lever launched the product under the Persil name primarily to trade on the well established brand image. The risks of doing this were that:
- It might be difficult to clearly differentiate this product from the rest of the Persil family
- consumers might not notice the new product amongst the rest
- the brand image of the new product is constrained by the established Persil brand image and values
- retailers might only give the new product shelf space at the expense of existing Persil products?
- if anything were to go wrong with the new product, the whole Persil family suffers.
The benefits were that:
- The established Persil image would rub off onto the new product
- the manufacturer does not have to invest so much time and effort in developing a totally new identity
- retailers might find a product presented as a range extension more acceptable than something completely independent of the existing range
- consumers do not have so much learning to do as they are already familiar with the core brand, and thus ...
- the new product launch is less risky for the manufacturer.

2   How, and to what extent, do you think P&G was successful in spoiling Lever's new product launch? What counter-attack measures did Lever have to take?

P&G was successful in:
- Quickly finding a major flaw in the product

- commissioning the research to prove the flaw
- ensuring that the flaw received publicity
- investing in a high profile aggressive comparative advertising campaign.

P&G managed to spoil the new product launch in that its actions managed to sow sufficient doubt in consumers' minds to make them think twice about using the product. In the process of doing this, P&G also managed to enhance both its corporate image as 'the consumers' champion' and the image of its own products. P&G certainly started the ball rolling, but could not have achieved so much damage to Persil without the willing co-operation of the media. P&G were instrumental in feeding information to the press, but media interest kept the story alive and ongoing. The media would be seen as more impartial by consumers than P&G alone, and thus could have been more powerful in turning customers against Persil. The result of all this was that Lever had to:

- Spend an extra £25 million on advertising and promotion
- develop a very defensive tone
- reformulate the product and relaunch it
- compensate consumers for damage.

Lever was treading a very fine line between trying to dampen the negative aspects of the stories about the product, yet still be seen as being open and honest about problems. The last thing it needed was accusations of an uncaring, sinister 'cover up'.

3   Was Lever right to maintain the Persil Power brand for as long as it did? What are the problems associated with deleting a brand like this?

If Lever felt that there was a chance of rescuing the brand, and that it could develop a viable repositioning strategy to do so, then it was right to maintain the product, as to abandon it would be:
- Seen as an admission of major fault
- an admission of defeat to P&G, leaving them clear space for their new product launch
- to write off some £300 million. When so much has been invested, to drop is a brave decision.

As well as these problems of deletion, once the product is dropped, the inquests really begin, and someone has to be prepared to take responsibility for the failure. For as long as there is a possibility of salvaging the product, this issue might not be so pressing. It can be very difficult in reality to know when enough is enough, and when to make the ultimate decision. A pressing factor in this case would have been the loss of a major supermarket multiple as a distributor. This kind of product cannot afford to be absent from any one of the big name retailers. Once one has lost faith in the product, others are likely to follow. To maintain the product, however, carried its own risks of:
- Further damage to the Persil name
- alienating or exasperating the retail trade
- continued hostile publicity
- needing major investment just to stop it declining any further without any guarantees of future success.

4   What are the lessons to be learned from this case about new product development?

- It can be very risky
- it can be very expensive
- it can be very unpredictable even for a major multinational with all its R&D and market research resources and all its experience of new product launches
- there are no guarantees of success, even for what seems to be a routine launch of a brand extension
- if the product is flawed or unsuitable to the market, all the marketing skills and investment in the world are unlikely to save it
- sometimes you just have to admit defeat!

Marketing in Action Rubbing Salt into the Market (p 334)

Discussion question
What benefits do you think Kallo was trying to achieve by launching PanSalt into the UK consumer market and into the processed food sector simultaneously?

- Economies of scale?
- Synergy in spreading awareness and acceptance:
  - ⇒ If consumers buy processed foods that feature PanSalt, it might encourage them to try the product for themselves
  - ⇒ if consumers can buy PanSalt for themselves, the food processors might better see the sales benefits of featuring PanSalt in their foods.
- Trying to ensure that PanSalt becomes almost the generic name for low sodium salt
- trying to leave no clear gap in the market for a rival product's entry.

Marketing in Action Neutraceuticals (p 336)

Discussion question
What do you think are the problems of developing and launching a new neutraceutical product?

- Ensuring that any health claims can be substantiated
- ensuring that the product does not technically become a 'medicine', subject to much more stringent regulations on formulation, testing and distribution
- ensuring that there is a sufficiently large health conscious segment that will buy it
- finding the right price which is:
  - ⇒ high enough to reinforce the impression of it being something special, thus higher than the 'ordinary' products in its market
  - ⇒ not so high that it only appeals to the hard core health freaks
  - ⇒ attractive to the retail trade in terms of their margins.
- Securing the enthusiastic co-operation of distribution channels, probably major supermarket, pharmacy and health food multiples through trade promotion, personal selling, and point of sale display support
- developing a marketing communications campaign that clearly explains the product benefits, differentiates the neutraceutical from 'ordinary' products, and encourages trial of the product.

Marketing in Action Recycled Paper (p 342)

Discussion question
Why has it taken so long for recycled paper to move out of the introduction stage of its PLC into growth?

Recent technological improvements have increased the attractiveness of recycled paper:
- Improvement in the quality of the end product
- ability to achieve a quality end product from lower grade inputs

Customer/market needs can now be met better than before because of:
- Technological advances, as above
- the end product can now be used for a much greater range of applications
- using recycled materials is now seen as a tangible sign of being 'a responsible and caring organisation'
- recycled papers now more cost effective than before.

Economic reasons:
- Virgin fibre pulp prices have risen
- ability to use lower grade raw material for recycling has lowered the price.

Marketing in Action Business Forums (p 359)

Discussion question
What are the advantages and disadvantages of business forums for the small entrepreneur?

Advantages:
- Feedback on the idea, proposals for improvement, and reaction on its likely feasibility
- contact with sources of help and funding
- a confidence booster
- meeting like-minded entrepreneurs and sharing experiences.

Disadvantages:
- Feedback could be discouraging.

SUGGESTED ASSIGNMENTS

- Questions for Discussion 9.1
- Test marketing is an outdated concept that has no relevance to today's fmcg manufacturers. Discuss.

Chapter 10
PRICING: CONTEXT AND CONCEPTS

LECTURE PLAN

A lecture based on this chapter should help the student to:
1. Define the meaning of price;
2. understand the different roles price can play for buyers and sellers and in different kinds of market;
3. appreciate the nature of the external and internal factors that influence pricing decisions; and
4. understand the impact of the single European market on pricing.

The key sections of this lecture should be:

Introduction (pp 369-375):
- Definition of price
- customer perceptions of price, including OHP 29, figure 10.1 (p 371) Factors Influencing Customers' Price Assessments:
    ⇒ Discuss each factor and how it affects price
    ⇒ the importance of consistent price messages from all the factors
    ⇒ the importance of emphasising key factors as a means of justifying price within the marketing mix.
- The seller's attitude to price: relationship between revenue and profit; price and positioning; customers' switching costs.

Pricing contexts (pp 375-380):
- *Consumer markets:* disposable income; price perceptions; price sensitivity.
- *Retail and wholesale markets:* supply prices and profitability; price discipline.
- *Services markets:* problems of perishability and intangibility.
- *Non-profit markets:* different pricing objectives.
- *Organisational markets:* relationship between price and costs; value management.

External influences on pricing (pp 380-391):
This section is based on OHP 30, figure 10.2 (p 381) External Influences on the Pricing Decision:
- *Customers and consumers:* pricing discretion; demand and elasticity; price sensitivity.
- *Channels of distribution:* need to cover costs; value added to products; desired margins.
- *Competitors:* pricing under different market structures.
- *Legal and regulatory:* freedom to set prices; unfair pricing practices; sales taxes, VAT etc and their impact on prices.

Internal influences on pricing (pp 391-395):
This section is based on OHP 31, figure 10.8 (p 392) Internal Influences on the Pricing Decision:
- *Organisational objectives:* the role pricing can play in achieving long- and short-term corporate objectives.
- *Marketing objectives:* the role pricing can play in achieving long- and short-term marketing objectives; price and product positioning.
- *Costs:* the relationship between price and costs; the need to apportion costs fairly across products; balancing the need to cover costs against the price the market will bear.

European aspects of pricing (pp 396-398):
- The impact of the SEM on pricing
- why there are price differentials in different geographic European markets
- problems of managing European prices
- problems of parallel trading.

QUESTIONS FOR REVIEW

10.1   What factors affect the customer's interpretation of price? (pp 371-373)

- *Functional:* the product's ability to fulfil its desired function.
- *Operational:* the ability of the product to increase operational efficiency, either in the factory or in the home.
- *Quality:* the perceived quality of the product or of the corporate image of its producer.
- *Financial:* the ability of the product to generate cost savings and efficiency gains.
- *Personal:* the ability of the product to enhance the purchaser's self-image, status or comfort.

10.2   In what kind of circumstances might a high price actually be better for a seller than a low one? (pp 373-375)

A high price might be better if:
- The seller wants to build a quality image for the product
- the seller wants to build an exclusive image for the product
- the buyer is purchasing a gift and wants to feel that they have spent a reasonable sum on it
- the segment is generally not price sensitive. In this case, the seller might as well price towards the top of the acceptable price band rather than towards the bottom.

10.3   How can a seller distract the customer's attention from a high price? (pp 373-375)

- Reinforce the quality image of the product
- reinforce the desirability of the product's benefits
- augment the product/service package to make the customer think that they are getting more for their money, for example an extended warranty or customer helpline which are relatively cheap to provide, but are of immense value to the customer and help to enhance a 'good service' image
- emphasise the longer term cost savings derived from using this product compared with the cheaper competition.

10.4 Define price discipline and explain what it means to both manufacturers and retailers. (pp 377-378)

Price discipline means conforming to the unwritten rules of pricing within the trade. It might mean being consistent with other organisations' pricing approaches, or it might mean being able to justify any price differential clearly. To manufacturers, it means:

- Not selling direct to the public at significantly lower prices than a retailer
- not selling goods to one retailer at cheaper prices than to another unless it can be justified in commercial terms.

To retailers it means Not selling manufacturer brands below cost.

10.5 What are the particular problems of pricing service products? (p 378)

- They are intangible, thus it is difficult for the customer to 'see' the quality
- it can be difficult for the customer to make direct comparisons between competing products
- they are perishable and pricing can be instrumental in determining whether, for example, a hotel is full one night, or an aircraft takes off with half its seats empty.

10.6 List the internal and external influences on pricing decisions.

Internal factors (pp 391-394)
- Organisational objectives
- marketing objectives
- costs.

External factors (pp 380-391)
- Customers' and consumers' price attitudes and perceptions
- demand and price elasticity
- channels of distribution
- competition
- legal and regulatory constraints.

10.7 Define price elasticity. Why is this an important concept for the marketer? (pp 384-386)

Price elasticity measures the sensitivity of demand to price changes. The higher the elasticity, the greater the price sensitivity. For an elastic product, a small change in price leads to a disproportionately large change in demand. For an inelastic product, a change in price leads to a disproportionately small change in demand. It is an important concept because it shows how important precise pricing is within the marketing mix. In a sensitive (elastic) market, a price which is just a little bit higher than that of the competition could lead to a large loss in market share. An elastic market might also be more prone to price wars. In an insensitive (inelastic) market, can concentrate on emphasising factors other than price, and set a price that is towards the top of the acceptable price band.

10.8 In what ways can competition influence pricing decisions? (pp 387-389)

Pricing is affected by:
- The number of competitors and the power of any one of them to influence pricing in the market significantly
- the pricing framework established within the market by the combined effects of competition
- the efforts of oligopolists to maintain a pricing status quo
- the willingness or otherwise of competitors to get drawn into price wars.

10.9   To what extent and why do you think that costs should influence pricing? (p 394)

Costs should affect prices because the organisation does want to make a profit, but:
- It can be difficult to calculate and apportion shared or centralised costs for each unit of a product
- considering the price that a customer is prepared to pay for a product is more important than a cost recovery approach, otherwise there is a risk of under- or over-pricing the product
- short term losses might be acceptable if the longer term strategic aim is to build market share or customer loyalty.

10.10   What factors influencing European prices are likely to increase or reduce price differentials over the next five years? (pp 396-398)

- Market development in different regions
- exchange rate fluctuations or stability
- distribution channel and logistics developments
- regional differences in trade margins and operating costs
- harmonisation of tax and excise rates
- differences in regional lifestyles and price perceptions among consumers.

QUESTIONS FOR DISCUSSION

10.1   Choose a manufacturer that produces a range of products serving different price segments in a consumer market. How does the manufacturer 'justify' the different prices?

From this question, students are developing an appreciation of the reasons why manufacturers should target different price segments, and applying the concepts of influences on pricing. The kinds of products that might be interesting for this exercise include:
- Cars
- hi-fi, televisions and other household electrical goods
- possibly cosmetics and toiletries
- possibly boxed chocolates?

A point to reinforce is that segments will probably be defined in terms of price banding, and the size and consumer perception of those bands will vary from market to market. A consumer might, for example, consider a box of chocolates in the £5-£6 range as significantly 'better' than one in the £4-£5 range. That same consumer, however, might regard all cars in the £7,000 to £10,000 bracket as 'similarly priced'. The justification for higher prices might include:
- Higher raw material/labour costs in producing of a better quality product
- higher distribution costs through using more select outlets
- greater levels of customer service and care
- loss of economies of scale in the higher priced niche market
- consumers equating price with quality
- reinforcing an upmarket image.

10.2   Find an example of a price sensitive consumer market. Why do you think this market is price sensitive and is there anything that the manufacturers or retailers could do to make it less so?

Students should be able to justify their choice of market in terms of:
- The nature of the product, which is likely to be a low involvement, functional kind of product with little to differentiate it from its competitors other than price
- the marketing strategies of competitors in the market
- the actions of retailers or other intermediaries in emphasising price.

In trying to find ways of de-sensitising the customer, students should be encouraged to examine their chosen product in terms of the factors listed in table 10.4 (p 385) to see if the manufacturer or retailer can exploit any of them.

10.3   Compare consumer and organisational attitudes to price, explaining how and why they differ.

This discussion should bring out a range of points, including:
- Rational *vs.* emotional decision making processes
- functional/financial *vs.* psychological product benefits sought
- the customer's perceived level of risk in the purchasing decision
- accountability for the purchasing decision
- the frequency of purchase
- the necessity of the purchase
- focus on short *vs.* long term benefits
- willingness and ability to negotiate
- relative power of buyer and seller.

10.4   To what extent do you think the classic demand curve as shown in Fig 10.3 is a useful guide for the marketing manager in practice?

It is not very practical because:
- It assumes a linear relationship between price and quantity which is too simplistic
- to draw one relies on managerial judgement of the price/quality relationship
- too many other factors, both controllable (for example advertising, distribution strategies, and point of sale promotion) and largely uncontrollable (for example, competitors' marketing activities the emergence of new competitors, the emergence of substitute products, changing customer needs and wants, the changing economic environment, and the marketing activities of intermediaries) can affect attitude towards price and willingness to buy.

10.5   Choose a consumer product and explain the role that pricing plays in its marketing mix and market positioning.

This is a straightforward exercise to ensure that the student understands:
- The need for pricing's messages to be consistent with the rest of the marketing mix
- the effect of price on consumer attitudes and behaviour
- the concept of price sensitivity and the reasons why competitors in a market try to emphasise or de-emphasise price
- the ability of price to help define market segments
- the role of price as a differentiator
and can see how these factors might work in practice.

CASE STUDY 10.1 The Net Book Agreement (p 401).

Teaching Objectives

1. To ensure that students understand the influences on price;
2. to discuss the desirability or otherwise of artificial price maintenance;
3. to examine the practical consequences of deregulating prices.

1   Summarise the reasons for the NBA's collapse.

- Falling book sales
- some publishers felt that the NBA was reducing sales volumes achievable on hardbacks

- UK book prices were out of line with those of other countries
- supermarkets wanted to get into bookselling, but only if they could discount on bestsellers
- some High Street multiple booksellers wanted to be able to use discounted bestsellers promotionally to entice customers to spend more
- two powerful players, Hodder Headline, a major publisher and ASDA a major supermarket multiple joined forces to break the NBA deliberately. Eventually others felt they had to follow suit and the pressure on the legislators to abolish the NBA officially became too great to withstand
- media pressure against the NBA was also a powerful force.

2   What are the internal and external influences on a book's price from a publisher's perspective?

Internal:

Organisational and marketing objectives: the need to
- Meet and defend specified sales volume and market share targets
- achieve growth targets
- service the needs of target segments
- establish and reinforce corporate image within the market.

Costs: the need to
- Recoup investment costs in developing a title
- cover distribution, marketing and other fixed and variable costs associated with a title
- meet profit targets.

External influences:

Consumers' price attitudes, perceptions and sensitivity in the context of their needs and wants: this will vary according to the type of book and the type of customer:
- Some books, for example light romantic novels, are almost impulse buys and thus need to be reasonably inexpensive
- consumers might regard more expensive books as infrequent self-indulgent treats or as gifts
- consumers might compare the price of books with alternative treats or gift. How does the book's price compare with a CD or a box of chocolates?
- If a hardback is considered too expensive then the customer might be content to wait until the paperback comes out before buying it
- students buying textbooks, however, will be painfully aware of the price, but feel obliged to buy anyway.

Channels of distribution:
- What level of profit does a retailer expect to make on a title? A retailer selling a bestseller in huge quantities might be happy to accept a lower margin per book on that compared with a slower moving glossy 'coffee table' book.

Competition:
- How are similar books priced by competitors?
- Are there many other books on the market that the consumer might view as direct alternatives?

Legal and regulatory constraints: the impact of the NBA while it was in force.

3   Summarise the advantages and disadvantages to (a) the book buying public and (b) the booksellers arising from the ending of the NBA.

a)   Advantages to the public:
- Cheaper bestsellers
- availability of books in supermarkets as well as bookshops.

Disadvantages to the public:
- Risk of reduced choice if publishers concentrate on mass market guaranteed bestsellers
- risk of reduced choice if retailers concentrate on mass market guaranteed bestsellers
- risk of reduced choice if retailers can no longer stock books on a 'sale or return' basis to test customer response

- risk of reduced service levels in bookshops if narrower margins force cutbacks
- risk of loss of smaller bookshops
- risk of rising prices on some books to compensate for reduced prices on others
- publishers unwilling to take risks on new talent.

b) Advantages to the bookseller:
- Ability to price books as they wish independently of the publisher's influence
- ability to use books promotionally as loss leaders or traffic builders
- potential rise in profit from bestsellers through increased sales volumes from reduced price.

Disadvantages to the bookseller:
- Loss of sale or return arrangements to reduce the risk on taking on unknown titles
- reduction in the range of titles available
- increasing the price sensitivity of consumers generally
- risk of price wars among retailers
- pressure to maintain volume sales to generate profit
- increased competition from supermarkets and discount orientated outlets
- threat of driving small independents out of business or into even more niche markets.

4   Is the wine analogy appropriate? How do you see the book market in the UK developing over the next few years?

To some extent it is appropriate in that like wine, the book market:
- Can support a wide range of price segments
- can offer psychological benefits that reduce price sensitivity
- can provide products at the top end of the market that consumers buy to enhance their status
- can support a constant stream of new products to stimulate and maintain consumer interest
- can support retailers who augment the product with high service levels.

It is not appropriate, however, in that:
- The wine market is much more pretentious and status orientated at the top end than the book market
- in some market segments, price of wine is more likely to be equated with quality than in the book market
- the consumer needs much more help at the point of sale with wine choices than they do in buying books
- the underlying trend in the wine market was for growth in consumption in any case. With books, it was fairly stagnant or even falling in some segments
- the wine market in the UK has seen the entry of producers such as Chile, Bulgaria and South Africa with good quality, reasonably priced products to boost the bottom/middle of the market
- the wine market was sufficiently under-served to support the entry of mass market retailers.

The development of the book market in the UK over the next five years is likely to see:
- Concentration of discounting, with only the supermarkets and major multiples able to afford it
- increasing specialisation among small independents
- rising prices for all but the very best sellers, thus an increasing price gap between the lowest and highest priced books
- more price sensitivity in the mass market
- rationalisation of the number of titles offered and fewer new authors and titles.

5   Can there be any justification for the artificial maintenance of price levels, such as those represented by the NBA, or should all prices be driven by market forces?

In the case of the NBA, in favour of the artificial maintenance of prices:
- It ensures price stability and consistency in the retail market
- maintains profit margins for both publisher and bookseller
- allows publishers to publish 'risky' or marginal works
- allows the small independent to compete with the big multiples.

Against the artificial maintenance of prices:
- It is anti-competitive
- it milks the consumer
- it restricts the retailer's ability to develop its own marketing strategy
- it puts too much power in the hands of the publishers.

Similar points may be applicable in any kind of market - compare it with over the counter medicines, for example.

CASE STUDY 10.2 Eurostar (p 403)

Teaching Objectives

1. To ensure that students understand the nature of the factors that influence pricing decisions;
2. to show how different market segments can have different price perceptions and sensitivities;
3. to begin to examine the use of price as a strategic weapon.

1   How might the business traveller's attitude and reaction to price differ from those of the leisure traveller?

The business traveller:
- May not be paying for his/her own ticket
- may be more concerned about timing and convenience than about price if comparing Eurostar with an airline
- regards the time of travel as crucial, and will pay more to travel at convenient times
- may have an urgent need to travel at short notice and thus might pay more for a seat
- may be prepared to pay extra for services that mean less hassle, less time wasted and more comfort both before and during the journey
- might not be prepared to accept the need to stay away over a Saturday night in order to qualify for a cheaper fare.

The leisure traveller:
- Is paying for his/her own ticket and may be price sensitive
- may accept a lower level of service to gain a fare reduction
- may be more flexible, and thus be prepared to travel off-peak for a lower fare and similarly ...
- is more likely to accept the need to stay away over a Saturday night in order to qualify for a cheaper fare
- may not be obliged to travel at all; their decision to take a trip on Eurostar may be stimulated by the advertising of prices that are perceived as 'reasonable' for a leisure break
- might find the price of 'all-in' packages, to include travel and hotel, more attractive.

2   Why did Eurostar begin its services in 1994 with a premium price? Do you think that this was the right strategy?

The premium price was probably a result of Eurostar's feelings that:
- Many passengers would be business travellers and would not be price sensitive
- such passengers would value the convenience of Eurostar travel (city centre - city centre) highly
- such passengers would value the time saved through Eurostar travel (taking into account getting to the airport, check in procedures, disembarkation time, baggage handling, air traffic delays, then getting from the airport to the final destination) highly
- travelling by Eurostar, because of its novelty and because the public had spent so long looking forward to it, would have a certain cachet
- passengers would value the reliability of the service, in that it is not subject to weather disruption.

The risks of premium pricing in this case could be that:
- Travellers were used to flying and might need encouragement through low prices to break their habits and try Eurostar

- because Eurostar was new, travellers had no experience of its benefits, and this underlines the need to encourage low-risk trial of the service
- it left the airlines plenty of room to respond to the opening by undercutting their prices.

In the event, the poor publicity about technical problems and delays would probably have left travellers just what it was they were being asked to pay a premium price for!

3   What are the internal and external influences on Eurostar's ticket pricing?

Internal influences:

Organisational and marketing objectives: the need to
- Meet and defend specified sales volume and market share targets compared with the airlines
- achieve growth targets in terms of capacity utilisation and the number of trains run per day
- service the needs of target segments
- establish and reinforce corporate image within the market.

Costs: the need to
- Recoup investment costs in developing the Eurostar service
- cover operating and marketing costs, including the levy payable to Eurotunnel for each train using the tunnel
- meet profit targets.

External influences:

Consumers' price attitudes, perceptions and sensitivity in the context of their needs and wants, as discussed in question 1 above.

Channels of distribution:
- How are tickets sold, and what level of commission would a travel agent or booking facility wish to make on a ticket sale?

Competition:
- How are the airlines pricing on the same routes?
- Can any price differences be clearly justified through benefits delivered?

Legal and regulatory constraints: EU approval needed for any pricing decisions.

4   Should Eurostar continue to use price as a major weapon in competition with the airlines?

This should lead to some debate about the role and wisdom of price competition. Points that might be raised include:
- As a new product, it does need to take customer away from the airlines, but price is only one way
- if it goes too far, it could result in a price war that serves only to damage all parties concerned
- price changes are too easily copied
- price competition does not encourage customer loyalty, because customers focus on price and switch to the cheapest option
- it does not encourage the service providers to invest in non-price differentiation
- a balanced programme of short term price promotions coupled with a drive towards improving the service and communicating improved benefits to potential passengers might give Eurostar a more secure basis for longer term stability.

Supplementary question
Following an incident such as the Channel Tunnel fire and the subsequent disruption to passenger services in November 1996, what role do you think price could play in bringing customers back?

This kind of incident shakes customer confidence, as well as getting them out of the habit of travelling by Eurostar for a time. Promotional low pricing to signal the return to normal service could be helpful, but travellers are likely to need much more reassurance than that of safety and reliability. This implies a concerted advertising and PR campaign to restore confidence and the service's image.

Marketing in Action Putting You in the Picture (p 372)

Discussion question

When assessing the price of cameras, consider the relative importance of the five benefits detailed in figure 10.1 (p 371) in the two main price segments for cameras.

Budget price segment:
- *Functional:* features such as built in flash, auto-focus and automatic advance and rewind would be expected to minimise effort. The overall design should suggest simplicity. Not much attention is likely to be given to the technical features, and thus the consumer's general technical understanding may be low.
- *Quality:* customers probably accept different price points as indicators of the different performance and product quality. The corporate image of such brands as Olympus, Minolta and Nikon may all strengthen quality perceptions, despite the low prices
- *Operational:* ease of operation is a major requirement in this segment. It needs to be 'point and shoot' with acceptable results, whatever the conditions.
- *Financial:* other than the total outlay, the customer might expect the durability of the product to be reflected in the price. At one end of the market, the low priced 'disposable' camera has been introduced for maximum flexibility and convenience.
- *Personal:* psychological factors might not be that important in this segment, but perhaps the security of reliability and the joy of capturing precious family moments will affect the consumer rather than status and ownership.

High price segment:
- *Functional:* considerable attention is likely to be given to functional concerns, as the more serious photographer will appreciate the impact of the range of features and their flexibility (for example the ability to change lenses, add a flash gun or manually set the shutter speed) could have on the quality of the final photograph.
- *Quality:* a deeper understanding of different price points and perhaps a wider search including the assessment of alternative offerings might still lead to judgement of quality being linked to price. Brand loyalty might exist in this segment and trading up a manufacturer's range might also take place.
- *Operational:* some photographers might not necessarily need the full range of features offered for the type of photographs being taken, but will still enjoy the possibility of experimentation and having the full range at their disposal. Ease of operation may be less important than adaptability to different circumstances, for example speed, lighting, focus etc.
- *Financial:* the more serious photographer may regard the camera as more of an investment and be prepared to pay a higher price for better consistency of photographic output.
- *Personal:* status and self image factors could apply. The amateur photographer might be in group situations, for example at sports events or the photographs could be used for publication, for example in hobby magazines.

Marketing in Action Budget Tyres (p 377)

Discussion question

Are the tyre manufacturers right to assume that the two price segments are discrete?

In the short term the strategy appears to be valid, as price is used as an indicator of quality in the market. This is linked with, and emphasised by the importance of safety, car manufacturers' recommendations and the strong brand image of tyres such as Michelin and Continental. There is a customer view that a performance car requires a performance tyre and that low priced tyres may be suspect. There is also the advantage that the tide of cheap imports can be stemmed by adopting a competitive stance in the budget segment while still protecting the higher margin markets. The longer term danger could be in the durability and performance of the own brand tyres. If there are no perceived differences between own brand and manufacturer brand tyres, a shift could take place and the budget segment could expand. The motor industry is well covered with magazines, road tests and independent commentaries, so a greater awareness of relative performance of tyres could be assumed than in some other sectors. The battle in the wider fmcg retail sector between own brand and manufacturer brands should teach a cautionary lesson to tyre manufacturers as they seek to trade in own brands with some large European tyre retailers.

Marketing in Action Sweet Smell of Success (p 387)

Discussion question
Is the Chinese government right to restrict export licences in order to stabilise world honey prices?

China as a leading producer has a strong impact on world supply and prices, and its industry appears to be capable of meeting challenging international standards. However, because there are many small producers, production might not be very efficient and distribution could be more complex and costly. Much, therefore, depends on how the supply industry will change over the coming years. If Russia becomes organised and efficient enough to enter world trade, prices could destabilise. Will small scale Chinese producers be able to compete? China is already leaving the European 'back Door' open by undersupplying the market.

By restricting producers and keeping prices artificially high, China is not encouraging the restructuring of the industry. This could have damaging consequences in the long term as leading producers that can compete on a worldwide scale are less likely to emerge. Other nations such as Mexico, Argentina and Australia may therefore be able to pose a more serious threat as quality standards and consistency improve. A similar situation has emerged in the wine industry in Europe as home producers have lost share to nations such as New Zealand, South Africa and Chile.

Marketing in Action Pricing a Pinta (p 395)

Discussion question
What role does Milk Marque play in all this. What might happen if Milk Marque did not exist?

Milk Marque's role is to:
* Negotiate better prices for farmers for milk than they could achieve on their own
* try to create and maintain price stability for farmers
* give the farmers sufficient collective power to allow them to deal with the supermarkets
* act as a central distribution intermediary between the farmers and the supermarkets, and thus ...
* allow the farmers to concentrate on production rather than marketing.

Without Milk Marque:
* Farmers would have to negotiate their own prices with individual buyers leading to price fluctuations in the market
* farmers would have to process and market their own milk, pushing costs up
* supermarkets would have far more power than their suppliers, and would probably thus drive supply prices down
* supermarkets would have more difficulty with the logistics of getting milk from the farm to the store, thus pushing distribution costs up. This means that the supermarkets either (a) increase the price of milk to the consumer or (b) put downward pressure on suppliers' prices.

Given all these factors, without Milk Marque, supermarkets would find it a lot more difficult to use milk as a loss leader, which might be welcome news to the doorstep delivery milk trade.

SUGGESTED ASSIGNMENTS

* Questions for Discussion 10.1 could be adapted as an assignment thus: choose a manufacturer that produces a range of products serving different price segments in a consumer market. Referring to

as many of the internal and external influences on pricing as you can, how can the manufacturer 'justify' the price differentials?
- A price is a quantitative calculation that should be based on costs. It has no place in the marketing mix. Discuss.

Chapter 11
PRICING STRATEGIES

LECTURE PLAN

A lecture based on this chapter should help the student to:
1. Understand the managerial process that leads to price setting and the influences that affect its outcomes;
2. appreciate the multiple and sometimes conflicting objectives impacting on pricing decisions;
3. define a range of available pricing strategies and their application in different market and competitive situations;
4. understand the available pricing methods and tactics, and their most appropriate use; and
5. appreciate some of the special issues affecting pricing in organisational markets.

The key sections of this lecture should be:

Introduction (p 407):
Most of this lecture is based on OHP 32, figure 11.1 (p 408) Determining a Price Range - Overview:
- A very brief introduction to each stage
- how the stages flow from the broad strategic considerations to the practical, operational issues.

Pricing objectives (pp 409-413):
- What the organisation is trying to achieve through pricing, including OHP 33, figure 11.2 (p 409) Conflicting Price Objectives:
  ⇒ What each group of objectives involves (see below)
  ⇒ why they might conflict
  ⇒ their practical impact on pricing decisions.
- *Financial objectives:* profit; cash flow generation.
- *Sales and marketing objectives:* emphasis on volume or value share; price and product positioning; desire to maintain the status quo, including OHP 34, figure 11.3 (p 412) Price - Quality Matrix:
  ⇒ Need for consistency between perceived price and perceived quality offered
  ⇒ problems of too high a quality and too low a price
  ⇒ problems of too low a quality and too high a price.
- *Survival:* short term revenue generation.

Pricing policies and strategies (pp 414-423):
- Definition of policies and strategies
- skimming
- penetration
- pricing within the product mix
- managing price cuts and increases
- responding to competitors' price moves.

Setting the price range (pp 423-432):

- *Cost - volume - profit relationship:* breakeven and marginal analysis. This may be omitted if students have already covered it in finance modules.
- *Cost-based pricing methods:* how they are calculated; the advantages and disadvantages.
- *Demand-based pricing:* why it can be used to manipulate demand; psychological pricing; problems of implementation.
- *Competition-based pricing:* why it is done; how it is done; advantages and disadvantages.

Pricing tactics and adjustments (pp 432-434):

- Why adjustments are made
- types of discount and other adjustment.

Issues in pricing in organisational markets (pp 434-440):

- Negotiation, including OHP 35, figure 11.11 (p 436) Negotiation Variables:
  ⇒ Why negotiation takes place
  ⇒ product and service aspects that might be subject to negotiation
  ⇒ importance of win - win price negotiation
  ⇒ importance of conceding on areas that cost the supplier little, but are valuable to the buyer.
- Tendering and bidding
- transfer pricing.

QUESTIONS FOR REVIEW

11.1   Define the various stages involved in setting prices. (pp 407-408)

- *Pricing objectives:* what is the organisation trying to achieve through its pricing strategies and tactics?
- *Demand assessment:* what is the product's market potential and how price sensitive is the market?
- *Pricing policies and strategies:* the guiding philosophical framework within which pricing decisions are made.
- *Setting the price range:* ensuring that prices set generate satisfactory profit and fit appropriately into the competitive context.
- *Pricing tactics and adjustments:* the application of pricing in reality, and its use as a short term competitive weapon.

11.2   List the financial objectives that might be achieved through pricing decisions and outline the ways in which pricing might help to achieve them. (pp 409-411)

Profit:

- Return on investment: a high launch price might help to generate a quicker payback period on the development costs of a product, whereas a lower price might take longer unless it builds up much higher sales volumes.
- Profit maximisation: in the short term this might tempt the organisation to price the product as high as possible to maximise the margin on it. A longer term view, however, might a lower price will build customer loyalty and repeat sales, thus leading to higher cumulative sales volumes that will eventually generate higher profit levels.

Cash flow: lowering prices might help to stimulate sales of slow moving products to generate cash in the short term for strategic or survival purposes.

11.3   How can pricing help to achieve marketing and sales objectives? (pp 411-413)

- By expanding market share through lower pricing
- by reinforcing the product's market position through appropriate and consistent pricing
- by stimulating short term volume sales through price reductions

- by stimulating long term volume sales through aggressively low prices
- by creating stability through the organisation's refusal to get drawn into price wars
- by differentiating the product through positioning it in a different price bracket from the competition.

11.4   In what circumstances might a high price be justified for a new product launch? (pp 415-416)

- Where customers are not price sensitive
- where a quality image is required
- where the organisation is not certain what the price ought to be. Lowering a price later is easier than raising it.
- Where the market has absolutely no experience of this kind of product and does not really know what it is worth.

11.5   What factors might prompt an organisation to initiate either a price cut or a price rise? (pp 418-423)

A price cut could be initiated in order to:
- Clear excess stock
- reinforce 'value for money' image
- stimulate sales to utilise excess production capacity
- put pressure on competitors
- defend a segment from competitor entry.

A price rise could be initiated in order to:
- Cover rising costs
- reduce or maintain demand at manageable levels.

11.6   What are the possible responses for an organisation facing a competitor's price cut? (pp 420-421)

- Ignore the price cut
- undercut the competitor's new price
- deflect the impact of the cut through non-price marketing tactics.

11.7   What contribution can (a) marginal analysis and (b) breakeven analysis make to the pricing decision? (pp 423-425)

Marginal analysis demonstrates the relationship between additional unit sales and the extra costs they incur, and shows at what point the revenue gained from an extra sale does not cover the cost of producing it. It is most useful in predictable, stable markets where cost schedules and demand sensitivity are known. Breakeven analysis shows the relationship between total costs and total revenue and at what sales volume profit begins to be generated. It is useful in a price-competitive market so that the organisation knows just how low it can afford to set prices without making a loss.

11.8   What are the advantages and disadvantages of cost based pricing methods? (pp 426-428)

Advantages:
- Simple to calculate
- guarantees profit margin
- logical to justify.

Disadvantages:
- Internally focused, ignoring competition and ...
- ... ignoring what the customer is prepared to pay
- could lead to under- or over-pricing and thus ...

- might not lead to optimum sales volumes or cumulative profit over time.

11.9   Why are discounts an important feature of organisational product pricing for both the seller and the buyer? (pp 433-434)

- They give both buyer and seller scope for negotiation, with both parties gaining some benefit from the discounts given
- they allow a seller to reward a buyer for bulk buying or long term loyalty
- they encourage buyers to buy more cheaply at 'off-season' times, evening out the seller's cash flow
- they allow a seller to reward a buyer for services rendered to the product at the point of resale
- they can be used to encourage prompt payment from the buyer.

11.10   Define transfer pricing and summarise the various available methods of calculating a transfer price. (pp 439-440)

Transfer prices are charges for goods and service traded across internal boundaries within organisations. Transfer prices can be:

- Negotiated between the business units concerned
- set to be the same as the external market price for the good or service would be
- equal to the actual cost of producing and delivering the good or service.

QUESTIONS FOR DISCUSSION

11.1   Define penetration pricing and find an example of an organisation that has used it for one of its products.

A penetration pricing strategy is used to gain as much sales volume as possible as quickly as possible through undercutting competitors' prices. The student should be able to justify the choice of product in terms of:

- Comparison with competitors' prices
- any evidence of market share figures
- evidence of market positioning.

11.2   How can organisations justify charging different prices for different products within their product ranges?

Students might raise issues such as:

- Products offer different sets of benefits
- products offer different quality levels
- products are targeting segments with different needs and price sensitivities
- products targeting different segments face different competitive price scenarios
- organisations want to offer a complete range of products so that customers can trade up to 'better' more expensive products as their needs and level of affluence evolve.

11.3   Define three methods of psychological pricing, then find and discuss examples of each one in practice.

- *Prestige pricing:* a high price to make the buyer feel special and elite. Students might offer products like perfumes, jewellery, designer clothing as examples.
- *Odd-even pricing:* ending the price with .99 or .09 to make the customer think it is cheaper than it really is and that the retailer is a 'good value' operator. Examples are likely to be found in discount food, clothing or variety stores.
- *Price lining:* setting a specific price point which is applied to all products, thus a clothing retailer might sell ladies' blouses at £20. Because all products are priced alike, the consumer makes a

choice based on other criteria. A retailer might operate a number of such price points to allow for higher or lower quality merchandise.

- *Bundle pricing:* assembling a group of products or services to be sold as a complete package at one price. Package holidays, for example, include flights, hotels and specified meals in the price.
- *Promotional pricing:* short term offers, for example £1 off for this week only, to stimulate consumer interest and encourage prompt action. Used extensively by fmcg manufacturers and retailers.
- *Time specific markdowns:* end of season sales, for example, that again stimulate the consumer into buying. Used extensively by retailers of shopping or speciality goods.
- *Price differentiation:* charging different prices to different segments, justified perhaps through variations in service or distribution methods.

11.4   To what extent and why do you think that a marketing manager's pricing decision should be influenced by the competition's pricing?

Issues that might be raised include:

- The number of competitors
- the perceived similarity between the products in terms of non-price based features, benefits and additional services
- the desired market positioning
- the degree of customisation in the market
- the price sensitivity of the target segment
- the extent to which competitors are trying to focus the consumer's attention on price
- the desire to be a cost leader or follower.

11.5   Develop a checklist of five important points that you would like a sales representative to bear in mind when trying to achieve a favourable outcome from price negotiation with a potential customer.

There are many potential points that might be raised in this discussion, including:

- The supplier's cost structure and margins
- the cost of any concessions made in return for a more favourable price
- the value of those concessions to the customer
- the supplier's ability to deliver on those concessions
- the importance of the customer concerned
- the urgency of the need to make a sale
- the implications for future negotiations with this customer
- the ease with which the customer could switch suppliers
- the effect on the customer's attitude towards the supplier and thus on the buyer-seller relationship.

Students should be encouraged to debate their relative importance in different kinds of buying situation and the problems of using them as negotiation variables.

CASE STUDY 11.1 Summer of CD Price Discontent (p 443)

Teaching Objectives

1. To demonstrate how a pricing strategy is implemented in practice;
2. to examine the effects and implications of implementing a particular pricing strategy;
3. to discuss the effects of pricing decisions on customer attitudes and behaviour.

1   What pricing strategy are the manufacturers adopting on CDs and what conditions allow them to maintain this strategy?

It could be argued that the situation in the UK represents a skimming strategy, or at least a very up-market strategy that just stops short of all-out skimming. It exists and can be maintained because:

- The supply side of the market is dominated by a few large producers, each of which has exclusive rights to big name artists. None of these producers, therefore, would see price competition as necessary or desirable.
- The retail side is dominated by a few big names, none of which would probably want to risk being de-listed by any of the big producers, for fear of damaging their ability to compete on the High Street. Thus it is possible that the retailers are not pushing too aggressively on trade prices.
- There is no realistic substitute for CDs, partly in terms of sound quality, and partly because if the consumer has bought a CD player, then the only thing it is good for is playing CDs!
- The consumer is prepared to pay these prices, despite complaining about it, and both the manufacturer and the retailer can make reasonable margins from sustaining these prices.

2   What do you think of the BPI's defence of CD prices?

The main points of the defence are that:
- In real terms, prices of CDs have actually fallen
- producers need reward for the risks they take
- production costs have risen
- artists' advances and royalties have risen
- comparison with US prices is invalid
- the limited size of the UK market prevents economies of scale
- the breadth of range expected by the UK public prevents economies of scale.

Students should be encouraged to debate the merits of these points critically. The particularly questionable elements are:
- The basis for the calculation of production costs
- the basis for the calculation of artists' earnings
- the ways in which economies of scale could be achieved
- the contradiction between the first point mentioned and the rest!

Supplementary question
What role is played by the retailers in CD price setting?

Again, this is open to debate. Points that could be raised include the fact that the retailer has to negotiate a trade price from the CD companies, and then set a resale price that:
- Covers the retailer's administration and internal distribution costs
- considers the price sensitivity of the customer
- considers the level of the 'must have' desirability of the CD to the target customer
- considers the likely length of the CD's life cycle
- considers whether a particular CD should be priced as a promotional incentive
- takes into account how other retailers are pricing the same CD
- generates an acceptable profit margin.

Thus although retailers do have some pricing discretion, they do have their own pricing objectives and strategies to consider, and they are trapped between the trade price that they can negotiate from the manufacturer, and the ultimate ceiling of what the market will bear.

3   Evaluate the options open to the manufacturers in terms of (a) short-term pricing tactics and (b) longer-term pricing strategies.

a)   In the short-term, they can respond to criticism by:
- Lowering the trade price to give the retailers more pricing discretion
- introduce or improve discounts (for example bulk discounts) given to retailers, again to increase the retailer's pricing discretion
- giving the retailers more support in terms of totally or jointly (with the retailer) funding promotional offers at the point of sale to bring down the price to the consumer

- standing their ground, maintaining prices at current levels and reiterating the arguments in favour of those prices.
b) In the longer-term, they can try to move towards a pricing strategy that is less orientated towards skimming and more of a mass market approach closer to penetration pricing by:
- Finding ways of reducing production costs
- ensuring that titles offered have international appeal to try to capitalise on economies of scale
- working more closely with retailers to reduce distribution and selling costs
- streamlining the range offered through concentrating on big name best sellers and offering fewer expensive niche titles
- stopping the cross-subsidisation of niche titles that are expensive to produce from the mass market popular titles
- increase sponsorship on expensive titles
- maintaining a skimming strategy in some segments of the market that will bear it, but putting more emphasis on budget titles in others to dampen criticism.

Given what was said in answer to question 1 above, there may be no particular reason why the producers should want to bring prices down unless something happens that radically changes the marketing environment, for example the introduction and mass acceptance of a new music format that directly competes with CD.

Supplementary question
What are the risks of dropping or cutting down on the niche titles that are expensive to produce?

- It alienates an upmarket segment that might be prepared to pay even higher premium prices for obscure repertoire
- it could damage the recording company's credibility or reputation for comprehensiveness of market coverage for all tastes.

4   To what extent do you agree with the sentiment expressed by *The Times* columnist in the last paragraph?

This should provoke some debate about the willingness and ability of the consumer to accept or reject prices offered in the market. The questions that could be raised by the quote and debated are:
- Are CDs really a luxury item?
- How would the individual consumer benefit or suffer from refusing to buy a particular CD, financially, socially, or psychologically?
- Can the actions of one consumer affect the thinking of the producers and retailers?
- How can mass consumer feeling and action be provoked?
- To what extent are consumers locked into buying CDs because of what they have invested in CD-based hi-fi systems?

CASE STUDY 11.2 Lucerne Hotel and Conference Centre (p 444)

Case Note: this case can be used either as a normal case study for class discussion or, when accompanied by detailed briefing notes, as a role play exercise that encourages students to experience a 'real' negotiation in which price can be traded against a number of variables.

Teaching Objectives

1. To establish the role of price in negotiation;
2. to begin to appreciate the range of non-price variables that can be used in negotiation;
3. to understand the process of negotiation.

1   How should Mr Fischer respond to the client? Should he simply quote them a price for the conference or should he be prepared to negotiate a price for the conference?

It is advisable for Mr Fischer to be prepared to negotiate a price as there could be a better deal for both parties if they are prepared to give and take. There are advantages in arranging a meeting with the potential client, not just to sell the facilities, but also to discuss a whole range of issues that need to be resolved. If there is no meeting there is a strong chance that some things will be overlooked that would result in either unforeseen costs or client dissatisfaction. Hurrying to reaching a deal is likely to result in added complications later.

The range of issues that have to be resolved through negotiation are presented in Q2 and Q3.

2   If he decided to negotiate, what factors would Mr Fischer have to consider in preparing for the meeting?

Mr Fischer needs some fundamental information before a detailed meeting:
- Whether there is availability on the required dates
- the likelihood of renting the facilities to another customer
- what his policy is to be on changes or cancellation after the contract has been agreed
- what terms of payment he wants (when, how much, in what currency etc)
- the cost profile of all the additional elements in the package to be offered. Refer to figure 11.11 (p 436) for a general range of variables that might have to be considered. Mr Fischer will have to know his maximum, minimum and desired position on each of the variables in terms of cost and services offered. In this case, the variables could be:
  ⇒ Room specification for conference and meeting rooms, bedrooms, and syndicate rooms
  ⇒ meal plans, including required menus
  ⇒ sports and leisure provision required
  ⇒ exact numbers of guests on different days
  ⇒ likelihood of future business from this client
  ⇒ any transportation requirements, for example from and to the airport
  ⇒ tourist services required
  ⇒ any special services required, for example interpreters, audio-visual facilities etc
  ⇒ any special decorations or hoardings required
  ⇒ parking arrangements.

All of these variables have a cost dimension for Mr Fischer and a value dimension to the client and thus can be used as a means of building and negotiating a mutually agreeable price. They also provide a means of trading, for example, Mr Fischer might provide a free airport shuttle in return for payment in full at the start of the conference. Mr Fischer will also have to consider how to conduct the negotiation, for example when to bring up each of the points and in what order. He also needs to understand and emphasise the total package rather than discussing each item in turn as a discrete element. It is always best to seek a win-win deal (Mr Fischer gets profitable business and the client gets the ideal conference) as a basis for creating long term satisfied customers. However, Mr Fischer also needs to be able to recognise the point at which the deal looks like becoming lose-win (the potential client demanding too much and giving nothing in return) and it is best for him to walk away.

3   What information would each party ideally like to have about the other before negotiations begin?

Both parties would ideally like to know the other party's strength of desire and their tolerance limits in any negotiation, both in general and on each of the main variables. Some of this information can be acquired from prior research, some from the first meeting between Mr Fischer and the client, and some may have to be inferred or assumed. That is part of the fun of a negotiation. Mr Fischer might like to know:
- What alternatives do Swiss Foods have? The deadlines are relatively short.
- How many such conferences do they hold each year?
- What items do they really value? Areas that they value highly but are not costly for Mr Fischer to deliver are attractive negotiating points. They can be traded for items of value to Mr Fischer.
- What standards does the client expect?

- Which locations have they used previously for similar events?
- What is their bottom line?

The Swiss Food Company might like to know:

- How desperate is Mr Fischer for the business?
- In what areas is Mr Fischer likely to be more willing to concede?
- What are the cost profiles on each of the variables that are likely to come up?
- What can Mr Fischer offer which is easy for him to concede but valuable to us?
- On what items is he likely to find it difficult to be flexible if we must have some movement?
- What is his bottom line?

For use as a class exercise: students could be split into two groups representing the two parties to the negotiation. The maximum team size should be three to enable all participants to play a full role. Students may elect to play roles as part of the team, for example Managing Director or Events Manager etc. A two hour period would be necessary to allow adequate preparation and debriefing. Students will have to consider in detail their responses to the case questions as part of the planning process. Additional information will have to be provided on a confidential basis to each side before the negotiation begins to enable more meaningful discussion. Most of the main variables are discussed above. It is important that each party has the basic information on their own situation provided by the tutor. This should include:

- Recent prices paid in a package per head basis (Swiss Food Company - SFC)
- typical prices charged for a similar package (Lucerne Hotel and Conference Centre - LHCC)
- typical costs for some of the ancillary services (LHCC)
- what alternatives, if any are available (SFC)
- other customers (LHCC).

The situation can be varied according to the expertise of the groups. In some situations a wider variation between the seller's expected price and the buyer's expected price can create tougher negotiating conditions as can one or other party being more desperate for the order. To create a more balanced situation each party should need the other equally to reach a win-win deal i.e. no other serious customers or suppliers in the frame. In the feedback session, students should reflect on the pattern of concession making, and precisely what was conceded and gained. A cost, however notional, should be attached to every item. Each party can be asked how satisfied they were with the outcome. If no deal has been reached after the negotiation period then it must be concluded that a lose-lose situation has been created.

Marketing in Action Premium Sausages (p 414)

Discussion question
What are the main marketing ingredients enabling Lazenby's to occupy the premium niche?

- Price positioning ahead of mass market sausages to indicate product differentiation on quality
- play on old-fashioned butchers' values to denote quality and imply a safe, traditional product
- the use of unusual flavour variants to support differentiation further
- the use of top quality raw materials
- communication of quality in all that Lazenby's does, i.e. packaging, advertising etc.
- deliberately aiming not to generate volume sales.

Marketing in Action Apple Turnover (p 418)

Discussion question
How sustainable is the premium price position sought by Apple Computers?

The industry has grown significantly on a world wide scale over the past ten years. This has enabled both standards to develop side by side with profit opportunities for both. With growth, many software producers have emerged supplying increasingly specialised applications. The greater market penetration of the IBM PC format has encouraged wider software choices and lower total system costs.

This has eroded the competitive advantage of the Apple format. If Apple is to remain in the low priced segment, especially for entry level, it may increasingly be forced to accept lower prices and margins to compete. The aim may be to encourage trading up if customer loyalty can be encouraged. The specialist applications sector such as publishing may still enable a price premium to be gained. This segment could provide sufficient margins to compensate for losses in the lower price end of the market. Further use of geographical pricing may also be needed to maximise price levels where aggressive pricing is less prevalent. If the market continues to grow and becomes more specialised, it may still be possible for a premium price position to be held, but in world wide niche applications.

Marketing in Action Channel Tunnel and Freight Costs (p 429)

Discussion question
What demand based factors should Eurotunnel consider when setting freight prices?

- Sensitivity to different speeds of movement from collection to delivery
- the importance of reliability and consistency
- the size (volume/bulk) of the product movement, i.e. bulk loads
- the ease with which customers can pass on higher freight costs through enhanced customer service
- the preparedness of customers to trade off higher freight costs against lower delivery times
- the range of other choices available.

Marketing in Action Deutsche Telekom (p 435)

Discussion question
Do you think that the German telecommunications minister's decision to allow the new discount structure was contrary to the general deregulation initiative?

There is no one answer to this question. In favour of the decision:
- An effort by government to keep out of normal competitive marketing
- cross-subsidisation across product ranges and market segments is a normal part of marketing management for many larger organisations
- it could be regarded as an individual company decision to price, whatever the state of profitability
- lower prices may well generate increased volume
- the total system will benefit from the 'linked' investment in digitalisation.

Against the decision:
- The market is still effectively controlled by DT (market share) and new competitors could suffer either losses in their hard-won market share or in profitability if they are forced to meet the cuts
- DT should always win a price battle given their resources and dominance ,so the long term aim of creating at least an oligopolistic market may be delayed
- the discounts will reinforce customer loyalty to DT.

SUGGESTED ASSIGNMENTS

- Questions for Discussion 11.4
- What is the difference between price skimming and penetration pricing? In what kinds of circumstances might each be appropriate and what are the risks and benefits of using them? Cite examples.

Chapter 12
MARKETING CHANNELS

LECTURE PLAN

A lecture based on this chapter should help the student to:
1. Define what a channel of distribution is;
2. understand the role of the channel and its important contribution to efficient and effective marketing effort;
3. differentiate between types of intermediary and their roles;
4. appreciate the factors influencing channel design, structure and strategy; and
5. understand the potential for co-operation and conflict within channels, and the effects of both positive and negative uses of power.

The key sections of this lecture should be:

Definition of marketing channels (pp 450-456):
- What a channel of distribution is
- overview of types of intermediary
- consumer channels, including OHP 36, figure 12.1 (p 452) Channel Structures for Consumer Goods:
  ⇒ Discuss different lengths of channel
  ⇒ overview of role of each intermediary
  ⇒ give examples of each in practice.
- Organisational channels, including OHP 37, figure 12.3 (p 455) Channel Structures for Organisational Markets:
  ⇒ Discuss different lengths of channel
  ⇒ overview of role of each intermediary
  ⇒ give examples of each in practice
  ⇒ contrast with consumer channels.

The role of intermediaries (pp 457-461):
- Rationale for using intermediaries, including OHP 38, figure 12.4 (p 457) The Role of Intermediaries:
  ⇒ Reducing complexity
  ⇒ reducing costs
  ⇒ allowing specialisation within the channel.
- Intermediaries' tasks and value added, including OHP 39, figure 12.5 (p 458) Value Added Services Provided by Intermediaries:
  ⇒ discuss the scope of each group of factors
  ⇒ emphasise how they reduce complexity
  ⇒ emphasise how they can reduce costs
  ⇒ emphasise how they can make the distribution channel as a whole offer better service and improve efficiency.

Channel strategy (pp 461-469):
- Market coverage strategies, including OHP 40, table 12.1 (p 462) Alternative Distribution Intensities: General Characteristics:
  ⇒ Define each type of strategy
  ⇒ the kinds of products each is appropriate for
  ⇒ the kinds of customers each is appropriate for

$\Rightarrow$ the competitive advantage to be gained from each.
- Influences on channel strategy: internal organisational factors; market size and spread; buying behaviour; product characteristics; the marketing environment.
- Selecting channel members.

Competition and co-operation within channels (pp 470-474):
- *Competition:* horizontal; intertype; vertical; channel system competition.
- *Co-operation:* the concept of the VMS; corporate VMSs; contractual VMSs; administered VMSs; the advantages and disadvantages of each.

Behavioural aspects of channels (pp 474-482):
- Importance of co-operation and partnership
- sources of conflict
- power and its abuse.

This section could be omitted, and students encouraged to read the material for themselves.

QUESTIONS FOR REVIEW

12.1   What are the different types of intermediary that might be found in a distribution channel? (pp 451-452)

- Wholesalers
- retailers
- distributors and dealers
- franchisees
- agents and brokers.

12.2   What is the short channel of distribution in consumer markets and what benefits does it offer the manufacturer? (p 453)

The short channel of distribution consists of direct supply from producer to consumer with no intermediaries involved. Its benefits include:
- Closer relationship between producer and consumer
- producer retains control over the selling and distribution of the product to the end buyer
- can cut the cost and time involved in distribution in some cases.

12.3   Why might agents be used in organisational channels of distribution? (pp 456-457)

- Agents are used in organisational markets to allow the selling organisation to:
- Avoid the costs and commitment of setting up a direct selling effort
- take advantage of the agent's knowledge and expertise in a particular geographic market
- take advantage of the agent's knowledge and expertise of a particular product market
- take advantage of the agent's established business contacts
- gain synergy from the other complementary products that the agent might deal in
- enter a market quickly
- gain the flexibility to get out of a failing market with as few losses as possible and as quickly as possible.

12.4   In what ways can intermediaries make a channel of distribution more cost efficient? (pp 457-461)

- Streamlines administration
- streamlines logistics
- breaks bulk

- brings related and complementary products into one location
- gains economies of scale in storage and related costs through centralisation.

12.5   What specific functions can intermediaries undertake that are of benefit to the manufacturer? (pp 457-461)

- Making bulk orders that are delivered to a single location
- providing wide geographic coverage for the manufacturer's product
- reaching a large number of small retailers
- selling and marketing
- selling this manufacturer's products alongside related and complementary items
- product storage and further distribution
- bulk breaking
- sorting products and grading them
- providing feedback from the market.

12.6   What are the five factors influencing channel strategy? (pp 464-468)

1. Organisational objectives, capabilities and resources
2. market size, dispersion and remoteness
3. buying complexity and buying behaviour
4. product characteristics
5. the changing marketing environment.

12.7   In what ways might product characteristics influence channel strategy? Give examples. (pp 466-467)

- High value or technically complex products tend to be distributed direct or through a short channel e.g. computers, cars, fighter aircraft, designer jewellery
- perishable products need short, fast specialised distribution e.g. dairy products, fresh fruit and vegetables, meat products, and even daily newspapers
- well packaged, robust, routinely purchased long shelf-life products tend to be intensively distributed through a variety of channels.

12.8   Define the different types of channel conflict. (pp 476-478)

- *Incompatible goals:* different channel members are trying to achieve different things.
- *Role conflict:* there is disagreement as to who should be taking responsibility for what tasks.
- *Decision domain conflict:* disagreement as to who should be taking which decisions.
- *Perceptions of reality:* channels members interpret what is going on in incompatible ways.
- *Expectations:* hannel members have different view about what should be done in the future.

12.9   What are the relative advantages and disadvantages of an administered VMS compared with the other two types? (pp 472-474)

The advantages of an administered VMS include:
- Gaining the benefits of close co-operation often without the formal commitment of contracts or loss of autonomy
- the formation of close mutually beneficial links
- the weaker members benefit from the expertise and knowledge of the dominant member.

The disadvantages of an administered VMS include:
- Undue pressure and dominance from the stronger member
- if there are no contractual ties, it might become difficult to hold the VMS together
- if there are no contractual ties clearly allocating responsibilities, conflict might be more likely.

12.10 Define the different sources of power and explain how each might influence the atmosphere within which a channel conducts its business. (pp 478-480)

Where A and B are the two parties involved in the relationship:

- *Reward power:* B thinks that A can provide rewards for B, for example in terms of higher margins or increased volume sales. This could lead to B becoming dependent on A and conceding to A in order to protect the flow of rewards, although B's attitude to A is likely to be a positive one.
- *Coercive power:* B thinks that A can punish B, for example in terms of reducing order size or delisting a product. Again, this could lead to B doing what A says, for fear of punishment, and thus B's attitude to A is likely to be negative, and A's attitude to B is likely to be demanding and perhaps aggressive.
- *Legitimate power:* B thinks that A has the right to tell B what to do, perhaps because of a contractual arrangement between them. As long as both parties work within the agreement and deliver their part of the bargain, the atmosphere between them should be positive.
- *Referent power:* B respects A and wishes to be closely associated with A perhaps to enhance B's standing. It might also arise where A and B are inextricably linked and must succeed or fail together. The atmosphere is thus likely to be close, intimate and co-operative.
- *Expert power:* B thinks that A has greater expertise or knowledge and thus B accepts A's right to dictate terms. Since B thinks that B can benefit from this expertise in positive ways, it is similar to reward power.

QUESTIONS FOR DISCUSSION

12.1 To what extent and why do you think that the creation of a VMS can improve the performance of a channel and its members?

The broad points that will arise in discussion include:

- More commitment between members
- better communication between members
- members learn from each other
- members likely to be working towards agreed goals to their mutual benefit
- less duplication of tasks and functions in a VMS
- the VMS as a whole can be more effective and efficient than its constituent parts alone i.e. exploit synergies
- the VMS as a whole can exert more power (for example, voluntary chains) than its constituent parts alone.

Students might take these points further, discussing how they might apply to a greater or lesser extent in the different types of VMS.

12.2 What kind of market coverage strategy might be appropriate for (a) a bar of chocolate, (b) a toothbrush, (c) a home computer, (d) a marketing textbook, and why?

This discussion question ensures that students understand the different kinds of distribution strategy and how they might be applied in reality. Basing their answers on the kinds of points raised in table 12.1 (p 462) students should be able to demonstrate how and why these four specific products have different and contrasting distribution needs.

12.3 Using Table 12.2 as a starting point, develop lists of criteria that a manufacturer might use in defining (a) 'good' retailers and (b) 'good' wholesalers to recruit for consumer market channels.

Many issues could be raised, including:

a) Good retailers:

- Provide wide geographic coverage (e.g. supermarkets), or ...
- ... help to intensify coverage (e.g. smaller chains or independent outlets)
- can access the target segment
- can store, handle and display the product appropriately
- can provide necessary customer service pre- and post-sale
- is willing to commit to the product on a long term basis
- will maintain price discipline (see pp 377-378).

b) Good wholesalers:
- Can help to distribute the product more widely and to a greater range of retailers than the manufacturer could manage alone
- can get the product to retailers faster and more cheaply than the manufacturer could
- can store, handle and display the product appropriately
- can provide necessary customer service pre- and post-sale
- is willing to commit to the product on a long term basis
- will maintain price discipline (see pp 377-378).

The debate could be made more specific by looking at different sorts of product (perishables *vs.* durables; fmcg products *vs.* shopping products; foodstuffs *vs.* toiletries, for example) or different kinds of suppliers and/or retailers in terms of size or specialism, for example.

12.4   List the potential areas of co-operation and conflict between (a) a large brand manufacturer and a large supermarket chain and (b) a small manufacturer and a wholesaler.

a) Between the large brand manufacturer and the large supermarket chain:
Potential areas of co-operation include:
- Automated re-ordering
- joint promotional packs
- in-store displays and product demonstrations
- joint advertising
- joint promotional activities, for example contests
- own-label products.

Potential areas of conflict:
- Amount of shelf space compared with competing products
- competition between the manufacturer brand and the own-label equivalent
- price and terms of supply
- poor in-store display and sales support
- reliability of supply continuity from manufacturer to retailer.

b) Between the small manufacturer and the wholesaler:
Potential areas of co-operation
- Joint advertising and selling
- own-label products for the wholesaler
- local market research
- joint promotions
- logistics systems.

Potential areas of conflict:
- Price and terms of supply
- quality and quantity consistency and continuity from manufacturer to wholesaler
- delivery schedules
- wholesaler's selling effort.

12.5   Discuss how a power - dependency relationship might work between (a) a large brand manufacturer and a large supermarket chain, (b) a small manufacturer and a large supermarket chain, (c) a multinational manufacturer of hi-fi equipment and a UK-based

high street electrical retailer, and (d) a small manufacturer of high technology, specialised components and an export agent.

The four scenarios presented are different, but can be analysed using a common set of issues. The challenge to the students is to work out what these issues are, and then how they might work within each relationship to create power or dependency. The issues that should be considered include:
- The relative size of the parties
- the complexity of the product concerned
- the availability of alternative suppliers (for the buyer) or customers (for the seller)
- the switching costs involved in finding alternatives
- the degree of customisation involved in either the product or services associated with it
- the depth of knowledge and expertise by either party
- the extent to which the buyer controls access to the next level of the distribution channel (for example a retailer's market share amongst consumers, or the percentage of small retailers reached by one wholesale chain).

CASE STUDY 12.1 Monaghan Mushrooms (p 484)

Teaching Objectives

1. To ensure that students understand the different kinds of market coverage strategy and their applicability;
2. to examine the benefits gained from membership of a VMS;
3. to think in a practical way about the ways in which suppliers and retailers try to develop positions of power over each other.

1   Outline the kind of channel structure appropriate for supplying mushrooms from the producer to (a) an individual consumer and (b) your university or college catering department. What kind of market coverage strategies do you think these channels represent?

a) To the individual consumer there are two alternatives:
- Through smaller retail outlets e.g. High Street greengrocery stores: producer - wholesaler - retailer - consumer.
- Through large supermarket multiples: producer - retailer - consumer.

Between them, these two alternatives represent fairly intensive distribution in that as many outlets as possible that are likely to want to sell fresh produce/mushrooms will be covered. The product will also be easily and conveniently available to consumers with the minimum of search effort on their part, either as planned or as impulse purchases.

Supplementary question
Why involve a wholesaler at all?

- There are too many small retailers to deal with individually
- it streamlines the producer's distribution to central points
- cash and carries might be more cost and time effective for the producer and the smaller retailer
- wholesalers can buy in bulk and pass on some of the savings to small retailers
- wholesalers can bring related merchandise together under one roof - not just mushrooms!

b) To the catering department:
Producer - distributor - customer, where the distributor is likely to be a specialised catering supplies/fresh produce wholesaler who delivers, or a general cash and carry. This is a kind of selective distribution, in that for this kind of customer, the purchase is planned and they will be looking for

specialist outlets to serve their needs. In any area, there will be a small number of such outlets, serving a relatively limited number of (probably) known customers.

2   What do you think are the particular problems of producing and distributing a product like mushrooms?

The problems are:
- Guaranteeing the right quantity at the right time
- guaranteeing consistent quality and specification
- the distance from growing areas to markets
- the short shelf life means that they need efficient and quick harvesting, packing and distribution
- the need too for temperature controlled distribution
- the large range of potential outlets for the product
- packaging for protection, yet retaining optimum condition.

3   What kind of VMS is represented in this case, and what benefits do you think it gives (a) Monaghan Mushrooms and (b) the individual growers?

In terms of the relationships between Monaghan and the growers, it's closest to a contractual VMS, 'a kind of franchise'. The relationship between Monaghan and the UK multiple retailers could be an administered VMS, if the supermarkets are using their buying power to exercise undue influence over the supplier, but it is difficult to tell from the information given in the case. Concentrating on the contractual VMS involving Monaghan and the growers: Monaghan could gain:
- Reliable production quantities because they control the growers
- reliable and consistent quality from different growers
- more stable, and agreed prices between the growers and Monaghan
- more cost effective production
- improved product shelf life
- freedom from worry about the actual growing and can concentrate on processing and distribution
- improved grower loyalty as they are locked into the system
- close co-operation with long term suppliers to improve the growing system and the level of integration between Monaghan and the growers
- control over the types of mushroom produced to balance with retailer demand and longer term product development plans.

The benefits to growers are that they could gain:
- A guaranteed outlet for their produce
- freedom from worrying about selling and marketing
- freedom from worrying about transportation as Monaghan collects the mushrooms from the grower's coldstore
- the benefit of a tried and tested growing system
- help with quality and grading systems.

4   Where do you think the balance of power lies in the relationship between Monaghan Mushrooms and the UK supermarket chains? What could either party do to increase their power?

In favour of Monaghan, Monaghan can:
- Deliver a quality product to customer specifications
- grade and pack to customer specification
- deliver efficiently and reliably into JIT systems
- apparently dominate the Irish producers
- produce a longer shelf-life mushroom because of the unique system.

In favour of the supermarkets, the supermarkets can:
- Play off the Irish against the Dutch

- exert power because each supermarket multiple represents significant business to Monaghan. A threat to switch suppliers would be a serious blow to Monaghan, thus ...
- ... supermarkets can pressurise prices downwards
- exert power because it is not going to be easy for Monaghan to find alternative customers to fit easily into its existing distribution structure
- exert power because Monaghan has invested a lot in developing a distribution system tailored to the supermarkets' needs.

Looking at this, it would seem that Monaghan needs the supermarkets more than the supermarkets need Monaghan, although switching suppliers might still involve some uncertainty and the potential loss of some significant benefits. The supermarkets would not do it lightly.

Monaghan could increase its power by:
- Working hard to reduce its costs (production, processing or logistics) in order to give them more price flexibility with the supermarkets
- ensuring that its quality of product is clearly better and more consistent than any other supplier's
- ensuring that its quality of customer service is second to none
- working very closely with the supermarkets to develop tailored products or offerings that could not easily be sourced elsewhere, for example own-label ranges of premium canned or bottled mushrooms.

The key thing is to prevent the supermarkets from thinking that mushrooms are fairly generic products that can be sourced from anywhere purely on price.

Supermarkets could increase power by:
- Multiple sourcing and ...
- ... ensuring that each supplier is aware of the others
- ensuring that they take such a large percentage of Monaghan's output that Monaghan dare not lose their custom
- encouraging Monaghan to invest in systems/logistics tailored to the supermarkets' needs so that Monaghan is locked in.

CASE STUDY 12.2 French Hypermarkets and Their Smaller Suppliers (p 485)

Teaching Objectives

1. To examine the risk of power abuse that might occur when a large customer is dealing with a small supplier;
2. to look at ways in which the small supplier can prevent such abuse;
3. to look more closely at the benefits gained by small suppliers from own-label products.

1   What kind of power do the hypermarkets tend to exert over their small suppliers?

The situation could be viewed in a number of ways. It might be seen as:
- Reward power, because the retailer has the ability to give the supplier high volume orders and a route into mass markets.
- Coercive power, because if the supplier fails to meet the retailer's increasing demands, its products might be threatened with delisting.
- Expert power, because the small supplier might see the hypermarket as having extensive knowledge of what consumers want and how best to sell to them.

Whatever the interpretation, it seems that the power is all on the hypermarket's side - the small suppliers need them more than the hypermarkets need the suppliers. A hypermarket controls a massive potential distribution opportunity for the supplier.

2   What are a small supplier's risks and rewards in dealing with a hypermarket?

The small supplier's risks are of:
- Over dependency (cf. Duarig selling 80 per cent of its output through hypermarkets)

- being squeezed on prices and terms of supply (cf. Cipem)
- taking on greater volume orders than the organisation can really cope with
- being used effectively as a test marketing exercise. If the product sells well, then the hypermarket might drop the original supplier and source the same stuff as an own brand more cheaply from elsewhere (cf. Palladium)
- damage to quality if supply prices are driven down (cf. Lewinger)
- developing a survival mentality if margins become too thin, rather than looking for a longer term growth and development strategy
- getting dragged into a mass market segment that conflicts with desired market positioning (cf. Palladium)
- not getting paid promptly.

The small supplier's rewards are that:
- They are dealing with only one major customer, and thus there is less marketing and less administration to be done
- they are gaining national coverage of a mass market
- once they have been listed by the hypermarket, the amount of in-store competition is limited
- if the arrangement works well, it can provide a stable background while the organisation develops new products and markets
- the supplier gains experience and a reputation among big league retailers
- the supplier gains experience of mass market supply and quality consistency
- because of this experience, any new products from this supplier are likely to be more acceptable to the retailers
- it can open up opportunities for own brand supply.

Supplementary question
Why did Routin and Metronic do better in dealing with the hypermarkets than Duarig and Cipem?

Duarig and Cipem:
- Allowed the hypermarkets to focus on price and squeeze
- did not manage to offer the hypermarkets anything that they valued over and above price.

Routin:
- Got into the hypermarkets via own-label products, giving Routin the chance to develop a relationship with the hypermarkets, as working on own-labels means greater involvement and commitment on both sides
- the own-label supply was a valuable learning experience for aspects of dealing with a hypermarket
- carefully positioned Fruiss not to cannibalise the own-label product's sales, and might even have designed it deliberately to fill a gap in the hypermarket's range
- Fruiss was sold to the hypermarket with a generous margin
- was committed to point of sale support material, thus offering a useful non-price service to the hypermarket.

Metronic:
- Also switched the hypermarket's focus away from price to a complete product and service package
- was selling a bigger margin, more technical product and thus the hypermarket would appreciate the support even more
- was feeding valuable marketing information to the hypermarkets which the hypermarkets would miss if the supplier was lost.

Clearly, neither Routin or Metronic was trying to achieve too much too soon. Their approaches were strategically planned and implemented, and they had planned and costed any extra support and services into their offering to the hypermarkets right at the start. Companies like Duarig and Cipem seem to have been forced into providing services reactively at the demand of the hypermarkets, and then wondering how they were going to pay for them. The main morals to all this seem to be:
- Do not take on more than you can handle
- plan your involvement and what you can and can not realistically provide
- learn how the hypermarkets think and design an offering that gives them what they want

- divert the hypermarkets' attention away from price, and make yourself indispensable to them.

3   How can own-label products provide an opportunity for the small manufacturer?

As seen in the example of Routin, own-label supply provides the small manufacturer with the opportunity to:
- Build relationships with retailers
- learn what retailers (and their customers) want and how they think
- get help with developing quality systems and distribution expertise
- focus on refining the manufacturing and logistical sides of the business rather than marketing and brand building - that is the retailer's initiative
- gain guaranteed shelf space
- build production expertise
- utilise excess capacity with regular and reliable orders
- broaden its product range at low risk
- gain a stepping stone (cf. Routin) to launching a manufacturer brand of its own.

4   Other than going down the own-label route, what can a small supplier do to improve its chances of getting its products listed by the hypermarkets? Are there any potential problems with the strategies you are suggesting?

A small supplier could try to:
- Demonstrate a proven track record of supply to other retailers or in other markets, but this is not easy if the supplier is very small or just starting out
- demonstrate proven demand for the product and the competitive advantage to the retailer of stocking it, but this could require a depth of market research that a small organisation could not afford to do
- position its product in a gap in market to make it more attractive and show the retailer how it could complete the range offered, but again this could involve heavy investment in market research
- offer to adapt the product to suit retailer's precise needs, but this might involve time delays and investment that the organisation cannot afford, and additionally it might make the supplier very dependent on the retailer
- offer a full marketing support package, but the cost will have to be considered
- offer exclusivity, but the implications of this for dependency would have to be carefully considered
- offer a trial supply period which reduces the risk to the retailer, but does not guarantee longer term acceptance of the product
- offer an attractively low price, but this puts too much focus on price, and as discussed earlier in this case, leaves the supplier vulnerable.

Much depends, of course on what sort of product or market segment is involved. If the supplier is offering yet another brand of biscuits or baked beans in a saturated market supplied by well established manufacturers, getting listed is going to be virtually impossible. If, however, the small supplier's product is complementary, if the target segment is currently under-served, if it has clear synergy with the retailer's existing lines, then there is a fighting chance. Nevertheless, it must be emphasised that remaining unique is not easy! If a small supplier's unique product is seen to be successful, then sooner or later it is going to be challenged by 'me too' imitations and own-label competition.

Marketing in Action Telmat (p 457)

Discussion question
What value added is provided by Telmat?

To the manufacturer:
- Finding new customers
- delivery services

- concentration on a new, difficult market
- risk sharing
- information provision
- storage, bulk breaking.

To the direct customer:
- Sourcing expertise
- information and translation
- certification of drugs
- fast, reliable delivery.

Marketing in Action Going Dutch (p 460)

Discussion question
What advantages are expected to be offered by the VTN compared with the auction system?

- Buyers will be less vulnerable to price fluctuations
- long term price agreements will be possible
- ease of enquiry and information gathering
- more efficient order processing
- reduced delivery periods
- added services, for example packing and grading which are important to supermarket buyers
- greater opportunity for quality assurance of service with the greater involvement of growers.

Marketing in Action Borsalino (p 466)

Discussion question
What factors have influenced the channel structure and strategy adopted by Borsalino?

External factors:
- Changing demand patterns from mass markets to specialist provision
- the growth in the relative importance of demand from outside Europe
- the move towards the 'store within a store' concession concept.

Internal factors:
- The shift upmarket of the product range and its image led to a greater emphasis on retailer exclusivity
- the need to open up a range of segments such as the youth and women's markets
- the need for stronger branding and its link with store image development to carry through a co-ordinated look
- the need for strong marketing at the point of sale in terms of space allocated and designer-led displays
- the need for greater contact with customers as an opportunity for new product trials
- the development of directly owned stores enabled a co-ordinated store identity to be developed and the acquisition of prime locations in major cities.

Marketing in Action Daewoo (p 470)

Discussion question
Why did Daewoo choose to avoid franchised dealers when they launched in the UK?

As a small, new brand on the UK market it would have been difficult to attract the right kind of dealers who would be prepared to put the required effort into selling Daewoo. It would be interesting to ask whether Daewoo have made a virtue (or marketing proposition) out of a difficult channel strategy situation! It would not have offered any distinctiveness in the customer's mind. The car itself had few unique points, and the alternative approach adopted enabled the simplicity and customer care service message to be reinforced as a positive selling point. A direct relationship could be developed with the customer. Although most car dealerships also establish equally good relationships with customers, in this case, the manufacturer retains control over the relationship. Despite these developments it is interesting to note that Daewoo found it necessary to supplement their market presence and broaden consumer awareness through the Sainsbury's experiment and the customer support centres at Halford's. Perhaps the challenge to Daewoo will emerge fully when they seek to expand their market penetration further and thus represent a greater threat to established dealers.

SUGGESTED ASSIGNMENTS

- Questions for Discussion 12.1
- To what extent and why do you think that a trend towards direct supply in consumer markets poses a threat to traditional intermediaries?

Chapter 13
RETAILERS AND WHOLESALERS

LECTURE PLAN

A lecture based on this chapter should help the student to:
1. Understand the role and importance of retailers and wholesalers within the distribution channel;
2. classify retailers according to a number of different organisational and operating dimensions;
3. differentiate between types of retailer, appreciating their individual contribution to the retailing scene and their problems;
4. analyse the particular strategic and operational marketing concerns of retailers; and
5. understand the role played by different types of wholesaler.

The key sections of this lecture should be:

Definition of wholesaling and retailing (pp 490-493):
- The difference between wholesalers and retailers
- their functions: assembling a range of goods; providing storage and transportation; giving advice and information; transferring title; providing an appropriate selling environment.

Retail structures (pp 493-499):
- *Forms of ownership:* independents; corporate chains; contractual systems.
- *Levels of service:* full service; limited service; self-service.
- *Merchandise lines:* breadth and depth of range, including OHT 41, figure 13.2 (p 499) The Mixed Approach:
  ⇒ Space constraints on what can be stocked and displayed
  ⇒ importance of assessing how fast-moving a line will be
  ⇒ importance of assessing customer needs in terms of size and colour (or other variables) choices.
- *Operating methods:* store *vs.* non-store retailing, a very brief overview.

Types of retailer (pp 499-511):
- Department stores (including concessions)

- variety stores
- supermarkets (including discounters)
- hypermarkets
- out of town speciality stores
- town centre speciality stores
- convenience stores
- discount clubs
- markets
- catalogue showrooms.

Non-store retailing (pp 509-510):
- In-home selling
- mail order
- teleshopping
- vending.

This section could be omitted, and students encouraged to read the material for themselves. Non-store retailing is more fully covered in chapter 19.

Retail strategy (pp 511-521)
- *Location:* the importance of the right location, including OHP 42, figure 13.3 (p 512) Factors Influencing the Location Decision Making Process:
    ⇒ The strategic importance of the location decision
    ⇒ the complexity of the factors that impact on it.
    ⇒ trends within the marketing environment affecting retailers' location choices.
- *Product range decisions:* assortment; product type including OHP 43, figure 13.4 (p 514) Factors Influencing Product Assortment Strategy:
    ⇒ Brief overview of the factors
    ⇒ importance of balancing practical issues against customer needs and image building requirements.
- *Positioning:* importance of differentiation in the eyes of the target market.
- *Store image and atmosphere:* the impact on the customer's senses of the physical and psychological aspects of the store and its marketing.
- *Merchandising:* layout and display, including OHP 44, figure 13.5 (p 518) Factors Influencing Layout and Display:
    ⇒ Brief overview of factors
    ⇒ again, the importance of balancing practical considerations against customer ideals and image building.
- *Technology:* its impact on retail efficiency and customer service; EPOS; EFTPOS.
- *Retailer own brands:* brief overview of why they exist and what they add to store image.

Retail Europeanisation (pp 521-523):
- Why internationalisation is happening
- push - pull factors influencing internationalisation
- the role and benefits of strategic alliances.

This section could be omitted, and students encouraged to read the material for themselves.

Wholesalers and distributors (pp 523-524):
- Full service wholesalers
- limited service wholesalers.

This section could be omitted, and students encouraged to read the material for themselves.

QUESTIONS FOR REVIEW

13.1   Summarise the main functions of wholesalers and retailers. (pp 490-493)

- Assembling an appropriate range of goods
- providing storage and transportation facilities
- giving advice and information
- transferring title to goods, i.e. reselling
- providing an appropriate selling environment.

13.2   Define place utility and time utility. Why do these concepts matter to customers?
(pp 490-491)

Place utility means having the goods at a convenient location for easy access by the customer. Time utility means making the goods available when the customer wants them, and minimising the amount of time the customer has to spend in the purchasing process.

13.3   What factors might be considered in providing an appropriate selling environment? How might the importance and the decisions made about these factors differ between retailers and wholesalers? (pp 492-493)

- *Atmosphere:* a retailer might want to create an atmosphere that creates a psychological mood, for example relaxing or stimulating and this will be a very important aspect of their marketing effort. A wholesaler might prefer a more businesslike, functional atmosphere that allows the buyer to complete their transactions as quickly as possible.
- *Layout and ease of goods selection:* again, a retailer might use layout to enhance image and help to create mood. More expensive consumer goods might be displayed in such a way that the customer has to be helped by a sales assistant. A wholesaler might focus more on functional self-selection of goods, and concentrate on designing a layout that makes it as easy as possible for customers to find what they want and move it the minimum distance to their vans or other means of transport.
- *Convenient parking:* wholesalers and supermarkets would certainly consider this to be very important. Customers must be able to move large quantities of goods from the outlet to the car or van easily. Dedicated parking is often less important and indeed less feasible for high street retailers, such as fashion stores, but proximity to public car parks could be useful.
- *Credit and delivery services:* the wholesaler, dealing with trade customers buying in bulk, would consider these things to be much more important than most retailers, although retailers do operate store-specific credit cards to encourage customer loyalty. Retailers might offer delivery on bulky expensive items, such as furniture or washing machines, for example. A wholesaler might deliver orders more routinely to trade customers' premises.
- *Assistance with purchasing:* both wholesalers and retailers might consider sales assistance essential for more expensive or for more technically complex goods.

13.4   What are the predominant forms of retail ownership, and what are the major problems facing each of them? (pp 493-495)

- *Independents:* cannot compete on price or breadth of range with chains; can often be in poor locations; have lost out in the trend towards out of town shopping.
- *Corporate chains:* cannot easily tailor themselves to suit local needs.
- *Contractual systems:* franchisee's loss of operational and strategic discretion.

13.5   What are the advantages and disadvantages of allowing concessions within a department store? (pp 499-501)
Advantages:
- Adds a different character to the store
- utilises excess floor space
- generates extra customers
- broadens the product range or gives greater depth

- generates extra income.

Disadvantages:
- Ties up floor space
- might conflict with store image
- might take customers away from the store's ranges
- might create a cluttered look.

13.6 What is a variety store and what particular advantages does it offer to the shopper? (pp 501-502)

A variety store stocks a limited number of ranges, but in some depth. Its advantages are that it:
- Offers a degree of specialisation
- offers a lot of choice within a product area
- can sell sufficient volumes of a product to gain from economies of scale, which might be reflected in the prices charges to customers.

13.7 What advantages does out of town retailing offer to a speciality retailer and its customers? (pp 505-506)

- The sites are cheaper to operate, thus ...
- ... product prices can be lower
- deliveries are easier to make
- bulk deliveries can be made
- parking and access are easy and convenient for the customer
- stores can be large and thus stock and display more merchandise.

13.8 Why is choice of location so important for a retailer, and what factors are likely to be taken into account when making a location decision? (pp 511-514)

Location is important because:
- Customers need to be able to access the store easily
- a large enough catchment area has to be available to generate required sales
- the store might have to be able to attract passing consumer traffic
- the store's proximity to competition or key retail names might affect its level of business
- it could affect the operational costs of the store.

The broad categories of factors to be taken into account are thus:
- Population and demographic profiles
- accessibility
- competition
- location costs.

13.9 What factors influence the assortment of goods stocked by a retailer? (pp 514-515)

- Store image
- stock control systems
- branding strategy
- risks and costs
- staff expertise and ability.
-

13.10 What are the advantages for a retailer or wholesaler of internationalisation through strategic alliances? What are the potential drawbacks of such an approach? (pp 521-523)

Advantages:
- Increased buying power

- access to local knowledge and expertise
- trading under established local retail names
- creating allies out of what might otherwise be aggressive competitors
- less risk.

Drawbacks:
- Potential conflicts of interest
- potential cultural clashes
- achieving the unanimity required to exploit joint buying power
- limiting the partners' ability to expand.

QUESTIONS FOR DISCUSSION

13.1   Find examples of (a) full service, (b) limited service and (c) self service stores in the same retail sector. What contribution does the level of service make to each of those stores' marketing approaches?

This discussion question ensures that the students understand the difference between alternative service levels and their appropriate application. The choice of retail sector is unimportant as long as clear examples relevant to the three categories of service are presented. Issues that the students should consider in analysing service levels include:
- Complexity of products
- price of products
- frequency of purchase
- likely level of customer knowledge about products
- store image and positioning in the market
- whether different service levels occur in different parts of the store.

13.2   What is a category killer and how might its activities affect other retailers? Give examples.

The examples chosen should clearly demonstrate that a category killer is (usually) an out of town speciality retailer that offers such depth and breadth of choice within its chosen specialist market at such competitive prices that other smaller retailers cannot compete. A category killer's activities might well drive other retailers out of business, or push them into very narrow niche positions, because the category killer gains competitive advantage through:
- Massive buying power
- economies of scale in operation
- an image of being 'the ultimate specialist'
- customer convenience.

13.3   In what ways and to what extent do you think that non-store retailing poses a threat to conventional retailers?

This is a broad question, and students might find it useful to look at different types of non-store retailing, for example in-home selling, mail order operations, telemarketing, and vending in assessing the level of threat. In general terms, the issues that should be addressed include:
- Operating costs compared with store-based retailing
- size of potential market
- geographic spread of potential market
- type of product
- level and type of pre- and post-sale services associated with the product
- frequency of purchase, and purchase occasions
- logistic considerations
- degree of customer's psychological involvement in the purchasing process

- social aspects of shopping.

13.4   Choose a retailer and analyse how its store atmosphere is made up.

Choice of retailer is immaterial as long as the analysis covers issues such as impact made through:
- *Sight:* colour; lighting; displays.
- *Sound:* use of silence; use, volume and mood of background music.
- *Scent:* product smells; background smells.
- *Touch:* materials; fabrics; fixtures and fittings; temperature.

The student should also demonstrate an appreciation of how all these factors interact with each other and are integrated to create a coherent atmosphere that makes the 'right' impact on the shopper.

13.5   Find examples of retailers that use (a) grid layout, (b) free flow layout and (c) boutique layout. Explain how each layout seems to affect shoppers' behaviour within those stores and what contribution it makes to the overall image and atmosphere of the stores.

Points likely to be raised for each type of layout include:

a) *Grid layout:*
- Leads shoppers round the store on a largely pre-determined route
- maximises shopper exposure to merchandise
- could create a functional, regimented feel to the store.

b) *Free flow layout:*
- Leaves shoppers free to browse as they wish
- allows shoppers to move towards the merchandise that looks most appealing to them
- can create a strong visual image
- can create an aesthetically pleasing or stimulating feel for the store.

c) *Boutique layout:*
- Leaves shoppers free to browse as they wish within the designated area
- can denote a trading area with a very different character from the rest of the store
- can create a strong visual image
- can create a more intimate atmosphere within a large trading area.

CASE STUDY 13.1 Sainsbury's (p 527)

Teaching Objectives

1. To emphasise the importance of store location;
2. to explore the problems faced by multiples in balancing centralised marketing decision-making against local needs;
3. to analyse the role of own-label products in a supermarket's product mix.

1   Why is store location so important for a grocery retailer? Assess the way in which Sainsbury's evaluates potential locations.

Store location decisions are important for a grocery retailer because:
- They are selling mainly fmcg products that need intensive distribution and thus the retailer wants to make sure that full geographic coverage is achieved
- stores have to be convenient for shoppers to access
- new stores need to minimise the amount of business they take away from existing stores
- stores need a sufficiently large catchment area to generate satisfactory turnover
- precise choice of location can have a big effect on potential sales and operating costs
- proximity to competing supermarkets, out of town retail parks or malls, or shopping centres might affect its level of business.

Sainsbury's uses a system that incorporates:

- Drive times within a catchment area
- demographic and economic data within an area
- average grocery expenditure within an area
- consideration of competitors' locations within an area.

The benefits of such a system are that:

- It contains most of the key data to allow an accurate assessment of a location's potential
- presumably it has been refined through usage and experience
- it has proved its abilities
- it provides a powerful, trustworthy and objective aid for managerial decision-making
- it allows quick and easy comparison of a number of alternative locations.

The potential problems are ensuring that:

- Its data remain accurate and up to date
- any assumptions about the nature of the marketing environment are monitored and updated
- the accuracy of its outputs are constantly monitored and evaluated
- it does not lull managers into a false sense of security
- it remains a decision-making aid rather than becoming the decision-maker.

2 How would you define Sainsbury's market segment? What are the marketing implications of that definition?

It is a broad segment, difficult to define in as detailed and precise a way as perhaps segmentation theory would like! It might be useful to ask students to revise the parts of chapter 5 relating to segmentation in consumer markets, and ask them to consider the relevance of each of those segmentation variables to a supermarket retailer. The general characteristics of Sainsbury's target segment are that it consists of:

- Anyone who finds the store location conveniently accessible (close to home; close to work; close to the town centre; close to major out of town shopping developments)
- anyone who wants a reasonably broad selection of goods, both staple groceries and more unusual or exotic lines, to choose from within a single store
- anyone who seeks reasonably good quality at a reasonable price.

It does not seem to have any particular:

- *Age appeal.*
- *Gender appeal:* although it is likely that the majority of its shoppers will be female or heavily influenced by females.
- *Family life cycle stage appeal:* it provides pack sizes suitable for families, couples or singles.
- *Socioeconomic group appeal:* its product ranges cover a variety of price points, from premium brands to very low priced economy lines. A store's catchment area is also likely to be wide enough to encompass a variety of more or less affluent areas.
- *Lifestyle appeal:* its product ranges include the ordinary, the functional, the traditional, the familiar and the mundane as well as the new, the exciting, the exotic and the experimental!
- *Occasions appeal:* its product lines can service the ordinary day to day needs of a household, a formal dinner party, or a buffet for 60 guests! Its stores are also located and laid out to be used either for a planned weekly major shopping trip, or for a quick dash around for a few essentials on the way home from work.

In short, cutting out the very extreme edges of the market (the highly discerning, relatively rich and exclusive shopper at one end, and the extremely price conscious, relatively poor shopper at the other), the supermarket is designed to appeal to virtually anyone who needs to buy food.

3 What factors might encourage a grocery multiple to vary the product mix, promotional offers or pricing from store to store?

Relevant considerations might include:

- Specific local needs, for example high concentrations of ethnic groups
- varying store sizes, for example large stores can stock more product lines than small ones

- the need to respond to aggressive marketing tactics from nearby competing stores
- the ease with which local shoppers can patronise a competing store
- the need to hold on to current customers when competitors are opening new stores in the area
- the need to clear slow-moving stock in a particular store
- the need to stimulate sales in a poorly located store or in a 'tired' store which needs refurbishment
- promotional initiatives relating to a new store opening or the re-opening of a store after refurbishment.

Supplementary question
Why do retailers prefer to retain central control over most aspects of retail marketing?

- Centralised buying and distribution gains economies of scale
- centralised buying ensures that products are suitable for the market and creates buying power
- it allows national and cost effective marketing communications initiatives
- it creates consistency between different stores in terms of their day to day operation
- it creates a uniform and consistent store image
- it ensures that a suitably high level of management expertise is involved in decision-making
- it creates an efficient and coherent system overall with the minimum of duplication of tasks
- it allows best practice to be disseminated and implemented throughout the chain.

4   **Why are own-label products so important to Sainsbury's? Can a grocery outlet have too many own-label products?**

Own-label products are important to Sainsbury's because such products give the retailer:
- More control over quality and supply
- the opportunity to fill in price gaps in the ranges stocked
- the opportunity to create products to suit their customers' needs
- products that can not be stocked by their competitors
- the opportunity to rationalise the number of different brands stocked within a product type
- more control over their shelf space allocation
- more bargaining power with suppliers
- better profit margins
- more tangible reinforcement of their 'quality, but good value' image.

It could be possible for a grocery outlet to have too many own-label products, in the sense that at some point consumers will start to feel that their choices are being unduly restricted, especially if the shelf space seems to be dominated by own-labels. Customers perhaps want to feel that they have had the option of examining and rejecting other brands, and that they have made a positive choice to buy the own-label, rather than having it forced on them.

CASE STUDY 13.2 Amstrad Sells Direct (p 528)

Teaching Objectives

1. To ensure that students understand the benefits of retailing;
2. to examine the kinds of problems that can cause conflict between suppliers and retailers;
3. to explore the benefits and problems of direct supply as an alternative to traditional retail channels.

1   **Why did Amstrad decide to stop selling products through retailers such as Dixons? Is this any great loss to Dixons?**

Amstrad might have decided to stop selling through retailers such as Dixons because:
- Sales targets were not being met
- the retailers were squeezing the trade price

- the retailers were making demands for advertising support from the manufacturers
- retailers were demanding more favourable supply terms (for example sale or return)
- the retailers were benefiting from expensive extended warranties on the products
- Amstrad products were being sold alongside competing products
- given the range of goods that retailers like Dixons sell, Amstrad might have questioned the level of commitment and attention given to selling Amstrad goods
- sales depend to some extent on the quality of the catchment areas of the retailers' stores.

Dixons might have regretted the loss of a major name like Amstrad, but if it was so eager to hold on to Amstrad, it might not have been quite so demanding in terms of price and conditions. Since the market for PCs is extremely dynamic and competitive, it is likely that Dixons would soon find an alternative supplier, offering more attractive prices to fill the gap in Dixons' range left by Amstrad.

2   What can retailing offer in the PC market that direct supply cannot?

Retailing can offer:
- Personal contact and dialogue with a customer
- customers who have bought other things from that retailer and thus already have a relationship
- seemingly impartial advice and a sales approach tailored to the customer's needs
- an opportunity for the customer to handle the goods before buying
- an opportunity for the customer to compare competing offerings directly
- attractive credit terms to the customer
- additional warranties
- a point of contact for after-sales service
- attractive product displays
- national distribution through the retailer's own logistics system
- additional marketing support, in that by being on display in the store, the product is visible to consumers, and is benefiting from the retailer's name and reputation
- a natural focal point for consumers thinking of buying a PC.

Supplementary question
What benefits could direct supply offer the manufacturer?

Direct supply can offer:
- Direct contact between manufacturer and customer
- no geographic constraints on catchment
- the ability to save on the intermediary's profit margin
- total control over the marketing and selling of the product
- a selling operation fully committed to one manufacturer's products.

3   Initially, Amstrad targeted its direct supply at small businesses. What would be the problems of extending the direct supply concept to individual consumers?

The potential problems include:
- *Targeting consumers:* locating and contacting them. Should they use purchased mailing lists? Direct response advertising in PC magazines? Television advertising?
- *Delivery logistics:* getting products quickly and safely to domestic addresses all over the country
- *The cost of selling and delivery* to a potential market of thousands.
- *Supporting consumers through the decision-making process adequately:* small businesses are likely to buy on more rational criteria, such as price, or on technical specification. Consumers might need more persuasion and reassurance on various issues, both rational and emotional.
- *The appropriateness of the product to consumers rather than small businesses:* consumers might be looking for a multi-purpose machine that can play games and serve educational purposes as well as managing the household accounts.

- *Providing adequate after-sales service* and support to as potentially large number of individual buyers.

4   Do you think Amstrad has made the right move? What else could it have done?

It is difficult to give a definitive answer to this. Much depends on Amstrad's ability to design, resource and implement a direct selling campaign, and how well it understands its target market. It also depends crucially on why sales through the retailers were disappointing. To what extent was it the retailers' fault, and to what extent was there something lacking in the product and its associated marketing mix? If the product is not competitive, then perhaps it could be argued that sacking the retailer and moving into direct supply is the wrong solution to the wrong problem! Alternative courses of action, therefore, might include:
- Finding alternative retail channels
- rethinking the product
- developing parallel channels, i.e. retaining existing retailers but selling direct as well.

Supplementary question
What would be the problems of using parallel channels, i.e. continuing to sell through a retailer, but also selling direct?

The problems would be:
- Alienating the retailers
- confusing the customer
- increased costs and management time and attention trying to manage both properly.
Some of these problems might be overcome by:
- Ensuring that any price differential can be justified
- perhaps ensuring that the products offered in each channel are different
- perhaps trying, if possible, to ensure that the direct supply targets a different group of customers from those reached by the retailer.

Marketing in Action Menswear (p 495)

Discussion question
What marketing advantages do independent menswear operators have over the multiples?

- Carefully selected merchandise closely matches the needs and tastes of a narrow target market
- the merchandise selection helps build a strong and distinctive store image
- the independent can build premium position through either own or exclusive labels
- the independent can build its range with the local area and target customer in mind, in terms of range depth, breadth or complementary accessories
- as a group independents offer wider variety than the high street multiples
- the independent can build closer relationship with customers
- the independent can be more flexible in offering additional customer services
- the independent can differentiate through a themed environment.

Marketing in Action Small Retailers in Portugal (p 504)

Discussion question
Is the independent sector in Portugal destined to contract as the hypermarket format expands?

Despite the lobbying efforts of the independents, it is likely that the hypermarkets will expand and continue to take market share. The actual rate of expansion and overall impact might not follow exactly the French experience. The key issue is not so much population size, but the catchment area of different locations. The Portuguese population outside the main centres, such as Oporto, Braga and Lisbon is widely dispersed, with some very remote towns. The catchment needed by hypermarkets is generally very large, to provide the necessary volume. More remote locations, especially where the road systems are well below European standards, might be less attractive to potential investors. The independents could, therefore, survive in some more remote locations, but otherwise as suggested in the vignette, there will have to be changes in strategy to achieve group buying, wholesaler branding, the raising of display and service standards and a continued emphasis on convenience and sensible prices. These changes might enable the specialist retailer of food products, for example vegetarian or ethnic specialists, and the convenience format to survive alongside the hypermarket. However, this could still mean considerable changes in their marketing approaches.

Marketing in Action Tie Rack (p 511)

Discussion question
What are the main elements of the retailer strategy that have led to the success of Tie Rack?

- *Location:* concentration on airport locations as well as high street; captive audience at airports.
- *Number of outlets:* international expansion in 14 different locations to spread risk.
- *Product assortment:* Concentration on ties and scarves; narrow product line and mid range pricing rather than exclusive prices.
- *Store image and atmosphere:* standard approach to store design, fascia, product presentation, despite the varied locations; small intimate stores; ease of self selection and browsing.

Marketing in Action Polish Distribution (p 522)

Discussion question
Why is Poland an attractive market for expansion by western European retailers and wholesalers?

Students should be referred to table 13.6 (p 521):
- An underdeveloped retail structure is dominated by independents (80%) with variable standards
- the market is large, with a 38 million population
- new entrants have a competitive advantage over existing independents
- new entrants need to enter the market early to build market strength. Most other competitors entering the market are large and powerful with the capacity to build and sustain a market share. They may be difficult to compete against in a few years' time
- there are only limited growth opportunities in the main EU markets which are mostly mature
- the poor wholesaling structure provides opportunities for cash & carry to supply independents
- a limited range in terms of breadth and depth are offered by the independents.

However there could be problems with expansion. These include:
- Low salary levels
- high unemployment with economic restructuring
- the need to find and train appropriate management staff
- poor transport infrastructure
- lower car ownership levels
- the need to change shopping habits
- a sometimes chaotic distribution system.

SUGGESTED ASSIGNMENTS

- Questions for Discussion 13.5 could be used as a group assignment, with either a report or a verbal presentation or both as the output.
- What strategic benefits do retailers derive from developing own-label products?

Chapter 14
PHYSICAL DISTRIBUTION AND LOGISTICS MANAGEMENT

LECTURE PLAN

A lecture based on this chapter should help the student to:
1. Understand the distinction between physical distribution management and logistics;
2. appreciate the importance of customer service as an integral part of logistics and distribution;
3. analyse how customer service elements can be built into the distribution channel;
4. identify the functions involved in logistics and to appreciate the decisions contributing to their management; and
5. assess the importance of physical distribution within an integrated marketing mix.

The key sections of this lecture should be:

Definition of physical distribution and logistics (pp 531-533):
- The importance of PDM and logistics
- the differences between them.

PDM (pp 533-535):
The role of PDM in the distribution channel, including OHP 45, figure 14.1 (p 533) Channel Management and Physical Distribution Management:
- The extra tasks involved in PDM
- the extra intermediaries introduced
- why a strategic approach to PDM is necessary.

Logistics management (pp 535-540):
- The role of logistics management and its importance
- the complexity of logistics, including OHP 46, figure 14.3 (p 536) Influences on the Logistics Process:
  ⇒ Discuss each group of factors
  ⇒ emphasise areas which tend to reduce costs and areas which tend to add costs
  ⇒ discuss how each group of factors adds to customer service.
- Total logistics cost concept
- main areas of logistics costs.

Customer service (pp 540-543):
- Pre-transactional variables
- transactional variables, including OHP 47, figure 14.5 (p 541) Customer Service and Transactional Variables:
  ⇒ Overview of the types of factors included
  ⇒ the importance of time efficiency
  ⇒ the importance of accuracy
  ⇒ the importance of tracking order and consignment status.
- Post-transactional variables.

Logistics functions (pp 543-560):
- *Transportation:* different modes of transport; their advantages and disadvantages; factors influencing transport mode selection.

- *Order processing:* including OHT 48, figure 14.8 (p 553) Stages in Order Processing
  - ⇒ Overview of each stage
  - ⇒ importance of speed and accuracy
  - ⇒ its contribution to customer service and cost saving.
- *Warehousing:* types of warehouse; the role of warehousing.
- *Materials handling:* what it involves; what it adds to logistics efficiency and speed.
- *Inventory management:* costs associated with inventories; why inventory is necessary; controlling inventory levels.

The impact of PDM and logistics on the rest of the marketing mix (pp 560-561):
- Product
- pricing
- promotion.

QUESTIONS FOR REVIEW

14.1   List the range of functions undertaken in physical distribution management. (pp 533-535)

- Receiving and processing orders
- picking and packing
- managing warehouses
- stock management and control
- transportation.

14.2   What are facilitators, and what specific functions do they provide within PDM? (pp 533-535)

Facilitators are intermediaries within a distribution channel who do not take title to goods, but help to ensure the efficient and safe flow of goods. Their functions include:
- Transportation
- warehouse operators
- insurance providers
- freight forwarding agents.

14.3   How does logistics differ from PDM? (pp 535-537)

PDM concentrates on the movement and handling of goods and materials outwards from the manufacturer to the point of consumption. Logistics includes the concept of PDM but also considers the inbound movement and handling of supplies, components and raw materials, and their management through to the production line.

14.4   What are the main cost areas of logistics? (pp 537-540)

- Order processing and administration
- inventory management
- transportation
- providing and maintaining storage and handling facilities.

14.5   What are the three groups into which customer service can be categorised, and what kinds of services does each group cover? (pp 540-543)

1. *Pre-transactional variables:* the setting of customer service standards and targets consistent with corporate policies and procedures. Areas covered include order processing, stock availability, speed of order fulfilment etc.
2. *Transactional variables:* services that enable the customer's order to be fulfilled and delivered. Areas covered include delivery time and reliability, invoicing, handling delivery problems such as incorrect consignments or damaged goods etc.
3. *Post-transactional variables:* services supporting the customer after the sale and while the product is in use. Areas covered include guarantees, installation, training, maintenance and complaints handling.

14.6 Outline the stages in order processing and discuss their contribution to customer service. (pp 551-553)

- *Placing the order:* customers must find it easy and convenient to make orders through a variety of media.
- *Entering the order into the system:* to enhance customer service, this needs to be done quickly and accurately. With computer based systems, placing and entering the order could be done simultaneously perhaps be the customers themselves.
- *Producing and checking documentation:* ensuring that the order has been recorded accurately and either confirming that the goods are available for immediate dispatch or giving the customer a future delivery date. The invoice is also produced at this stage.
- *Order picking, packing and dispatch:* the required goods need to be brought together and fitted into dispatch and delivery schedules. In terms of customer service, speed and accuracy are essential, as well as maintaining the good condition of the goods.
- *Delivery:* getting the goods to the place where the customer wants them at the time the customer wants them.
- *Post-delivery:* following up the order to make sure that the customer has received what they wanted, when and where they wanted it, and that there are no problems in using the goods or integrating them into production lines.

14.7 How and why does holding inventory incur costs? (pp 556-557)

- *Carrying costs:* if inventory is held, then it ties up cash which might mean higher borrowing to maintain cash flow.
- *Stock servicing costs:* the costs include insurance, for example. While inventory is being held, it must be insured against accident, destruction or theft.
- *Storage costs:* these costs include maintaining storage space in terms of heating, lighting, rent, business rates etc. Also included are the costs of managing and handling stock.
- *Obsolescence and wastage costs:* losses incurred through damage, pilfering or the natural perishability of goods.

14.8 How do JIT systems affect inventory control and management? (pp 559-560)

JIT means that:
- Minimal or no safety stock is held
- order processing must be rapid and accurate
- the supplier must be able to fulfil orders on schedule or even on demand and may thus need to carry ample safety stock
- picking and packing must be rapid and accurate
- delivery must be on time to the right place
- goods must be delivered in good condition.

14.9   To what kinds of problems can poor inventory management lead? (p 560)

- Having to sell off surplus or damaged stock cheaply
- stockouts and thus delays in fulfilling orders
- inability to meet delivery promises
- not knowing what products are or are not available from stock
- not knowing what stock has been promised to other customers
- increasing inventory costs (as outlined in question 14.7 above)
- falling stock turnover levels.

14.10   Summarise the ways in which PDM interacts with the elements of the marketing mix. (pp 560-561)

- *Product:* PDM strategy depends on the nature of the goods, for example their size, fragility, perishability etc. Product design and packaging can also ease goods handling and storage problems. The size of the product mix and the breadth and depth of ranges handled directly impact on the complexity of the PDM task.
- *Price:* has to cover the costs of PDM and the associated services offered. Efficient and cost effective PDM could actually help to keep overall prices down by improving stock turnover and thus sales volumes.
- *Place:* PDM helps to get products to the right place at the right time, but customer needs and demands in terms of time and place also influence the design of PDM strategies.
- *Promotion:* if marketing communications activities are making promises about product availability, then PDM has to be able to deliver on those promises. A direct response television advertisement, for example, might encourage consumers to phone in and order an item. Not only does the seller have to be able to handle all the incoming calls and record the orders, it also has to have stock available to fulfil those orders, and be able to dispatch them within a reasonable time.

QUESTIONS FOR DISCUSSION

14.1   Draw up a table which lists each of the five main modes of transport, summarises their advantages and disadvantages, compares their relative costs per kilometre, and gives an example of an appropriate use of each mode.

Students' tables might include the following considerations (see pp 544-547):
a)   Rail
- *Advantages:* can handle large heavy quantities of goods; can cover great distances quickly; relatively environmentally friendly.
- *Disadvantages:* can only move where track is laid; it can be difficult to cross international borders because of different rail gauges; getting goods to and from railheads.
- *Relative cost/km:* cost of goods movement is low for long distances, but the loading and unloading costs at either end are high.
- *Appropriate use:* heavy bulk loads such as coal and chemicals.
b)   Road
- *Advantages:* can undertake door to door delivery in all areas and over all terrains; can cross international borders relatively easily; can deal with large and small load sizes.
- *Disadvantages:* size of one load is limited; pressure of traffic; seen as environmentally unfriendly.
- *Relative cost/km:* low over short distances for door to door service.
- *Appropriate use:* relatively local movement of limited quantities.
c)   Air
- *Advantages:* fast international delivery; good for small, light, valuable items; good for perishable items.
- *Disadvantages:* getting goods to and from airports; very costly for large weighty loads.
- *Relative cost/km:* high.

- *Appropriate use:* emergency international deliveries, or for perishable goods over long distances.

d) Pipeline

- *Advantages:* environmentally friendly; can cover long intercontinental distances regardless of terrain or external conditions; protects the product in transit; can maintain a constant flow of bulk.
- *Disadvantages:* coverage limited to where the pipeline is laid; damage to pipeline may be hidden and difficult to repair; damage to pipeline stops the flow of goods completely.
- *Relative cost/km:* very low, once the pipeline has been set up.
- *Appropriate use:* bulk flows of oil, gas, water etc.

e) Water:

- *Advantages:* environmentally friendly; can transport bulk quantities over long distances.
- *Disadvantages:* limited by existence and maintenance of waterways; expense of moving goods to and from ports and wharves; relatively slow.
- *Relative cost/km:* very low, as long as the customer is not in a hurry to get the goods!
- *Appropriate use:* low value bulk products where speed of delivery is not of the essence.

14.2   What are the main criteria affecting transport choice and how might they impact on transporting (a) coal to a power station, (b) fruit to a supermarket, (c) components to a car factory, and (d) cash for wages from a bank to a factory?

The main criteria affecting transport choice are (see pp 548-550):
- Cost
- performance of the mode of transport
- transit time
- reliability
- security
- frequency of required deliveries
- capability of the transport mode
- accessibility.

In looking at the four scenarios offered, students should show a common sense appreciation of how each of these criteria might apply and which are the most important in determining transport mode, with due respect for the characteristics of the product and the types of organisation under consideration.

14.3   Road transport has come under increasing criticism on environmental grounds. To what extent do you think this should influence organisations' transport policy?

The debate stimulated by this question might consider the following points:
- Does the nature of the products being transported mean that alternatives are possible?
- Can alternative modes of transport be acceptably cost effective?
- Are governments likely to do more to discourage road transport, through fuel taxes or lack of support for road building programmes, for example?
- Are governments prepared to offer incentives to use alternatives?
- To what extent does the organisation want to promote a 'green' image for itself?
- Would the organisation's customers appreciate a greener but slightly less efficient or convenient transport policy?

14.4   To what extent and why do you think warehousing can contribute to effective and efficient PDM?

Points that might be raised in discussion include the facts that warehousing enables:
- Stocks of goods to be held ready
- stocks to be held close to where they are needed
- extensive geographic areas to be served efficiently and cost effectively through networks of warehouses

- stocks to be held under controlled conditions in terms of temperature, humidity etc
- seasonal produce to be released onto the market over time
- goods to be graded, picked and sorted
- improved customer service.

14.5   Critically evaluate the limitations of the stock control models presented on pp 556-560.

The reorder point model assumes that:
- Replenishment lead times are predictable and reliable
- required safety stock is predictable
- there will be no unexpected surges in demand during the replenishment lead time.

All of these could be dangerous assumptions. Additionally, this model does not indicate how much stock ought to be ordered at the reorder points.

The economic order quantity model assumes that:
- Minimising total cost is the prime objective
- compromising on safety stock carries no penalty
- the costs per unit can be calculated accurately
- the organisation can cope with the delivery and storage of the quantity specified
- if the model indicates that larger quantities should be ordered less frequently, the goods can be maintained in peak condition until sold on.

Pareto analysis assumes that:
- Some key product lines should be given greater priority because of their contribution to total sales
- some key products need higher safety stocks than others.

CASE STUDY 14.1 Putting Some Fizz into Supply Chain Management (p 564)

Teaching Objectives

1. To look at the role of IT in efficient distribution;
2. to analyse the contribution of distribution centres to cost effective logistics management;
3. to explore the benefits of centralised distribution management.

1   Why are sophisticated IT systems important for distribution centres such as those operated by Britvic and Cadbury's?

Sophisticated IT is important because of the need to:
- Manage the sheer size of the operation in terms of:
  ⇒ number of lorries per day (700 at Britvic)
  ⇒ number of different product lines and items (93,000 pallets of chocolate at Cadbury's)
- process orders quickly and accurately
- pick and pack orders quickly and accurately
- get the right goods on the right lorry at the right time
- turn lorries around as quickly as possible
- minimise stock holding levels
- ensure that oldest stock is dispatched first
- track the location and movement of stock within the facility and in and out of it
- ensure quick turnover of stock
- minimise labour and stockholding costs
- enhance customer service, not only through speed but also through computerised order reception and information flow from supplier to customer.

Supplementary question
What are the costs associated with holding stock?

- *Carrying costs:* the cost of working capital tied up in stock.
- *Stock servicing costs:* insurance for example.
- *Storage costs:* providing and maintaining the storage space
    - ⇒ Recouping the capital investment in providing space
    - ⇒ heating and lighting
    - ⇒ rent and/or local authority business rates
    - ⇒ building and facilities maintenance
    - ⇒ labour costs
    - ⇒ costs of handling and managing stock.
- *Obsolescence and wastage costs:* stock lost through accidental damage, perishability, poor administration or pilfering.

2   What services are these distribution centres providing to the retail trade?

The services provided by the distribution centres include:
- Storing products in good condition until the retailer wants to call on them. With chocolate in particular, temperature and humidity control are important.
- Allowing the retailer to place orders for specific quantities of a product rather than using 'truckloads' as the basic unit of ordering.
- Deliveries to the retailers' own regional depots
- up to date, accurate information about stock availability and delivery times
- providing retailers with products that are as fresh as possible
- shorter lead times between orders and deliveries
- on-line ordering
- more cost effective and efficient logistics overall
- delivery of the right goods in excellent condition.

3   In what ways might these distribution centres reduce costs for (a) the manufacturers and (b) the retailers?

a) Manufacturer costs could be reduced because the distribution centres:
- Minimise stock held
- maximise stock turnover
- achieve economies of scale in operation through centralisation and eradicate duplicated tasks
- minimise labour involvement
- allow faster order turn around
- create less wastage and fewer mistakes.

b) Retailer costs could be reduced because the distribution centres:
- Make it easy to place orders of any size at any time
- fulfil orders accurately and quickly, so the retailer does not need to hold big safety stocks at its own depots
- allow the manufacturers to reflect some of their cost savings in trade prices charged to retailers.

4   What are the relative advantages and disadvantages of having one large distribution centre rather than a series of regional centres when dealing with fmcg products such as chocolate and soft drinks?

The advantages of centralisation are:
- Economies of scale in investment and operation
- eradication of duplicated effort
- there is no need to worry about balancing and managing stock levels at different locations
- there is no need to worry about deciding which location a particular order should be serviced from
- delivery to and despatch from one location in bulk

140

- the size of the facility makes investment in state of the art technology worthwhile.

The disadvantages of centralisation are:

- If there are problems within the facility, for example fire, flood, technical breakdown or power failure, there are no other locations to which orders can be diverted
- the size of the facility might mean that much more effort has to be put into creating and maintaining control systems
- ensuring that the chosen site and its neighbourhood can cope with the comings and goings of 700 lorries a day!
- extra costs incurred through having to deliver goods over greater distances to customers (although these are likely to be more than off-set by cost savings in other operational areas).

CASE STUDY 14.2 Fording the Channel (p 565)

Teaching Objectives

1. To emphasise the need for efficient logistics management;
2. to explore the contribution to logistics of the Channel Tunnel;
3. to consider the benefits of close liaison between a manufacturer and a logistics specialist.

1   Why is a smooth and fast logistics operation essential for Ford in this case?

If the parts moved are essential for the manufacturing process at Ford any delays could result in considerable cost in down-time or in rescheduling production. The more reliable the transportation process the greater the opportunity for JIT deliveries despite the distances covered. This is standard practice within the motor industry and is used by such companies as General Motors to move components from Germany to its UK plant. If the parts are for the after-sales service market, then the faster and more reliable the service, the lower the stocks that would have to be either in transit or held as finished goods at Dagenham. In both cases a fast and reliable service can lower working capital requirements through lower inventory costs. It allows flexibility of transport, within wagon capacity constraints, and new trains can be operated.

2   What difference do you think the opening of the Channel Tunnel made to the European logistics operations of organisations like Ford?

- It enabled closer integration of manufacturing sites on JIT principles
- it enhanced service levels to customers on either side of the Channel through reduced lead times and less risk of delays
- it reduced logistic system costs due to more direct, faster product movement
- it helped organisations to move towards a stock free environment when operating across international borders
- it integrated UK operations more closely into continental Europe
- it opened up new possibilities for long haul bulk freight movement across most of Europe, eastwards to the border with the former Soviet Union (gauge change) and south to Italy.
- long haul rail traffic became highly competitive compared with the road alternative.

3   Why did Ford choose to award a contract for the Valencia - Dagenham logistics function to an outside company rather than handle it themselves? Are there any risks in doing this?

- There is no pan-European transport system. Different gauges and railway authorities means more complex negotiation, and product tracking as well as material handling.
- Transfesa has experience of bulk train operation.
- Material handling is complex because of gauge changes and different handling requirements.
- Experience of administrative and freight forwarding systems is needed.

- It allows Ford to concentrate on its key business, assembly and marketing.
- Ford avoided specific investment in wagons and container handling, but cannot control the consistency of effort and the reliability offered. It is dependent on a third party.
- Ford had to commit to a five year contract, regardless of volume of traffic to be shipped.

4   Transfesa have clearly invested a great deal of capital in this five year contract. What are the potential risks and rewards for them?

Risks:
- Transfesa might need a longer pay back period on specific investment.
- Transfesa is vulnerable to influences beyond its control, for example traffic delays, tunnel fires etc.
- that Ford might attempt to hold or reduce prices through bargaining.

Rewards:
- A long term relationship with major manufacturer
- both parties become equally dependent upon each other.

Marketing in Action Apple Hollyhill (p 537)

Discussion question
How have Apple Macintosh benefited from the development of an integrated logistics system?

Students should be referred to figure 14.2 (p 536). The system developed has:
- Reduced the barriers to ensure close integration between suppliers, manufacturing and field inventory, to ensure lower costs and improved customer service
- meant that there is no manufacturing work in progress
- reduced transit time
- reduced manufacturing costs
- led to just in time delivery from suppliers
- improved customer service
- reduced order processing costs
- created the ability to handle complexity in terms of 500 different product lines in 21 different languages.

The next stage is to move to a stock free environment.

Marketing in Action Benetton (p 539)

Discussion question
Consider the various cost trade-offs in the Benetton system.

- In-house manufacturing - subcontracted manufacturing.
- Order processing costs - work in progress costs: by higher investment in IT the supply chain is closely integrated to minimise inventory levels. Production schedules and customer demand are closely matched to ensure minimal work in progress and finished goods in the manufacturing system.
- Inventory - transport: by adopting one central finished goods warehouse, Benetton not need to carry so much stock due to faster throughput, but transport costs are likely to be higher.
- Single warehouse - local warehouses: although the facilities costs at one highly automated central warehouse are high, this is compensated for by not having a number of other warehouses each requiring stock, facilities, staff etc.
- Outlet - order processing: greater efficiency can be gained by having a highly automated central order processing system rather than a series of less efficient systems at outlet level.

- Local delivery cost - long distance trunking: local delivery costs are higher because there are no intermediaries to sell or stock the product but greater efficiencies can be achieved by having a well organised, planned distribution schedule across international boundaries.
- Direct - indirect distribution channel: direct distribution costs are higher, but no margin needs to be released to intermediaries for stocking or selling the product. The product moves straight into the retail network.

Marketing in Action EDI - A Central Part of the Logistics System (p 552)

Discussion question
Outline the benefits offered by investment in EDI within a logistics system.

- Improved communication.
- Linking demand with production schedules.
- Linking finished goods with the distribution system.
- Flexible purchasing on a standardised system.
- More efficient and faster order processing.
- More control over the supply chain including product tracking.
- Improved handling capacity.
- Ability to handle a wide range of varying products quickly and appropriately.
- Lower stock carrying costs.
- Improved stock management.
- Closer working relationships with suppliers and customers.
- Improved efficiency, cost savings and customer service levels from the above two areas.
- Wider use of JIT.
- More effective handling of international customers.
- Greater consistency in customer service.
- Faster invoicing resulting in improved cash flow.

Marketing in Action Efficient Consumer Response (p 558)

Discussion question:
What barriers might exist in supply chains to prevent ECR's full potential from being realised?

- The willingness of all parties to co-operate for mutual benefit.
- Many distribution channels in the food sector are retailer led.
- The need for manufacturers and retailers to co-operate, to give as well as take in negotiation.
- The dominant bargaining position of many retailers over smaller manufacturers.
- It is noticeable that it is the dominant retailers and large fmcg manufacturers that are taking a keener interest. They may seek to impose changes on other parties.
- If discounters are not seen as a long term threat there may not be same pressure to innovate.
- The level of investment needed to introduce ECR.
- To achieve efficient replenishment systems needs investment in EDI and new product handling capability. This could make it more difficult for smaller manufacturers to compete.
- Packaging and product handling methods may have to change to create greater handling capacity and more flexible movement.
- Ownership of warehouses may be an issue. A saving of 700 hours in stores is the result of an additional 200 hours invested in the warehouse.
- The ability of ECR to influence promotions and product strategy.
- The level of own brand penetration often means that retailer brands set the scene for other brands. This might not be acceptable to branded manufacturers.
- Will retailers be willing to pass on the price savings resulting from improved efficiency?
- Longer shelf life may mean less markdowns near 'sell by' dates.

- Cross-docking may mean a more consistent flow of product where lead times are short, for example as with perishable goods.

SUGGESTED ASSIGNMENTS

- Why is an understanding of PDM and logistics management important for the marketing manager?
- Questions for Discussion 14.3.

Chapter 15
COMMUNICATION AND THE PROMOTIONAL MIX

LECTURE PLAN

A lecture based on this chapter should help the student to:
- Understand the importance of planned communication in a marketing context;
- appreciate the variety and scope of marketing communication objectives;
- explain the use of promotional tools in the communication process;
- identify the factors and constraints influencing the mix of communications tools an organisation uses; and
- define the major methods by which communications budgets are set.

The key sections of this lecture should be:

Introduction (pp 569-571):
- Broad overview of the elements of the promotional mix, including OHP 49, figure 15.1 (p 570) The Elements of the Promotional Mix:
    ⇒ A few comments about what each element covers
    ⇒ each element has different strengths and weaknesses
    ⇒ importance of exploiting synergies between them
    ⇒ importance of creating an integrated and consistent mix.
- Importance of a planned approach to communications.

Communications theory (pp 571-575):
- Definition of communication
- developing a simple model, including OHP 50, figure 15.3 (p 572) A Simple Model of Communication:
    ⇒ Define each element of the model and its role
    ⇒ emphasise the importance of 'shared meaning' in successful communication
    ⇒ relate the model to a marketing example, for instance a television advertisement
    ⇒ emphasise the importance of 'shared meaning' in marketing communications
    ⇒ discuss why shared meaning is hard to achieve in a marketing context.

Communications planning model overview (pp 575-576):
Broad introduction to the rest of the lecture, including OHP 51, figure 15.4 (p 576) The Communications Planning Flow:
- Brief reference to each element
- following sections take each element in detail.

Situation analysis (1): The target market (pp 576-582):

- *Organisational vs. consumer markets:* characteristics and communications implications, including OHT 52, figure 15.5 (p 577) Organisational vs. Consumer Promotional Mix:
  ⇒ How the general balance of the mix changes from organisational to consumer
  ⇒ why it changes
  ⇒ influence of product type, creating grey areas where some consumer communications mixes behave more like organisational ones.
- *Choice of push or pull strategies:* definition of push - pull, including OHT 53, figure 15.6 (p 578) Push - Pull Strategy:
  ⇒ Circumstances in which each might be used
  ⇒ different promotional mixes for each, and why
  ⇒ advantages and disadvantages of each
  ⇒ benefits of a combined push and pull approach.
- *Buyer readiness stages:* cognitive, affective and behaviour stages; strong and weak theories of communication; the role of different promotional mix elements at each stage.

Situation analysis (2): The product (pp 582-586):

- *Organisational vs. consumer products:* refer back to previous discussion of OHT 52.
- *Product life-cycle:* difference in communications tasks at each stage; difference thus in promotional mixes at each stage.

Situation analysis (3): The environment (pp 586-587):

- A brief overview of how each of the STEP factors might impact on communications.

Objectives (pp 587-588):

- Overview of the range of different communications objectives
- their link with customer behaviour
- their implications for promotional mixes.

Strategies (pp 588-592):

- Need to design message content, structure and format
- source credibility, including the VisCAP model
- personal and impersonal media, including OHT 54, table 15.4 (p 592) Comparison of Personal and Impersonal Media for Communication:
  ⇒ Summarise key strengths and weaknesses of each
  ⇒ give examples of their use
  ⇒ summarise what each can achieve for the marketer.

Budgeting (pp 592-594):

- Why budget setting is important
- how it can constrain communications planning
- brief overview of judgemental budget setting methods
- brief overview of data-based budget setting methods
- particular advantages and problems of objective and task budgeting.

Implementation and evaluation (pp 595-596):

- The importance of planned and managed implementation
- importance of monitoring performance
- importance of flexibility.

QUESTIONS FOR REVIEW

15.1   What are the five main elements of the promotional mix? (pp 569-571)

- Advertising
- sales promotion
- personal selling
- public relations
- direct marketing.

15.2   Define encoding and decoding, and discuss their role within the communication model. (pp 571-573)

Encoding is the form into which a message, including the words used, any visual imagery, and the tone and mood of the message. It is important within the communications model because the way in which a message is encoded can increase its chances of being understood by the recipient and acted upon. Decoding is the way in which the recipient perceives and interprets a message and how they feel about it. Regardless of how carefully the sender encoded the message, if the recipient misinterprets it, then the sender is not likely to achieve the expected response.

15.3   How might an understanding of the theoretical model of communication help a marketing manager? (pp 573-575)

The model helps marketing managers to consider seriously:
- The target audience to be reached, their needs and how they might react to marketing communication
- the definition of the message
- the choice of appropriate media
- the desired response
- the kind of feedback needed to determine whether the message has succeeded.

15.4   What are the stages in the marketing communications planning flow? (pp 575-596)

- Situation analysis (environment; target market; product)
- objectives
- strategies
- budgeting
- implementation
- evaluation.

15.5   How does a push strategy differ from a pull strategy, and in what circumstances might each be appropriate? (pp 577-579)

A push strategy concentrates on communication with the next member of the distribution channel, for example manufacturer to wholesaler. It is appropriate where:
- The manufacturer might find it difficult or too expensive to communicate directly with the end consumer
- the manufacturer wants to 'load up' the distribution channel with goods as a competitive defence
- acceptance of a new product by distribution channel members is particularly important.

A pull strategy concentrates on communicating with the end consumer, by-passing other members of the distribution channel. It is appropriate where:
- The manufacturer wants to create consumer demand to prove to other distribution channel members that the product is worth stocking

- the manufacturer wants to stimulate higher volume sales to intermediaries without giving them promotional incentives.

15.6 What are the three broad stages of buyer readiness, and how might the balance of the promotional mix vary between them? (pp 579-582)

1. *Cognitive:* gaining attention and generating awareness. Likely to involve an emphasis on mass market advertising.
2. *Affective:* creating or changing attitudes. Advertising is still a strong influence, but sales promotion can also help to gain trial, and therefore judgement of the product.
3. *Behaviour:* precipitating action through desire for the product. Personal selling becomes a much more effective tool at this stage.

15.7 How and to what extent might the product life cycle concept influence the balance of the promotional mix? (pp 584-586)

- *Introduction:* large spend on the promotional mix to generate awareness and trial of the product; emphasis on advertising and sales promotion to consumers; emphasis on personal selling and sales promotions to intermediaries to ensure product availability.
- *Growth:* perhaps a slightly lower promotional spend, aimed partly at creating new customers and partly at reinforcing image and positive attitudes among repeat buyers; still a strong emphasis on advertising and sales promotion to consumers; still a strong emphasis on personal selling and sales promotions to intermediaries to ensure continued product availability and to defend against competition.
- *Maturity:* perhaps an average promotional spend, with the objective of maintaining or holding a position in the market by reminding customers about the product and reinforcing its image and benefits; main emphasis on advertising with occasional sales promotions to consumers; occasional sales promotions to intermediaries to maintain interest in the product.
- *Decline:* low level of promotional spend to milk the last sales out of the product.

15.8 What are the main categories of marketing communication objectives? (pp 587-588)

- *Cognitive:* affecting consumer needs and awareness.
- *Affective:* affecting perceived brand image and preferences.
- *Behaviour:* affecting consumer actions.
- *Corporate:* affecting the organisation's reputation and standing with various publics.

15.9 What are the six main methods of budget setting? (pp 591-594)

Judgmental methods:
- Arbitrary
- affordable
- percentage of past sales
- percentage of future sales.

Data based methods:
- Competitive parity
- objective and task.

15.10 Why is the post-implementation evaluation of marketing communication plans important? What areas should the evaluation cover? (pp 595-596)

It is important because it analyses:
- To what extent objectives were met
- what went well and what went badly
- whether the exercise was cost effective

- whether the chosen plan was the best one.

The areas it should cover are:

- Effects on sales
- consumer and trade response
- consumer and trade attitudes
- effects on longer term loyalty
- performance and effectiveness of different media, campaigns or techniques
- implementation problems
- budgetary analysis.

QUESTIONS FOR DISCUSSION

15.1   Within a marketing communications model, give three specific examples of noise, outlining how it might disrupt the communications process.

- Physical interference with the communication, for example poor print quality or a distorted broadcast signal. Either of these could destroy part of the message or make the receiver less attentive to it.
- Distractions which divert the receiver's attention away from the message, for example a phone call while television advertisements are on or the arrival of a train preventing them from reading a poster.
- The noise created by competing messages which either overloads the receiver to the point where messages are filtered out or lessens the impact of, or distorts the receiver's perception of any one message.

15.2   How and why might the balance of the promotional mix differ between (a) the sale of a car to a private individual and (b) the sale of a fleet of cars to an organisation for its sales representatives?

In differentiating between these scenarios, students should be addressing the following factors (see also table 15.1, p 576):

- The number of potential customers to be reached
- the complexity of the product and the customer's required benefits from it
- the customer's perceived level of risk
- the frequency of purchase
- the value of the purchase to the seller
- the customer's information needs
- the nature of the decision-making unit involved.

This can then be put into the context of the relative strengths and weaknesses of each element of the promotional mix, using for example figures 15.5 (p 577) and 15.8 (p 582) to help determine the optimum promotional mix.

15.3   For each of the STEP factors of the marketing environment, give three examples of influences on the promotional mix.

Issues raised might include:

Sociocultural:

- Acceptability of certain approaches to advertising
- acceptability of certain personal selling techniques
- the popularity or fashionability of different media, communication techniques, or promotional methods
- the need to avoid offensiveness in terms of portrayal or references to gender, race or creed etc
- the use of stereotypes
- the targeting of vulnerable groups.

Technological:
- The creation of new advertising media
- the potential for handling mass market direct response campaigns
- the ability to communicate direct with millions of customers through database creation and analysis.

Economic and competitive:
- The promotional strategies of competitors
- the relative cost of media
- the changing affluence of the target audience which might, for example, change their media consumption habits, or their attitude towards price based sales promotions.

Political/legal:
- Restrictions on what can be advertised through what media
- restrictions on what product claims can be made
- restrictions on how vulnerable groups, for example children, can be addressed
- differing regulations in different countries.

15.4 **What are the main advantages and disadvantages of objective and task budget setting compared with the other methods?**

Advantages:
- Unlike other methods, it links directly with the product's communications needs
- it looks ahead rather than back
- it does not rely on arbitrary percentages
- it does not make assumptions about direct relationships between sales and advertising
- it spends no more and no less than what is required
- it acknowledges that marketing communication objectives might vary significantly between budgeting periods
- it provides clear justification for the requested budget
- it forces managers to think ahead about what they are really trying to achieve with a product, and what is realistic.

Disadvantages:
- It takes time to calculate
- it relies to some extent on being able to forecast precisely what inputs are needed to achieve specified outputs
- because it is not a routine, formulaic calculation, it might cause a great deal of internal argument.

15.5 **To what extent do you think that the advantages of using a systematic planning process for marketing communications outweigh the disadvantages?**

Advantages:
- Implies a sense of purpose and direction
- ensures common understanding of aims and objectives
- streamlines budget allocations
- justifies resource requests
- establishes priorities
- allocates responsibilities
- defines monitoring and performance criteria.

Disadvantages:
- The planning process can become an end in itself, with the resulting plan largely ignored
- planning can become the territory of specialist planners, with the resulting plan largely ignored
- plans can become too rigid and inflexible to deal with unforeseen circumstances
- plans can be unrealistic if the background analysis is poorly carried out.

Generally, if managers understand the proper role of planning and involve staff at all levels in a thorough and rigourous planning process, the disadvantages can be minimised or overcome completely, and the benefits will outweigh any remaining risks.

CASE STUDY 15.1 Riverdance (p 599)

Teaching Objectives

1. To differentiate clearly between push and pull strategies;
2. to analyse the problems of developing marketing communications strategies for a largely intangible product;
3. to explore the impact of market perceptions of a product on its communications planning.

1   Is the Riverdance phenomenon more of a 'push' or a 'pull' strategy?

The 'product' in this case is the show, the video and associated merchandise. It is, therefore, a combination of a physical product and a service experience and this has an impact on marketing communications objectives and the feasibility of push or pull approaches.

The show:

A push approach is possible for this kind of product through the theatres and their booking and promotional activities. Once a theatre has undertaken to stage the show, it is in its interests as well as those of the show's promoter to ensure full houses. The theatre, therefore, might advertise the show through local media, leaflets and posters on display on the premises, and through mailshots to its regular attendees. A pull strategy, by raising consumers' interest in the Riverdance show, means that they are more likely to seek out tickets for a full length show. A pull approach was used by Riverdance, begun by the impact of the Eurovision sequence and followed by some further appearances. The audience was very large and pan-European and the powerful imagery and dance routines clearly had a major impact in penetrating viewer indifference during a programme full of music. It also appeared to make consumers more receptive to further information generated by the press and further media coverage. This all helped to build demand for the shows and associated products. In the early period, the shows were frequently sold out.

The video and merchandise:

A push strategy would involve considerable effort by the Riverdance promoters to ensure that the video and merchandising was available in retail stores. Heavy point of sale promotion could then be used to generate sales, involving special displays, posters etc From a distribution perspective, Riverdance did make sure that fairly intensive retail distribution was achieved to help sustain interest in the show. As with the show itself, the impetus for a pull strategy was the original Eurovision appearance. Sufficient interest and desire was created among consumers to give retailers confidence that Riverdance videos could sell in significant numbers.

Thus for both the show and the video, a combination of push and pull strategies was necessary, working in synergy with each other.

Supplementary question
Was the Riverdance show a marketing response to customer needs or was it in fact creating interest and demand through its existence?

In one sense, the communication strategy, through the Eurovision exposure, involved a direct push on to the audience of a new product in the hope that it would be acceptable. Interestingly, the following year's Eurovision interval entertainment, a combination of Irish music and a supporting choir of monks failed to make any lasting impact. At best, it could be argued that Riverdance was appealing to latent needs and interest in Irish music and culture, feeding the audience a common Irish stereotype but spiced up with the influences of ballet and Flamenco. Either way, we did not know that we wanted the Riverdance phenomenon until it was thrust upon us! This is a typical problem for music and cultural event organisers and media programmers contemplating radically new departures.

2   Outline the promotional mix likely to have been used to sell the video of the show.

A lot of the generic promotion for Riverdance has effectively been done for it through media coverage and exposure. The impact of the show and its origins created an activated media looking for stories, new angles and coverage. The main problem for Riverdance was to decide on how best to capitalise on that interest. By the time the video was released the interest and demand was already there. The promotional mix was thus likely to be:

Public relations:
- Extensive use of television shows, media events and editorial coverage to inform an alert public that a video had been launched. Extracts may well be shown as part of this media coverage.
- The main artists, Michael Flatley and Jean Butler, both Irish Americans, would need to be very active in guest appearances. The preference would naturally be television given the potential for visual impact.

Advertising:
- The main priority would probably be awareness generation, letting people know that it had been released.
- National newspapers would enable a wide coverage to be gained in a short period of time.

Sales promotion:
- Point of sale promotion would be critical both for passing trade and to guide those consumers making a purposeful search. This could mean special display stands and posters to draw the shopper's attention to the video and stimulate interest and impulse sales.
- Price promotions would not be a priority, because of the lack of any serious competition, and the high level of consumer interest in the show, but a link to a competition for free tickets to a forthcoming show could create some additional interest.

Personal selling:
- Would not play a role in direct sales to the public, but certainly would be necessary to deal with the retail trade. This aspect should not be difficult, because of the high public interest in the show and the difficulty in obtaining tickets in the early period.
- Once negotiations have been completed for price/volume, merchandising support etc, a direct telephone repeat ordering service may be sufficient to maintain retailer stocks.

Direct marketing:
- A possible channel for selling the video could be direct selling through mail order book, video and music clubs.

3   What are the particular problems of marketing communication for a stage show and what kind of promotional mix is this likely to indicate?

A stage show is a service experience that cannot be stored for a later day and requires a regular, changing audience if it is to survive. Some shows fail even though well known artists may be in the cast or line-up. As an experience itself, a reasonable sized and supportive audience is also needed to generate an atmosphere. There are three critical phases in the development of a stage show.

Phase 1, The pre-launch: interest needs to be generated to secure advance bookings. This is especially important if it is a one-off or short lived show rather than the launch of a new show schedules to run for a full season or more.
- *PR:* for theatre and shows, the opinion of the critics in the press and specialist media can be important in stimulating interest and demand for tickets.
- *Advertising:* the show must be advertised sufficiently far in advance of its opening to generate the necessary awareness and interest.

- *Direct marketing:* theatres may send direct mailshots to regular theatre-goers to tell the of the show. Booking offices also have to ensure that the telemarketing operation can cope with the telephone bookings.

Phase 2, the launch: initial audiences and the critics could have a major bearing on its eventual success. In the Riverdance case many of the launch problems in generating awareness and interest were minimised due to the major initial impact. While there were some critics, strong public acceptance had already been secured through the television impact. It may have only been seven minutes long, but in advertising terms, that is the equivalent of an enormous spend on pan-European television. However, a rapid build up of demand is still necessary to exploit fully what could be a fairly limited life cycle. Thus key marketing communication activities could include:
- PR aimed at securing reviews and positive media coverage of the show and interviews with its stars.
- promotion through the ticket reservation agencies and the theatres.
- Further selected advertising, especially in local entertainment guides to attract transient traffic.
- Direct mail to previous customers could encourage return visits or positive word of mouth recommendation to friends.

Rarely do stage shows have such a powerful launch as Riverdance. Some struggle to build audiences especially if the early audience, who can act as opinion leaders, are less than enthusiastic.

Phase 3, the maturity stage: if the show survives the first few months and audience levels are maintained, then the maturity stage may be reached when the more committed audiences have been exhausted and the wider public and occasional theatre-goers may have to be targeted. Sometimes this is achieved by going 'provincial' and taking the show on tour or opening parallel productions in different cities of the world. The length of the maturity stage can vary widely, with some shows lasting only a few months and others, such as Sir Andrew Lloyd Webber's *Cats* running for over ten years without any apparent wane in their popularity. The communication problem in the maturity stage is continually reaching new, wider audiences. It remains to be seen whether Riverdance has the staying power to become a long-term fixture.

4   There has been much debate as to whether Riverdance is 'a showbiz fad' or a serious piece of culture. What difference would it make to the communications planning flow if it was thought to be culture rather than showbiz?

Situation analysis:
- The target audiences are different with culture more likely to appeal to an older, wealthier, more elite audience (this is, of course, a gross generalisation)
- the potential competition will differ, with a showbiz product competing with other mainstream musicals, shows and leisure activities, while a 'culture' positioning will be competing with opera, orchestral concerts, ballet etc
- the potential for 'volume sales' through size of potential audience is greater for something marketed as showbiz
- the potential for spin-off merchandise is greater in the showbiz area
- the product life cycle for showbiz is likely to be shorter, but with a much higher peak and a shorter maturity plateau than culture, which should last longer, peak at a much lower level of sales, but also have a longer, flatter plateau at maturity
- both showbiz and culture, however, offer a high involvement, exciting experience to the customer.

Objectives:
- Product positioning will differ, with showbiz looking for a more mainstream position within the entertainment world
- target audience will differ (as mentioned above)
- targets for awareness and sales will also differ because of the differing target segments.

Strategies:
- Because of the different positioning and the different target segments, different messages and media will be appropriate.

Budgeting:
- If the product is seen as a short-term, short life cycle showbiz event, then a correspondingly short-term, but very large budget might be justified to reach a relatively dispersed mass market
- for a cultural approach, the communication might be more tightly targeted, and involve much lower levels of spend but over a longer period of time.

Implementation and evaluation:
- In either case, once the marketing communications campaign has been designed and implemented, its outcomes need to be carefully monitored to ensure that the right image is being put across and that the required number of tickets or videos are being sold. This is especially important if the life cycle is expected to be short. Any problems or shortfalls have to be spotted and rectified very quickly.

CASE STUDY 15.2 Le Shuttle (p 600)

Teaching Objectives

1. To emphasise the importance of marketing communication;
2. to explore the links between target segments and communications;
3. to examine the impact of the competitive environment on communications decisions.

1   Why is marketing communication so important for Le Shuttle?

There are several reasons why marketing communications is so important for Le Shuttle:
- Establishing the brand name and image of Le Shuttle in its own right, differentiating it clearly from Eurostar and the Channel Tunnel, both of which are owned and operated by different companies.
- Although there is a high level of awareness of the Channel Tunnel, potential customers unfamiliar with Le Shuttle need detailed information on prices, schedules, procedures, booking etc.
- Le Shuttle has to convert existing users of the cross-channel ferries to try Le Shuttle's services and then to become regular customers.
- Le Shuttle needs to show new cross-channel travellers the Le Shuttle option and how it makes the whole process easier and more convenient.
- Le Shuttle is in competition with the ferries, and thus will have to counter their marketing communication messages and if possible 'shout louder' than the ferries.
- The best laid plans are liable to change in a dynamic competitive environment, and thus as the marketing mix is modified (for example, in terms of changing prices, new services, promotional offers) potential customers will have to be told.
- To generate repeat sales cost effectively, Le Shuttle can use a database of previous customers for direct marketing initiatives.

All of these reasons for focusing on marketing communications are designed to achieve the levels of usage and planned market share objectives that are crucial to the financial viability of the company.

2   How have the various elements of the promotional mix been used in Le Shuttle's marketing communications strategy?

- *Advertising:* advertising accounted for the main part of the promotional spend because of the need to reach a wide audience fairly quickly to build traffic. Television dominated the spend (£11m of which over £5m was spent in the UK). This medium was especially important for conveying the excitement and uniqueness of selecting the Le Shuttle option. Press advertising and inserts, although linked to the main theme, were able to go further in giving detailed information on price, short-term promotions and booking procedures.
- *Personal selling:* given the size of the mass audience that had to be reached within a relatively short period of time, the role of personal selling appears to have been negligible. There could have been some direct contact with the travel trade, freight operators and coach operators to negotiate terms and contracts. The main use of personal selling to the general public would be through

contact with staff either on the telephone whilst booking or during the actual travel experience. In this context, personal selling is closely linked to service delivery and customer service.

- *Sales promotion:* the main use of sales promotion has been through special price promotions outside periods of heavy traffic. This helps build to traffic that may not have previously used sea or tunnel options and to encourage customer to travel at off-peak times to even out demand. The promotional 'booze cruises' achieved a similar effect for the ferries. Other sales promotion techniques have been used, such as loyalty schemes to encourage repeat use and linked duty free promotions to broaden the benefits of Le Shuttle compared with the ferries.
- *Direct marketing:* the potential for direct marketing was limited at first until a customer database could be established. This would allow direct communication, but its full potential would take up to one year to become firmly established. Direct mail was used, probably using purchased lists targeted at known cross-channel users. Inbound telemarketing featured from the outset for handling bookings and enquiries etc.
- *Public relations:* this promotional mix element had a major positive and preventative role to play. From a positive perspective, the use of press releases, special launch travel for the media helped to ensure that the broader marketing communication objectives were achieved. However, a lot of time was also spent in countering negative publicity, either in damage limitation or presenting rational explanations for mistakes and operational or financial difficulties. Despite their efforts in this area, the press seemed to consider even relatively minor problems highly newsworthy. If these same problems had occurred on the ferries, the media would not have been interested.

3   What do you think is Le Shuttle's main target segment and how has that influenced its communications?

The main target segment is the existing cross-channel ferry user, whether for holiday, leisure or business use. This target group can be targeted more easily in the UK than perhaps in continental Europe for obvious geographical reasons. Existing users do not need to be told about the attractions and benefits of crossing the Channel. The communications focus with this group is, therefore, the relative benefits of alternative transport modes rather than building traffic in the first place. The message content will cover issues such as:
- Relative price and value for money
- speed
- comfort and safety
- reliability
- frequency of services
- ease of use and booking etc
rather than the pleasures of a day or weekend in France or the UK. By attacking this segment, Le Shuttle pitches itself into a direct confrontation with the ferries as they also regard this segment as core business. There are other segments:
- The novelty user or experimenter who may try the service once and then decide to repeat the experience
- the casual traveller
- those currently travelling by air.
All of these are segments based on the reasons for travel and benefits sought.

4   How has the launch of Le Shuttle changed the ferry companies' approach to communication, and why?

The ferry companies' communication has been geared towards countering the impact of Le Shuttle. Implicit within this has been a range of marketing changes to make the ferry option more attractive. These changes have been designed to slow down the rate of loss of existing customers as well as to attract new segments based either or price or the 'total experience', including shopping and entertainment. All of these propositions need to be communicated to potential and regular customers.

Le Shuttle's launch has, therefore, stimulated a raised level of marketing communications activity from the ferry companies:

- Spend has had to increase in line with the threat and the effort to retain share.
- Heavy price discounting is designed to tempt customers to trade off any extra time saved by using the tunnel against a lower price. Those valuing speed and convenience will probably still switch to Le Shuttle, whereas leisure travellers and budget conscious groups might think twice before changing.
- A greater emphasis on building the quality image of the 'cruise' experience and the total service package offered by the ferries. The on-board duty free and other shopping facilities are often especially attractive to the leisure traveller, which, along with the possibility of the walk on deck, are in stark contrast with the enclosed space of the tunnel.

These messages have to be communicated to an audience and to a degree that is not drowned out by the high launch spend associated with Le Shuttle.

5   **What are the potential risks of focusing on advertising in particular as a major competitive weapon in a head-to-head battle between two large operators such as Le Shuttle and P&O?**

It is considered that Le Shuttle will ultimately win the cross-channel battle because of speed and reliability. The problem for Le Shuttle is that it is a battle that must be won because of its large fixed investment, whereas if the worst came to the worst, a ferry could be moved on to other routes elsewhere. Ferry services from Portsmouth to Le Havre, Weymouth - Cherbourg and Plymouth - Roscoff are considered to be reasonably immune from the effects of Le Shuttle because of their distance from the tunnel. Given this major difference, the ferries can be as disruptive, in a marketing sense, as they like. With high fixed costs in the short-term, heavy price promotion and aggressive advertising can be used to generate as much traffic as possible with no real concern for the longer-term impact. This is especially true while the duty free loophole exists which makes the margins from on-board retailing and catering highly attractive and takes some of the pressure off generating revenue from ticket prices. The main danger arising from an advertising war is the potentially escalating cost, especially if both sides choose to match the other's spend. This, combined with lower ticket prices, will inevitably depress profit margins without necessarily generating significantly higher volumes (see figure 11.1, p 419). That, in the long run, could hurt Le Shuttle more than P&O because of the difference between mobile and fixed investments.

Marketing in Action A Model Market (p 578)

Discussion question
Evaluate the communications strategy adopted by Airfix to promote its model range.

- *Target audience:* although the 8-14 year olds are the main target group, given the level of product complexity and the competing claims for teenagers' attention, it is likely that the actual buyers might well be adults, buying for themselves as a hobby or as gifts. This could be important for message design. With the 8-14 year olds, the message is likely to be that Airfix can offer an opportunity to be creative, to achieve and be entertained, whereas adults might prefer to be reminded how much fun building an Airfix actually was!
- *Push or pull strategy:* there has been a deliberate switch to 'pull' rather than 'push' with the decision to pursue consumer orientated advertising. However, trade support will still be necessary with display stands, in-store promotions and catalogues to achieve maximum impact at the point of sale. Airfix will need to think this area through very carefully to create a balance between push and pull that stimulates both intermediaries and consumers.
- *Marketing environment:* this has become much tougher because of new entrants and the changing nature of indirect competition. There is a need to emphasise traditional brand values and build on loyalty to create a strong brand image.

- *Product:* the basic product concept has changed little over many years. Only individual models rise and fall in popularity. The move to the complete kit, including accessories and paints is welcome although care must be taken with comparison with alternatives.
- *Main objectives:* the main objectives are not clearly specified and still appears related to reminder and brand recognition rather than stimulating interest.
- *Communication strategies:* the means of getting the message across appears dubious. The role of the 'human model' must be questioned in terms of the perceptions and interests of the target audience. Whether the message is powerful enough also needs to be questioned as many alternative options exist for escapism for the target age group, not least of which is the home computer. It is perhaps questionable how effective media advertising would be given the diversity and non-specialist nature of the target audience. Perhaps more should be spent on push and pull at the point of sale including displays, packaging, free exciting catalogues, special offers etc to cut through the 'noise' of competitors' pressure on the target audience.
- *Budgets:* it is difficult to evaluate the relative significance of the spend, but in media advertising terms, £500,000 is unlikely to go far considering the scale of the communication task and the need to rebuild image and attitudes afresh.

Marketing in Action Hooper's Hooch (p 584)

Discussion question
Should Hooper's Hooch proceed with the same communications mix now that the product has been successfully launched?

The approach adopted for launch could be considered to have been deliberately controversial in order to gain attention and trial. The media interest, in part generated through careful public relations to raise the ethical debate could have worked to the advantage of Hooper's Hooch. It even helped to create a cult following of early adopters to stimulate further demand by word of mouth. The shift towards heavier media advertising that has now already started seems inevitable. Although the controversial theme is continued with the packaging, the launch of competitors' 'me too' brands means that more attention has to be given to branding and reinforcing the positive attributes of the Hooper's Hooch brand. Posters may eventually have to give way to other targeted media to reach the young adult market and if appeal broadens, the chosen media will have to reach the majority. The manufacturers have been able to generate considerable interest to date, but as the novelty wears off and repeat business becomes the main priority, packaging, sales promotion and flavour variants may become more significant. The brand will certainly have to be well supported through the promotional mix to maintain its impetus and its share.

Marketing in Action Olive Oil (p 589)

Discussion question
Were the agencies correct in their belief that marketing olive oil is a fairly straightforward task?
The marketing strategy for promoting generic products as opposed to specific brands is the same to the extent that it can follow similar decision principles. The differences lie in the emphasis and content of the message. In this case, the main differences would be in the message content, and this is where there appears to be a flaw in EU thinking. Different EU nations clearly have different traditions, experience and usage of olive oil. In the Mediterranean countries, per capita consumption already appears to be high, while in northern Europe, including the UK, the market is growing yet consumption and the level of understanding appear still to be much lower. This is reflected in the competitive state of different EU markets.

The 'EU equity and compromise' approach to spending across each EU nation does not seem to be appropriate. The communication task in the heavy usage countries may be best handled at brand level rather than generically, as manufacturer brands compete with own label and are already generating supplier marketing activity, one of the EU's broad objectives. A general campaign would probably do little to increase overall consumption or to change attitudes and behaviour in the use of olive oil in a relatively mature market. In the northern countries there may be a case for a generic campaign to inform a public which still appears to be experimenting and does not have the in-depth appreciation of the benefits of using olive oil. Stimulating generic demand in other food areas such as milk, butter, cheese meat and eggs have had some benefit in increasing total sales, from which all producers benefit. The campaign could provide new information that could guide consumer choice towards olive oil.

It is not only the targeting and objectives of a pan-European campaign that would have to be carefully considered. The mix of activities would also vary according to the two markedly different segments. Advertising in the media, whether in specialist cookery or women's magazines or more general media would enable the benefits of olive oil's use to be communicated. This might not, however, be strong enough to influence preferences and behaviour, especially when typical brand advertising expenditure in the fmcg sector is considered. Public relations, books, television cooking shows, menu tips and in-store tasting could all be used to encourage a wider appeal among light users. The healthy food aspect could also be communicated though this medium along with information about the types of oils used for different cooking purposes. In the heavy user situation, again public relations and promotions could be useful in highlighting even more versatile cooking applications using the product. However, the relative impact is likely to be much lower than in the growth segment where attitudes and preferences are still being formed.

Marketing in Action Crocodile: Will Consumers Snap it Up? (p 590)

Discussion question
Is the mixed push and pull strategy appropriate for The Freedown Food Company?

The main problems in promotional terms for Freedown are generating awareness of the new meat alternatives, and persuading a wider range of customers to (at least) try the products. This will be essential for retaining and expanding supermarket distribution. The barrier to development, in addition to the normal difficulties of a small supplier trying to make an impact in the fmcg sector, such as promotional spend needed, gaining shelf space etc, are likely to be related to overcoming consumer ignorance and prejudice about eating 'unusual' meats. Offering these exotic meats through some restaurants and selected butchers can reach a select group of innovators, prepared to innovate and explore new tastes, but generating a wider, more mass market appeal among less experimental consumers is a very different task.

In targeting the mass market, a pull strategy alone would probably be well beyond the resources of Freedown, given the cost of large scale promotion. Careful use of PR through experts and specialist media editorial may stimulate some interest, but word of mouth recommendation is likely to be just as important in spreading a willingness to try. A push strategy would need the full co-operation of the retail trade. The large supermarkets may need some convincing if Freedown relied on them to promote a new product to a potentially dubious audience. Even Tesco is likely to experiment with the product in a few stores before committing itself to more widespread adoption. Supermarkets do not want difficult or slow sellers.

Many of the actions taken by Freedown are, therefore probably appropriate. The mixed approach provides synergy between the push and pull elements. Retailers might be more confident if a supporting merchandising and promotional campaign is planned. Freedown may thus have to consider more point of sale activity. In-store testing, information sheets, sample packs, and special price promotions may also need to be introduced to support the retail store (if they want it!) and to encourage trial. The process of information dissemination and eventual trial and adoption could, however, become protracted and Freedown will have to ensure that the retailers do not run out of patience.

- Questions for Discussion 15.5
- Compare and contrast the effectiveness of judgemental budget setting methods with data-based methods.

Chapter 16
ADVERTISING

LECTURE PLAN

A lecture based on this chapter should help the student to:
1. Define advertising and its role within the promotional mix;
2. appreciate the complexities of formulating advertising messages and how they are presented for both print and broadcast media;
3. differentiate between types of advertising media, understanding their relative strengths and weaknesses;
4. appreciate the role played by advertising agencies and the importance of cultivating good agency - client relationships; and
5. understand the stages in the management process of managing advertising activities.

The key sections of this lecture should be:

Introduction (pp 604-609):
- Definition of advertising
- pioneering advertising
- competitive advertising
- reminder and reinforcement advertising
- institutional advertising
- the role of advertising within the marketing mix.

The advertising message (pp 609-612):
- The importance of understanding the audience
- link between message and objectives
- problems with message execution.

Creative appeals in advertising (pp 612-618):
- Rational appeals
- emotional appeals
- product-orientated appeals
- customer-orientated appeals
- communicating appeals.

Print presentation (pp 618-622):
Copywriting, including OHP 55, Illustration from p 620, Shogun Advertisement:
- Importance of good headlines
- how the advertisement sells the benefits
- how the advertisement communicates to the target reader
- how the advertisement creates credibility for itself

- how the message remains simple, clear and concise.
- importance of print layout.

This section could be omitted, and students encouraged to read the material for themselves.

Broadcast presentation (pp 622-624):
- Stages in developing a broadcast advertisement
- guidelines for attracting and retaining attention.

This section could be omitted, and students encouraged to read the material for themselves.

Advertising media (pp 624-633):
- *Media terms:* reach, ratings, frequency, OTS.
- *Television:* advantages; disadvantages; trends and developments.
- *Radio:* advantages; disadvantages; trends and developments.
- *Cinema:* advantages; disadvantages; trends and developments.
- *Magazines:* advantages; disadvantages; trends and developments.
- *Newspapers:* advantages; disadvantages; trends and developments.
- *Hoardings, transport and outdoor media:* advantages; disadvantages; trends and developments.

Advertising agencies (pp 633-636):
- Types of agency: full and limited service.
- Choosing an agency, including OHP 56, figure 16.2 (p 634) Criteria for Selecting an Advertising Agency:
  $\Rightarrow$ Overview of the criteria
  $\Rightarrow$ importance of a 'comfortable' match
  $\Rightarrow$ importance of trust and good communication.

This section could be omitted, and students encouraged to read the material for themselves.

Developing a campaign (pp 636-645):
This section is based on OHP 57, figure 16.3 (p 637) Stages in Developing an Advertising Campaign:
- *Campaign responsibilities:* ensuring that an appropriate range of managers are involved and that tasks and responsibilities are clearly defined.
- *Target audience:* ensuring deep understanding of the target audience.
- *Campaign objectives:* defining what the campaign is to achieve in line with the overall marketing plan.
- *Setting budgets:* refer back to the previous section on budgets.
- *Media selection and planning:* selecting appropriate media, including OHP 58, figure 16.4 (p 640) Factors Influencing Media Selection:
  $\Rightarrow$ Discuss effect of each factor
  $\Rightarrow$ problems of balancing out conflicts, for example between budgets and desired reach
  $\Rightarrow$ importance of external factors (for instance competition) as well as internal factors (for instance campaign objectives).
- *Advertising development and testing:* role of pre-testing and post-testing.
- *Implementation and scheduling:* implementing the campaign and scheduling, including OHT 59, figure 16.7 (p 643) Factors Influencing Advertising Schedules:
  $\Rightarrow$ Discuss scope of each factor
  $\Rightarrow$ potential conflicts between them
  $\Rightarrow$ their effects on reach and frequency choices
  $\Rightarrow$ their effects on drips and bursts choices.
- *Evaluation:* importance of interim and post-campaign tests and evaluation; aided recall; unaided recall; attitude tests; enquiry tests; sales tests.

QUESTIONS FOR REVIEW

16.1   In what ways can advertising support the other elements of the promotional mix? (pp 604-609)

- It can be used as part of a PR campaign to reinforce corporate image
- it can be used as a means of informing customers about sales promotion activities and of distributing small free samples and coupons
- it generates awareness among potential customers of an organisation's image and products to pave the way for sales representatives
- it is a vital part of direct marketing as a means of generating responses.

16.2   What is comparative advertising and what are the risks of using it? (pp 606-607)

Comparative advertising is a form of competitive advertising that makes direct comparisons between the advertiser's product and those of the competition. The risks are of:
- Making unreasonable claims that cannot be proven
- provoking aggressive responses from competitors
- making the consumer think more seriously about the competition
- failing to differentiate the advertiser's produce from the competition on criteria that actually matter to the target audience.

16.3   What are the different ways in which product-orientated appeals can be used? (pp 613-615)

Product-orientated appeals can show the consumer:
- How to solve a problem
- a comparison between different products
- a slice of life, showing how the product fits in
- hard information and proof through news, testimonials, or advertorials.

16.4   Define reach and frequency. Why might there be a conflict between them in practice? (pp 625-626)

Reach is the percentage of the target market exposed to the message at least one during the relevant period. Frequency is the average number of times each member of the target audience reached is likely to have been exposed to the advertisement There might be conflict because it would be very expensive to achieve high levels of both reach and frequency. The organisation then has to decide which one has to have priority.

16.5   What can radio offer as an advertising medium to a small business? (pp 628-629)

- It has local reach that might well coincide with a small business' catchment area
- it is relatively cheap in terms of both production costs and airtime
- it can achieve high frequency levels.

16.6   What advantages might cinema advertising have over television? (pp 626-629)

- A captive audience
- a clearly defined and profiles audience
- a different audience every time the same film is shown
- high attention levels
- good quality sound and pictures
- can sometimes screen advertisements that would not be permitted on television.

16.7   In what ways can magazines be a better advertising medium than newspapers? (pp 629-632)

- Magazines have a longer life than newspapers
- a magazine tends to be passed around a number of people
- magazines are read more carefully and when the reader is relaxed
- magazines can be tightly segmented
- magazines can have more international appeal
- reproduction quality can be very high.

16.8   What are the relative advantages and disadvantages of (a) full service advertising agencies, (b) limited service agencies and (c) handing advertising in-house? (pp 633-634)

a)   Because everything is within one agency, full service agencies:
- Can undertake a wide range of advertising tasks
- are easier to manage and control
- allow a strong and close agency-client relationship to develop
- bring a fresh objective view to the client's advertising problems,

but:
- The client might miss out on the special creativity of small specialist agencies
- if the relationship sours, the client risks losing the full range of services.

b)   Because they are specialists, limited service agencies:
- Can become extremely good at what they do
- bring a fresh objective view to the client's advertising problems,

but:
- The client has more management and co-ordination to do in bringing the services of a number of agencies together
- the more agencies that are involved, the greater the chance of breaches of confidentiality.

c)   In-house advertising:
- Retains ultimate control over the whole advertising process
- prevents over-dependency on external bodies

but:
- The right expertise might not be available
- the advertising approach may become too blinkered
- such a department could be expensive to maintain.

16.9   Describe the stages in developing an advertising campaign. (pp 636-645)

- *Deciding on campaign responsibilities:* who is authorised to make what decisions? Who should be responsible for implementing and managing what tasks?
- *Selecting the target audience:* defining and profiling in detail the audience at which the communication is to be aimed.
- *Defining campaign objectives:* setting out objectives which are specific, measurable and time related.
- *Setting campaign budgets:* ensuring that the resources are available or will be made available in order to allow the objectives to be achieved. If not, then objectives might have to be prioritised.
- *Media selection and planning:* choosing the appropriate media, the relevant vehicles within each media type, and the dates, times and spaces required.
- *Advertising development and testing:* creating the advertisements themselves, and testing them to ensure that they have the desired effect.
- *Implementation and scheduling:* finalising the advertisements and delivering them through the chosen media to the target audience.
- *Campaign evaluation:* assessing whether the campaign objectives have been achieved and analysing any variations from what was expected.

16.10   What can an advertiser gain from pre-testing advertisements? (pp 641-642)

The advertiser can check whether:
- The content is appropriate
- the message is understood by the target audience
- the advertisement creates the desired images and attitudes
- the advertisement will positively affect the target audience's behaviour
- any adjustments need to be made.

QUESTIONS FOR DISCUSSION

16.1   Find examples of advertising that uses (a) a rational appeal and (b) a fear appeal. Why do you think the advertisers have chosen these approaches?

The chosen advertisements should show that the student understands the difference between rational and fear appeals. Points that might be raised in discussing why these approaches have been chosen might include consideration of:
- The nature of the product
- the target audience
- the core message
- the extent to which the advertiser wants to make an emotional impact on the target audience
- the extent to which the objectives include changing attitudes.

16.2   What are the guidelines for good copy for a print advertisement? Find a print advertisement and discuss the extent to which it conforms with those guidelines.

The guidelines are:
- Sell the benefits
- communicate to the individual
- be credible
- keep the message clear, simple and concise
- clearly identify the sponsor of the advertisement.

The student's discussion of the chosen advertisement should show an appreciation of how all these elements work within the advertisement. The student should also present a critical analysis of the advertisement's strengths and weaknesses with due respect for the target audience and the nature of the product.

16.3   Find a current advertising campaign that uses both television and print media. Why do you think both media are being used? To what extent is each medium contributing something different to the overall message?

Issues that might be raised include:
- Extending reach and frequency
- maximising cost effectiveness
- the print advertisement can include more detail
- the television advertising can capitalise on music and movement
- the print advertisement can be used to remind the target audience of the television version or ...
- ... the two media can give slightly different messages that create synergy
- between them, they can offer a potential customer a range of different direct response mechanisms.

16.4   Find out the cost of (a) a 30-second advertising slot on your regional commercial television channel at 8 p.m. on a weekday evening, (b) a 30-second slot at the same time on your local commercial radio station, (c) a full-page advertisement in your local newspaper, and (d) a full-page advertisement in a national daily newspaper.

This discussion question encourages students to explore their own local and national media scene. They might need guiding towards relevant reference works such as BRAD. They can also be encouraged to analyse why the price differences have arisen and the extent to which students think that advertisers actually pay the stated price.

16.5 Develop a checklist of criteria against which a prospective client could assess advertising agencies. Which criterion would you say is the most important, and why?

Relevant criteria include:
- The size of the agency relative to the client
- the agency's location and accessibility
- the agency's ability to provide the type of advertising and related services that the client is seeking
- the extent to which the agency specialises in advertising in the client's markets
- the agency's history and track record
- the extent to which the client feels that the agency is compatible with them and can work with them
- the agency's ability to manage itself and its clients' business efficiently and cost effectively.

The extent to which any one of these criteria is more important than the rest is debatable, but nevertheless, students should be encouraged to discuss why these criteria are important and how they work with each other.

CASE STUDY 16.1 Nike (p 648)

Teaching Objectives

1. To examine the problems of communicating with youth audiences;
2. to analyse the problems of using celebrities in advertising;
3. to explore the reasons why an advertiser might not wish to use straightforward product-based imagery.

1 Why do you think the youth market is a particularly difficult one for advertisers to communicate with?

The advertisers' key objective is to reach the youth audience in order to generate brand awareness and build brand image and credibility. But:
- 'The youth market' is not homogeneous
- short attention spans, selective attention, and selective perception mean that the audience will screen out some advertisements and 'misinterpret' others
- the target audience may have limited and narrow television viewing habits, as there are many other leisure pursuits competing for their attention
- there may be low readership of traditional print media outside highly specialised vehicles
- the youth market is generally better informed and more judgmental of advertising
- the youth market has developed deep cynicism over advertising approaches and claims
- many organisations are trying to reach this audience and thus there is a lot of competitive 'noise'.

Thus the advertiser is having to compete hard for youth's attention and has to develop its messages carefully, creatively and originally in order to attract attention in the first place, and then to avoid patronising the audience or alienating them. Many organisations, however, think that the pursuit is worthwhile. If they can attract young customers, then they hope to keep them brand loyal throughout their lives.

2 What are the potential advantages and disadvantages of using a celebrity such as Eric Cantona in advertising?

Advantages:
- Credibility by association; if the product is good enough for him/her, then it's good enough for me
- the perceived power and uniqueness of the celebrity might rub off onto the product
- it reinforces the authenticity of the message
- it identifies the product with the emotions of the sport
- for products such as Nike's, the use and wearing of the product creates further exposure
- it creates an element of excitement and helps the advertisement to grab attention
- it helps to provide strong visual images
- it provides useful continuity across different media and marketing activities, for example posters, press, television, competitions etc
- it can tie in with sponsorship.

Disadvantages:
- The product becomes linked with the fortunes of the celebrity. Poor form, bad behaviour, not being selected for the team etc reflect badly on the product
- it can be very expensive
- the communications focus could become centred on the celebrity rather than on longer term brand attributes
- the creative approach can become limited and rather boring
- if many competitors in a market use celebrities, then the impact is less and the competitive environment simply becomes a battle of the big names
- some celebrities are somewhat 'promiscuous' in that they will advertise anything and everything. Again, this lessens the impact for any one advertiser
- few celebrities have widespread appeal and universal approval. The advertiser thus suffers from negative attitudes towards the star as well as benefiting from the positive ones.

Supplementary question

What current advertising campaigns are you aware of that use celebrities? Why do you think those particular celebrities were chosen for those particular campaigns? To what extent are these campaigns at risk from the disadvantages you have just outlined in question 2?

3   **Why do you think Nike chose not to focus more on product-orientated advertising, for example showing the shoes and explaining their technical superiority over the competition?**

Leisure shoes are not purchased on technical criteria but fashion and lifestyle reinforcement. Nike were not interested in just the sports shoe market, but in the wider fashion/lifestyle segment. This meant an appeal beyond the obvious applications and the technical product features relating to grip, comfort, stress etc. Nike has been established long enough in the market for its technical quality standards to be largely assumed. The majority of the target audience would, therefore, not be interested in an advertising approach that was essentially product orientated. Any such campaign might well be ignored and make little impact as being too 'cold' and technical. Direct comparison with competing products on technical grounds would be particularly dangerous, because:
- If the audience is not that interested in technical features, then the comparison is meaningless and boring
- it might serve to make the audience more interested in technical features and dilute the Nike lifestyle image
- it implies that Nike is basically on a par with its competitors, whereas Nike would prefer to be seen as being in a class of its own
- it invites an aggressive response from the competition.

The success of Nike's campaign has been the appeal to the emotional and aspirational aspects of wearing Nike, not the technical composition of the product. By moving towards an emotional approach, there is considerably more scope for creative advertising. Whatever product information is required can be gained at the point of sale, and the role of advertising is to concentrate on developing positive connotations and attitudes towards the Nike brand name. This involves developing a strong image and positioning in the consumer's mind. This would be difficult with an audience like the youth market, as discusses in question 1 above.

4   Analyse the 'forces of darkness' advertisement in terms of its target audience, its objectives, the message itself, and the creative appeal used. Can the use of this kind of frightening or controversial imagery be justified?

In terms of the advertisement itself:

Target audience: the youth market is the main target segment for Nike, and thus for reasons outlined earlier, a very powerful approach is necessary. The audience is probably also interested in sport, particularly from the spectator's view of it as a powerful emotional social experience.

Objectives: to create and reinforce brand awareness and loyalty to Nike and to inject strong emotional values into the Nike brand name.

Message: that Nike is an essential tool in a hero's armoury to help good to triumph over evil. The implications are that:

- Nike is a quality brand
- Nike is a tough, uncompromising and rugged brand that wins through
- Nike is the choice of top professionals
- Nike enhances personal status and image
- Nike is on the side of 'the good guys'
- Nike understands the soul of sport as well as the mechanics of it.

Creative appeal:

- The use of black and white and frightening monsters emphasises deep-seated attitudes and desires for good to win through.
- The choice of a soccer theme and the coincidence of the campaign's timing with the European Cup capitalised on the build-up of excitement before the tournament.
- The ability to emphasise different players depending on the country in which the advertisement was screened ensured that local heroes with whom the audience could identify were prominent.
- The life and death battle between good and evil reflects the attitude that many fans have towards soccer matches!
- The whole sequence makes compelling viewing with such overt and stunning symbolism and imagery that the retention of viewer attention throughout the sequence is almost guaranteed. It is also transferable across national boundaries with little loss of meaning.

In terms of the use of frightening imagery:

There are widely differing views on this subject ranging from highly liberal 'anything goes' attitudes to almost Victorian standards of public decency that would stop most advertisements that use any hints of sex, violence or anarchy. There is a serious issue, however, focusing on the impact of such advertising on young minds. Television viewing is very difficult to control and "the forces of darkness" advertisement could cause distress to young children. Advertisers do have some responsibility in that regard.

The cinema was also used for the Nike advertisement, but in cinema, the audience profile is more predictable and such an advertisement can easily be restricted to audiences over 15 years old. On television, however, despite the 9 p.m. watershed, as many children have televisions in their bedrooms and access to videos, it is almost impossible to restrict viewing of advertisements. Even among the target audience, there is the danger that the message could become distorted. One person's enemy is another's friend. The symbolism of one group annihilating another could easily reinforce conflict behaviour between rival groups. It is questionable, however, just what impact one advertising campaign can have when the public is exposed to a wide variety of messages that could be misinterpreted or seen as encouraging anti-social behaviour.

CASE STUDY 16.2 Anti-drugs Advertising (p 649)

Teaching Objectives

1. To explore the problems of using advertising for public health education;
2. to examine how one campaign worked in terms of its advertising imagery;
3. to consider the problems of reaching different target audiences through advertising.

1 **What messages are the anti-drugs campaigns trying to get across, and what are the problems of turning those messages into advertisements?**

The messages about the dangers of taking drugs are targeted at one of four possible audiences:

1. Prevention of drug use among non-users, mainly young people:
Message: This could be considered a high priority group, as the best way to beat drugs is perhaps never to start. This means generating awareness of what the drugs journey can lead to. The message needs to show how low-level, what could be regarded as harmless experimentation can end in tragedy. Sometimes, actual examples of case histories can show the journey while information campaigns can indicate the side effects on the way.
Difficulties in conveying the message: youth's natural curiosity and taste for experimentation, self-expression and group conformity are strong countervailing forces. The arrogance of youth also tends to lead them into thinking that "this will never happen to me". The message may thus be screened out as irrelevant.
2. Soft drug takers, mainly young people, but not exclusively
Message: the "know the score campaign" outlined the possible side effects, even when the habit is regarded as being under control. The focus on general appearance, attractiveness to the opposite sex, and general health could make the audience look at the problem in a different way and lead to some restraint. It is hoping to appeal to self-interest and youth's natural anxiety to belong and be accepted by peers.
Difficulties in conveying the message: the direct messages may be screened out as not being relevant. "It won't happen to me" or "I have things under control" are classic lines for self denial of the health messages being sent. Peer group pressure and word of mouth counter arguments can be powerful nullifying forces.
3. Hard drug takers, tend to be younger but can be older
Message: The serious dangers of moving into hard drugs. The 'Heroin screws you up' campaign typifies the dramatic and hard hitting messages needed.
Difficulties in conveying the message: existing hard drug takers are likely to screen out messages that they find uncomfortable. Denial is almost certain and a resentment of being preached at. If the habit is established, then sheer despair and apathy could block out the advertising messages.
4. Parents (especially mothers) and advisors who can assist in prevention
Message: It could happen to your child. How to spot the signs and what to do about it.
Difficulties in conveying the message: many parents do not want to believe that their children are capable of getting involved in drugs and so may not take the message seriously.

2 **Do you think the message approaches described in the case are appropriate?**

The major difficulty with the campaign is the need to communicate with at least four different audiences. Many members of the target audiences might have a cynical view of advertising and will not follow traditional media vehicles. The soft sell approach seems sensible because:

- If the audience perceives the examples as being too extreme, they will ignore them as irrelevant to them
- the audience would also reject deeply boring or conceptual technical, legal or moral arguments
- the messages have to talk the same language as the audience and ensure that they make the necessary impact rather than being wasted

- it could be argued that the dramatic images of pimples and poor hair condition, because they are perceived as closer to the realms of reality, could have a greater impact on the target audience than images of extreme drug addicts.

The decision not to glamourise drug takers at parties is also important, and the black and white images perhaps highlight the starkness of the message. There are dangers in information provision in that it assumes an open audience willing to receive the messages. This may not be the case. Some of the advertising must be aimed at assisting problem recognition and overcoming attitudinal barriers rather than information provision. That is the second phase in seeking to change attitudes and behaviour, the whole purpose of these campaigns.

3   What media are best for communicating these messages to the target audience, and why?

All media used have to be private and relevant to the individual. Family viewing is a non-starter. The problem with traditional media is that they cannot be assumed to be reaching the target audience.

- *Television advertisements* have to be carefully scheduled to hit the audience during more popular programmes, without drifting into times that could be seen to raising the profile of drug taking with younger, impressionable non-users. The messages using this medium have to be simple, non-glamourous and designed to gain attention.
- *Print media* can convey more complex messages, often through better targeted media vehicles. The problem is that only a small number of specialist media are actually read by the target audience, but once these have been identified, the messages can be more uncompromising and harder hitting than perhaps would be permitted on television.
- *Posters and information leaflets* at schools and colleges are essential for reach the audience in forums where they congregate. This could be followed up by 'personal selling' involving health advisors and counsellors who are trained to deal sympathetically and non-judgmentally with the target audience.
- *Radio* is also used as this can reach the target audience effectively and convey simple messages with impact and imagination. Radio can also be used for more informed discussion, involving peer groups in a non-confrontational manner.

4   Why is it more difficult to make a success of a public health advertising campaign than an ordinary consumer product campaign?

The peculiarities of public health campaigns are that:
- They are trying to tackle complex major social problems on limited budgets
- they do not have the clear purpose of building brand image and loyalty
- there is a lack of receptiveness to highly personal messages
- there is a lack of institutional credibility i.e. this is 'authority' telling us what to do
- they involve a political dimension, trying to appeal to the interests of many groups
- consumers do not want to be educated
- there are interested parties i.e. drug pushers and perhaps some more liberal-minded individuals within the environment opposing the very basis of the concept being proposed. This does not tend to happen in most consumer markets; there are no lobby groups out trying to counteract manufacturers' advertising by promoting the message that baked beans are essentially a bad thing and you should not buy them!
- The benefits of adopting anti-drugs messages are not immediately obvious, and indeed listening to the messages may actually cause short-term pain
- there is a high level of public ignorance to be overcome
- the 'product' being sold is essentially intangible, and is rather negative and depressing and about self-restraint. The message is "don't" and "stop". With normal consumer products, the audience is buying positive benefits and listening to encouraging messages such as "indulge yourself" and "if you want it, then have it".

Marketing in Action Foden Trucks (p 606)

Discussion question
Is comparative advertising as adopted by Foden a sound basis for an advertising campaign?

This is a controversial area. The comparative approach is widely used in the USA, but has had far less impact in the UK and the rest of Europe. There have been some noticeable exceptions such as Flymo vs. Qualcast in the lawn mower market, but generally, more subtle image and benefit based advertising has dominated. There are some good reasons why comparative advertising might not be an effective strategy:

- It invites retaliation and an equally aggressive response that may cause a downward spiral with ever increasing budgets
- the potential customer may not appreciate such a negative approach
- it does not emphasise the positive benefits of product to build loyalty
- it indirectly creates more awareness of the competitor's offering.

In the Foden case a very careful selective approach has been developed to build upon perceived brand strengths, in this case the cost of spares. Iveco in the same magazine suggest in their advertisement that Foden are much poorer on fuel efficiency. Which of the two will win the comparative battle depends on what the target market's priorities are in terms of benefit criteria, although both companies appear to be targeting the value for money group.

Marketing in Action Pan-European Advertising - East and West (p 611)

Discussion question
Consider some of the barriers facing organisations such as Pizza Hut and Xerox when developing pan-European campaigns covering both east and west.

Pan-European campaigns have only become a feasible proposition relatively recently. The added complexity of Central and Eastern Europe may not suit all organisations. In organisational markets, the convergence between east and west might be quicker, because organisational markets:

- Are more exposed to international suppliers and customers
- consist of many international companies operating across Europe
- are involved in international technology transfer
- involve smaller numbers of major customers to be contacted and influenced
- are less dominated by advertising and more reliant on personal selling and sales literature dominated.

However there are problems in organisational markets because of:

- Staff and management training needs
- developing after-sales quality that is consistent and can meet claims
- markets varying in sensitivity to price
- buying sophistication is only slowly emerging.

In consumer markets more difficulties may be experienced, such as:

- Wide variations in disposable incomes, lifestyles, culture and eating habits
- inconsistencies in media availability
- language differences are more pronounced
- different levels of sophistication in market information
- different retail and distribution systems and levels of sophistication.

However there are benefits in broadening the geographic scope of advertising, such as:

- Reduced costs in creative development and production
- the development of some segments that are transnational, for example the Pizza Hut target audience.

Marketing in Action Christian Cable TV (p 638)

Discussion question
Is there real potential for advertisers in using targeted media such as Christian TV?

A number of factors need to be considered when selecting specialist media. These include:
- Their match with the target audience and segment
- their ability to achieve frequency impact through media
- the need to be sure how well researched viewing profile actually is
- the additional reach possible with using highly specialist media
- the match between the mood and style of the medium and the nature of the message
- the danger of spreading the advertising spend over too wide a range of media
- the additional benefits and costs associated with advertising in a specialist medium
- the profile of other advertisers using the medium and whether that will add to or subtract from credibility.

The Christian Channel appears to offer positive benefits in terms of association, but the audience may be diffuse i.e. the 70 per cent who believe in God. The common thread linking the medium's audience, which is at present uncertain, is likely to relate to common values and attitudes to certain types of advertising approaches. The Ark 2 experience suggests that the main attraction is for advertisers selling religious products rather than mainstream long term brand building. Many of the other advertisers seem to be more interested in the benefits of association.

SUGGESTED ASSIGNMENTS

- Choose and research a current advertising campaign for a consumer product that uses several different media. Analyse and evaluate the campaign with reference to media choice, synergy between media, scheduling, message content and target audience for each medium, and campaign objectives. This could be used as an piece of group work, involving a written report, a verbal presentation or both.
- Why should organisations use advertising agencies? Are there any circumstances in which using an agency would be inappropriate?

Chapter 17
SALES PROMOTION

LECTURE PLAN

A lecture based on this chapter should help the student to:
1. Define sales promotion and appreciate its role in the communications mix through the objectives it can achieve;
2. understand the range of sales promotion methods in consumer markets and their objectives;
3. understand the range and objectives of sales promotion methods used by manufacturers to stimulate retailers;
4. appreciate the role of sales promotion in other organisational markets and how sales promotion overlaps with other elements of the communications mix; and
5. gain an overview of the issues involved in the sales promotion planning process and their implications for the application and practice of sales promotion methods.

The key sections of this lecture should be:

Introduction (pp 653-663):
- Definition of sales promotion.
- trade promotion, including OHP 60, figure 17.2 (p 654) Manufacturer - Intermediary Sales Promotion Objectives:
    ⇒ Overview of each reason
    ⇒ types of promotion that might achieve them.
- Retailer promotions, including OHP 61, figure 17.3 (p 656) Retailer - Consumer Sales Promotion Objectives:
    ⇒ Overview of each reason
    ⇒ types of promotion that might achieve them.
- Manufacturer promotions, including OHP 62, figure 17.4 (p 659) Manufacturer - Consumer Sales Promotion Objectives:
    ⇒ Overview of each reason
    ⇒ types of promotion that might achieve them.
- Business promotion: brief overview of role, methods and links with personal selling and exhibitions; see also p 684.
- Summary of sales promotion objectives: incentive; communication; invitation.

Money-based consumer promotions (pp 663-667):
Overview of types, including OHP 63, figure 17.6 (p 664) Money-based Sales Promotion Methods:
- Brief description of each type
- examples of each type
- advantages and disadvantages of each type
- impact on the consumer.

Product-based consumer promotions (pp 667-672):
Overview of types, including OHP 64, figure 17.7 (p 668) Product-based Sales Promotion Methods:
- Brief description of each type
- examples of each type
- advantages and disadvantages of each type
- impact on the consumer and the intermediary.

Gift, prize or merchandise based consumer promotions (pp 672-678):
Overview of types, including OHP 65, figure 17.8 (p 672) Gift, Prize or Merchandise Based Sales Promotion Methods:
- Brief description of each type
- examples of each type
- advantages and disadvantages of each type
- impact on the consumer.

Store based consumer promotions (pp 679-680):
- Point of sale displays
- demonstrations.

Trade promotions (pp 680-684):
- Allowances and discounts
- selling and marketing assistance
- sales force support.

Managing sales promotion (pp 685-690):
This section is based on OHP 66, figure 17.10 (p 685) The Sales Promotion Management Process:
- *Objectives:* target audience; what the promotion is to achieve.

- *Programme:* with objectives in mind, choosing appropriate techniques, creative planning, budgeting, planning implementation and adhering to guidelines.
- *Management:* allocating tasks and responsibilities.
- *Implementation:* undertaking the promotion.
- *Evaluation:* analysing outcomes compared with objectives.

Joint promotions (pp 688-690):
- What they are
- benefits to both parties
- risks
- good management.

This section could be omitted, and students encouraged to read the material for themselves.

QUESTIONS FOR REVIEW

17.1   What is sales promotion and in what ways does it differ from advertising? (pp 653-654)

Sales promotions are marketing techniques that add extra value to a product, over and above the normal offering. Their use is often tactical, but some promotions can play a longer term strategic role too. Sales promotion differs from advertising in that it:
- Is usually used as a short-term tactical incentive
- adds value to the product
- is usually used to prompt the customer into specific courses of action rather than just creating awareness and attitudes.

17.2   What are the main objectives of manufacturer sales promotions aimed at consumers? (pp 658-660)

- To encourage product trial
- to expand usage of the product
- to disseminate and emphasise information about the product
- to attract new customers
- to get customers to trade up to bigger sizes or to more expensive products in the range
- to load up customers with product to protect them from being tempted by a competitor
- to even out fluctuating or seasonal sales
- to counteract the competition's promotional efforts.

17.3   Why do manufacturers offer sales promotions to retailers? (pp 654-656)

- To increase stock levels within the distribution chain
- to launch a new product and ensure availability for consumers
- to even out fluctuating or seasonal sales
- to increase shelf-space given to a product or to get better positioned shelf-space
- to counteract competitors' promotional activities.

17.4   How do the objectives of retailer - consumer sales promotions differ from those of manufacturer - consumer sales promotions? (pp 656-660)

- Both might want to increase sales volumes
- both might want to increase an individual customer's purchasing frequency
- both might want to even out fluctuating sales
- both might want to protect their customers from the competition
- both might want to attract new customers
- both might want to encourage trial

- both might want to nurture customer loyalty.

In very broad terms, therefore, their objectives do not differ at all. What does differ is how these objectives are achieved and the relative difficulty of achieving them.

17.5   What are the main forms of money based sales promotions aimed at consumers and what are their advantages and disadvantages? (pp 663-667)

Reduced price (either on-pack or at the point of sale):
- Has a sense of urgency about it
- gives the consumer an immediate, quantifiable reward
- is quick and simple to implement

but:
- could cheapen the product image
- are not very imaginative
- are easily copied by competitors
- could make the consumer more price sensitive.

Coupons:
- Can be distributed in a wide variety of ways
- can help to build repeat purchases
- give the consumer a quantifiable reward
- can draw the customer's attention to a product they might not otherwise consider or be aware of
- can be personalised for specific customers' use
- are not viewed as price cuts that might damage image

but:
- they can be misredeemed
- they might simply be rewarding loyal customers who would have purchased the product anyway
- they are very commonly used.

Rebates:
- Make the consumer work harder for the reward, thus the promoter gets more sales
- give a quantifiable reward
- can help to generate a customer database, because consumers have to mail in to claim the rebate
- are not viewed as price cuts that damage image

but:
- the consumer might see the reward as too small for the effort
- the consumer might see them as inconvenient.

17.6   What specific objectives can BIGIF and similar types of sales promotion achieve?
        (pp 668-669)

- Loading up customers with product
- getting customers into the habit of using the product
- rewarding the customer without cheapening the product image.

17.7   How do self-liquidating offers differ from free mail-in offers, and in what circumstances might each be appropriate? (pp 672-674)

Self-liquidating offers ask the consumer to pay money to cover the cost of the gift, handling, postage and packing, whereas the maximum charge for a free mail-in is postage. Self-liquidating offers might be more appropriate where the promoter wants to feature better quality promotional merchandise or wants to create an image of exclusivity and desirability for the merchandise.

17.8   What is count and recount? Why might a retailer prefer it to a buying allowance?
        (pp 680-682)

Count and recount offers the retailer a retrospective rebate on stock units sold within a specified period. Retailers might prefer it to a buying (or volume) allowance because:

- They do not have to commit to purchasing large volumes of stock in order to qualify
- the size of the reward is performance-related, directly linked the retailer's selling effort.

17.9   Outline the key stages in the sales promotion management process. (pp 685-688)

- *Setting objectives:* what is to be achieved and with which target audience?
- *Defining the programme:* deciding on the content of the sales promotion campaign, its timing and its costs
- *Allocating responsibilities:* ensuring that the right things will be done at the right time with appropriate management and control, whether in-house or through an agency
- *Implementation:* finalising the duration, coverage, intensity, and terms and conditions of the campaign and then putting it into action
- *Evaluation:* assessing the degree of success and effectiveness of the campaign in the context of the original objectives and analysing any unexpected variations.

17.10   Once the broad form of a sales promotion has been determined, what specific details need to be sorted out before it can be implemented? (p 687)

- Checking its legality
- determining how long the promotion will run
- setting any qualification criteria (for example the number of tokens to be collected)
- deciding the size of the reward.

QUESTIONS FOR DISCUSSION

17.1   Research a recent new product launch by a manufacturer in a consumer market. What role did sales promotions play in that launch?

Students should be able to make the connection between the range of sales promotion techniques used and their objectives. With a new consumer product launch, the likely objectives are:

- Drawing the consumer's attention to the product, either in the store or by door to door coupon drops, for example
- giving product information, perhaps through coupons or door to door samples
- encouraging trial and assessment of the product, through samples
- reducing the risk to the consumer of trial through various kinds of money-based sales promotions, trial sizes. trial prices, samples etc
- making the first repeat purchase easy through on-pack coupons or perhaps rebate schemes.

17.2   Choose an fmcg product area (breakfast cereals or hot chocolate drinks, for example) and analyse the sales promotions currently offered on the range of available brands in terms of the methods used, duration, size of reward etc.

This question encourages students to take an overview of promotional activity within a product sector. They should be analysing not only what the individual brand is trying to achieve for itself through a promotion, but how that fits into a wider competitive picture. Issues to consider include:

- To what extent are different brands targeting different segments, and how is this reflected in the type of promotion?
- To what extent are different brands competing directly through the same types of promotional the same time?
- To what extent are the promotions on offer trying to be different from each other?
- To what extent do you think manufacturers might be trying to co-ordinate their promotions so that only one or two brands are being promoted at any one time?

- If there are several promotions running simultaneously, what effect do you think this has on the consumer?

17.3   To what extent are the sales promotion methods used in consumer markets equally applicable in organisational markets?

In terms of the manufacturer - retailer promotions, their broad objectives will be equally applicable in organisational markets where a manufacturer is selling direct to an organisational customer. The way in which these objectives are achieved and the size of the incentives might differ, however. Money-based incentives, product-based incentives, and gifts are all part of the selling and negotiation package. Where a manufacturer is selling through an intermediary, such a distributor, to a large number of organisational customers, the situation is very similar to that of selling to consumers through retailers. Thus many of the consumer-orientated promotional techniques will be appropriate, as well as the manufacturer-retailer and the retailer-consumer techniques. Again, however, the fine detail of the size of the incentive, the frequency of promotions and the choice of most appropriate technique will vary according to the character of the market concerned.

17.4   What kinds of sales promotion are (a) '20% extra free', (b) 'send in £9.99 plus 5 proofs of purchase to get a branded sweatshirt', and (c) 'when you open the product packaging, look to see if there is a cheque for £5,000 inside'? Why might manufacturers use them?

- *'20% extra free'* is a product-based promotion (see pp 667-668). It is a way of giving the consumer a positive reward, something in addition to the normal offering, without resorting to anything directly linked with price. It can be used in response to a competitor's price moves to reinforce a value for money image without starting an all-out price war. It can also be used to load customers up, if they decide to stock up with the product in bulk while it is such good value, as a defence against the competition.
- *'Send in £9.99 plus 5 proofs of purchase to get a branded sweatshirt'* is a self-liquidating offer (see pp 672-673). It allows the promoter to offer better quality promotional merchandise, as the consumer is paying for it. Collecting proofs of purchase encourages brand loyalty from the consumer, and the merchandise itself can feature brand logos to act as a constant reminder to the consumer of the product and its values. Because it is a mail-in offer, it also allows the manufacturer to build a database of interested customers.
- *'When you open the product packaging, look to see if there is a cheque for £5,000 inside'* is effectively a sweepstake. It is the luck of the draw whether the consumer buys a winning packet or not. Because it is a sweepstake, however, in the UK the promoter cannot make product purchase a condition of entry and has to make provision for non-purchasers to have a promotion pack opened on their behalf. Such promotions add extra excitement for the consumer because there is an element of uncertainty about whether there is any reward in the pack at all. They can also encourage more frequent repeat purchases, "this pack wasn't a winner, but maybe the next one ...".

17.5   Find three examples of joint sales promotions and discuss the benefits for the organisations concerned and their customers.

The sales promotions can be jointly run by a manufacturer (or service provider) and a retailer, or by two manufacturers (or service providers). The benefits to the organisations are likely to be:
- Exploiting synergy between the products, for example coffee and biscuits
- synergy through targeting a common segment
- pooling resources to spend more on a more extensive promotion
- providing a far more interesting promotion
- providing incentives that are more valued by the customer because they involve high quality, well known brand names
- shared costs and risks.

The benefits to their customers are likely to be:

- Developing awareness of, and perhaps even trial of products that they would not otherwise have thought of
- bigger and better rewards
- more interesting incentives.

CASE STUDY 17.1 Student Banking (p 693)

Teaching Objectives

1. To ensure that students understand the different kinds of sales promotion and their appropriate use;
2. to analyse the role of sales promotions in a competitive market;
3. to explore the problems of using sales promotions for service products.

1   What kinds of sales promotions do the banks use in the student segment and what are they trying to achieve?

The problem with student banking is that the financial products offered to students by banks are virtually indistinguishable from each other, and any sales promotion can be easily copied by a competitor if it looks attractive. The main objective of sales promotions in this market is to attract students at a critical stage in their careers. An undergraduate account could mean a customer for life, so the stakes are high and the competition fierce between the leading banks. Sales promotions add short-term value to the offering and could help a student to differentiate between one bank's offering and another's and to make a final decision as to where to bank. Sales promotions have to be analysed within the context of the underlying product being offered and the broader marketing campaign that involves the use of:
- Standard financial products tailored to the student segment
- sales presentations during the induction period
- localised cash dispensers and access points can be especially important for more remote 'green field' campuses
- subsidised banking (pricing) while the customer is a student
- a more generous attitude to overdrafts than would normally be the case for younger people.

The sales promotion methods used include:
- *Gifts:* gift vouchers; filofaxes; clothes; CDs.
- *Price promotions:* interest-free overdrafts; reduced interest on credit; cash incentive to open account; free student insurance; credit cards with annual charges waived; travel money deals.
- *Competition-based promotions:* free rent scratch card promotion.

Supplementary question
What sales promotions were banks running when you were opening your bank account as a student? To what extent did these promotions influence your decision?

2   Why do you think the banks have tended to move away from gift-based promotions to money-based offers?

The move to money-based promotions reflects the changing patterns of financing in higher education in the UK. Although participation in higher education in the England and Wales is approaching 30 per cent (much higher in Northern Ireland and Scotland), student grants have not kept up, so there is less to go round per student. The grant falls a long way short of living requirements, and while parental contributions have increased, they still often fall short of requirements. In any case, with a maturing student population, such funding becomes less relevant. All of this adds up to the financial pressures that many students experience and can lead to some extreme cases of student poverty. The banks have responded to these changes in the economic environment by switching from frivolous and luxury items to more serious essentials, i.e. cash. Thus the reasons for the switch in promotional techniques are:

- Students see the cash as more valuable than the gifts
- students feel that they need the cash more
- it makes students feel that the banks understand their circumstances.

Additionally, money-based promotions have advantages for the banks:

- The promotion remains entirely within the bank's control, since they do not have to worry about sourcing and maintaining supplies of merchandise
- the banks do not have to worry about whether the gift will be attractive to the target audience
- the promotion relates closely and directly to the bank's core business
- it overcomes any cynical attitudes about banks being money-grabbing!

3   What are the problems of using sales promotions in such a highly competitive, concentrated market?

The attractions of using money based promotions in a segment that is normally short of money are obvious. The problem with many sales promotion techniques is that the pressure is on to be the first in the market with a new, innovative idea that captures the interest of the target population. The second or third organisation to adopt a similar promotion rarely makes the same impact. Any lead, however, is short-lived and thus a constant flow of new ideas is needed to maintain the freshness, innovation and impact. An allied problem concerns the spiralling costs associated with planning and implementing a series of short-lived promotions. This is especially true if the promotions move away from the straightforward money-off type of offer. Money-off promotions can, however, become a standard part of the offering and they are easily replicated. Competitions are limited, live activities that are not so easily replicated. There are also issues related to social responsibility, as there are few choices for the stusent. Care must be taken not to allow the package of student debt to rise to a level that creates a major financial burden on the student for many years. However, it could be argued that with an otherwise indistinguishable product offering, sensible sales promotion does allow some short term differences and attractions to be built into a difficult differentiation exercise.

4   How might the use of sales promotion methods differ for a financial services product compared with an fmcg product?

- Financial services are intangible products and so there is a strong role for gift-based promotions to add a tangible element.
- Some decisions on financial services might not lead to noticeable benefits for several years and will involve a long term cost. A short-term promotion would thus have to be very powerful to overcome the consumer's natural fears. Money-based promotions, perhaps reduced premiums or lower interest rates for the first year, for example, could be most appropriate.
- With financial services, there could be heavier emphasis on the social responsibility aspects of sales promotion, particularly money-based methods. Banks and other financial institutions cannot be seen to be encouraging people to take on more debt than they can cope with or to be giving them incentives to buy inappropriate products.
- Financial services cannot really undertake on-pack promotions (!), but what they can do is to use communications with existing customers (for example when statements are mailed out) to offer them incentives to buy other financial products.
- Financial services can use alternative currencies. Some credit cards give customers points depending on the sums spent using the card. These points can then be redeemed for goods and services.

CASE STUDY 17.2 Supermarket Loyalty Cards (p 694)

Teaching Objectives

1. To examine the reasons behind customer loyalty schemes;
2. to explore the operational problems of setting up and maintaining such schemes;

3. to consider ways in which loyalty schemes can provide a foundation for other promotional activities.

1   What factors have led the supermarkets towards these kinds of loyalty scheme and what do they hope to achieve from them?

The fundamental rationale stems from the fact that the UK supermarket sector is an oligopoly which is extremely competitive, mature and saturated. This environment has led to the need to:

- *Appeal to price conscious customers:* the loyalty card means that customers feel that they are getting financial rewards and value for money, but the supermarkets do not have to become embroiled in all-out price wars to deliver it.
- *Increase each customer's spend:* if a supermarket has loyal or regular shoppers, then clearly the more they spend per visit, the better. The loyalty card means that the customer feels that extra spending on a visit is worthwhile because it increases the points tally.
- *Increase customer loyalty:* the retailer wants the same customers to keep coming back, because repeat selling to an existing customer is a lot easier and cheaper than finding a new one. With a loyalty scheme, customers are more likely to patronise the same retailer regularly in order to build up points.
- *Build relationships with customers:* this is not just about loyalty and generating repeat business, but also about image building and winning customer goodwill. The retailer wants customers to feel that they are valued and listened to, and that their needs are understood. Regular and well targeted communication through the scheme's database can help to achieve this.
- *Create a focal point for coherent and strategically planned promotional activities:* it is too easy for one-off promotions in a large, fast-moving retail environment to be missed or to become boring (ceaseless 10p off or BIGIF promotions). The loyalty scheme allows promotions to be targeted at individual customers and to have a common thread (extra points on this product, or double points on all your shopping this week) within the bigger picture of ongoing points collection.
- *Create a focal point for alliances and joint promotions with other non-food retailers:* this creates synergy between retailers in different sectors which can deliver benefits and competitive advantage for both.
- *Gain valuable market research information:* knowing the customer is an important task for any retailer, but particularly difficult in fmcg situations. The database created by the loyalty scheme gives information about shopping habits, preferences, frequency and value, as well as responsiveness to promotional activities. This can help the retailer to refine its marketing strategy to increase its competitive advantage.

Supplementary question
How and why might the rationale for an airline's frequent flyer loyalty scheme differ from that of a supermarket?

In broad terms the rationale is very similar, and all the points raised in the supermarket context above apply just as much to an airline. Additionally, airlines:

- Provide a less frequently purchased product, and thus maintaining contact with customers between purchases is extremely important
- have to find promotional approaches that appeal to a wide range of internationally dispersed customers
- can use the frequent flyer club as a way of providing better quality services to some customers and not to others.

2   What are the practical problems of setting up, managing, and maintaining a promotion like this?

The problems include:
- The cost of the IT needed to set it up
- installing the IT in every checkout in every store and making sure it works reliably

- ensuring that the system can cope with the expected response
- training staff in the use of the system and training them to answer customer queries
- setting the size of the discount
- forecasting how much money is going to be given away in discounts
- setting up and managing a pilot scheme to test the system, fine-tune the marketing of it, and to gauge the customer response
- ensuring that customers are aware of the scheme and that they understand its scope and its benefits
- managing the inflow of customer details quickly and efficiently as they sign up to the scheme
- collecting, storing and analysing day to day shopping data by customer
- managing the production and distribution of the quarterly newsletter and statement to each scheme member
- using the data to make tailored offers to sub-groups of members
- tracking customers, including the detection of light users or fading users so that they can be encouraged to increase their purchases
- keeping the database up to date and 'clean'
- keeping customers active and interested in the scheme
- maintaining the scheme's differentiation from anything similar run by competitors
- extra staff costs needed to manage and administer all this.

3   Tesco has already segmented its cardholders by age and family status. What other variables could it use and how might these be used in other promotional activities?

Tesco could use any segmentation variable, but some are going to be more relevant than others. Apart from age and family status, there are several relevant variables which could provide a foundation for cost effective promotional campaigns:

- *Average spend per member of the household:* when a customer signs up to a loyalty scheme, they are asked about the structure of the household. The retailer can thus calculate on average how much a two-, three- or four-person household spends per person over a period based on an analysis of all the households on the database. The retailer can then target all households spending less than the average to encourage them to spend more. This could be through money-off vouchers, or through extra points for higher spends. If the customer only spends £40 a visit, for example, the retailer could offer to double their points on any spend over £50 during a certain period.
- *Frequency of visits to the store:* if, overall, a customer is spending an average or above average amount in the supermarket, then the retailer might not mind whether that amount is made up of large infrequent shopping trips, or small frequent ones. Some customers, however, might be shopping infrequently and spending too little. Incentives such as extra points for doing a £30 or more shop at least once a week over five weeks might help to stop any store switching that is going on and get the customer into more regular patronage habits.
- *Timing of visits to the store:* one of the big headaches for supermarkets is trying to cope with the peaks and troughs in the number of customers in the store at particular times of the week. The retailer might select customers from the database who habitually shop at busy times (for example Sunday mornings) and offer them extra points for shopping at a quieter time (on a Wednesday evening, for example) instead.
- *Percentage of own-label items purchased:* own-label products are important to supermarkets who will certainly want to encourage customers to buy more of them. The database might help to identify light users of own-labels who can then be given specific incentives (money off or extra points) to increase their purchases of them.
- *The number of different items purchased over a period:* as a means of increasing a customer's total spend, the retailer might analyse the breadth of range of items purchased. If this is narrow, predictable and very brand loyal, again, incentives might help to broaden the customer's scope and vary their routine purchasing behaviour.
- *Patronage of different departments within the store:* some customer might be heavy users of some parts of the store (for example canned foods and the in-store bakery), but only light users of other parts (for example chilled ready meals and the delicatessen). If the retailer can give incentives to

increase the customer's purchases in the lightly patronised areas, then there is a strong chance that the consumer's total spend will rise.

- *Geographic segmentation:* this could also be interesting, in that it might allow the retailer to spot peculiar trends in individual stores which could be remedied or exploited by targeted offers to the store's local customers.

4 **To what extent and how do you think that the retailers and consumers might benefit or suffer from the long term continuation of these schemes, once the novelty has worn off?**

Retailers will benefit from:
- The power of the database for promotional purposes
- the power of the database for relationship purposes
- improved knowledge of the customer
- the spin-offs, for example the alliances with other retailers and the expansion of financial services made possible by the database.

Retailers will suffer from:
- The costs of running and maintaining the scheme
- the costs of the discounts offered
- the existence of competitors' schemes lessening the impact and competitive advantage of any one scheme
- customers coming to view such schemes as a normal and expected part of a supermarket's offering.

Customers will benefit from:
- Rivalry between retailers for their custom, possibly increasing the size of incentives
- ongoing guaranteed discounts
- better targeted promotional offers.

Customers will suffer from:
- Junk mail overload from many retailers?
- Feeling that if their shopping habits change or step out of line, the retailer will be on to them?
- The existence and costs of the scheme being reflected in higher prices.

Supplementary question
Do you have a store loyalty card? How has it changed your shopping habits?

Issues to discuss might include whether it has changed:
- How much you spend
- where you shop
- how often you shop
- what you buy
- your attitude towards the retailer
- your responsiveness to promotional offers.

Marketing in Action Trade Promotions (p 655)

Discussion question
How do the trade promotion objectives differ between Sellotape, Cellnet and Unipath?

Sellotape offered a collection-based potential prize system, and even if it failed, charities would still benefit. The idea capitalised on the initial interest in the UK's National Lottery. The main objectives were:
- To generate general awareness and interest in the product from wholesalers, including cash and carry operators
- to increase stock levels within the distribution channel
- to encourage intermediaries to sell harder. The promotion may just encourage the sales representative to talk a little more about Sellotape when visiting retailers.
- to create more interest in Sellotape than in competing brands.

Cellnet: the objectives of this promotion were likely to have been to:

- Improve image through the link with the glamour associated with motor racing
- increase sales volumes
- improve restocking rates.

The prize system was linked with volume, and the added bonus of becoming 'the best selling dealer' created further interest for those in strong locations with a successful sales team. This promotion could certainly have affected competitors' sales in the short term.

Unipath: the approach adopted by Unipath is perhaps more subtle than the previous two cases. The main vehicle, the regular magazine:

- Contains product information that is considered essential for more informed selling. This should work through to ...
- better advice to customers and therefore increased sales and stock holding.
- contains competitions as an extra incentive for readers to take in the product information.

However, it is not clear how powerful these competitions actually are and what the take-up rate is.

Marketing in Action Sampling Kids (p 669)

Discussion question
Should the guidelines adopted by the confectionery and food manufacturers apply to all sampling programmes with kids?

There is no one answer to this question. Regulations and codes of practice will also differ around Europe. Class discussion will reveal a wide range of attitudes. Particular issues that might emerge will include:

- Is 16 a realistic age limit and how do you know they are that age anyway? Adults often get it wrong!
- Should different approaches be selected for different age groups?
- Where the product might actually give positive benefits to the child, for example cleaning teeth, health awareness etc, should the code of practice be relaxed?
- Who makes these decisions?
- Is the main issue the product being given away or the principle of receiving gifts?
- What forums are legitimate for giving? Should it be permitted only through churches, clubs, or schools?
- What is the real difference between the distribution of samples by strangers through the post or when parents are present and the handing over of a sample by a stranger to the child directly?
- Is the whole principle of seeking to influence minors ethically wrong in the first place? If so what difference is there between sampling and other forms of promotion?

Marketing in Action JCB (p 685)

Discussion question
Is the offer of a few days away in Spain just a nice holiday or is it a serious attempt at organisational sales promotion?

The approach adopted by JCB is very typical in organisational markets where there are real benefits in selling the product through demonstration. The trip to Spain is more than a holiday because:

- If reasonably attractive and exotic locations were not used it would be difficult, if not impossible to gain buyer's undivided attention for such a concentrated period of time. This would also be true of the trade press.
- When combined with other activities, such as the sales conference, a high level of interest can be generated. The use of associated excursions, golf competitions etc all help the social bonding and relationship building.
- It can also be very effective in developing selling efficiency. Having potential customers come to you on a captive basis helps to reduce selling time, travelling time, demonstration time etc. With a

group of potential customers together, the demonstrations can be bigger, better and much more impressive. The serious negotiation can take place later back in the home country with a lot of the pre-selling done already.

- In any case, an organisation might feel obliged to provide this kind of event if its competitors are also offering a similar type of arrangement!

SUGGESTED ASSIGNMENTS

- Questions for Discussion 17.3
- Sales promotion has traditionally been thought of as a poor relation of advertising. Is this a fair assessment? In what ways is the strategic role of sales promotion changing?

Chapter 18
PERSONAL SELLING AND SALES MANAGEMENT

LECTURE PLAN

A lecture based on this chapter should help the student to:
1. Appreciate the role that personal selling plays in the overall marketing effort of the organisation;
2. define the tasks undertaken by sales representatives;
3. differentiate between types of sales representative;
4. analyse the stages involved in the personal selling process and understand how each one contributes towards creating sales and developing long-term customer relationships; and
5. appreciate the issues, responsibilities and problems involved in sales management.

The key sections of this lecture should be:

Introduction (pp 698-701):
- Definition of personal selling.
- Advantages of personal selling: impact, precision, cultivation and cost.

Tasks of the sales representative (pp 701-704):
This section is based on OHP 67, figure 18.1 (p 702) Typical Tasks of the Sales Representative:
- Briefly define each task
- emphasise that it is not just about selling
- stress importance of all these tasks in providing a full service to the customer
- stress strategic importance to the seller of some of these activities.

Forms of personal selling (pp 704-708):
- Order takers
- order makers
- sales support
- relate each type back to the tasks in the previous section.

The personal selling process (pp 708-721):
This section is based on OHP 68, figure 18.3 (p 709) The Personal Selling Process:

- *Prospecting:* definition; problems of locating and screening prospects; cold calling.
- *Preparation and planning:* importance of understanding the prospect's needs and concerns and creating an appropriate approach.
- *Initiating contact:* the importance of making the right impression at the right time; getting the prospect's attention and interest.
- *Sales presentation:* the importance of customer orientation; the benefits of need satisfaction rather than formula selling; the importance of flexibility and listening to the prospect.
- *Handling objections:* types of objection and appropriate responses.
- *Negotiation:* the importance of negotiation; the importance of win - win rather than competitive negotiation; relative power; limits and boundaries.
- *Closing the sale:* the importance of assessing when the prospect is ready; type of close.
- *Follow-up and account management:* the importance of checking that all promises made to the customer have been fulfilled; the importance of maintaining ongoing relationships, including OHT 69, figure 18.4 (p 720) The Role of Personal Contact in Maintaining Good Customer Relationships:
  ⇒ Brief overview of each point
  ⇒ the strategic importance to the seller's organisation
  ⇒ the benefits to the sales representative for ease of gaining future orders from the same customer.

Sales management issues (pp 721-731):
- *Sales planning and strategy:* setting sales objectives; deciding on the size, structure and deployment of the sales force.
- *Training:* what, how much and when.
- *Motivation and compensation:* how to motivate; compensation schemes.
- *Performance evaluation:* why do it; how to do it; implications.

QUESTIONS FOR REVIEW

18.1   What is personal selling and how does it differ from other elements of the promotional mix? (pp 698-701)

Personal selling involves face to face interpersonal communication undertaken by individuals on behalf of an organisation. It informs, reminds or persuades clients, customers or other groups with the objective of directly or indirectly making sales and building relationships. It differs from the rest of the marketing mix because:
- Advertising is a mass medium; personal selling is selective
- advertising and sales promotion are essentially impersonal; personal selling is face to face
- sales promotion offers short-term incentives; personal selling is about relationship building
- personal selling can deliver more complex messages
- personal selling can tailor messages to repond to direct feedback from the potential customer.

18.2   What are the major advantages of personal selling and what can they contribute to the marketing effort? (pp 698-701)

Its major advantages are that it:
- Makes a direct impact on the potential customer and is hard to ignore
- can precisely target individuals
- can tailor the message to suit the individual customer's needs
- can allow two-way live dialogue between buyer and seller
- can build deep and complex relationships between individuals as well as between organisations
- can be a very cost effective way of converting a customer's uncertain interest into sales especially for high value high risk purchases.

Their contribution to the marketing effort is:
- Better understanding of customers and their needs

- better buyer-seller relationships and thus more loyalty
- creating sales
- defendable competitive advantage through interpersonal relationships.

18.3 What are the typical tasks of a sales representative? (pp 701-704)

- Prospecting for new customers
- informing customers about products and benefits
- installing and demonstrating products and systems
- co-ordinating their own organisation's efforts on behalf of the customer
- maintaining longer-term relationships with customers even when they are dormant
- gathering market information and customer feedback
- monitoring competitor actions within the market.

18.4 How might the implementation and importance of each of those tasks vary between organisational and consumer markets? (pp 701-704)

- *Prospecting for new customers:* in organisational markets, it is likely to be easier to define prospects. In consumer markets, there will be a lot more cold calling and rejection and in some areas, such as selling cars, the organisation will wait for the prospect to approach them rather than vice versa. New customers are important in both kinds of markets, especially for infrequently purchased goods where a constant supply of new business is essential.
- *Informing customers about products and benefits:* an important task in both markets as it is the key to making sales. Organisational customers might prefer to hear about economic and 'rational' benefits, whereas a consumer might be persuaded by psychological benefits.
- *Installing and demonstrating products and systems:* important in any market, consumer or organisational, involving complex products which involve high risk investment by the buyer or with which the buyer is not familiar. Cars, computers, production machinery are all products that need a high degree of demonstration pre-purchase and immediate after-sales support.
- *Co-ordinating their own organisation's efforts on behalf of the customer:* in either consumer or organisational markets, the customer's first and perhaps only point of contact is likely to be the sales representative. It is therefore up to the sales representative to find answers to customer queries, solve problems, and ensure that promises are delivered.
- *Maintaining longer-term relationships with customers even when they are dormant:* probably more important in organisational markets where repeat purchases of the kinds of products sold through personal selling are more likely.
- *Gathering market information and customer feedback:* again, probably more important in organisational markets where one customer can represent a large amount of potential business. Consumer markets are more likely to rely on standard market research programmes for information and feedback.
- *Monitoring competitor actions within the market:* important in both kinds of market. In organisational situations in particular the approaches and marketing techniques used by competition could make a serious impact on an important customer. In consumer markets, it would be useful to know whether competitors have reached that customer first, and what sort of offers they are making.

18.5 Why might a sales representative's role include co-ordination within the selling organisation? (pp 702-703)

Co-ordination is important because:
- The customer needs a familiar and reliable point of contact with the organisation rather than being pushed around from department to department
- any promises made by the representative re specification or delivery etc must be communicated internally and met

- two-way buyer - seller dialogue might be necessary to fine-tune the order and its delivery.

18.6   What is the difference between an order taker and an order maker? (pp 704-706)

An order taker either has a set pattern of customer contact (external order takers) or waits for customers to contact them with the ordering needs (inside order takers). Their role is administrative rather than selling as such. An order maker has a more active role in locating new prospective customers, identifying their needs and then selling them an appropriate product package. They also take an active role in expanding sales to existing customers by selling them different product lines.

18.7   What are the stages in the personal selling process? (pp 708-721)

- Prospecting
- preparation and planning
- initiating contact
- sales presentation
- handling objections
- negotiation
- closing the sale
- follow-up and account management.

18.8   Why is preparation and planning so important a part of the personal selling process? (pp 710-711)

It is important because it:
- Develops a better understanding of the prospect's needs
- develops a better understanding of how the seller's product solve the buyer's problems
- allows the representative to design a relevant and appropriate sales presentation
- allows the representative to negotiate more intelligently with the prospect.

18.9   How might the sales representative tell whether or not a prospect is ready to close a sale? (pp 718-719)

The representative should watch the prospect's body language and listen to what they are saying in order to assess whether they have made a decision. The representative can also test the buyer's readiness with the following techniques:
- *Alternative close:* "do you want the red or the black?"
- *Assumptive close:* "we'll deliver in two weeks then".
- *Time pressure close:* "I can only hold this offer open until Friday for you".

18.10   What are the main issues that the sales manager must consider as far as sales planning and strategy are concerned? (pp 721-725)

- Specifying sales objectives, including sales targets and quotas for individual representatives
- sales force structure and organisation
- size of the sales force and territory allocation.

QUESTIONS FOR DISCUSSION

18.1   Give examples of three different kinds of sales support staff and analyse their contribution to the personal selling effort.

- *General support staff:* help sales representatives by locating prospective customers; screening prospects for ability and willingness to think about buying; compiling background information for the sales force; providing sales training; taking responsibility for after-sales service.
- *Missionary sales staff:* help sales representatives by implementing a pull strategy, creating interest and demand among the customer's customers to makes the sales representative's job easier.
- *Sales engineers:* help sales representatives by helping to define a customer's technical problems and needs; getting involved in installation, maintenance and technical training.

Students should be encouraged to find real examples of these support roles in action and to discuss their contribution.

18.2   In what ways do you think a sales representative could make the sales presentation more relevant and interesting for the prospective customer?

The discussion could include consideration of:
- Proper preparation so that the presentation directly addresses issues of concern to the prospect
- the need for an emphasis on benefits rather than features
- the inclusion of audio-visual aids
- including an opportunity for the customer to get their hands on the product
- allowing the customer to talk to previous satisfied customers or to visit their premises to see the product installed and in use
- involving members of the sales support team to handle more technical queries.

Students might be encouraged to look at how these issues might apply in different kinds of markets and selling situations, for example consumer vs. organisational markets, or highly technical vs. 'ordinary' products.

18.3   What techniques might a sales representative use to counter the following objections: (a) "Your competitor's product is a lot cheaper ...", (b)"I don't think my wife would like it if I bought this ...?, and (c) "I've heard that your service engineers are very inefficient"?

- *"Your competitor's product is a lot cheaper ...":* ask the objection back; agree and counter.
- *"I don't think my wife would like it if I bought thi s...":* ask the objection back; feel, felt, found; denial (dangerous!).
- *"I've heard that your service engineers are very inefficient":* denial (if the substance of the objection is not true); agree and counter (if there have been problems which are now solved).

Students could explore these situations through a mini-role play, trying out and analysing the effectiveness of different kinds of response and the exchanges that follow.

18.4   Summarise the relative advantages of allocating sales responsibilities on the basis of (a) geographic regions, (b) product-based criteria and (c) customer-based criteria.

Defining selling responsibility in terms of geographic regions:
- Minimises travelling time
- avoids call duplication
- allows representatives to become familiar with local conditions and competition

but:
- representatives have to be able to handle the full product range.

Defining selling responsibility in terms of product based criteria:
- Allows the representative to develop specialist expertise and deep product knowledge and thus ...
- ... to become more involved in the customer's problem solving

but:
- travelling times and costs increase
- there is the potential for call duplication
- representatives cannot become deeply knowledgeable about each customer's local conditions.

Defining selling responsibility in terms of customer based criteria:

- Allows the sales representative to become familiar with specific applications of the product or types of customer
- encourages long-term buyer-seller relationships
- allows a more tailored sales approach
- reduces the chances of call duplication

but:

- travelling times and costs increase.

18.5 **Find 20 job advertisements for sales representatives and summarise the range of characteristics and skills sought. Which are the most commonly required and to what extent do you think that they are essential for a successful sales representative?**

This question is designed to stimulate debate about what is desirable in a sales representative and the difficulties of defining and measuring some of these characteristics. Students might also compare the needs of different markets or of different sized employers. Students might wish to compare the advertised characteristics with the attributes outlined in table 18.3 (p 727) and then discuss the extent to which success is a result of training rather than breeding!

CASE STUDY 18.1 Buying a Car (p 734)

Teaching Objectives

1. To explore the complexity and difficulties of personal selling to consumers;
2. to consider what constitutes 'good practice' in personal selling;
3. to examine the role of price negotiation in a consumer personal selling situation.

1 **You are Darren, and you arrive on Tuesday morning to hear from the Fleet Sales Representative what happened on Monday. What are you going to do?**

As firm a potential customer as it is possible to have is on the verge of being lost. The customers have made it clear that their preference is for the 1.6GL, and they would not have persisted so long if their interest was not real. Darren thus needs to contact Jane or Peter as a matter of urgency in order to:

- Apologise profusely for the confusion
- clarify how they felt about the test drive experience
- if the feedback is positive, make a real attempt to close the sale, even if it means collecting Jane from her home or place of work.

Darren appears not to have learnt the lesson that customers are valuable, need to be serviced properly and most of all that any promises made need to be kept. Darren, as the sales representative should have been responsible for organising things at Smiffy's Cars so that even if he was not available himself, a fully briefed substitute would be there to deal with the buyer. Instead, Darren is in a situation where his own credibility and his company's efficiency and quality of service are being questioned, and he is going to have to work very hard just to get back to where he started.

2 **As the Sales Manager, how would you have handled the situation on Monday?**

The sales manager appears to be even less interested in Jane and Peter than Darren was! Instead of taking full command of the situation, organising the test drive, giving attention to the buyers and even trying to close the sale, he appeared to be more concerned with the inconvenience and paint work problems. The buyers should not have had to create a scene to make any progress. Although the Sales Manager has a different role from Darren's, he is still part of the same team. As a manager he must be prepared to take responsibility for the actions, expertise and results achieved of any member of the sales force. Appropriate behaviour, systems, procedures and customer handling approaches may have to be trained into the sales force otherwise there will be many more incidents similar to what Jane and Peter experienced. Thus appropriate actions from the Sales Manager would, therefore, have been to:

- Apologise for the confusion
- reassure the customer that everything would be sorted out with the minimum of delay and inconvenience
- sit the customer down with a cup of coffee while a test drive is organised
- accompany the customer on the drive, find out more about the customer's needs and then sell the appropriate benefits of the car
- close the sale and get a signed order, even if then left up to Darren to process it all when he returns.

3   Assess Darren's approach to selling. What did he do right and what did he do wrong?

Darren will have to learn fairly quickly if he is going to build a career in sales. He will have to correct his mistakes and develop the following good habits:
- Never knock your own products, it makes the customer wonder what is really going on
- find out in some detail what the customer is looking for before starting to sell
- try to match the product's benefits to the customer's needs
- try to find out what the customer's decision making criteria are
- if the customer is not alone, find out who is playing what roles within the decision-making unit and what influences are prevalent
- try to move towards product involvement with a test drive
- never wait for the customer to telephone you; you always contact them as a follow up
- never let the customer leave the showroom without giving you a name and contact number
- do not promise discounts until you are sure of the customer's intentions and priorities
- beware of the danger of telephone negotiations, as the sale cannot be closed (i.e. a contract signed)
- always keep promises to customers
- ensure full co-ordination within the selling organisation, and keep the manager informed of the possible sale and arrangements made.

Overall, he appears not to want to persuade, but just take orders (and he cannot even do that very well). What Darren did do well was to agree to go on a sales training course!

4   Why do you think that Peter took over the negotiation on Thursday (even though it was Jane who was buying the car) and why did he not accept the £10,400 offer immediately?

Peter was seeking to get the best deal possible for Jane:
- It may have been tactical that Peter decided to take over the negotiation, as it tends to conform to the typical stereotype of the male dealing with the price. Jane could be closely following the negotiation, observing what is said and not said in order to strengthen the position.
- It could make it more difficult for the salesperson, as the negotiator is likely to be less enthralled with the emotional aspects of the purchase than the actual buyer. That would give the negotiation a purely price-orientated focus with less opportunity to trade off price against expected benefits.
- It makes it harder for the sale representative to pressurise the customer into accepting a deal on the spur of the moment. Peter really only has the authority to take away any offer that sounds reasonable and discuss it with Jane. That allows Jane time to think about the pitfalls of acceptance, to make a more measured response and to keep Darren sweating about whether the sale is to be closed or not.
- Peter might simply be a more experienced negotiator than Jane.

In a price negotiation it does not always pay to accept the first price quoted. It is often difficult to defend in a situation where competitive prices are used as a weapon to beat your own price down. If there is a package involved various elements can be traded to arrive at a balanced deal. There are some variables in a car purchase such as accessories, service options, financing etc, but once a model has been selected, the customer's focus tends to be on gaining the best price. Darren did not make the task any easier for the negotiation by giving a clear impression that he would be very flexible.

5   What should Jane and Peter do next? What can they learn from their experience and how can they turn it to their advantage?

They have a number of options:

- As long as they are still prepared to purchase the 1.6GL, they might even be able to drive a harder bargain. By emphasising how unhappy they are about Monday's debacle, they might be able to negotiate the price down further, perhaps to £10,000.
- They could return to Evans' cars to see whether a better deal could be obtained. Even if they did not want to close that deal, they could quote the price offered as a further test of Darren's resolve. Sometimes taking a little longer over the negotiation, being prepared to shop around, checking on alternative offerings and testing the resolve of the other party might help the customer to negotiate a better deal.
- In a car buying situation, neither side really knows what the other is thinking, and what are the obstacles, barriers and limits to the other party's tolerance. Although many car buyers have a rough appreciation of the margins on new cars they are not familiar with special model discounts, short term manufacturer promotions or the annual volume loadings agreed. Neither do they know how desperate the individual salesperson is to make a quota during that month. Similarly the car salesperson does not know the real preferences of the other party, what prices have been quoted and how desperate they are to own the model being offered. Careful questioning and probing helps, but an element of gamesmanship always exists in the negotiation. Jane and Peter should keep pushing Darren, step by step, until they find his bottom line.

CASE STUDY 18.2 Irish Fire Products (p 736)

Teaching Objectives

1. To examine the implications of sales force remuneration packages;
2. to emphasise the importance of sales training;
3. to look at the implications of the competitive environment on personal selling.

1   What kind of remuneration package is used with the sales representatives? What are the problems with it?

The package offers:
- Commission only, after initial period on the territory
- expenses to cover the running of a car.

Its strong points are that it:
- Provides extra incentive to the sales representative to pursue sales actively
- acts as an incentive to undertake extra calls, including cold calls to fill time
- is cost effective for smaller business, as the sales representative is effectively self financing
- means that the sales representative is likely to respond more enthusiastically to special offers or promotions if they makes sales easier to achieve
- keeps the sales representative focused on selling tasks rather than non-selling tasks.

Its problems are, however, that the sales representative:
- Might not be willing to spend time cultivating long term business
- might be more interested in making a short-term sale rather than building long-term potential
- might not have customer's interests at heart
- not be willing to spend too much time on non-selling activity, including product updating meetings and training
- might see higher staff turnover and general stress and dissatisfaction in sales force, which can create fear and poor morale
- will minimise time spent on administration, sometimes to an unacceptable level
- might not be willing to spend time selling new products or products which take longer to sell.

2   IFP wants to encourage sales representatives to do more cold calling. Is the company going the right way about achieving this? What else can be done?

Cold calling is often seen as the toughest part of the sales representative's task. It can:

- Be a waste of time
- be psychologically challenging
- fail to offer the required degree of penetration of a sales area.

Cold calls can:

- Be made to the wrong buyer
- expose the sales representative to competitive or usage problems that they are not prepared for
- suggest a lack of professionalism and a pressure selling approach that could cause buyer resistance.

The major advantage of using cold calling is that it is direct and can be efficient when calling on very small businesses where appointment selling may not be appropriate. Fire products are widely used by large and small businesses alike, but the niche that IFP appears to be occupying appears to be in the small business sector and covers less complex, all-embracing fire prevention systems. In Ireland the majority of business, whether retail or industrial, tend to be small. However new approaches have been developed to assist enquiry generation and cold calling. This would leave the sales team free to work on converting enquiries into sales. Other actions that IFP could take are:

- The use of telemarketing for enquiry generation
- the use of targeted direct mail with a response mechanism
- the use of specialist canvassers to generate lists
- the use of exhibitions or local shows to generate leads
- the use of direct response advertising
- the use of local PR, including press releases on fire risks and regulation changes.

IFP appears to have been increasingly left behind in developing an integrated promotional campaign, which would make the sales representative's job easier at least be generating awareness. Non-personal communication can even be used to generate enquiries and sales leads. Little effort appears to have been made to create a valuable customer database that can be used to sell a wider range of products and services to existing and past customers.

3 Is the training programme adequate? What should go into a formal sales training programme?

Training in sales is a means to an end, not an end in itself. It is designed to build a competent, professional sales force that can compete with other suppliers, and gain an edge in situations where the rest of the offerings are similar. Training is an investment in the future, but in the case of IFP, the high staff turnover and remuneration package suggest that such an investment is not valued. This could become an even more serious problem as IFP is squeezed at either end of the market. A number of areas need to be covered in a comprehensive skills development and training programme. Some will be taught during induction, others through a series of interventions during the year. The attitude and message need to be that a day's training increases selling effectiveness, not that it represents a lost day's selling. In many situations facing IFP sales staff, the customer is obliged to buy because of regulations, but the key issue is from whom to buy. A better trained sales force could have an edge over competitors in helping the prospective customer to make that decision. There are several skill and knowledge areas that have to be developed:

- Product knowledge: currently handled by the owner during induction.
- New and forthcoming regulations.
- Account management: nothing formal currently exists.
- Competitor knowledge: representatives currently learn on the job with no formal inputs.
- Application/usage knowledge: there is some coverage during induction, but it might not be comprehensive. The idea is to pick up more insights through experience. This area is vital when dealing with new prospects.
- Selling skills: previous selling experience is valued, but this can include bad as well as good habits. These skills are only occasionally covered during *ad hoc* training.
- Negotiation skills: not covered currently.

More attention needs to be given to this whole area. There are limitations in the 'sitting with the sales manager' approach. 'Learning from experience' can be costly when mistakes could have been avoided with proper training. Even *ad hoc* training courses might not address the real needs of the sales force. Skill needs have to be identified, and refresher training could involve selling simulations as well as inputs focusing on areas of skills deficiency.

4   How can Mike Dalton fight the pressure from the more sophisticated integrated systems at one end of the market and the cowboys at the other? What are the implications for the sales force?

There are serious strategic marketing problems developing for IFP as it is squeezed at one end of the market by the sophisticated and fully integrated fire prevention systems, often sold direct by the manufacturers, and the 'cowboy' operators at the other end of the market selling purely on price. This leaves the mid-range sector which might shrink over time as it polarises towards the other two areas. The sales force lacks the products, sophistication and even the motivation, with commission-only selling, to become more involved in the systems selling sector. Many of the products, once specified, are essentially commodities which prepare you for an eventuality which you hope never happens. The key skill lies in helping the customer to match perceived risk with appropriate protection. The sales staff appear to be competent in this area. Regular sales calls enable upgrading to take place and unless the customer starts shopping around, IFP is well placed to take orders. The low price operators, however, could increasingly make gains in this area. As with any low price operator, the basis of the lower price needs to be understood. In this case, it could be either lower overheads, or as IFP would like to believe, poor or no after-sales service. Much will depend on whether their belief is correct. If it is not, then there could be a serious competitive option. In order to differentiate themselves from the lower priced operators, there has to be an increased emphasis on sales professionalism, where representatives effectively become external advisors on fire prevention. They must be able to combat buying on price by demonstrating the importance of diagnosis. There are many industries where lower price operators exist but are not the dominant force.

The more worrying long term concern for IFP must be the integrated systems. These may well eventually spread to more complete cover in smaller businesses as more comprehensive risk protection is needed. IFP might have to seek alliances or distribution arrangements for more sophisticated systems to augment its existing range. This will mean a fundamentally different approach to the sales management policy. The focus on systems will demand high technical skills, considerable negotiation for higher value orders, and a commitment to longer term relationships. This could mean less focus on commission-only remuneration, more sales training, more specialisation in the sales force for different risks and systems, as well as a higher profile in the industry to develop a reputation as a credible supplier. This will make considerable demands on the company's management capabilities.

Marketing in Action Is the Sales Rep. an Endangered Species? (p 707)

Discussion question
Are the changes in the way that fmcg companies handle their sales forces' selling roles likely to extend to organisational marketing applications?

The main changes in the fmcg sector relate to the reduction of the number of order takers. In routine selling situations, once the main contract has been negotiated with the retail headquarters, the role of personal selling is concentrated on merchandising and providing local support. The growth of on-line ordering and the use of contract staff has clearly enabled more cost effective alternatives to traditional order takers. Most fmcg organisations still, however, retain top flight sales staff for negotiating, managing and representing clients' accounts internally and for maintaining the longer-term ongoing relationship. The contract and field marketing staff support that overall role.

In organisational markets, the nature of the sales task is different particularly where product and applications complexity is higher and the number of potential customers is much smaller. This tends to favour direct contact between buyer and seller. Informing, persuading and negotiating can demand a high level of technical or commercial expertise and thus these tasks cannot be transferred easily to less well trained and less experienced staff. Relationships between buyer and seller tend to be long lasting and can involve a wide range of personnel in the selling and buying unit. However, there are some selling situations that could be ripe for change. In frequent repeat business situations, direct ordering could be possible using telemarketing or IT systems. Other areas might favour greater use of direct marketing, for example catalogue selling for office furniture. Prospecting for non-specialist products is one task that could be undertaken by specialist staff.

Marketing in Action The Sales Force and IT (p 719)

Discussion question
How might the use of IT in support of the sales force develop further in the next few years?

The main areas highlighted in the example are:
- The input and processing of orders
- recording basic marketing information
- route planning and territory management systems
- access to basic product information.

The next stage could include:
- Faster access to more comprehensive databases that can better inform the salesperson when preparing for a customer visit
- providing live information during the sales call, including:
- additional customer applications data
- detailed product comparisons
- more rapid costing and pricing systems.

Links to the main selling organisation's MIS from the customer's premises reinforces the role of the salesperson as the interface and account manager when dealing with larger clients. There could, however, be a number of problem areas:
- The level of sales analysis possible with an MIS is only as good as the data that is entered
- too much data, and information overload can soon develop
- poorly structured databases will not enable fast, on-line access to the right information; poorly recorded information is of little use to anybody.

Nevertheless, by providing access to a more comprehensive system, a sales representative can plan the sales approach more carefully including the appeals to use and who to contact. They can also have better information on competitor activity, either in that account or gained elsewhere. IT will never replace the order making salesperson, but will provide the tools to enable more effective selling.

Marketing in Action 'The Man From the Pru' (p 725)

Discussion question
Are the days of 'the man from the Pru' numbered?
Not according to the Pru itself. Considerable effort is being made to train the sales force better and to support them with more effective marketing. However, it is a tough business. Insurance selling often involves a commission-only sales force and sometimes a high turnover of staff which is costly in terms of recruitment and training. The advantage of the current system is that it enables direct selling to take place and makes contact with a segment that otherwise would be difficult to reach and influence. Telephone selling is still not widely accepted in the UK for the complete selling process (only for prospecting) and direct marketing would take away any distinct advantage that the Pru might have in promotional terms. The problem is of course cost. This can be kept down through commission-only remuneration, but with the high costs of developing and maintaining a field sales management structure, costs are high, with a 25 per cent premium suggested. This is not compensated for by higher turnover.

It is likely that the contraction of the sales force will continue as the sophistication and acceptability of direct marketing grows. In an age of direct banking and direct insurance in other areas, the product is increasingly being sold over the telephone. If the trust can be built between the regular telesales person and the customer, progress can be made. However, such changes are not without risk. The target group might not respond so well to direct marketing. They might need the prompt of the face to face contact to encourage them to subject themselves to questioning and probing on their specific needs. The data base at the Pru does not even appear to be capable of easily providing a sophisticated database that would assist with targeting particular promotions to existing customers that may need them. The most likely outcome is, therefore, gradual rather than radical change. Telesales can support the sales representative's effort. Certainly, there could be more sophistication in targeting promotions. Again, however, the purpose would have to be to prepare the way for the direct sales contact. This would help the efficiency and productivity of a smaller, more highly trained, professional sales force.

SUGGESTED ASSIGNMENTS

- Questions for Review 18.8 could be adapted as an assignment thus: discuss how preparation and planning can provide an important foundation for the other stages in the personal selling process.
- Analyse the ways in which the role of the sales representative is changing in organisational markets.

Chapter 19
DIRECT MARKETING

LECTURE PLAN

A lecture based on this chapter should help the student to:
1. Understand what direct marketing is and why it has risen in importance in recent years;
2. review the various methods used in direct marketing, appreciating their relative strengths and problems in implementation;
3. analyse direct marketing's contribution to achieving marketing communication objectives, and how direct marketing can integrate with other elements of the promotional mix;
4. appreciate the broad issues involved in managing a direct marketing campaign; and
5. appreciate the importance of creating and maintaining a database of customers and understand the importance of using the database as a direct marketing tool.

The key sections of this lecture should be:

Introduction (pp 739-741):
Definition of direct marketing.

The rise of direct marketing (pp 741-743):
- Changing customer lifestyles and demographics
- changing consumer attitudes to direct marketing
- changing nature of competition
- media fragmentation
- increasing media and selling costs
- changing distribution channels
- improvements in database capacity and management techniques
- new communications technology.

Direct marketing techniques (pp 744-762)

This section is based on OHP 70, figure 19.1 (p 744) The Range of Direct Marketing Techniques:

- *Direct mail:* definition; customer attitude problems; advantages of direct mail; important stages in campaign development.
- *Direct response advertising:* definition; types and different media; importance of making it easy for the consumer to respond; management problems.
- *Telemarketing:* definition; applications; ACH; limitations and regulations.
- *Mail order:* definition; role; advantages and disadvantages; current strengths, including OHP 71, figure 19.3 (p 759) How Modern Catalogues Overcame Mail Order's Weaknesses:
  ⇒ How catalogues are more user-friendly
  ⇒ how they have adapted to better meet the needs of changing customers
  ⇒ how they have exploited developments in database technology
  ⇒ how they have capitalised on improved distribution techniques.
- *Teleshopping:* definition; applications; trends.

The direct marketing campaign (pp 763-769):

This section is based on OHP 72, figure 19.4 (p 766) Managing a Direct Marketing Campaign:

- *Campaign objectives (including pp 763-766):* types of objectives that direct marketing can achieve; links with wider marketing objectives.
- *Target audience selection:* classifying prospects for direct marketing; sources of lists; problems with international audiences.
- *Media selection:* finding the right medium for the audience; importance of cost effectiveness; importance of buyer readiness stages.
- *Creative development:* designing the campaign, including OHP 73, figure 19.5 (p 768) Issues Influencing Creative Development:
  ⇒ Overview of the issues
  ⇒ importance of getting them all right
  ⇒ importance of ensuring consistency between them.
- *Response management:* importance of ensuring that the organisation can cope with the expected response.
- *Evaluation:* ratios for assessing responses and campaign success.

Database creation and management (pp 769-772):

The database as a foundation for ongoing relationship marketing, including OHT 74, figure 19.6 (p 769) Database Creation and Management:

- Recap problems of recruiting customers through direct marketing
- importance of detailed and up to date customer information
- necessary information about customers
- role of data in facilitating repeat sales, up-selling and cross-selling
- importance of regular data analysis for both operational and strategic purposes
- importance of maintaining ongoing relationships.

QUESTIONS FOR REVIEW

19.1   What is direct marketing? (pp 740-741)

Direct marketing is an interactive system of marketing that uses one or more advertising media to effect measurable responses which can then be used as a basis for ongoing relationship building between the organisation and its customers.

19.2   What general issues have led to the rise in popularity of direct marketing? (pp 741-743)

- Changing demographics and lifestyles
- increased customer confidence in direct marketing

- increasing competition
- media fragmentation
- increasing media and sales costs
- the opening up of new distribution channels
- increasing computer power
- lower data processing costs
- new communications technology.

19.3   Summarise what you consider to be the key success factors for a direct mail campaign. (pp 744-749)

- Maintaining a 'hot' mailing list
- ensuring that the envelope gets opened
- tailoring the content to suit the target customer
- using attention grabbing devices
- making it easy for the recipient to respond.

19.4   What is direct response advertising and what are the relative advantages and disadvantages of using (a) television, (b) radio and (c) print media for it? (pp 749-753)

Direct response advertising uses standard media and formats, but is designed to provoke a response from the target audience in terms of orders or requests for further information.
- *Television* can reach a huge audience, but is expensive, and the telephone number or address might have to be repeated many times before the audience remembers and acts on them. With potentially huge numbers of responses, the organisation must be sure that it can deal efficiently with them.
- *Radio* can reach large local audiences relatively cheaply. Again, however, much repetition might be necessary to get the response mechanism across.
- *Print media* can reach large, highly segmented audiences and provide the widest range of alternative response mechanisms (phone, mail-in, send off a coupon, e-mail). The advertisements are less transient than their broadcast counterparts, and so the customer can follow them up when they are in the mood. Because of this, however, there could be less sense of urgency to respond.

19.5   In what ways can telemarketing support and enhance the other elements of the promotional mix? (pp 753-758)

Telemarketing can:
- Be used for competitions and responses to other promotions
- provide customer care support
- provide back-up information to enhance advertising efforts
- be used for personal selling
- be used to screen prospective customers and make appointments for sales representatives
- create databases for future direct marketing campaigns.

19.6   How do 'modern' mail order operations differ from the 'traditional' approach? (pp 758-760)

Modern mail order operations:
- Do not run on the agency system
- are more narrowly segmented
- are more efficient at order processing and delivery
- deliver more quickly
- do not necessarily offer long-term credit
- offer better quality merchandise.

19.7   Why might High Street retailers want to run mail order operations in parallel with, and under the same trading name, as their stores? (p 760)

- They extend the shop window into the customer's home
- they can expand the retailer's geographic coverage
- they can trade on the retailer's name and reputation
- they advertise the retail operation.

19.8   What is teleshopping and through what media can it be offered to customers? (p 763)

Teleshopping enables the consumer to select products and to order interactively from home. Teleshopping media include:
- The Internet
- cable and satellite television channels
- direct computer links between buyer and seller through a modem.

19.9   Explain the role that direct marketing can play in both creating and retaining customers. (pp 763-766)

Direct marketing can:
- Provide opportunities for potential interested customers to contact a supplier for information or to buy
- make it very easy for customers to order and re-order
- create tailored offerings that better match customers' needs and buying habits
- create opportunities for cross-selling or up-selling
- persuade customers to visit retail premises or dealerships
- persuade customers to try products.

19.10   Define the main stages in managing a direct marketing campaign. (pp 766-769)

- *Defining campaign objectives:* specifying what the desired outcomes of the campaign are.
- *Selecting the target audience:* defining who should be targeted, their characteristics and needs.
- *Media selection:* finding the most appropriate means of reaching the target audience and stimulating responses.
- *Creative development:* finding the most appropriate means of stimulating responses.
- *Response management:* ensuring that the logistical frameworks are in place to cope with the expected response efficiently and effectively.
- *Evaluation:* analysing actual outcomes compared with expected outcomes.

QUESTIONS FOR DISCUSSION

19.1   Collect three pieces of direct mail and for each one assess (a) what you think it is trying to achieve, (b) how that message has been communicated, (c) what involvement devices have been used to encourage the recipient to read the mailshot, and (d) how easy it is for the recipient to respond in the required way.

This question is designed to allow the students to review the material on pp 766-769 with a practical slant. Students should show that they have thought through how each chosen mailshot 'works', and how its various creative elements interact with issues of target audience and objectives to create a powerful piece of communication. Students might also be encouraged to compare mailshots to analyse why some seem to work better than others. Are these differences caused by:
- More 'difficult' target audiences?
- Poor targeting?
- More complex messages?

- Less intrinsically emotionally appealing messages?
- Poor or unimaginative creative skills?
- Lack of involvement devices?
- Poor response mechanisms?

19.2   Using Table 19.2 as a framework, carry out your own analysis of the advertising in a magazine. Discuss examples of good and bad direct response advertising from that magazine. What overall conclusions can you draw?

Students should categorise advertisements according to whether they encourage:
- Postal responses
- coupon filling and return
- telephone responses

and additionally whether the respondent or the promoter pays the cost of response.

'Good' and 'bad' advertisements might be defined in terms of:
- The cost to the consumer of replying
- the range of choice of response mechanisms offered
- what they are promised if they do respond
- the ease of response (for example do they just have to pick up the phone? do they just have to fill in their name and address on a coupon?)
- the level of encouragement to respond contained within the advertisement
- clarity of instructions
- clarity of promises
- any incentives to respond NOW.

19.3   To what extent, and why, do you think that outbound telemarketing should be controlled by legislation or codes of practice?

Issues that might be raised during this debate include:
- Invasion of privacy
- the irritation and annoyance factor
- the role of a telephone preference service
- voluntary self-regulation *vs.* legislation
- whether cold calling is acceptable
- whether automatic dialling systems should be permitted
- in what ways telemarketing is 'worse' than direct mail.

19.4   For each of the techniques of direct marketing outlined in Fig. 19.1, assess their relevance to (a) consumer markets and (b) organisational markets.

The techniques under consideration are:
- Direct mail
- direct response advertising
- telemarketing
- mail order
- teleshopping.

Students should discuss their relevance to consumer and organisational markets taking into account:
- The characteristics of the products that might be being sold
- the risks and benefits of eliminating intermediaries
- the size of the potential market
- the complexity of the purchase
- perceived risk to the buyer
- locating and contacting the potential customer
- reasons for buying

- potential for future repeat and expanded business
- potential for relationship building.

19.5 **Imagine that you are a customer of a mail order CD club. Specify what information about yourself the club's database should ideally hold. Which bits of that information would be of greatest use to the organisation in designing an appropriate offer for you?**

Required information might be:
- Name
- address
- age
- length of club membership
- how you were recruited
- musical preferences, both style of music and by artist
- preferred price band (e.g. full price or budget)
- frequency of purchasing
- value of purchases
- response to promotional mailshots.

Once the organisation has you as a member, the most valuable pieces of information that will help to design specific offers are those relating to past purchasing history and preferences. If you have been a member for some time, and have been sent previous offers, your pattern of responses to them will be important. Students should be encouraged to discuss what effect each of the above prices of information could have on a promotional offer.

CASE STUDY 19.1 Hyatt International Hotels (p 775)

Teaching Objectives

1. To consider the kind of information needed to build a database for direct marketing purposes;
2. to examine ways in which direct marketing might be applied to different kinds of customer;
3. to analyse the problems of implementing international direct marketing campaigns.

1 **What kind of data could a hotel capture about its guests and how might this be of use to the hotel's marketers?**

Background characteristics:
- Name and address
- party size
- private or company booking
- leisure or business trip
- pre-booked or walk-in
- smoking/non-smoking rooms
- geographical location, linked to neighbourhood analysis.

Usage characteristics:
- New or repeat business
- frequency of visits
- length of stay
- spend (both total and by category, for example fitness centre, restaurant, laundry)
- payment method
- mode of travel
- food, wine, minibar, video choice
- room price, special discounts.

All these data help to describe customer profile and can be used to target special promotions as well as maintaining an ongoing customer relationship by regular communication through corporate magazines etc. Data could therefore be used to:

- Encourage more visits to the hotel or chain
- encourage visits to different sites within the hotel chain
- encourage longer stays
- encourage more in-house spend.

2   In what ways might the direct marketing approach to a £10,000 a year customer differ from the approach to an £800 a year customer?

The retention of regular, high-spending customers is crucial. The marketing objectives would be to attract the customer back and to provide excellent service during the actual visit.

For the £10,000 customer, the direct marketing approach might mean:

- Regular, high quality, personalised mailshots
- trying to build a strong relationship
- encouraging high value customers to think of themselves as a select, discerning elite
- offering high quality extra services
- offering high value incentives to broaden the customer's geographic range of hotels used
- offering high value incentives to broaden the customer's off-season usage of hotels.

For the £800 customer, the direct marketing approach might mean:

- Regular personalised mailshots
- trying to build a strong relationship
- offering moderate incentives to increase usage and spend
- offering moderate incentives to try to expand geographic and off-season usage.

The main difference between them is the amount that the organisation is prepared to invest in cultivating them. Clearly the £800 group have the potential for spending more, and this needs to be encouraged, while the £10,000 group is already very valuable and the focus is more on relationship maintenance and reward rather than overt attempts to increase their spend.

3   What advice would you give to Hyatt's marketing department about what problems to look out for in setting up a centralised, co-ordinated database?

Need for simplicity:

- Hyatt must not create a monster system that few can use
- it could be best to start with essential information and then expand the range of data as the system's use grows
- the system has to be IT based with data captured automatically from the reservation and/or check out system
- a standardised approach will have to be developed so that information can be integrated from all over the world.

Database management:

- The database will have to be 'cleaned' and updated regularly, for example keeping track of changes of address
- the database must be used to segment and prioritise customers, probably on more detailed criteria than simply heavy and light users. The more segmentation that takes place, the more appropriate the special marketing promotions can be.

Usage training:

- Marketing staff need to be trained to ensure that the data are used to guide marketing decisions
- staff at individual hotels might have to be trained in the day to day use of the system for both inputting and accessing customer details
- guidelines on marketing information applications should be developed
- individual hotel locations should be able to access data for local promotions

- the hotel should be able to identify heavy users before they arrive so that they can be given special service.

4   What are the potential problems facing Hyatt when eventually it is able to think about a co-ordinated international direct mail campaign?

Mailing list management: building an international mailing list could be a tough challenge for Hyatt, not so much in its construction, but being able to use it effectively to develop campaigns. Particular issues could be:
- Ensuring careful targeting of mailing campaigns to appropriate customers
- reassessing the basis of targeting on more sophisticated lines than just volume usage. Other factors could also define guests worthy of special communication.
- Problems with different international conventions on address formats, for example
- complex database management problems arising from the sheer scale of the operation
- regular updating of the database to record who has received what offers, and the responses
- database analysis for planning future promotions
- maintaining some flexibility and access at a local level while retaining central control.

Creative Development: developing appropriate creative themes and messages is always a challenge for the direct mail campaigner. Any failure to gain attention and then encourage reading and action will result in a less than effective campaign. Issues to consider will include:
- Personalising mailshots in the customer's native language with appropriate salutations
- if the material sent is not relevant, it can have a negative impact on brand perceptions. The chances of this happening are increased when a broad appeal is being adopted.
- Significant differences could exist in the role and effectiveness of direct mail campaigns across the world
- campaigns must be sufficiently flexible to allow for local messages and local campaigns, even if local is defined as nation, region or state.

Objectives and implementation: the purpose of the direct mail campaign could vary in different countries, depending on the nature of the trade (for example resort hotels vs. airport hotels) and the local competitive scene. Catering for all these variations as part of a overall marketing strategy could be difficult. Issues to consider will include:
- Deciding on the purpose of the campaign to guide implementation. If a campaign is being used for information only and just as a means of maintaining contact as part of a relationship building campaign, the message and implementation could be capable of a transnational approach. Loyalty programmes are also frequently centralised. However, special promotions to fill capacity, give additional rewards for loyalty, or to open up new segments might need a more localised approach.
- Special promotions that call for a response will have to allow for different response mechanisms and times around the world.
- The legislation on the use of unsolicited mail also varies around the world, so some care will have to be exercised.
- Decisions will have to be made as to whether the centralised mailing database should mainly be used for a standardised international mailing programme or whether it needs a greater degree of flexibility for regionalised (for example Europe or North America) or localised (by country, region or city). The centralised resources could still, however, be used to handle high speed mailings.

CASE STUDY 19.2 Into the Internet (p 776)

Teaching Objectives:

1. To examine the current problems of selling over the Internet;
2. to explore the appropriate use of the Internet as a selling tool;
3. to consider the role of the Internet as a toll for relationship building.

1   What are the main barriers to Internet shopping and how can they be overcome?

Technology:
- The use of technology is not widespread although it is increasing
- not that many organisations are using the Internet extensively for selling
- the range of products available on the Internet is not yet broad
- the Internet can actually be very slow, especially compared with teleshopping
- the costs of setting up a selling site on the Internet are perceived as high.

Customer Resistance:
- The Internet is more acceptable to younger, better educated than older, lower socioeconomic groups
- it is not always easy to find and access new sites
- sites that are available may not be well designed or easy to use
- there is a general level of ignorance of the Internet's full potential
- there are perceived security problems with on-line credit card usage
- it is a poor quality shopping experience, since the customer cannot touch or experience the goods or benefit from the excitement of a retail atmosphere.

Time and innovation will assist in the adoption process. The number of selling sites should increase and the quality of sites should improve. New technology and features such as cryptography should improve security and reassure the customer. Development costs should fall as the volume of subscribers increases and more companies create sites and ensure that they are communicated to potential customers. Consumer resistance could be more difficult to overcome. It could take some time. In the longer term, the younger, early adopters will spread the innovation across a wider cross-section of the population and a new younger age group will be even more familiar with the technology. This might not be fast enough for Internet to achieve its full potential. Internet advertisers might consider:
- Encouraging the development of education guides and directories
- ensuring that sites are easily accessible and are capable of either extensive or quicker use
- opening up a price differential for Internet purchasing, passing on some of the savings in marketing and administration in the form of lower prices
- developing new direct ordering formats that enable browsing, the checking of availability and easy ordering
- ensuring better integration of Internet marketing initiatives with mainstream marketing campaigns in order to provide support material as well as high quality site material
- develop better communication to explain the benefits of using Internet for shopping/ordering etc.

2   What kinds of products do you think can best be sold direct over the Internet, and why?

The Internet can be used for buying and selling both high and low involvement products.

High involvement:

The Internet will play an essential supporting role within the overall marketing effort in the searching and information provision stage. Although ordering can not be expected, some products would benefit from fast access to detailed information such as product features, prices, dealership locations, after-sales servicing arrangements, guarantees, etc. This information would be useful for helping the customer to narrow down the range of choices before looking for more focused demonstrations, product viewing and negotiation. Examples could include cars, home buying, electrical goods, furniture and holidays.

Low involvement

In low involvement purchasing situations, the routine and sometimes tedious aspects of purchasing can be relieved by the use of the Internet. To what extent the use of the Internet will increase the proportion of non-store retailing significantly remains to be seen. A lot will depend, ironically, on the Internet's ability to deliver cost effectively and consumers' willingness to change their buying habits and behaviour. A situation could be envisaged where product items are selected from a supermarket site page and orders placed for home delivery. A minimum order charge or home delivery charge would have to be introduced. Generally, items that benefit from inspection before the sale, such as fresh fruit and vegetables, are less likely to be well received for Internet shopping. However, as quality grading systems become better understood, even these kinds of product might eventually become amenable to Internet selling. Such a move could also favour bulk buying to gain volume discounts, which would make electronic ordering more profitable. Other areas would also benefit from the browsing capability and direct ordering. Bookshops, stationery suppliers, parts suppliers, and record stores for example could all find a role for the Internet. In short, most areas could use Internet for marketing purposes, but a smaller number would use it for the complete selling and ordering process.

3   How can the Internet help to improve relationships between companies and their customers and potential customers?

This is an important development area. The Internet provides a new medium for a direct relationship that builds on all the strengths of the current methods such as direct mail, mail order and direct response. The Internet enables:
- Low cost, regular and interactive communication
- the collection of vast quantities of information about customers who visit an Internet site
- the targeting of special communication and offers to different groups
- the development of a news site updating customers on latest developments, which is especially important with products that attract special attention, such as hobbies, holiday packages, usage tips for IT etc
- a direct response capability so that the customer can make full use of the service and e-mail enquires
- potential customers to be dealt with in a direct manner, whether for enquiries, information needs, after-sales helplines etc.

4   Will the Internet ever take over from other forms of direct marketing and from conventional retailing?

Some types of retailing could be vulnerable, as already highlighted, if:
- The retailer needs to communicate to a geographically dispersed customer group who currently buy by mail order the product does not have to be touched or handled before purchase
- purchasing can be routinised and can be tedious
- visual inspection of the product by the customer is not essential
- customers know what they want before they go shopping
- travelling is difficult
- new information is regularly required
- subscription services are used.

In reality, the Internet will probably supplement existing retail operations rather than replacing them in the near future. In the short-term, there will not be sufficient numbers of customers prepared to use interactive technology. For many, shopping is not a functional task but a leisure experience in which half the fun is in browsing and enjoying the retail atmosphere.

Marketing in Action Automated Call Handling (p 757)

Discussion question
What are the applications of ACH systems and what factors have to be considered in managing them?

The main areas of application for ACH are:
- Taking orders
- handling customer enquires
- customer care lines
- competition entry.

The main issues that need addressing are:
- Ensuring a consistent speed of response despite the volume of calls
- capacity handling with uneven demand

- the ease and speed with which the system steers the customer through the menus
- an efficient link with interactive dialogue with the computer
- the relevance of the response to the customer's problem
- the majority of customers' unwillingness to use an automated system, especially for the first time
- the impersonal nature of the system.

However, ACH can:

- Be very cost effective
- handle more customers, more quickly
- be used to extend the range of services to customers, for example telephone banking at weekends.

Marketing in Action The Next Generation of Mail Order Catalogues (p 760)

Discussion question
How does the 'Next' type of catalogue exploit the strengths and overcome the weaknesses of more traditional mail order operations?

Mail order's traditional strengths are shown in figure 19.2 (p 759) and include:
- *Convenience:* new style catalogues are still used for convenient home shopping for a wide range of merchandise.
- *Comprehensive range:* new catalogues are better targeted and more narrowly focused in terms of product range, but they offer depth within the range.
- *Credit:* payment by weekly instalments can still be found, but more upmarket catalogues accept credit card payment in full for goods ordered.
- *Commission:* this is now less relevant, given the changing nature of the target market. Promotional discounts on specific merchandise are perhaps more acceptable.

Mail order's traditional weaknesses are shown in figure 19.3 (p 759), and include:
- *Lack of speed:* new technology impacting on ordering and distribution systems has speeded up the whole process and guaranteed 48 hour delivery can often be offered.
- *Downmarket image:* catalogues have improved their image through links with high street names; brand name merchandise; better quality merchandise.
- *Lack of targeting:* catalogues are now clearly targeted at age, gender, lifestyle, and product-orientated segments
- *The agency system:* this has largely disappeared, allowing customers more discretion about whether to buy just for themselves and their family or to buy informally for interested friends.

Marketing in Action Castle Cement Sweeps Telemarketing Awards (p 764)

Discussion question
How has Castle Cement used telemarketing to augment its overall promotional effort?

Castle had found that traditional promotional methods were ineffective in generating awareness of Multichem. Telemarketing enabled:
- Information to be given giving on the new product
- direct contact with 13,000 builders
- the flexibility to be linked with a sales promotion to generate further interest
- information gathering to build a database and to find out about customer purchasing habits.

SUGGESTED ASSIGNMENTS

- To what extent can direct marketing play a role in the promotional mix of an organisational market?
- Questions for Discussion 19.3.

Chapter 20
PUBLIC RELATIONS, SPONSORSHIP AND EXHIBITIONS

LECTURE PLAN

A lecture based on this chapter should help the student to:
1. Define what PR is and the areas of marketing activities it covers;
2. understand its role in supporting the organisation's activities and in reaching various groups, or publics, with differing interests and information needs;
3. outline the techniques of PR, their appropriateness for different kinds of public, and how they might be evaluated;
4. appreciate the importance of corporate identity, why organisations might wish to change identity, and the processes involved in change;
5. understand the role of sponsorship in the marketing communications mix and the benefits and problems of different types of sponsorship; and
6. appreciate the contribution that exhibitions can make to achieving marketing objectives and how to exploit them to the full.

The key sections of this lecture should be:

Introduction (pp 779-787):
- Definition of public relations
- overview of activities covered
- definition of publics, including OHP 75, figure 20.1 (p 782) Publics:
  ⇒ Brief definition of each group
  ⇒ overview of their interest in the organisation
  ⇒ necessity for communication with each group
  ⇒ necessity for consistent communication between different groups.
- The difference between marketing and corporate PR.

Techniques in PR (pp 787-793):
This section is based on OHP 76, figure 20.2 (p 787) Techniques in Public Relations:
- Brief overview of what each technique involves
- which publics each can reach
- circumstances in which each might be used
- each technique's contribution to the PR effort
- advantages and disadvantages of each.

Evaluating the PR effort (pp 793-795):
- The range of evaluation techniques
- the appropriateness for various types of PR activity
- the problems of evaluating PR.

Corporate identity (pp 795-799):
- Why change identity, including OHP 77, figure 20.4 (p 795) Reasons for Changing Corporate Identity:
  ⇒ Overview of the reasons for change
  ⇒ emphasise importance of identity

⇒ emphasise need for identity to be more than skin deep.
- Stages in the change process, including OHP 78, figure 20.5 (p 797) Stages in the Corporate Identity Change Process:
  ⇒ Overview of the stages
  ⇒ importance of good change management
  ⇒ importance of clear identity communication internally and externally.
- Problems with the change process.

This section could be omitted, and students encouraged to read the material for themselves.

Sponsorship (pp 799-810):
- Definition.
- Types of sponsorship: sport, broadcast, arts, cause related marketing.
- Advantages and disadvantages of each type.
- Choosing sponsorship type: including OHP 79, figure 20.7 (p 809) Factors Influencing Sponsorship Choice:
  ⇒ Overview of each factor
  ⇒ examples of each
  ⇒ potential constraints and conflicts between them
  ⇒ importance of overall fit with corporate image and wider marketing objectives.
- Evaluating sponsorship: evaluation methods and their problems.

This section could be omitted, and students encouraged to read the material for themselves.

Exhibitions and trade shows (pp 810-817):
- Definition and scope of such events
- benefits of exhibition attendance
- relationship between exhibitions and personal selling
- reasons for attending exhibitions
- management problems, including OHP 80, table 20.7 (p 816) Reasons for Poor Exhibition Performance:
  ⇒ Overview of reasons
  ⇒ importance of good planning and management
  ⇒ importance of adequate investment
  ⇒ importance of strategic fit between an exhibition and the rest of the marketing mix.

This section could be omitted, and students encouraged to read the material for themselves.

QUESTIONS FOR REVIEW

20.1   What is PR and in what ways does it differ from other elements of the promotional mix? (pp 780-781)

PR is the deliberate, planned and sustained effort to institute and maintain mutual understanding between an organisation and its publics. It differs from the rest of the promotional mix in that it:
- Does not directly try to sell anything
- focuses on the nature and quality of relationships between the organisation and various groups
- communicates with a much wider range of groups than just customers.

20.2   Differentiate between marketing PR and corporate PR. To what extent do you think this is a useful distinction? (pp 784-787)

Marketing PR is designed to enhance the organisation's profile and credibility in support of more mainstream marketing activities. It might be short-term and product-specific PR. Corporate PR is a part of long-term relationship building strategy enhancing the organisation's profile and credibility generally. It might also be used in response to a commercial crisis. It is a useful distinction because the two types of PR:

- Have different objectives
- play different roles in marketing mixes and corporate strategy
- operate over different timescales
- might be aimed at different publics.

20.3   List the advantages and disadvantages of publicity. (pp 787-790)

Advantages:
- It is relatively cheap, if not free
- it has credibility
- it can reach a very wide audience
- it generates excitement and interest.

Disadvantages:
- It is uncontrollable
- its coverage can be patchy
- it is short-lived.

20.4   In what ways can organisations feed material to the media, and in what kind of circumstances might each be appropriate? (pp 787-788)

- *Press releases:* written material, perhaps backed up with photographic or video footage used to inform the media of events or news.
- *News conferences:* gather media representatives together on a special occasion to hear big announcements, or to be updated during corporate crises.
- *Press briefings:* perhaps happen more regularly for periodic updates and routine background information. Often used by government departments.
- *Press receptions:* a more informal, social event at which media can mingle with the organisation's staff. It helps to develop and maintain good press relations generally.

20.5   Outline the potential benefits of developing a corporate magazine, such as those discussed at p 791. (pp 791-792)

Corporate magazines:
- Can be distributed to a wide range of publics
- can communicate complex information
- can help to create and maintain relationships and loyalty
- can be used to advertise or promote products and services
- keep the corporate name in the reader's mind
- can enhance and reinforce corporate image.

20.6   Why might an organisation want to change its corporate identity? (pp 795-797)

- The current image is dated
- the organisation has changed and evolved to the point where the existing image is inappropriate
- the organisation wants to be more clearly differentiated from existing or new competition
- a new identity is needed to unify diverse activities more clearly
- reinforcing corporate image and communicating corporate values better
- as an internal motivator, creating a renewed sense of purpose and direction.

20.7   Briefly describe the stages an organisation should go through in changing corporate identity, explaining why each one is important. (pp 797-798)

- *Internal and external research:* to establish what the organisation's current image is, and what it should be in the eyes of key publics. Without this, the exercise can have no clear purpose.

- *Defining objectives and criteria:* what characteristics is the new identity to reflect and what should it achieve. This provides the foundation for the next stage.
- *Design and image development:* translating the concepts into a visual image. This is important because the organisation is going to have to live with its outcomes for a very long time!
- *Implementation and launch:* ensuring that the new identity is appropriately applied and that publics are aware of it and what it means. If this is not done properly, it could lead to confusion and a scrappy launch.
- *Monitoring and evaluation:* ensuring that the new identity is understood and is working well in practice. It allows any last fine-tuning of the identity, and the resolution of any minor problems in its application.

20.8   Why might the lack of top management commitment to a corporate identity change mean the failure of the whole exercise? (pp 798-799)

Without top management commitment, the identity change might:
- Not be given sufficient resources
- not be managed by someone with sufficiently high-level authority to make it work
- not be taken seriously by anyone
- not be anything more than a half-hearted cosmetic exercise.

20.9   What can sponsorship offer that media advertising cannot? (pp 799-810)

- Associating a brand or corporate name with something deemed 'worthy'
- associating a brand or corporate name with an activity or interest close to the target market's heart
- a means of expressing 'corporate citizenship'
- a wide range of spin-off publicity opportunities
- a means of reaching different or hard-to-reach audiences
- a platform for corporate hospitality
- a means of communication that is not quite so overtly 'commercial'.

20.10   What factors might contribute to successful exhibition attendance? (pp 816-817)

- Thorough planning
- adequate investment in stands etc
- securing a good site within the exhibition area
- fully briefed and motivated staff
- clear performance objectives
- ensuring that enquiries are recorded and fully followed up.

QUESTIONS FOR DISCUSSION

20.1   At p 781 a range of different publics are mentioned with which a university might have to create and maintain relationships. Draw up a similar list for your own university or college and (a) briefly outline what aspects of the institution's activities might be of particular interest to each of those publics and (b) suggest appropriate PR methods for each of them.

The publics mentioned on p 781 include:
- Students
- potential students
- schools and colleges
- staff
- the academic community
- funding bodies
- industry

- the media.

Rather than simply addressing this question in an abstract way, students should be encouraged to find out what their own institution is doing to foster relationships with these and any other publics identified. They should analyse critically:

- The range of PR methods used
- which publics are targeted with which methods
- why these publics are so important to the institution
- what each method is trying to achieve
- what message each method is giving about the institution's activities
- the extent to which the messages are consistent
- whether any particular publics seem to have been left out.

20.2 **Find a corporate story that has made the news recently. It might be a 'crisis', a takeover battle, job losses or creation, new products or big contracts, for instance. Collect reports and press cuttings from a range of media on this story and compare the content. To what extent do you think that (a) the media have used material provided by the organisation itself? (b) the story has developed beyond the control of the organisation? (c) Imagine yourself to be the organisation's PR manager. Write a brief report to the managing director outlining what you feel to be the benefits and disadvantages of the coverage your organisation has received, and what you think should be done next regarding this story.**

This question encourages students to explore and analyse the workings of PR through the media. The exercise underlines many of the characteristics of press relations and publicity as PR tools. Issues raised might include:

- Uncontrollability
- inconsistencies between different treatments of the story
- the various slants on the story depending on each medium's own target audience and its interests
- selective use of detail and information provided by the organisation
- the life span of the story
- the differing amount of coverage in different media
- the editorial interpretation of the story and the extent to which it is supportive or otherwise of the organisation's view.

20.3 **Assess the Midland Bank's approach to choosing the charities that benefit from its cause-related marketing outlined on p 808.**

Points that might be raised include:

- It ensures that both parties get something out of the arrangement
- it ensures that cause-related marketing fits in with the bank's broader communications and marketing strategy
- it commits both parties to a three year, planned project with specific objectives
- it directs a significant amount of cash towards a focused area
- it ensures that the money will be well used and efficiently used
- it creates a partnership with defined mutual responsibilities.

However:

- It might discriminate against smaller, struggling charities
- it concentrates cash into only one charity within a sector
- it might discriminate against 'unfashionable' causes
- there is a small risk that the three year tie might become a burden to either party.

20.4 **What are the dangers of sponsorship from the recipient's perspective?**

Points that might be raised include:

- The risk of sponsorship being cut or withdrawn completely because of the sponsor's changing financial situation
- the risk of sponsorship being cut or withdrawn completely because of the sponsor's changing marketing strategy
- the risk of sponsorship being cut or withdrawn completely because of the recipient's poor performance or event delivery
- interference by the sponsor in terms of how events should be organised or on what the sponsorship should be spent
- meeting obligations to the sponsor, for example providing corporate hospitality opportunities
- conflict between different sponsors of the same event
- potential conflict if, for example, a team participating in a sports tournament is sponsored by a competitor of the event's major sponsor
- trying to sign up so many sponsors that no sponsor feels that it is gaining significant benefit from the exercise
- 'ambush marketing' - with a televised major sports event, for example, sponsors' competitors (who are not themselves sponsors of the event) can legitimately buy up advertising air time while the event is being screened and thus make the audience think that they are associated with the event
- failing to attract sufficient sponsorship to make an event viable.

20.5   Draw up a table outlining alternative methods for evaluating PR, sponsorship and exhibitions, and the potential pitfalls of those methods.

Some of the methods of evaluating PR are:
- *Awareness generation:* how much and within what target audiences has awareness increased?
- *Attitude change or creation:* to what extent has the PR message penetrated attitudes?
- *Media coverage and tone (column cm, airtime etc):* how much coverage has been generated? How much would that amount of coverage have cost if it had been advertising? Was it supportive?
- *Effect on positioning:* how has it affected the way in which we are perceived in comparison with our competitors?
- *Responses generated:* how many enquiries or sales leads have been generated?
- *Share price changes.*
- *Effect on sales:* the problem with this is separating the PR effect from that of the rest of the marketing mix.

Some of the methods of evaluating sponsorship are:
- Media coverage and tone
- awareness generation
- effects on attitude
- effect on sales
- feedback specifically from participating groups, in terms of awareness, attitude, behavioural response etc.

Some of the methods of evaluating exhibitions are:
- Media coverage and tone of the event and our participation in it
- number of visitors to the exhibition
- number of key decision-makers attending the exhibition
- awareness generation within the industry or among potential customers
- effects on attitude within the industry or among potential customers
- number and quality of leads generated
- effect on sales.

General points to note when undertaking evaluation in order to avoid pitfalls are as follows:
- Ensure that the chosen evaluation methods are appropriate for the original objectives
- be aware of the problems of measuring things like attitudes and be prepared to invest in 'professional' research in order to get a true picture
- avoid making unrealistic assumptions about cause and effect. There are many other factors out these affecting attitudes, awareness, sales etc.

- quantitative measures are just part of the picture. The amount of media coverage gained is a meaningless measure unless there is some qualitative assessment of its tone and level of supportiveness
- combinations of measures are likely to be necessary to build a more complete picture. Media coverage needs to be looked at in terms of its appropriateness to the target audience and the extent to which it has changed or influenced their attitudes.

CASE STUDY 20.1 Shell, Greenpeace and Brent Spar (p 820)

Teaching Objectives

1. To ensure that students understand the range of publics targeted by PR activities;
2. to consider the use and effectiveness of different PR techniques;
3. to focus on the interaction between commercial organisations and pressure groups.

1   Which 'publics' was Shell having to deal with during the course of this issue?

Both parties in the Brent Spar confrontation were using deliberate PR strategies with the publics they considered to be important in shaping the outcome of the dispute. It could be argued that Greenpeace probably won the first round in the battle through the publics they reached and the nature of the activities they pursued.

- *The general public:* in the markets that Shell operates in, it is difficult to distinguish between the general public and potential and actual end customers. Greenpeace, however, is also appealing to a similar audience although it knows that it only needs a response from a small but active minority in order to attract sufficient attention to endorse a claim of 'representing public opinion'. It was public pressure, perhaps cultivated by the media, that eventually encouraged the politicians to make a stand on the issue.
- *Customers:* Shell's customers started boycotting Shell garages, especially in Germany. This was a major cause of concerns for Shell's board of directors. This boycott was a major factor in causing Shell to reconsider its policy.
- *Other environmental groups:* both large and small environmental groups, through their own lobbying and motivation of interested parties, help the 'cause dissemination' process. These groups, therefore, can act as opinion formers following Greenpeace's lead. There are several environmental groups concerned with nuclear power restriction, the degradation caused by the spread of motorways, preservation of the countryside etc which could all find a common cause in supporting Greenpeace's fight against big business to prevent what they regard as environmental spoiling. It might, after all, be their area that is under threat next.
- *The UK government:* the government appeared to take a strong pro-Shell view in the dispute and ironically in the end it was they who appeared to feel let down by Shell's reversal of the dumping decision.
- *Other European governments:* given the strong green lobby in continental Europe, especially in Germany, it is perhaps not surprising that a number of governments appeared to support the Greenpeace position, even if they did not agree with their methods.
- *The Green Party:* a powerful political force as an opinion leader and opinion former in Europe.
- *The Church:* this was perhaps a surprising source of support for the Greenpeace stand, but clearly if religious leaders can be motivated to express a view, it would have a significant impact on some members of the general public and would certainly legitimise the cause.
- *Internal:* in a large multinational there are many internal publics with potentially different perspectives on the same issue. The German operation was particularly badly hit by the boycott. The engineering area had a technical view on the most appropriate means of disposal for Brent Spar, while the board had to consider the global perspective. It is important that all parties should understand the issues, work in a co-ordinated manner, and present a united front.
- *The media:* the media are the main target group to influence public opinion. They are perceived as being independent and neutral on many issues. Greenpeace went to great lengths to prepare and

present both emotional and factual information to the media in order to generate the maximum favourable coverage.

⇒ *Television:* Greenpeace's activities made excellent television footage. Early in the dispute this media group was targeted and the communication infrastructure put into place to make sure that television got what it wanted.

⇒ *Press/magazines:* this group appeared to be crucial. After a lack of interest in the UK, the continental press activation was a major vehicle in activating public opinion.

2   What different PR techniques have been used by the various parties in this case and how effective were they?

- *Events:* the occupation of Brent Spar was a form of media event. It created a highly visual example of the small guy fighting off big business trying to spoil the environment. The fact that it was an illegal occupation was perhaps sometimes forgotten. This was perhaps the most effective PR activity undertaken by Greenpeace as it provided the newsworthiness and focus needed to raise the issue in the mind of Europeans. Shell was always going to be on the defensive on this issue. On the one hand, the ejection of Greenpeace would reinforce Greenpeace's argument, but on the other hand, if Greenpeace was allowed to remain, so too would the media focus. In short, it was a no win issue for Shell.

- *Media relations:* this was the second part of the Greenpeace strategy. It was essential to exploit the Brent Spar occupation and raise public awareness of the issues. They used a variety of techniques: film and photography releases; press releases on the issues and news updates; and regular press conferences to ensure smoother dissemination. Again, Shell never really appeared to be able to get its side of the argument across. The focus on technical issues has little appeal to the public and thus media interest was also low.

- *Lobbying:* there is no direct evidence of Greenpeace's lobbying, but it might well have taken place behind the scenes. It might not be easy for mainstream politicians to identify with the Greenpeace movement, because of some of their unorthodox measures, but they can identify with the issues when it suits their broader interests. Shell appeared to be far more active in lobbying. It certainly appeared to have been highly successful with the UK government, as it remained supportive throughout the episode. It would appear that the legal and technical arguments were a powerful factor in retaining their support. Lobbying other European governments, if it took place at all, was clearly far less successful.

- *Publications:* through the use of the Internet and other literature, Greenpeace was very effectively able to communicate their conviction that there were real dangers in dumping at sea.

3   What advantages and disadvantages does a pressure group like Greenpeace have in dealing with a large global company such as Shell?

The advantages that a pressure group has in dealing with large global companies are:
- They can play the David *vs.* Goliath role in the public's mind
- they are not bound by conventional rules and 'corporate responsibility'
- they can break the rules, within reasonable limits
- public sympathy is more easily generated
- they can play on potential differences of opinion within the global company.

The disadvantages that a pressure group has in dealing with large global companies are:
- The larger company can lobby more support from government
- protection of jobs, investment and assets often seem to overrule environmental considerations
- the larger company can mobilise far more resources
- if the pressure group makes a misjudgement, it can expect litigation
- even if the pressure group does not make mistakes, their judgement can be questioned by the 'establishment', in this case including leading scientists.

4   What lessons can both Greenpeace and Shell learn from this situation?

Greenpeace can perhaps learn that:
- The end sometimes justifies the means
- you should always check the facts before going public, as they will be challenged
- careful planning and implementation of a campaign always pays
- it could pay to target specific nations on global or European issues, as the early stages of Greenpeace's campaign, when the focus was on the UK, proved to be very difficult
- it pays to cultivate good media relations
- if you can affect the sales of a global company, change will soon be forthcoming
- expediency is a poor weapon against motivated conviction.

Shell can perhaps learn that:
- The best technical argument is not necessarily the best commercial option
- consideration of PR consequences should be a factor in strategic and operational decision making
- technical arguments have to be presented in such a way that the wider audience understands them
- keep the messages simple
- the PR case for the preferred option should be prepared before implementing that decision
- the power of pressure groups and those with a cause should not be underestimated
- however large, well-established and well-respected your organisation is, you are not immune from damage
- Greenpeace should not be provided with even further media footage i.e. what might be interpreted as offensive use of helicopters and water cannon
- the meaning of a confrontation in political, PR and commercial terms should always be thought through
- 'what if?' questions should be explored
- the power of a consumer boycott should not be underestimated
- the PR price and cost should be calculated before embarking on an issue
- high profile targets should not be left unguarded!

CASE STUDY 20.2 Antique Exhibitions (p 821)

Teaching Objectives

1. To explore the circumstances in which exhibitions might become an appropriate way of selling;
2. to look at the advantages to both buyer and seller of exhibitions;
3. to examine the practicalities of staging these kinds of events.

1   What factors have led to the growth of exhibitions as a means of selling antiques?

Push factors:
- The rising cost of maintaining retail premises, especially in expensive areas
- the difficulty of reaching a geographically widespread customer base that is made up of specialist interests
- maintaining retail premises involves considerable expense for relatively small traffic flows, and the cost per enquiry high.

Pull factors:
- Exhibitions reach a large number of potential customers in a concentrated period
- a large numbers of interested and motivated buyers are available in one place
- exhibitions create easier browsing conditions for customers.

2   What are the potential advantages and disadvantages to (a) the dealer and (b) the customer of buying and selling in this way?

Advantages to the dealers:
- The sheer volume of potential customers
- reduced selling costs, reduced cost per order
- may generate better quality prospects
- customers are prepared to buy
- attracts consumers from a much wider area
- exhibitions could be used to build a mailing list for catalogue selling.

Disadvantages to the dealers:
- They need high quality stands to create an impact
- the event may be badly organised
- poorly targeted consumers might be attracted to the exhibition
- while high profile exhibitions are often well marketed, smaller ones can be more variable
- dealers cannot give customers much time when they are busy and this could lead to poor sales presentation
- the dealer cannot identify good prospects from rest very easily
- more staff might be needed to deal with the number of potential customers
- there is less chance to negotiate
- growing costs of exhibition attendance
- the risk of customer boredom with the format
- it becomes harder to build personal relationship.

Advantages to customers buying and selling:
- Less pressure to buy
- easier to browse
- a wide range of products under one roof
- lower costs of travelling to see different dealers
- customers selling can see a wide range of dealers and play them off against each other
- easier for comparison shopping.

Disadvantages to customers buying and selling:
- Do not get salesperson's attention when you want it
- do not get information or reassurance when buying
- it could be difficult for non-experts to find their way around the different dealers
- little chance to negotiate
- may make buying mistakes
- if something goes wrong, it might be difficult to locate the dealer afterwards

3   **What can the exhibition organiser do to try to ensure the success of an event?**

The exhibition organiser should try to ensure that:
- There is a clearly defined purpose for the exhibition in terms of its theme and scope
- there is a clear match between that purpose and the participating exhibitors
- the target market segment is clearly defined and identified
- the exhibition is clearly promoted to both the trade and potential customers
- exhibitors understand what they are paying for
- basic services and facilities are sufficient and appropriate for keeping visitors at the event for as long as possible
- the layout is clear, visitors can circulate freely and can easily locate the dealers they want to see
- there is appropriate signposting and adequate parking.

4   **What other consumer goods could be sold in this way?**

The products that are or could be sold using exhibitions are items that:
- Benefit from perusal, display and comparison shopping (cars)
- are not readily available through retail networks (art, crafts, specialist books, etc)

- are complementary to each other and when brought together in an exhibition, will attract a critical mass of sellers and a large number of potential customers (ideal home exhibition, bridal exhibitions)
- need to generate leads and enquiries so that selling can take place later at home (glazing, bathrooms and other home improvements)
- specialist products (hobbies, for example model railway exhibitions).

Marketing in Action Mad Cows and Englishmen (p 786)

Discussion question
Which publics does the MLC have to deal with? How are the communication objectives likely to differ between the various publics?

The MLC's publics can be divided into two main groups:
- Members of the industry who are at worst neutral but many of whom, despite a socially responsible stance, have an interest in continued beef sales.
- Other publics who are more volatile and are concerned with other agendas, including public opinion and the interests of the wider community.
The MLC will need different messages and approaches for each of these publics.

Industry Related:
- *Farmers:* farmers were very concerned at the perceived lack of support from the trade and government in the face of major operational problems imposed by a threatened slaughter programme, declining prices for beef, loss of export markets and unwanted (and costly) cattle having to be kept on the farm. The MLC needs to keep the support of this group both directly and indirectly through the support of the National Farmers' Union. The MLC must be able to demonstrate that it is fighting for the farmer while at the same time keeping farmers patient and persuading them to change some farming practices to restore the reputation of the beef industry.
- *Meat processors:* they are in similar position to the farmers, with a vested interest in the British beef industry.
- *Large retailers:* these could be considered more neutral in that their prime desire is to achieve turnover on their stock in line with customer demand. They would be happy to buy beef from whatever source provided it is perceived as safe and acceptable by their customers. The MLC needs to keep reassuring retailers that the necessary steps have already been taken to safeguard supplies of quality, disease free meat.
- *Independent butchers:* they similar concerns to those of the larger retailers, but they may not be less able to source freely from a disease-free environment and to convince their customers of the quality of their meat. The MLC could support them with arguments as to why British beef is safe as well as promoting any additional quality assurance schemes.
- *Trade media:* the trade media are in a difficult situation. They need to be in tune with the opinion of their readers and advertisers, but they also have to report the facts and give guidance to the trade. The MLC needs to keep them informed of developments and stories that will be of interest to their readers. This would include the latest news and restrictions, tips on how to cope, market price trends etc.
Non-industry publics are a tough group to communicate with. Lobbying, news conferences, good news stories, positive industry information etc all have to be disseminated.
- *General media:* this group is especially difficult to influence because its main interest is in selling extreme, emotional stories which can have a dramatic impact on public opinion. The MLC must fight hard to ensure that a balanced, factually accurate case is presented, and thus might release its own or independent positive scientific findings. It might also show the social and economic impact of the various governmental responses on the livelihood of the industry to try to gain public and media sympathy.
- *The UK government:* the MLC appears to have some support from the UK government although the Minister and some others were severely criticised by the press for misjudging the strength of

European public opinion and for their handling of the crisis. The MLC might thus want to keep government informed of the impact of their decisions, and to lobby key MPs and MEPs with agricultural constituencies or even those who would delight in being critical of the responses of other European governments to the crisis.

- *European Commission and foreign governments:* these publics are the most difficult to influence. They have little empathy or sympathy with the needs of the UK meat industry. They are likely to ignore directly supportive measures. Lobbying through MEPs, government ministers etc is probably the only way to attack this group.
- *Export buyers:* with many choices, this group will again be difficult to influence. Their interest is primarily in customer demand and all beef sales suffered as a result of the crisis. Without the removal of the export ban, it would be difficult to influence this group. However countering negative views through the press and feeding direct information is necessary to retain the goodwill of this group, ready for when the ban is eventually lifted.
- *Large meat buyers:* this group includes the restaurant and fast food chains. They may have little loyalty to the UK beef industry, so again, keeping them informed in a balanced way prepares the way for a return of confidence.
- *Health pressure groups:* this group would probably be highly resistant to any messages from the industry. The communications task might have to be to meet them head on, to counter and disprove claims and to seek to make them appear as honest do-gooders that do not really understand the scientific facts. The MLC did have some success in this area.
- *General public:* the main priority revolves around maintaining public confidence in eating beef and providing consumers with a justification for ignoring other negative publicity. There is some evidence that after some initial setbacks, public opinion was coming round to a more balanced view. Through press releases, media appearances, newsheets etc, counter messages could be provided.

Marketing in Action Corporate Magazines (p 791)

Discussion question
What are the advantages and disadvantages of House magazines as promotional vehicles?

Advantages:
- They are very useful for relationship building with customers
- they allow presentation of company news and product benefits in a 'soft sell' environment
- they can be carefully targeted at different groups
- they are useful for database building and maintenance.

Disadvantages:
- There is a danger of information overload if too many companies use them and a loss of novelty value
- they need a constant flow of interesting news in relevant areas
- they must not present a 'hard sell' or else they will alienate the audience
- they need to consider editorial costs as well as publication costs, and they can become expensive
- they may eventually be replaced with new media such as Internet which could be more cost effective.

Marketing in Action Music Sponsorship (p 806)

Discussion question
Evaluate the rationale adopted by organisations such as Mastercard and Virgin in sponsoring music events.

The rationale could be:

- *Compatibility with objectives:* if they are trying to generate favourable attitudes and beliefs within the youth market, then other promotional vehicles may be less effective.
- *The target audience are not exposed to mainstream media, or they ignore it or screen it out etc:* music sponsorship is thus a useful vehicle for reaching this market. Some actually attending while others will see the television coverage, the video, the music press coverage and the recordings.
- *The length of impact from one-off events:* this can be problematic and short, but it probably suited Virgin, as they were trying to coincide with the launch of the new record label.
- *Relevance to target audience:* such events reach a youth audience that is otherwise difficult to reach. In the case of Virgin there is a clear link with type of sponsorship. The Mastercard link is less clear but could it might suit its objectives in boosting credit card applications and use within the target group. The Hyde Park event had a much wider appeal than just the youth market.
- *Uniqueness/exclusivity of sponsorship within the events:* there were no problems with conflicting sponsors or too many sponsors in these examples, as both Mastercard and Virgin dominated their respective events.
- *Spin-off promotion in terms of hospitality and incentives:* Virgin very cleverly ensured that tickets were only available through their own stores, thus offering an opportunity to improve sales. Mastercard took telephone bookings by credit card of course! Special seating was available at the Hyde Park event for the more progressive corporate audience.

SUGGESTED ASSIGNMENTS

- Questions for Discussion 20.2 could be used as a group assignment.
- PR cannot achieve anything that cannot be done through advertising. Discuss.

Chapter 21
MARKETING MANAGEMENT

LECTURE PLAN

A lecture based on this chapter should help the student to:
1. Define marketing strategy and the internal and external influences affecting it;
2. understand the various types of portfolio model used to develop a strategic view of the organisation and the competitive context within which it operates;
3. outline different strategies for achieving growth and their appropriate use;
4. differentiate between types of competitors, appreciate the perspectives from which they can be analysed, and start to define appropriate strategies for dealing with them; and
5. understand the concept of competitive positioning and the range of strategies and tactical actions broadly appropriate for achieving and maintaining a position.

The key sections of this lecture should be:

Introduction (pp 827-836):
- Definition of marketing strategy
- overview of the concerns of marketing strategy
- the relationship between marketing and corporate strategy, including OHP 81, figure 21.1 (p 830) The Two-way Influence Between Marketing and Corporate Strategy:
  ⇒ Comparison between their areas of concern
  ⇒ the ways in which each informs the other
  ⇒ necessity for consistency.

- Definitions of terms: competitive strategy; marketing strategy; marketing plan; marketing programmes.
- Influences on marketing strategy: organisational objectives and resources; attitudes to change and risk; market structure and opportunity; competitors.

Strategic marketing analysis (pp 836-845):
- Concept of the product portfolio
- the Boston Matrix, including OHP 82, figure 21.3 (p 838) The BCG Matrix:
  - $\Rightarrow$ Define the structure of the matrix and its cells
  - $\Rightarrow$ explain the significance of the product positions
  - $\Rightarrow$ explain the significance of the circle sizes in (b)
  - $\Rightarrow$ outline the assumptions behind the Box
  - $\Rightarrow$ summarise its weaknesses.
- The GE matrix: structure; strengths and weaknesses.
- The Shell directional policy matrix: structure; strengths and weaknesses.
- Problems of developing and implementing portfolio models generally.

Growth strategies (pp 845-849):
- The Ansoff matrix, including OHP 83, figure 21.6 (p 845) Ansoff's Directional Policy Matrix:
  - $\Rightarrow$ Define the structure and the cells
  - $\Rightarrow$ the implications of each cell
  - $\Rightarrow$ examples for each cell.
- Integrative growth
- Summary of growth options, including OHT 84, table 21.1 (p 848) Alternative Growth Strategies:
  - $\Rightarrow$ Differences between them
  - $\Rightarrow$ summary of appropriate use.
- No growth options.

Competitive strategy (pp 849-859):
- Competitor analysis: Porter's five forces model; identifying competitors; competitive clusters; competitors' strengths and weaknesses; competitors' objectives and strategies; competitors' reactions; the competitive information system.
- Generic strategies, including OHP 85, figure 21.9 (p 854) Generic Strategies:
  - $\Rightarrow$ Overview of each strategy
  - $\Rightarrow$ advantages and disadvantages of each
  - $\Rightarrow$ appropriate use of each
  - $\Rightarrow$ examples of each in practice
  - $\Rightarrow$ factors influencing choice of strategy.

Competitive positions and postures (pp 859-867):
- Competitive positions, including OHP 86, figure 21.10 (p 859) Competitive Position and Strategy:
  - $\Rightarrow$ Define different positions
  - $\Rightarrow$ outline appropriate strategies and actions for each
  - $\Rightarrow$ discuss briefly how each can be implemented
  - $\Rightarrow$ advantages and disadvantages of each position.
- Competitive postures: aggressive strategies; defensive strategies.
-

QUESTIONS FOR REVIEW

21.1 Define the main factors influencing organisations' marketing strategy. (pp 833-836)

- *Organisational objectives and resources:* what the organisation as a whole is trying to achieve and what skills and assets it has at its disposal.

- *Attitude to change and risk:* whether the organisation and its managers are risk-takers or risk-averse.
- *Market structure and opportunities:* the level of competitiveness, the rate of change and the future potential.
- *Competitor strategies:* the strength of competitors, their dominance and their ability to defend their position.

21.2   What is a product portfolio and what is the point of portfolio analysis? (pp 836-838)

A product portfolio is the complete set of products or services offered by the organisation, each of which makes a discrete contribution to the organisation's overall performance. Portfolio analysis helps managers to define weak and strong products in terms of their financial contribution, their competitive position and their life cycle stage. Managers can then ensure that they have enough rising and emerging products for the future and sufficient cash generators to fuel future growth. They can also make decisions about which products should be dropped or invested in.

21.3   Define the four cells of the Boston Box. (pp 838-841)

- *Dog:* a product with low relative market share, positioned in a low growth market.
- *Question mark (or problem child or wild cat):* a product with low relative market share, positioned in a high growth market.
- *Star:* a product with high relative market share, positioned in a high growth market.
- *Cash cow:* a product with high relative market share, positioned in a low growth market.

21.4   How does the GE Matrix define industry attractiveness and business position? (p 843)

Industry attractiveness is a composite of factors such as:
- Market size
- rate of market growth
- degree of competition
- pace of technological change
- legislative impacts
- profit margins.

Business position is composite of factors such as:
- Relative product quality
- relative product performance
- brand strength and image
- distribution strength
- relative price competitiveness
- customer loyalty
- production efficiency.

21.5   What are the problems of implementing portfolio models in practice? (pp 844-845)

The problems include:
- Models do not give solutions to problems
- some models have rather simplistic decision rules associated with them
- simplistic definition of the variables contributing to the axes
- subjective definition and weighting of variables
- subjective measurement of the organisation's rating against those variables
- models do not consider synergies between products
- size of market share might not be a prime consideration for all organisations
- growth might not be a prime objective for all organisations.

21.6 **Which three cells of the Ansoff Matrix offer intensive growth opportunities?** (pp 845-846)

- Market penetration (current products in current markets)
- market development (current products in new markets)
- product development (new products in current markets).

21.7 **Differentiate between three different types of integrative growth.** (pp 847-848)

- *Backward integration:* buying suppliers or undertaking in-house production of items previously sourced from an external supplier.
- *Forward integration:* buying intermediaries or taking over their functions in order to control distribution more tightly.
- *Horizontal integration:* absorbing competition, either by full acquisition or by buying up the relevant product areas from them.

21.8 **What issues might an organisation take into account when undertaking competitive analysis?** (pp 849-854)

- Who are our competitors?
- How can our competitors be grouped meaningfully?
- What are our competitors' strengths and weaknesses?
- What are our competitors' objectives and strategies?
- How are our competitors likely to react to changes in the marketing environment?

21.9 **What are the three generic strategies and how might each be implemented?** (pp 854-859)

- *Cost leadership:* gaining competitive advantage through very tight analysis and control of costs, leading to improved productivity and/or more efficient and effective linkages both within the organisation and with suppliers or distributors.
- *Differentiation:* gaining competitive advantage through ensuring that the organisation's product and associated marketing and service package is significantly different from those of the competition. It can be implemented through any element of the marketing mix or through service.
- *Focus:* gaining competitive advantage by selectively targeting a relatively narrow niche in the market and serving it extremely well. This requires a thorough understanding of the niche segment in terms of its needs and its buying behaviour.

21.10 **Define the four different types of competitive position.** (pp 859-862)

- *Market leader:* one organisation is ahead of the rest in terms of market share and thus achieves a dominant position.
- *Market challenger:* an organisation with a market share smaller than that of the leader, but still big enough to pose a threat.
- *Market follower:* organisations who do not aspire to become challengers or leaders but are happy to trail along behind as 'me too' followers.
- *Market nicher:* a specialist organisation serving a narrow segment. A nicher might well have an insignificant share of the broad market, but within the narrowly defined segment it is likely to be dominant.

QUESTIONS FOR DISCUSSION

- **21.1 To what extent do the cells of the Boston Box reflect the stages of the product life cycle (PLC)? What does the Boston Box offer as an analytical tool that the PLC does not?**

There are some parallels between the Boston Box and the product life cycle:

- *Question marks:* are likely to be products in the early stages of the life cycle (introduction and possibly early growth) which have not yet developed their full potential. They need a lot of marketing investment to refine the product and to get its position in the market well established and strengthened.
  Stars: are likely to be products in the late growth stage of the life cycle who have established a strong position in a market which is itself still dynamic and growing. They still need a lot of investment to ensure that they maximise their market share while the market is still in growth and that their position is strong enough to withstand the shakeout that will happen as the market matures.
- *Cash cows:* are likely to be mature products that have reached a stable position in a market that has also settled down into a stable maturity. Marketing investment is likely to be steady and focused on maintaining position rather than building or developing it.
- *Dogs:* could be found at either end of the life cycle. A new product in a new market that is slow to develop could be seen as a dog. The key issues are whether the market will ever begin to grow and when, and whether the organisation is prepared to invest time and resources in developing better competitive strength for the product and in fuelling market growth. At the other end of the life cycle, a dying cow could be seen as a dog (?!) if it is a product in the decline stage losing share because the organisation has withdrawn marketing support and is happy to let it fade away.

The additional benefits of the Boston Box compared with the product life cycle include:

- The Boston Box makes it easier to view the whole product portfolio
- the Boston Box gives some insight into a product's competitive position
- the Boston Box gives some (if limited) insight into market conditions
- the Boston Box is not as rigid as the life cycle in assuming a linear sequence of events taking place within an ongoing timescale
- the Boston Box does not have the same fixed notions of 'beginning' and 'end' as the life cycle does.

21.2   For each cell of the Ansoff Matrix, find and discuss an example of an organisation which seems to have implemented that particular growth strategy.

This is a fairly straightforward exercise, designed to ensure that students understand the differences between the different cells within the Ansoff matrix. They should be able to justify their choice of organisation for each cell, and perhaps begin to explore the reasons why organisation chose that particular route in terms of factors such as:

- Market saturation
- emerging technology
- innovation capabilities
- emerging markets
- changing customer needs and wants
- competitors' threats and strategies.

21.3   Choose an organisation and apply Porter's five forces to its industry or market. What are the implications of your findings for your chosen organisation's strategic development?

This exercise is designed to ensure that students understand the five forces model, and that they can begin to appreciate some of the problems in applying it in reality. Issues raised might include:

- Problems of defining the market
- problems of defining the competition
- the subjective nature of a lot of the analysis
- the extent to which the model diagnoses problems rather than offers strategic directions
- the value of the model as a systematic analytical tool
- any gaps in the model, for example legal and regulatory constraints
- the ease with which major issues can be omitted or misinterpreted (deliberately or accidentally)!

21.4   To what extent do you think that market leadership is the best competitive position to aspire to?

Issues that might be raised in this debate include:
- The skills and resources available to the organisation
- whether leadership is compatible with the organisation's corporate objectives and strategies
- the strengths and capabilities of competitors within the market
- the number of competitors and the degree of dominance achievable within that market structure
- the vulnerability of the current leader
- the aspirations and vulnerabilities of current challengers
- the risks of leadership in terms of becoming a focal point for competitive attack
- the risks of leadership in terms of having to innovate to stay ahead of the rest
- the costs of attaining and then maintaining leadership.

21.5   Discuss the relative merits and appropriate use of each of the competitive postures described in this chapter.

- *Aggressive postures:* these pose a challenge to the existing situation in the market, and the different types of aggressive posture are described on pp 862-865. They have the advantage of perhaps taking a competitor by surprise or of hitting them directly and hard where it most hurts them or where they are most vulnerable. Through a short, sharp aggressive attack, a challenger can manoeuvre itself into a strong position and leave the competitor struggling to find and implement a response. Even a small organisation can use aggressive postures, since by-pass or guerrilla attacks for example need not be large-scale actions requiring massive resources. Regardless of whether the aggressor is large or small, however, the likely retaliation of the organisation attacked must be considered before an attack is launched.
- *Defensive postures:* these are mounted either to discourage attacks from competitors or in response to an attack. Types of defence are described on pp 865-866. Clearly, any organisation that has built a position within a market wants to maintain it. However, if that position is attractive or threatening to competitors, then it is vulnerable to attack. Ideally, the defender needs to be prepared in advance so that when attack comes, the response can be quick and decisive.
- *Co-operative and independent postures:* attack and defence can be costly, in terms of both resources and managerial attention, and run the risk of failing or bringing no major benefits for any party involved. Organisations might thus prefer to create alliances, either to pool resources and strengths to create a more defendable position, or to turn a potential enemy into a friend. Other organisations might wish to avoid direct competition as far as possible by carving out a quiet and non-threatening niche in a market.

CASE STUDY 21.1 Chuft Toys and Gifts (p 870)

Teaching Objectives

1. To look at the problems of business start-up;
2. to consider the factors leading to initial business success;
3. to explore the possibilities of strategic development.

1   What do you think are the problems facing two young graduates wanting to start a new business?

- *Personal ambitions:* they are at a stage in their careers where their personal objectives and needs are likely to evolve rapidly as they gain more experience of the world of business. Establishing a small business demands a level of commitment and staying power to realise any significant benefits. Rarely does success come instantly.

- *Skills, experience:* while they have acquired a solid engineering education and some limited experience of running a small business before Chuft, they still have much to learn about business management. Although they can gain from participation in training events, their lack of experience in the product area and in real life manufacturing and marketing may make them more vulnerable. They also would not have established market contacts and networks
- *External credibility:* although it cannot be condoned in any way, young people can meet prejudice from funders, suppliers and potential customers. They would have to be convinced that there is a commitment and that the expertise exists to create a viable enterprise.
- *Lack of resources:* to enter a new market requires investment of resources to create a meaningful niche. This niche can be achieved through a range of marketing decisions such as distribution, promotion and product design and development. Most areas of marketing require resources. When they are in short supply ambitions sometimes have to be tempered with realism.

However despite these potential limitations, young graduates could bring to a new business enthusiasm, freshness, creativity and commitment.

2   To what would you attribute Chuft's initial success?

Marketing:
- A focus on a narrow niche in market which had not been fully exploited
- a well differentiated product
- an incremental launch i.e. the product was piloted with the heritage railway
- developing a close match between the targeted niche and a selective distribution strategy
- the owners appeared to be able to manage the rapid growth
- careful attention to design, product image and packaging
- an appreciation of the value of point of sale displays as a substitute for heavy advertising in order to encourage impulse buys
- quickly developing a range of products to diversify risk
- they did not skimp on quality but achieved an above average price.

The owners:
- Total enthusiasm and commitment
- were able to assemble the necessary resources
- were not over ambitious about the returns they expected from the business
- undertook specialised roles to enable faster learning
- were flexible enough to cope with the change needed as the business evolved.

3   Assess Chuft's approach to market development.

- *The importance of defining what business they were in:* they shifted early on from 'the toy business' to 'the gift market'. This enabled them a lot more scope to apply their creative skills to a wider set of niches.
- *They developed the market through selective distribution strategy:* they targeted outlets that could command a higher price in support of the novelty value. They were happy to take pilot orders to make it easier for the customer to pilot.
- *Export markets:* their approach to exporting appeared to have been more haphazard. Initially, that was perhaps understandable given that foreign *ad hoc* enquiries and interest took them by surprise. However their policy might have drifted a little in terms of the role of exports and exploiting its full potential. While they would not have the resources to develop large overseas markets through direct sales, careful selection of intermediaries and a serious attempt at modifying the marketing offering could result in a significant growth opportunity for the business. However, their pricing and trade policy in export markets has not been thought through to enable higher margins where possible.

4   Where does Chuft go from here? What do you think might be the main dangers facing this firm?

Chuft could be at a critical stage in its development. It has survived the initial traumas of a new business launch and sales have reached what appears to be a healthy level. The owners have a number of strategic options:

To continue to develop new market segments, especially internationally: this is the most attractive growth option. The niche they appear to have found is based on novelty. The window of opportunity will not be open for ever. The barriers to entry are low and tastes and fashions may change. In selecting this route a more systematic attempt would be made to strengthen their position in foreign markets. Alliances could be formed to allow manufacturing under licence in some distant markets. However, despite the potential, the challenge would be to manage that growth from a personal and financial perspective. Strategy will have to be thought through and resources assembled to penetrate foreign markets seriously, while supporting the intermediaries. This could mean spending more time with the intermediaries in order to select the right ones and to supporting their sales effort. They would be moving more towards selling through, rather than selling to the trade. There might be some concern that the owners would be extending themselves too far in terms of the level of expertise and control necessary as the business expands. If they lose control of any one of several areas, such as production efficiency, quality, cash flow. distribution or marketing expenses, they could find themselves in some difficulty by effectively over trading.

To concentrate on developing new product lines that could have a wider appeal in the gift market: this would build upon their core strength in design and presentation. This route would encourage more steady growth and would appeal to the interests of the owners. They seem to enjoy the designing and making and, to some extent, to be happy for others to do the selling. By filling in the product range and taking on some new areas, sales could grow in a manageable fashion without some of the riskier aspects highlighted in the export option discussed above. Keeping the product range rejuvenated is important anyway, as life cycles become shorter and new entrants are likely. If some new winners are developed the portfolio could be strengthened and some resources could be released to support further managed expansion in export markets, even though commitment levels would not be high. If profitability can be improved this would also allow more investment in promotion and packaging, including the appointment of a sales person to support the owners' selling effort.

To consolidate for a few years while they build profitability: this option, while not having the same glamour and interest as the previous two, would enable the business to develop later from a far stronger base. Time could be spent on ensuring that the premises and production capability provide maximum efficiency. Staff could be better trained and new systems could be introduced. Attention could be given to the marketing methods employed and the margin and distribution policy could be re-examined to strengthen the company's position.

There are a number of factors that will influence the final choice of option, but each of them brings implied dangers to the business:

- The personal objectives and needs of the owners (money, risk, interests)
- their own assessment of their personal capability to sustain further development
- the level of available resources for further investment
- whether they really wish to focus on manufacturing or design and marketing
- the expectation of increased competitive activity
- their ability to think through the likely scenarios despite limited market information.

CASE STUDY 21.2 Boots' Strategic Headaches (p 871)

Teaching Objectives

1. To examine alternative growth strategies and the practical implications of using them;
2. to use the Boston Box as a diagnostic tool;
3. to encourage students to take an analytical approach to exploring future strategic directions.

1   **Which growth strategies has Boots employed? To what extent do you think they are appropriate? What problems do you think Boots might have faced in implementing them?**

Boots has adopted several routes for achieving growth. The current portfolio includes:
- Boots the Chemist (pharmacy/personal health care retail chain)
- contract manufacturing
- Boots Healthcare International (branded pharmaceuticals)
- Do It All (DIY)
- Halfords (car spares/accessories
- Children's world
- property development.

The *intensive growth* route has been used to build the traditional areas of the business. The chemist chain's market share is being defended by reformulated marketing approaches. New segments are being opened up through the launch of the community pharmacies. New product lines are always being introduced into the retail stores to retain and expand market share against increasingly aggressive competition.

Diversified growth has also been used to spread the portfolio of activities. Concentric diversification has been achieved through the move into Boots Healthcare International, where branded products are being sold to other pharmaceutical outlets around the world, building on the understanding of the retail and pharmacy business. The growth into contract manufacturing, also partially responsible for BHI, could be regarded as *backward integrative growth* in that it supplies the retail chemist chain as well as BHI.

Finally the moves into children's wear, car accessories and DIY are examples of *conglomerate diversification*, involving very different product and retail formats and market segments. It could be argued, however, that retail skills and expertise are being transferred and that the experience of merchandising, sourcing, site selection etc are associated with the core retail business.

The more Boots moves its portfolio into new areas, the greater the following risks become:
- Lack of knowledge of market segments and their dynamics
- retail formats may not transfer
- marketing formats may not transfer
- the portfolio can become too large and unwieldy with little scope for synergy
- if expansion is achieved through acquisition, business purchases might occupy weak market positions and need a lot of skill and resources to improve them.

These risks, however, must be countered with the benefits of aggressive growth:
- Reducing the risk of over-dependency on the retail pharmacy chain which is under threat
- it uses Boots' retail expertise in a range of markets
- it makes effective use of cash generated.

During the implementation of the portfolio expansion, Boots has to be able to defend its traditional areas of strength while absorbing the new enterprises efficiently and effectively. This will be highly demanding on management time and expertise. New strategic plans would have to be developed and some of the companies acquired would have to be relaunched and restructured to restore them to profitability. Learning would have to be very rapid, given the changing nature of competition, legislation and the economic environment.

2   **Using the cells of the Boston Box, roughly how would you categorise each of Boots' SBUs?**

- *Cash cow (high share, low growth):* Boots the Chemist is the market leader in the retail pharmacy and personal health care sector and although growth is low, considerable profits are being earned.

- *Question mark (low share, high growth):* the BHI division falls into this category. While some of the new branded products launched may become market leaders over time, there are other major European competitors who dominate many product sectors.
- *Star (high share, high growth):* Boots could still be seeking the star that could eventually rival the retail chain in terms of profitability and cash generation.
- *Dog (low share, low growth):* the DIY division fits into this category. Its competitive position is weak compared with specialists and better established retail chains.

There is insufficient information to classify Halfords, Children's World and the property division.

3   For each of those SBUs, what do you think is the most appropriate strategy for the future? What might cause problems in implementing those strategies?

Boots the Chemist is a cash cow, but is under major threat from aggressive competition from Superdrug, Lloyds and Unichem as well as the supermarkets' attempts to undercut OTC drug price levels. This area must be defended at all costs if the portfolio is going to expand and profitability be retained. This will mean more investment by Boots in marketing. Activities could include the price and product promotions mentioned in the case, introducing new lines, store refurbishment, careful category management, use of mass media to keep the Boots name alive and an expansion of new sites. They might even consider launching a new chain of cut price chemists to fight against the low price competitors. Despite such defensive measures it could be argued that the battle ground is already well defined and the main threats will not easily be overcome.

BHI offers real potential in the longer term, as long as Boots can build a portfolio of brands that are dominant in fairly narrow product sectors. While the larger manufacturers such as SmithKline Beecham are likely to remain market leaders, there still appears to be opportunities for well defined brands. To build share, BHI will have to brand heavily and ensure efficient distribution. This will mean heavy promotion both to the trade and to the consumer to generate loyalty. Alternative competitive products soon follow in this market, so it is essential to build share rapidly and then retain it. Shortening life cycles mean that a constant flow of upgrades and new products is needed. Product line extensions might also be necessary.

All of the above actions require heavy market investment, but there is little choice for BHI if it is to build in this growth market. Clear timescales will have to be agreed to establish when the investment can start to slow down and the products either become cash cows or stars. This does not appear to be happening yet.

Do It All seems to have been a bad acquisition. The difficult economic situation has not helped, as in a declining and static market gaining share can be extremely difficult and costly. Rarely will established competition sit back and let another competitor erode their market share seriously. Boots are already rationalising the store locations, but as yet has not found a formula that will enable it to grow. Intensive marketing does not appear to be the answer. Repositioning, perhaps with a greater focus on particular product areas within DIY could be useful, although this could further restrict volume sales and cause even greater short term difficulties. In the absence of a clear competitive advantage, divestment appears to be the best long-term solution.

Marketing in Action Grolsch (p 828)

Discussion question
Distinguish between the strategic and operational marketing decisions undertaken by Grolsch in the UK.

Strategic decisions include:
- Expansion by acquisition of brands
- building a premium position for brands as a means of creating competitive strength

- expansion into a different product sector
- being prepared to invest for long term brand building.

Operational decisions include:

- Using market research
- developing a marketing mix to sustain a premium price position
- identifying priority market segments.

Marketing in Action Tele Danmark Makes International Calls (p 835)

Discussion question

Identify the main influences on Tele Danmark's marketing strategy.

The four main influences identified in figure 21.2 (p 833) are well demonstrated in this MIA.

- *Organisational objectives and resources:* there are ambitious plans to develop a presence in international markets in order to reduce the dependency on the Danish market. The priorities in descending order are Scandinavia, Europe, and the rest of the world. This has encouraged a programme of growth through acquisition over the past few years.
- *Attitudes to change and risk:* Tele Danmark has a positive attitude, supportive of change and tolerant of the associated risk. This reflects the dramatic changes within the industry caused by deregulation, privatisation and rationalisation.
- *Market structure and opportunities:* Tele Danmark has focused on entering defendable niches in large markets such as Germany and by acquiring a stake in the former national telecom companies in smaller nations such as Ireland and Belgium.
- *Competitor strategies:* the competitive environment has not yet stabilised in many European markets (see the Deutsche Telekom Marketing in Action vignette on p 435). Prices charged by some telecom companies are, in the view of the EC, above expectations and innovation not as dynamic as it should be. Market forces, such as those experienced by Tele Danmark with Sonofon are increasingly likely to be focused in niches where dominance is sought. Tele Danmark would like to enter these growth segments early in order to build a strong long term competitive position.

Marketing in Action Williams Holdings Decides to Refocus its Product Portfolio (p 837)

Discussion question

What are the main considerations influencing the product portfolio development in Williams Holdings?

Three main product-market areas can be identified: fire protection; building products and security products. Williams might have different priorities in each of these areas. Williams appears to be seeking the following in their main portfolio areas:

- A strong market position, such as the 12 per cent international market share in fire protection and the number two position in the locksmiths market.
- New or growth markets, again such as the fire protection market, and parts of the advanced security products market.
- More established products that are capable of generating either cash or profits, mainly in the building products areas.
- Some consistency and fit between the areas of the portfolio, through the overall focus on buildings and their protection. This could offer some synergy in sales, distribution channels, type of customers to contact and linked promotions.
- Reasonable cash generating potential, either from existing brands or, with investment, emerging brands. Other product areas in the portfolio are being divested. Some clearly do not fit, such as electronics, office equipment etc, since they do not offer much overlap with the main portfolio activities. Others, such as home improvement related lines, do fit with building products but are

highly demanding and take the organisation into tough competitive markets from a weak competitive position.

Marketing in Action Aerospatiale and Dassault Take Off (p 841)

Discussion question
Do you think the French government is misguided in trying to force a marriage between two unwilling partners?

The decision appears to have been dominated more by political expediency than obvious business common sense. However, there are some major potential long-term benefits to be gained if the marriage is successful:
- A better opportunity to compete in world markets as a major world class company.
- An increased size with some diversity might make any merger or hostile takeover less likely.
- There is a general view that in the future both industries will demand larger, pan-European alliances pooling the expertise of a number of major players. One larger company will assist in that integration process.
- Some technical integration from combined R&D. This area is crucial for competitiveness in world markets when competing against Japanese and US companies.

The benefits outlined above are linked to strengthening the international competitive position rather than encouraging operational synergy in sales, distribution and marketing.

SUGGESTED ASSIGNMENTS

- Questions for Discussion 21.4
- To what extent are portfolio models useful tools in developing marketing strategy?

Chapter 22
MARKETING PLANNING, MANAGEMENT AND CONTROL

LECTURE PLAN

A lecture based on this chapter should help the student to:
1. Understand the different types of plan found within organisations and the importance of formal planning processes;
2. define the stages in the marketing planning process and their contribution to sound, integrated plans;
3. appreciate the various methods of estimating or forecasting both market and sales potential;
4. outline alternative ways of structuring a marketing department and their advantages and disadvantages; and
5. understand the need for evaluation and control of marketing plans and their implementation, and the ways in which this can be achieved.

The key sections of this lecture should be:

Introduction (pp 876-880):
- Definition of planning

- types of plan
- importance of marketing plans, including OHP 87, figure 22.1 (p 879) Benefits of Planning:
  ⇒ Discuss the areas within the diagram
  ⇒ emphasise the need for planning to be flexible rather than formulaic
  ⇒ raise the issue of the danger of planning for planning's sake
  ⇒ emphasise the need for sound and thorough marketing information as a planning foundation.

The marketing planning process (pp 880-892):

This section is based on OHP 88, figure 22.2 (p 882) Stages in the Planning Process:
- *Corporate objectives:* quantitative, philosophical and qualitative targets.
- *Marketing audit:* definition; importance; areas covered in internal and external audits.
- *SWOT analysis:* definition; relationship with audit.
- *Marketing objectives:* links with corporate objectives; links with SWOT; areas covered by objectives; characteristics of 'good' objectives.
- *Marketing strategies:* definition; links with objectives.
- *Marketing programmes:* definition; links with strategy.
- *Budgets:* importance of budget setting and cost control.
- *Control and evaluation:* necessity of monitoring ongoing performance and evaluating outcomes against expectations.

Market potential and sales forecasting (pp 892-901):

- Definition of market potential
- definition of sales potential
- overview of methods of estimating them
- forecasting methods, including OHP 89, figure 22.5 (p 898) Forecasting Methods:
  ⇒ Overview of qualitative methods
  ⇒ overview of quantitative methods
  ⇒ benefits of forecasting
  ⇒ risks of forecasting.

Organising marketing activities (pp 901-905):

- Role of marketing within the organisation.
- Alternative forms of marketing organisation: functional; product; regional or segment; matrix organisation.
- The benefits and appropriate use of each form.

Marketing control (pp 905-908):

- Strategic and operational control
- the process of control, including OHP 90, figure 22.7 (p 906) Marketing Control:
  ⇒ Trace the flow through
  ⇒ emphasise the need for realistic targets in the first place
  ⇒ importance of spotting gaps early enough to remedy the problem
  ⇒ importance of thoroughly analysing why deviations are occurring
  ⇒ importance of flexible plans to allow managers to take action in the face of unexpected events.
- Methods of analysing performance: sales analysis; costs and profitability analysis.

QUESTIONS FOR REVIEW

22.1   Why do organisations need marketing planning? (pp 879-880)

Marketing planning gives organisations:
- Greater control over marketing activities
- better co-ordination of marketing activities
- an aid to developing marketing activity for the future.

22.2   Define the stages in the marketing planning process. (pp 880-892)

- *Corporate objectives:* defining what the organisation is trying to achieve overall.
- *Marketing audit:* assessing the current situation both internally and externally.
- *SWOT analysis:* analysing the organisation's strengths and weaknesses and the threats and opportunities presented by the external environment.
- *Marketing objectives:* defining precisely what the outcomes of the marketing plan should be.
- *Marketing strategies:* defining the means by which the objectives will be achieved in broad terms.
- *Marketing programmes:* the detailed actions by which strategies are implemented.
- *Budgets:* specifying the plan's financial and other resource implications and constraints.
- *Control and evaluation:* ensuring that the plan is being implemented properly and that it is performing as expected.

22.3   What is a SWOT analysis? (p 886)

The SWOT analysis structures and organises the information from the marketing audit. Its four cells are:
- *Strengths:* the organisation's internal marketing and operational strengths.
- *Weaknesses:* the organisation's internal marketing and operational weaknesses.
- *Opportunities:* external factors or circumstances, usually within the marketing environment, which offer current or potential opportunities which can be exploited.
- *Threats:* external factors or circumstances, usually within the marketing environment, which create current or potential threats which have to be overcome or avoided.

22.4   To what general criteria should 'good' marketing objectives conform? (pp 886-888)

Good marketing objectives should be:
- Wide-ranging
- precise
- linked with corporate objectives
- consistent with each other
- attainable
- compatible with both internal and external environments
- measurable.

22.5   What is the difference between marketing strategies and marketing programmes?
(pp 888-890)

Marketing strategies take a broader, longer-term view of how objectives are to be achieved, whereas marketing programmes outline the precise actions in terms of the elements of the marketing mix, as well as specifying timescales and allocation of responsibility. Programmes allow strategies to be implemented.

22.6   Define market potential. (pp 892-893)

Market potential is the maximum level of demand that is available within a defined market, assuming that all customers within that market are buying the product as often as possible, using it as frequently as possible and using the maximum amount on each occasion.

22.7   What is the difference between breakdown and build up methods of assessing market potential? (pp 894-896)

Breakdown methods start from the aggregate level of the total market, and then break that down stage by stage until figures for individual segment potential reached. Build up methods start with the individual customer and then aggregate up to industry or market totals.

22.8   What are the (a) qualitative and (b) quantitative techniques of forecasting? (pp 897-901)

Qualitative techniques include:
- Management judgement
- sales force surveys
- panels of experts
- scenario techniques.

Quantitative techniques include:
- Time series analysis
- correlation methods
- leading indicators
- market tests.

22.9   What are the four main choices for structuring the marketing department? (pp 902-905)

- Functional organisation, structured according to specific marketing tasks
- product organisation, structured around different brands or products
- regional or segment organisation, structured in accordance with trading areas or different market segments
- matrix organisation, structured around teams made up partly of functional specialists and partly of those with product management responsibility.

22.10   How can operational performance be evaluated? (pp 907-908)

- Sales analysis
- marketing costs and profitability analysis.

QUESTIONS FOR DISCUSSION

22.1   What is the mission statement of the university or college at which you are studying? From your general knowledge of the organisation and your experience as a customer, discuss the extent to which you feel it is fulfilling its mission.

This question encourages students to take a more objective and perhaps critical look at an organisation of which they are a part! In discussing the mission statements, they should perhaps consider whether it conforms with Day's (1990) suggested criteria (see p 882) of:
- Being future orientated
- reflecting the values and orientation of the leader
- stating strategic purpose
- enabling, i.e. giving sufficient guidance for managers lower down the organisation.
- as well as the more obvious criteria of being:
    ⇒ short and simple
    ⇒ unambiguous
    ⇒ applicable to the whole range of organisational activities, and perhaps ...
    ⇒ ... inspiring!

Students might also be encouraged to collect and discuss the mission statements of a wider range of organisations.

22.2   Using whatever information you can find, develop a SWOT analysis for the organisation of your choice. What are the implications of your SWOT for the organisation's short- and long-term priorities?

This question ensures that students understand what goes into a SWOT analysis and that they can differentiate between the essentially internal focus of the SW and the essentially external focus of the OT. It also encourages them to go beyond the SWOT and begin to analyse what it means. In this exercise, they should be using their SWOT to help justify what their chosen organisation is seen to be doing now and for reasoned speculation about what it might do in the future. The student's SWOT should draw on as wide a range of sources as possible, such as company reports and information, trade press, and financial press as well as observation of the marketing strategy in practice. The analysis should also range systematically over the elements of the marketing mix, marketing strategy, management and organisation, and marketing and operational skills and resources for the internal analysis. The external analysis should range over the STEP factors in some detail.

22.3   Discuss the importance of market and sales forecasting in the marketing planning process and outline the relative advantages and disadvantages of three different forecasting methods.

Market and sales forecasting is important because:
- It puts upper limits on what is attainable
- it helps to determine whether a market is worth pursuing
- it acts as a basis for predicting profitability
- it helps to allocate resources and to focus effort
- it encourages analysis of the competitive environment
- it encourages analysis of trends in the market
- it helps to determine what kinds of strategies and marketing programmes might be appropriate.

The range of forecasting methods is described on pp 897-901.
Management judgement has the advantages that it:
- Takes advantage of a wealth of expertise and experience
- can touch on very qualitative and complex issues

but managers:
- might be too close to the problem
- might think too conservatively
- might make unreliable assumptions
- might not be objective.

A sales force survey has the advantages that it:
- Is built on information direct from the customer
- takes advantage of the sales force's expertise and experience

but:
- information from customers could be biased or naive
- the sales representatives might choose to distort the information for their own purposes.

A panel of experts has the advantages that it:
- Is perhaps less biased than internal managers or sales forces
- exploits a wide range of knowledge and expertise

but:
- it depends on the quality of the panel's knowledge and expertise.

Scenario techniques have the advantages that they:
- Involves an iterative and rigourous process
- can involve experts and tap into their knowledge

but:
- they depends on the quality of the panel's knowledge and expertise
- they depend on the underlying assumptions made about scenarios.

Time series analysis has the advantages that it:

- Builds on historic data
- can take account of cycles. trends, seasonality etc
- helps to explain cause and effect

but:

- it assumes that the past will carry on into the future in a fairly stable and predictable way
- it needs a detailed databank with a long history to feed it.

Correlation methods have the advantages that they:

- Build on historic data
- quantify the cause and effect relationship between variables

but:

- it assumes that the past will carry on into the future in a fairly stable and predictable way
- it needs an extensive, historic databank.

Leading indicators have the advantage that they:

- Are useful for short-term forecasting of trends and changes

but:

- they rely on managerial ability to define clearly what the leading indicators to look for are.

Market tests have the advantage that they:

- Give an insight into real behaviour in the marketplace

but:

- the conditions within which the test takes place have to be carefully specified and monitored
- the results might not be transferable to different geographic areas or markets.

22.4   What kind of marketing organisational structure would be appropriate for each of the following situations and why? (a) a small single product engineering company; (b) a large fmcg manufacturer selling a wide range of products into several different European markets; and (c) a pharmaceutical company manufacturing both prescription and 'over the counter' medicines.

A small single product engineering company might find a segment organisation most appropriate as:

- It only has the one product
- it will have relatively few customers but they might be working in different industries with different needs
- its customers might require a high level of customisation
- the focus will be on ongoing integrated technical and marketing relationships rather than specific marketing functions and tasks as such.

The large fmcg organisation might use a complex matrix, combining product, regional and functional organisation because:

- It has to manage a wide range of products
- it has to operate in different geographic markets with different characteristics and environments
- it has to ensure that brand images are consistent (or at least not contradictory) in different international markets
- the scale of the operation might warrant employing specialists in functional marketing areas
- products need 'champions' to fight for a fair share of the organisation's resources.

The pharmaceutical company might use a matrix combining product and segment considerations as:

- The prescription and over the counter segments will have very different marketing needs
- the organisation will have to ensure consistency between the messages given to the two segments
- the product will be fighting for a share of organisational resources.

22.5   Discuss the role played by control and evaluation in both the planning and implementation of marketing strategies and programmes.

Issues that might be raised about the role of control and evaluation are that:

- It ensures in the planning process that objectives are properly defined, as the control and outcome measurement mechanisms also have to be defined within the plan

- it helps the organisation to pick up problems and deviations from expected performance early and to implement remedial action
- it allows the organisation to identify unexpected successes and to exploit them fully
- it ensures that resources are used efficiently and cost effectively
- it ensures that someone takes managerial responsibility for implementing and overseeing the plan
- it forces managers to examine the planning process itself in retrospect to diagnose whether their original assumptions and targets were realistic.

CASE STUDY 22.1 DHL - A Global Brand (p 911)

Teaching Objectives

1. To emphasise the importance of marketing planning;
2. to examine the impact of factors within the marketing environment on planning;
3. to encourage students to think through and articulate strategic options.

1   Why is marketing planning so important for an organisation such as DHL?

Marketing planning is so important for an organisation such as DHL because:
- It is a very large organisation that generally needs to maintain co-ordination and control over itself
- it is a global organisation that needs to ensure that its geographically spread operations contribute consistently and synergistically to the wider corporate picture
- it has a policy of allowing local management a certain degree of autonomy, but still has to ensure that local plans are appropriate and reflect DHL's core values and objectives
- the DHL name is a strong and valuable corporate brand and the organisation cannot risk damaging that through poor management or marketing
- DHL has a clear sense of the market position it wants to occupy and planning is an essential part of creating that position and maintaining it in a very competitive market
- planning helps DHL to monitor the performance of its products and their marketing mixes and to gain an early warning of any problems
- it also helps DHL more generally to analyse its performance critically and to think seriously about the causes of deviations from expected performance over the year
- it forces DHL to consider the future and its threats, and to develop strategies for minimising threats, responses to possible scenarios, if they come to pass, or contingency plans if certain things go wrong
- it forces DHL to consider the future and its opportunities, and to develop strategies for capitalising on opportunities, and to think through likely competitor responses and how DHL will deal with them
- it thus also encourages DHL to think through any product modifications or new product development programmes early enough to implement them properly and to launch them proactively rather than as a panic reactive measure
- it allows DHL to consider its long- and short-term resource allocation priorities
- it is a means of communication that helps to ensure that all managers are working towards the same goals and know what their responsibilities and target are
- its managers across the world come from different cultural backgrounds and planning can help the organisation to ensure that they are all adopting consistent corporate values and goals, but also that the organisation as a whole benefits from the best ideas from this cultural diversity
- it allows managers to contribute to an important debate on what the organisation ought to be doing and can help to build better morale and a sense of corporate purpose.

2   Identify the key factors in the global marketing environment that are likely to have an impact on DHL's marketing planning.

Using the STEP factors as a framework:

Sociocultural:
- The cultural diversity of its markets
- the emergence of cross-border international segments
- increasing demand for the speedy and reliable international transfer of small packages generally
- the globalisation of other organisations creating demand for emergency deliveries of documents and small components across the world from site to site.

Technological:
- On-line links with major customers
- IT based tracking systems to ensure the safe and rapid delivery of the right package to the right place
- the growth and penetration of the Internet and e-mail as ways of transferring information internationally.

Economic and competitive:
- The ability and willingness of organisational customers to pay a premium rate for fast and reliable delivery, compared with the opportunity cost of that delivery *not* taking place
- the different economic conditions across the world that affect customers' ability to pay and their price perceptions
- the activities of major competitors such as Federal Express and United Parcel Service
- variations in the competitive environment in different markets and segments
- the market share taken by the Internet etc
- changes in the costs of operating its transport fleet, especially the aircraft.

Political and regulatory:
- Rules and regulations affecting its ability to operate in and out of international airports
- changing membership of trading blocs and emerging economies opening up new markets and opportunities
- variations in contract law across the world
- variations in taxes and duties across the world
- variations in import and export regulations
- variations in advertising and promotion approaches and regulations.

3   Is the global approach to branding the best strategy to take DHL into the next millennium?

This question is open for debate. In favour of global branding:
- It unites all DHL's worldwide operating units with a consistent image
- it provides a powerful and recognisable umbrella for all DHL's products, regardless of how diverse they are
- since DHL is operating internationally, it reassures customers that their package has been looked after by the same carrier regardless of its point of origin or its point of delivery
- since many of DHL's large organisational customers are global, they are likely to experience DHL in many different locations and need to see a consistent image
- it emphasises the size, power and spread of DHL across the world
- it means that the advertising and promotional approaches can be tightly focused on the umbrella brand and universally applicable with only minor adaptations
- it makes new product launches a lot easier.

4   How could DHL evolve to meet threats such as electronic mail?

E-mail and EDI are a serious threat, because they are cheap, reliable and instant ways of getting information across the world, and can be used to deliver copies of documents to a large number of geographically spread locations immediately. Their interactive nature also means that draft versions of documents can flow reasonably freely and be amended and checked 'live'. There are several strategic options that DHL might wish to consider:

- In the short-term, concentrate on document delivery to and/or from developing areas of the world where the telecommunications infrastructure or the penetration of networked PCs is less advanced but in the longer-term consider getting out of straightforward document delivery altogether.
- Develop a niche market, delivering documents that cannot be transferred electronically, for example some legal documents that have to be 'original copies' with real signatures and/or seals on them.
- Further develop value added services that EDI cannot supply, such as the help with export documentation mentioned in the case
- Focus on developing the business of transporting small, valuable physical goods or emergency supplies of parts and components to take over as the core activity.
- Further develop integrated IT links with key customers to make using DHL as easy as possible and to encourage them to think of DHL as an integral part of their inter-site communication system.

Supplementary question
Could Ansoff's matrix (p 845) be useful in this case and what would be the problems of using it?

It could be useful, and students might be encouraged to classify their responses to question 4 in terms of Ansoff strategies. The problems of using it are:
- How would you define 'market'?
- How would you define 'product'?
- It assumes that growth is the objective rather than portfolio consolidation or restructuring
- its cells are broadly defined and the analyst needs to be specific about the interpretation put on them within the organisation's own context.

CASE STUDY 22.2 Filofax (p 912)

Teaching Objectives

- To ensure that students understand the nature and importance of the marketing audit and the SWOT analysis;
- to explore the link between SWOT analysis and marketing strategies;
- to emphasise the importance of control and evaluation in marketing planning.

1   What kinds of factors is Filofax likely to cover in its external audit?

By using the STEP framework described in Chapter 2 the following factors should be covered:
Sociocultural:
- Changes in the fashionability of the Filofax as a status symbol
- the increasing acceptance of the personal organiser as a generic 'something for everyone' product
- the increasing acceptance and penetration of electronic media
- the rise and fall of the 'yuppie' segment
- the emergence of new market segments based on benefits sought and lifestyle
- tracking changing market demographics, such as the number of students.
Technological:
- Filofax itself is a low technology product, but new alternatives eliminate the need for paper
- new ways of recording and retrieving information through new technology
- the rate of acceptance and penetration of mobiles, electronic organisers, and personal links with larger IT systems.
Economic and competitive:
- Increasing competition, direct and indirect, in the Filofax market
- changing and emerging segments supplied by different operators i.e. low priced, premium priced etc
- tracking of changing price levels
- the erosion of clear differentiation in the customer's mind between different products

- identification of allied product areas for expansion
- the emergence of new, unexploited geographic markets.

Political and regulatory:
- While there are unlikely to be many restrictions, some general trade issues may have to be watched such as import/export regulations and tariffs, VAT levels etc.

2   From the information in the case, outline a rough SWOT analysis for Filofax. What do you think represents (a) its biggest opportunity and (b) its biggest threat, and why?

Strengths:
- A strong brand identity with the 'generic' name for the sector
- a dominant force in the market as the first and the original
- building a diversified product portfolio to capitalise on its distribution strengths
- spreading risk through geographic market diversification
- acquisition of its major competitor to achieve 85 percent share of the UK market
- consistent positioning and communication in diverse markets
- a quality product commanding a premium price.

Weaknesses:
- The common use of Filofax as a generic name might dilute the brand image and make customers 'blind' to Filofax as a brand in its own right
- over-concentration at the top end of market at a time when the customer is moving downmarket?
- it is still primarily a one product concept company. If the concept become redundant Filofax would be very vulnerable.

Opportunities:
- Horizontal and forward integration through acquisition in international markets
- further scope for penetration in currently under-exploited international markets
- the growing market for electronic organisers.

Threats:
- Competitive pressure from low cost or value operators
- market saturation as it moves from maturity into decline
- growth in the acceptance and use of electronic organisers.

The biggest threat is probably from the electronic organiser, as that could negate the whole Filofax product concept. The biggest opportunity is probably the further potential of international markets in which perhaps the electronic organiser is not yet a major force.

3   What marketing strategies might Filofax include in its planning to help it capitalise on its opportunities and overcome its threats?

Marketing strategies define the target markets selected, the mixes designed to be effective in those markets and the level of resourcing necessary for supporting those activities. Filofax has sensibly pursued a policy of international expansion to exploit its stranglehold over its main markets. It has found that the concept travels well across international borders within defined lifestyle and business groups. Further progress could be made in this area, although promotion and distribution problems would have to be considered. Using the existing target markets and the goodwill generated, the priority in the marketing strategy must be to sell a wider range of products to the same customer group. This could be extended to include electronic products to work either in competition with Filofax organisers or in conjunction with them. Various techniques could be used to generate customer loyalty including direct marketing, linked promotions, for example buy a Filofax and get stationery half price or buy an organiser and get a specialist Filofax at a reduced price.

Point of sale promotion may have to be enhanced to ensure mass distribution and heavy displays linking allied products and showing new applications. Promotion to emphasise quality and a premium price will have to continue to build additional value to maintain volume against lower priced alternatives. This would require further investment in marketing to keep the required presence.

However, the main priority must be to assess the impact of electronic organisers and other forms of IT. This is about 'what business are we in': selling Filofaxes or enabling consumers to organise their schedules effectively. The case does not make it clear whether joint venture opportunities could become available to allow synergy and joint brand development between Filofax and a major electronics specialist.

4   How might a company like Filofax control and evaluate its marketing activities?

The most effective means of controlling activities is to link them as closely as possible to an overall marketing plan. Such a task is not easy in a company operating in over 40 countries with a number of product lines. The marketing plan would involve a series of objectives and planned activities, by product and/or by region that could be assessed alongside actual outcomes. Where quantified, deviations in sales, products, territories and market shares for example can be analysed and the source of the deviations identified. Other variables such as the number of new accounts, distribution outlet average turnover and sales price levels achieved could also be assessed against objectives. The deviations form the essential basis for planned change and/or urgent corrective actions. Variation analysis could be undertaken for the organisation as a whole, or by geographical region. If, therefore, sales in the Baltic states for example were not meeting expectations, specific causes could be investigated and remedial action planned and implemented.

Objectives do not, of course, simply relate to sales or financial targets. Performance on issues such as the rate at which new markets are opened and penetrated, shifts in relative market share as a result of competitive strategies, the level of support offered to the retail trade and the strength of trade relationships, and the efficiency and scheduling of launching new products can all be compared quantitatively and qualitatively with planning intentions as a means of control.

All of this presupposes that a planning regime has been introduced into the company for short-, medium- and long-term horizons. The review of performance to plan is a central part of the management of the organisation. It could be especially important in the tracking of emerging difficulties early so that corrective action can be introduced with a better chance of success. Control can also be better implemented through a planning system that allocates responsibility and resources to named managers who are sufficiently skilled and/or senior to implement and manage activities on a day to day basis.

Marketing in Action Behind the Hollywood Glitter (p 880)

Discussion question
Is it possible for the US film industry to use forecasting and marketing planning systems?

The industry appears to be highly proficient in planning the marketing of a new film in terms of the use of techniques such as concept testing, test marketing, launch planning, public relations, merchandising etc. The Disney Corporation is an excellent example of professional planning for new film launches and commercialisation. The problem is that it appears to be almost impossible to forecast the success of a film. The reasons for this difficulty are:
- The unpredictability of the media and critics
- difficulty in pre-testing service products
- difficulty in predicting the word of mouth effect, form both critics and the general film-going public
- the emotional and psychological nature of the service experience
- changing viewing patterns with the rise of Multiplexes (a positive force) and video (a negative force).

Even well-tried formulae and well-known stars can not guarantee the success of a film. Forecasting can indicate a range of scenarios for planning purposes, but selecting the most likely outcome can be problematic.

Marketing in Action The Car Park Environment (p 884)

Discussion question
What can NCP do to minimise the impact of the external factors facing the business?

- To defend against competition, NCP can: build a strong brand identity; track competitors' actions and intentions; build customer loyalty for heavy users or high service users.
- Site acquisition is controlled by the land owners. NCP thus needs: early scanning for new sites; professional negotiation to secure longer term deals.
- In terms of management contracts, NCP needs: a more flexible response to accepting more lucrative management contracts; to build close relations with important site owners.
- For improved security, NCP should: invest in security, staff, systems and controls perhaps even linking them with a price premium for NCP's services.
- To respond to changing shopping habits, NCP could: open up new areas such as 'Park and Ride' sites; implement differential pricing to different segments, for example workers and shoppers.

Marketing in Action TI Rethinks its Portfolio (p 889)

Discussion question
How has strategic analysis assisted the development of TI?

Strategic analysis has helped by:
- Focusing on likely growth and share potential in each of the main product areas
- influencing TI's decision to divest in areas where profits were likely to be squeezed by international competition (cookers, kettles etc) and to divert resources to areas where they could build a strong position through market dominance and technological leadership
- identifying acquisition strategies rather than internal development as the best means to change the portfolio within a short period of time. These acquisitions were on a world wide basis.
- Developing a new focus on TI's real strengths and capabilities i.e. specialised engineering in international niches
- formulating a new mission statement to guide further acquisitions
- identifying key criteria for acquisition in terms of market share, technological leadership, added value services and a general ability to occupy the premium rather than the cheap end of the market.

Marketing in Action Bouygues Backs its Forecasts (p 895)

Discussion question
What factors are likely to influence: (a) the market growth in mobile phone usage in France and (b) Bouygues' share of the market?

There are many general influences within the socioeconomic and political environments which could have an impact on the expansion of the mobile phone market. In periods of economic downturn, for example, consumers might be less willing to invest in a mobile because of the total (subscriber and call charge) costs. More specific influences that would have to be addressed in any forecasts relate to the growth of the mobile market in France and Bouygues' expected share of the market. Issues relating to the market growth in mobile phone usage in France include:
- The rate at which connection fees and tariffs fall
- the main suppliers' marketing efforts focused on market expansion

- the rate at which new entrants join the market to stimulate total sales through increased marketing effort
- the rate of penetration in the better established business segment
- the rate at which consumer use expands
- the interest of intermediaries in stocking and actively selling mobiles
- the rate of technological innovation
- the level of 'notional' market saturation.

Issues relating to Bouygues' share of the total market include:
- The impact of their segmentation strategy aimed at non-business users
- the impact of their pricing and advertising strategy
- the speed with which they can expand their coverage across France
- the level and success of France Telecom and Generale des Eaux in their marketing activities
- the impact of new entrants in taking away market share
- the ability to find and keep good intermediaries
- the willingness of existing subscribers to switch to Bouygues
- the rate at which Bouygues subscribers switch to competitors (and vice versa).

Marketing in Action Restructuring Marketing Departments (p 904)

Discussion question
Outline some of the emerging issues that senior managers are having to consider when designing new structures for a marketing department.

The considerations, from a larger company perspective, could be broadly grouped into managerial efficiency and environmental relevance. In terms of managerial efficiency, they might consider:
- The danger of creating artificial boundaries with isolated empires within
- the danger of developing an inappropriate focus i.e. product or national organisation rather than a market or international orientation
- the need to combine teams of marketers from several countries to promote products in a reasonably consistent manner
- the need to work closely in focused teams across an organisation, involving design, service, production etc
- the general managerial fashions for downsizing, empowerment and multifunctional team working and whether these are really applicable
- more delegation and accountability down a reduced hierarchy with knock-on effect on staff capability and training.

In terms of environmental relevance, they should consider:
- That customers are becoming more demanding
- that customers are becoming more international in their sourcing whether they are manufacturers or intermediaries etc
- that markets are becoming pan-European and increasingly global which needs to be reflected in the structure adopted (cf. P&G)
- that there is a need for an appreciation of longer term customer relationships rather than just sales targets, which calls for a more integrated marketing approach
- that there has been growth in more specialised media, especially IT driven at same time as mass media effectiveness is being questioned, which creates a need for fresh ideas based on a sound understanding of the market.

SUGGESTED ASSIGNMENTS

- Questions for Discussion 22.5
- To what extent are the concepts of marketing planning equally applicable in small and large organisations?

Chapter 23
SERVICES MARKETING

LECTURE PLAN

A lecture based on this chapter should help the student to:
1. Define the characteristics that differentiate services from other products and outline their impact on marketing;
2. develop an extended marketing mix of 7Ps that takes the characteristics of services into account and allows comprehensive marketing strategies to be developed for services;
3. understand the importance of interactive and internal marketing for service products and their impact on issues of quality and productivity; and
4. understand the special characteristics of non-profit organisations within the service sector, and the implications for their marketing activities.

The key sections of this lecture should be:

Characteristics of service markets (pp 917-926):
- Definition of service goods compared with physical goods
- goods that combine elements of service with elements of physical goods
- characteristics of service markets, including OHP 91, figure 23.2 (p 919) Characteristics of Service Markets:
  $\Rightarrow$ Define each factor
  $\Rightarrow$ outline the problems each gives the consumer
  $\Rightarrow$ outline the problems each gives the marketer
  $\Rightarrow$ show the extent to which each of these is or is not applicable to purely physical goods.

The services marketing mix (pp 926-932):
This section is based on OHP 92, figure 23.3 (p 927) The Services Marketing Mix:
- *Product:* elements that make up a service product; comparison with a physical good; branding issues.
- *Price:* problems of setting and justifying service prices; the role of price in service demand management.
- *Place:* need for direct supply; problems caused by direct supply.
- *Promotion:* problems of services communication; role of communication in influencing expectations and actual experience of the service.
- *People:* the importance of both staff and customers ion the service delivery process; problems this causes.
- *Physical evidence:* definition; role in creating the service experience; difference between essential and peripheral evidence.
- *Processes:* definition; types of processes commonly found; their role in ensuring a smooth and efficient service experience.

Service quality (pp 932-934):
- The importance of service quality
- ten factors contributing to service quality, including OHP 93, figure 23.4 (p 935) Service Quality: Expectations, Perceptions and Gaps:
  $\Rightarrow$ Define the ten factors
  $\Rightarrow$ differentiate between factors mainly influencing the inputs into the service experience and those mainly affecting the outcomes of it
  $\Rightarrow$ explain how the comparison of expected and actual outcomes creates satisfaction or dissatisfaction

⇒ outline the reasons why dissatisfaction might occur

⇒ suggest what the marketer can do about it

⇒ emphasise how actual experience then affects expectations next time.

Internal marketing - training and productivity (pp 934-940):

- Importance of training in service markets
- definition of internal marketing
- types of staff: visible, invisible, direct and indirect.
- Definition of service productivity
- difficulty of measuring it
- ways of increasing productivity: staff; systems; reduced service; customer interaction; managing supply and demand.

Non-profit organisations (pp 940-945):

- Definition of non-profit organisations
- characteristics of non-profit organisations: multiple objectives; service orientation; accountability; multiple publics, including OHP 94, figure 23.5 (p 942) Non-profit Organisations: Multiple Publics:

    ⇒ Outline the range of publics

    ⇒ emphasise the difference between the revenue providers and the beneficiaries of the service

    ⇒ emphasise the multiple objectives

    ⇒ emphasise the need for marketing to all publics, regardless of whether they are providers or beneficiaries.

- The implications of all this for marketing mixes and strategies.

QUESTIONS FOR REVIEW

23.1   What are the main characteristics that distinguish services from physical products? (pp 918-926)

Services:
- Do not involve transfer of ownership
- are intangible
- are perishable
- are inseparable in the sense that production and consumption take place simultaneously
- are heterogeneous.

23.2   How can tangibility be introduced into service products? (pp 919-922)

Tangibility can be introduced through:
- The physical premises and location at which the service is delivered
- equipment and physical products used in the service delivery
- the appearance and manner of staff
- the efficiency and accuracy of systems
- a strong brand image
- advertising and promotional literature.

23.3   Define inseparability and its implications for the service product. (pp 924-925)

Inseparability means that consumption takes place at the same time as production and that the customer is likely to come into close contact with those 'manufacturing' the service. Its implications are that it:
- Makes it difficult to ensure consistent quality
- makes it difficult to plan production

- makes it difficult to control the conditions under which the service is produced
- means that human interaction is an important part of the service experience.

23.4   What are the 7Ps of the services marketing mix? (pp 926-932)

1. Product
2. price
3. place
4. promotion
5. people
6. physical evidence
7. processes.

23.5   What are the 10 criteria that affect customers' perceptions of service quality? (pp 932-934)

1. Access
2. reliability
3. credibility
4. security
5. understanding the customer
6. responsiveness
7. courtesy
8. competence
9. communication
10. tangibles.

23.6   Define the barriers to service quality. (pp 932-934)

- Misconceptions
- inadequate resources
- inadequate delivery
- exaggerated promises.

23.7   What is internal marketing and why is it important in service products? (pp 934-940)

Internal marketing means recruiting the right staff, remunerating them appropriately and training them to a sufficiently high level to be able to deliver the service experience to the customer effectively and efficiently. It is important because:
- Service products can involve a great deal of interaction between staff and customers
- service products are produced 'live' in front of the customer and must be right first time
- it is important to get as much consistency as possible in service delivery on different occasions and between different staff.

23.8   In what ways can service productivity be improved? (pp 936-940)

Service productivity can be improved by:
- Improved recruitment and training of staff
- more advanced systems and technology
- reducing service levels
- changing the nature of customer interaction (for example by introducing self-service options)
- reducing the mismatch between supply and demand (for example through reduced prices at quiet times).

23.9   In what ways do non-profit organisations differ from other types of business? (pp 940-943)

They differ because:
- They serve multiple publics
- they have multiple objectives targeted at different publics
- they have a service rather than physical goods orientation
- they are often open to public scrutiny and accountability.

23.10   Why might a non-profit organisation's approach to pricing differ from that of other types of business? (p 944)

Its approach to pricing might differ because:
- Its sources of income are different from its sources of revenue
- the service recipient's need comes first rather than their ability to pay
- its pricing has to be much more flexible, especially if service recipients are to be asked to 'make a donation' determined by their consciences and their financial means
- if it in receipt of public funds, its pricing discretion might be heavily constrained by external bodies and accountability.

QUESTIONS FOR DISCUSSION

23.1   Discuss the impact of perishability on the management and marketing of a service business.

Points that might be raised include:
- Both the customer and the service provider have to be in the right place at the right time
- the service provider has to do as much as possible to ensure that there is a customer for every single service delivery occasion
- the service provider has to try to manipulate demand flows to match the service provision rate and capacity
- the service provider might have to develop a more flexible approach to pricing as a demand management tool
- the service provider might have to develop a more flexible approach to production capacity as a response to fluctuating demand
- the service provider might have to be much more alert and responsive to what is going on in the marketing environment in case it affects short-term demand and supply
- the involvement of the customer or a group of customers might make any one service delivery much better or worse than another, giving the manager a certain amount of uncontrollable unpredictability to cope with
- the marketer is effectively selling a largely unpredictable product that has not been manufactured yet, and thus is making promises about product benefits in the hope that all the 'live' elements of the service product do indeed come together and work well at the point of sale and consumption.

23.2   Choose a service business and analyse its marketing offering in terms of the 7Ps.

Students should work systematically through the 7Ps, demonstrating that they appreciate the issues covered by each of them, and that they are aware of the interactions and synergies between them.

23.3   Design a short questionnaire for assessing the quality of service offered by a local dental practice.

Students should be encouraged to look again at chapter 6 to refresh their memories on the subject of questionnaire design. They should be encouraged to use as wide a range of question formats as possible, as long as they are appropriate for gaining the information required. As well as gaining basic details about the respondent, the questionnaire might well be based on the factors summarised in figure 23.4 (p 935) including:

- *Access:* convenience in terms of both location and surgery hours.
- *Reliability:* getting appropriate treatment that solves a dental problem with the minimum of pain and inconvenience; getting appropriate preventative advice and support.
- *Credibility:* any dentist should have professional credibility, but more generally, do the staff seem trustworthy? Are any 'after-sales' problems sorted out efficiently?
- *Security:* whether the practice reassures the patient, allays their fears and doubts, and respects patient confidentiality.
- *Understanding the customer:* making the effort to tailor the service to the customer's needs, perhaps with weekend and evening appointments, or with family appointments, or flexible payment plans for extensive treatment, for example.
- *Responsiveness:* whether the receptionist answers the telephone quickly or immediately attends to arriving patients; whether patients can get appointments when they want them; whether emergency treatment is quickly available; whether analyses or other work which has to be sent off to a laboratory or technician are returned quickly.
- *Courtesy:* of receptionists, nurses, and the dentist.
- *Competence:* of all staff (including external technicians) in delivering their part of the service experience efficiently, confidently and reliably.
- *Communication:* for example sending out letters informing the patient that it is time for a routine check up; if patients are kept waiting beyond their appointment time, apologising and telling them how long they might have to wait; providing appointment cards with written details of the next appointment and with contact telephone numbers and details of surgery hours and emergency dental provision.
- *Tangibles:* the ambience of the waiting room; provision of magazines while you wait; appearance of staff; quality and scope of dental health literature and literature sent out by the practice; cleanliness and age of the equipment, fixtures and fittings.

23.4   In what ways might the following service organisations define and improve their productivity: (a) a theme park; (b) a university, and (c) a fast food outlet.

The theme park might define its productivity in terms of:
- Number of visitors per period
- average spend per visitor
- throughput of customers per hour on each ride (or at kiosks, on-site stores or restaurants)
- length of queues at key times
- average waiting time in queues per customer
- number of enquiries dealt with per hour at information kiosks.

The theme park might improve its productivity by:
- Increasing the number of visitors at quiet times through sales promotions
- employing flexible part-time staff to deal with busy times of day or seasons
- staff training to handle enquiries more quickly; process customers more quickly (for example at ticket booths on entry, in stores or in restaurants); divert customers away from the busiest areas of the park to quieter ones; to entertain queues to make the wait less tedious
- increasing the number of staff to speed up customer service flows
- systems improvements to speed up customer handling and service
- reduced service levels, for example shorter ride times or shorter menus in restaurants to speed up customer choice and processing
- involving customers more in service delivery, for example introducing self-service restaurants or snack bars; installing vending machines for snacks; giving them more detailed maps and information to reduce the number of enquiries.

The university might define its productivity in terms of:

- Staff student ratios
- average class size
- number of awards made per academic year
- number of degrees within each classification band made per academic year
- research output and publications per member of staff
- research grants awarded and other external funds
- number of students recruited per course per academic year
- student drop-out rate
- average library usage per student.

The university might improve its productivity by:
- Recruiting better qualified staff
- investing in staff development
- using new technology to increase the amount of student-centred learning taking place
- re-defining staff roles to allow some to specialise in research or income generation
- investing in bigger lecture theatres and seminar rooms
- investing in library and IT resources
- investing in student recruitment drives.

The fast food outlet might define its productivity in terms of:
- Number of customers served per hour per serving person
- number of burgers (or whatever) served per hour
- average time taken overall to cook and serve an order
- average spend per customer
- length of queues at key times
- average waiting time per customer.

The fast food outlet might improve its productivity by:
- Staff training to process customers more quickly
- staff training to cook food more quickly
- increasing the number of service points
- employing flexible part-time staff to deal with busy periods
- review of systems to ensure that order processing and food production are as quick and as efficient as they can be
- streamlining menus to exploit production synergies between different items and to standardise as far as possible
- bundle pricing to increase customer spend and make order processing easier and faster
- promotional efforts to try to smooth out fluctuating demand.

Students might be encouraged to broaden the discussion by bringing in examples from their own experience of these types of organisation and their operations.

23.5   What do you think might be the main sources of revenue for the following types of non-profit organisation and what revenue generation problems do you think they each face (a) a small local charity; (b) a National Health Service hospital, and (c) a public museum.

A small local charity's main revenue sources are likely to be:
- Street collections
- a charity shop
- Christmas cards and other merchandise sales
- private donations
- fund raising promotional events
- sponsorship from local companies
- grants from other charitable bodies
- the national lottery.

Its main revenue generating problems are that:
- Its local nature gives it a limited pool of potential donors
- it is competing against higher profile national charities

- there is likely to be a lack of resources and skills to initiate major fund-raising efforts
- it cannot rely on a steady and predictable stream of income
- many of its revenue generating initiatives depend on the goodwill and hard work of volunteers.

A National Health Service hospital's main revenue sources are likely to be:
- National government
- transfer prices charged on the 'internal market' for services rendered to other units within the NHS, for example for laboratory analysis or radiography undertaken for general practitioners
- goods and services sold to private patients
- donation of equipment or volunteers' time by charitable bodies, commercial organisations or the general public.

Its main revenue generating problems are:
- Competing for funds against other hospitals and NHS units
- attracting full-fee paying private patients in competition against other, fully private hospitals
- pricing constraints imposed by the workings of the internal market
- ensuring that donated equipment in particular is appropriate and useful and that the funds are available to operate and maintain it.

A public museum's main revenue sources are likely to be:
- National government
- local government
- charitable bodies providing funds to purchase important artefacts, for example
- the national lottery
- entry fees
- merchandise or restaurant sales
- public and commercial donations.

Its main revenue generating problems are:
- Competing for governmental funds
- lobbying charitable bodies for funds
- uncertainty as to whether any one funding bid will succeed
- limits on entry fees imposed by public opinion or governmental influence
- ensuring a steady stream of visitors through the doors
- assembling and marketing an attractive range of merchandise.

CASE STUDY 23.1 The Education Catering Service (p 948)

Teaching Objectives

1. To emphasise that non-profit organisations have to deal with a wide range of publics with different vested interests;
2. to explore the necessity of marketing as a previously public sector service becomes open to free competition;
3. to evaluate the implementation of marketing strategy in a non-profit operation.

1 **One difficulty facing ECS was deciding who the customer was. Identify all the different groups who would have an interest in the product offered.**

The various interested groups are:
- The pupils
- their parents
- their teachers
- school managers
- the local authority
- school cooks.

2   **For each of the groups you defined in question 1, outline how their needs and priorities in terms of a school meals service might differ.**

- *The pupils:* this group is particularly concerned with the quality and variety of the food on offer. They do not want school dinners to be boring and predictable, nor do they necessarily want to be restricted by a set menu every day. A cafeteria system that allows them to overdose on chips every day if they want and to have a wide range of choice would probably be their preferred option.
- *Their parents:* primarily, parents are looking for value for money. Within that, however, they want reassurance that their children are getting a good quality, nutritionally balanced meal. Knowing that their children were able to spend their dinner money overdosing on chips might not please parents! Given all that, parents might prefer a set meal option or a limited choice cafeteria. Parents might also want to be reassured that any special dietary requirements (vegetarian, halal, kosher, or diabetic meals for example) would be provided. If the price of dinners is to reflect the true cost of their provision, however, a set meal might be priced higher than some parent would be prepared to pay. A cafeteria system at least allows the parent some price flexibility.
- *Their teachers:* teachers clearly have the children's welfare at heart and like the parents, want well-balanced meals that satisfy the children's needs. Pupils who have had a 'proper' lunch tend to work better in the afternoons.
- *School managers:* in administrative and logistic terms, school managers want to be assured that the school meals service can operate cost effectively, time-efficiently, and reliably day after day. They have to be sure that during the lunch period, every pupil can be fed and that the school hall (or other dining venue) can be cleared and returned to its proper use at the appointed time. School managers would also be interested in the cost to them of providing the various kinds of dining facilities, and the extent of their involvement in having to arrange and manage supervision within the dining hall and the collection and banking of cash.
- *The local authority:* the primary concern of the local authority is the most cost effective provision of a specified service to appropriate quality standards. Under compulsory competitive tendering, the authority is not necessarily concerned about whether the service continues to be provided by an in-house department or an outside contractor, as long as the decision can be justified and the provider matches performance expectations.
- *School cooks:* this group is currently employed by ECS and might have an interest in ECS retaining the contract rather than facing the uncertainty of being re-employed by an outside contractor or losing their jobs. In terms of the meals themselves, the cooks want to be able to produce interesting, enjoyable and varied meals that meet nutritional standards, with as big a budget as possible but keeping meal prices reasonable. Logistically, the cooks might find it easier to work to more limited daily menus to ease time pressures on production and to exploit economies of scale.

3   **Outline the 'competition' facing a school meals provider such as ECS. Can marketing help ECS to overcome the competitive threat?**

The immediate and direct competition comes from meal providers outside the local authority under the compulsory competitive tendering scheme. ECS has the advantages that:
- It has proved that it can provide the service!
- it knows the schools and the key decision makers
- it has the staff and the expertise in place
- it has established supplier networks.

The questions that the decision makers will be asking, however, include:
- Is there a meals provider outside the local authority that can do even better than ECS?
- Can ECS work within tight cost and performance constraints?
- Is ECS flexible enough and creative enough to meet the new, evolving needs of the various 'publics' efficiently and effectively?
- Is ECS too set in its ways to change?
- Can ECS survive in a free market economy as opposed to its previous virtual monopoly?

The less direct, but no less threatening competition, comes from pupils who:

- Go home for lunch
- bring food into school with them to consume on the premises
- are allowed to leave school premises to buy food from local shops and outlets.

In the light of these competitive concerns, adopting a marketing philosophy and developing a marketing strategy was absolutely essential for ECS if it was to retain its franchise and protect it in the future. Marketing could help ECS to:

- Communicate coherently and consistently with its various publics
- create a 'brand image' reflecting the positive and valued elements of its service
- develop a more businesslike approach to its operations and service provision
- streamline its offering to better match its customers' needs and wants
- manage the transition from public sector monopoly to free market competition
- win the contract
- make pupils and parents see a school dinner as the best lunchtime option.

4   Evaluate ECS's marketing strategy. Has ECS adopted the 'right' approach?

ECS has worked hard to develop a marketing strategy that best met the needs and answered the concerns of all its target publics and overcame the competitive threats. In the sense that ECS actually did win the contract, it clearly was the 'right' approach! Looking at the strategy in more detail, its positive aspects were:

- A flexible portfolio of dinner options was developed to allow schools to choose the one best suited to their facilities and pupil needs.
- The products developed also provided a range of pricing options, from the fixed price, fixed menu to the flexibility of the cash cafeteria.
- Internally, employees (managers and cooks) were involved in the strategy design, given marketing training and kept informed about what was happening to ECS.
- ECS targeted communication at pupils, through Eric the chef, in order to impress upon them the importance of good eating habits and the 'fun' factor of school dinners. This partly defends against the non-school dinner eating options, and turns pupils into influencers on behalf of ECS.
- ECS targeted communication at teachers, through the memo and perhaps through the influence of cooks, again to reinforce the healthy eating message, to establish ECS's image as a responsible and caring service provider, and to reinforce existing relationships.
- Presumably too ECS was active, within ethical constraints, in lobbying the local authority as the key decision-maker in awarding the contract.

The strategy described here is, of course, focused on winning the dinner contract. ECS has had to make certain promises and has had to commit itself to performance standards and targets. Its future marketing strategy has to focus on delivering all that, and on maintaining and further strengthening relationships with all its main publics in order to ensure that it can defend its position.

CASE STUDY 23.2 Day Visitor Attractions (p 949)

Teaching Objectives

1. To ensure that students understand the structure of the services marketing mix and how it might be implemented;
2. to explore the problems of designing targeted marketing mixes for services products;
3. to consider the marketing options and problems of increasing visitor numbers for a leisure services product.

1   Outline the issues facing a theme park under each of the elements of the services marketing mix.

Product:
- Keeping the product fresh and of interest
- developing a range of activities to appeal to a broad family segment and to create a fun experience
- maximising on-site sales, for example of merchandise, food and drink, around the core product experience
- injecting imagination to create fun and excitement.

Price:
- Setting prices that reflect the quality of the leisure experience, but do not make it too expensive for a family group
- pricing to reflect seasonality and predicted demand levels
- pricing to maximise the sales and profitability of merchandise etc.

Promotion:
- Generating awareness and interest in the attraction
- encouraging customers to visit
- keeping the public informed of new developments, for example new rides or changes in opening hours
- generating repeat business
- increasing demand during quiet or off-season periods
- making the best use of PR opportunities.

Place:
- Ensuring that the location is geographically accessible with a large catchment area
- ensuring good access by a variety of private and public transport modes
- proximity to large conurbations is useful for repeat trade.

People:
- Ensuring high service levels to enhance the product
- adding value to the product through service delivery
- setting clear performance standards and training staff thoroughly to deliver them
- motivating and remunerating staff adequately
- controlling other visitors to enhance atmosphere.

Processes:
- Keeping queues at the entrance gate and at rides, cafeterias etc as short as possible
- designing clear routes around the site that encourage customers to flow around the site in an orderly way so that they see and experience everything
- establishing quality assurance systems.

Physical evidence:
- Creating a good atmosphere around main attractions
- ensuring that physical facilities are clean and adequate for customer needs
- using physical evidence to provide a means of differentiation.

2   One of Aillwe Cave's target markets is groups of foreign tourists. How might Aillwe's marketing approaches to this segment differ from those aimed at the domestic Irish family segment?

The tourist segment members may not have any prior experience or information on the cave and its offering. The important challenge for Aillwe is to attract tourists once they are in the region. This is primarily a promotional task. As soon as the tourist enters Ireland via an airport or ferry terminal every effort needs to be made to encourage a visit. Brochures in hotels, roadside posters, advertising in tourist guides and signposting all help to generate a basic awareness and interest. Although Aillwe cave may not be the reason for a visit to Ireland, it does add to the total holiday experience. Tourists are in the frame of mind to seek to visit the main national attractions and once the basic awareness has been generated they will be aware of the type of experience they will undergo should they pay a visit. Aillwe does not have to wait until tourists are in Ireland before communicating with them. Through guidebooks and travel brochures, a general awareness can be generated before a visit. This can ensure that travellers build Aillwe into their schedules. The promotion seen by these travellers when they are in Ireland will reinforce the previous awareness and interest generated.

The Irish domestic tourist could be a repeat visitor and is probably less susceptible to promotion focusing on general awareness. New features or attractions maybe necessary to convince the domestic tourist to repeat visit. Different media might be appropriate too. The domestic visitor might be more exposed to television or national print media advertising. Other differences could relate to different price perceptions and typical spends while visiting the cave. For a local resident the cost of a day out or visit would be compared with a range of other alternatives so they might be less prepared to pay the full price. Family tickets, off season rates and weekday or weekend specials could appeal to domestic visitors without necessarily reducing prices to the tourist segment. On a one-off visit as part of a holiday tour, tourists might be less sensitive to comparative prices. Foreign tourists' spend on merchandise is also likely to be higher as they buy gifts or souvenirs to take home with them.

3   What are the benefits to the Tivoli Gardens of remaining 'quaintly old fashioned'?

The Tivoli Gardens are caught between the pressure for change to fit into a more 'high tech' leisure world, and the positive attributes of a well established brand name. Visitors have become more sophisticated, more experienced with a wide variety of leisure and theme parks, some of which combine high tech with outstanding customer service levels. In comparison, the Tivoli concept has hardly evolved at all and there are not the funds to undertake large scale investment. There are thus probably few choices other than building upon the old fashioned theme, yet that could still provide the opportunity for product enhancement. Costumed service staff and themed entertainments could support the basic concept and appeal to nostalgia, as the gardens cannot compete on the modern image. However, old fashioned should not mean outdated, antiquated facilities with poor service. The repositioning as an old fashioned, yesteryear theme park can retain the interest of visitors from Copenhagen, while not conflicting with the wider expectations of the international tourist.

4   If Lightwater Valley wanted to attract more visitors, what sorts of marketing actions could it take?

To expand the number of visitors, Lightwater Valley will either have to attract new customers to the park either from the core region or beyond or encourage repeat visitors. This latter group would be especially encouraged if new attractions are added to the portfolio. Either way, marketing thinking and techniques would be essential. The activities could include:
- Offering more off-season deals
- introducing and publicising new rides and/or replacements on an annual basis
- targeting groups with special packages during low usage days or months
- promoting more heavily to the margins of the core region
- arranging joint deals with local hotels to create weekend packages, including entrance fees
- introducing differentiated pricing, even lowering prices if the organisation is confident of increased spend within the park on merchandise etc
- increasing the opportunities for in-park retailing
- increasing reminder advertising within the core region.

Marketing in Action Multiplex Cinemas (p 921)

Discussion question
Why has the Multiplex cinema format become so successful?

The format has been successful because it meets the needs and lifestyle of the consumer better than the original cinema product. The service experience has been considerably upgraded to present cinema going as a leisure pursuit that can compete with alternative activities ranging from ten pin bowling to a visit to the theatre. Particular aspects of the service product and product service include:

- A wide choice of films to suit different tastes
- pre-booking possible to make an evening out more predictable for the customer
- easy parking
- easy access to a range of snacks etc
- a comfortable environment.

All of these deliberate efforts to upgrade the service experience have added value to the cinema outing so that although higher prices are being charged, more is being offered for the money. Although the service experience itself is intangible, the focus on tangible cues has improved perceived quality. Effective marketing has also played an important role, for example actively promoting forthcoming events through advertising and trailers. Large out of town sites use large displays to attract the attention of passing trade. Further developments could include greater use of direct marketing. Careful promotion is important given the perishable nature of a cinema seat. An unfilled seat is revenue lost forever.

Marketing in Action Novotel Design (p 931)

Discussion question
In what ways might a hotel use physical evidence to enhance the corporate image?

There are two main elements of physical evidence, essential evidence and peripheral evidence. Essential evidence is central to the customer's hotel choice criteria:
- Room, decor and furnishing
- car parks, reception areas, public areas and the general ambience created by materials, colour, texture, shape, and state of repair
- gardens and pools
- use of lighting, music and smell to enhance all the above points.

Peripheral evidence is less critical and covers relatively minor aspects, including bathroom accessories, menus, ashtrays, room stationary etc. All of these dimensions combine, along with staff, to create an image in the customer's mind. All elements should be consistent with each other and communicate the same values and themes.

Marketing in Action Fundraising and Image Creation (p 943)

Discussion question
What publics does the Hospice have to target for attracting funds? What methods does the Hospice use to attract resources from the general public?

The main publics are:
- The National Health Service for core funding provision
- the general public as the target for most of the additional funding
- institutional publics, such as schools and teachers for fundraising through personalised tea towels.

In attracting funds from the general public, the Hospice offers some tangible things for sale, such as products, and some less tangible things such as entertainment and a warm feeling of supporting a good cause with donations. The use of a friendly, readily identifiable logo supports the perceived value of the purchases by appealing to the giving instinct. The range of methods used include:
- Flag days
- instant prize scratch cards
- special fund raising events
- hedgehog toys
- Christmas cards
- tea towels and other products.

Marketing in Action The National Missing Persons Helpline (p 945)

Discussion question
Why is revenue generation more problematic for a charity than for a commercial organisation, and why does the NMPH have particular revenue generation problems?

Revenue generation is more problematic for a charity because unlike a commercial organisation:

- It cannot rely on a steady stream of predictable sales
- its revenue generation is separate from its service delivery, thus it does not have the close tie between production and sales volumes
- it cannot always price its services at commercial rates (see review question 23.10 above)
- it is generating revenue from a much more diverse range of sources
- those from whom the charity generates revenue do not always get any tangible benefit from it.

The NMPH's particular revenue generating problems include all of the above, and that:

- It does not have a strong public profile to trade on
- it is a relatively small organisation that does not have a great deal of resources to commit to funding revenue generation
- it is not involved in work that easily captures the public imagination
- to do its work it needs extensive media exposure and thus needs either a great deal of money to buy advertising airtime or generous 'donations in kind' from media owners and agencies.

SUGGESTED ASSIGNMENTS

- Questions for Discussion 23.1
- Analyse the ways in which a non-profit organisation's marketing problems differ from those of a similar profit-making organisation.

Chapter 24
MARKETING AND THE SMALLER BUSINESS

LECTURE PLAN

A lecture based on this chapter should help the student to:

1. Understand the special characteristics of a small business;
2. describe how marketing assists small business development from start up to maturity;
3. appreciate the impact of franchising as both a means of business expansion and a means of distribution; and
4. identify the main stages in setting up a franchise operation.

The key sections of this lecture should be:

The nature of small business (pp 952-957):
Defining small businesses by characteristics:

- Small share
- personal ownership
- independence
- other factors: uncertainty; innovation; fast evolution; resources; number of employees.

Stages in small business development (pp 957-969):
This section is based on OHP 95, figure 24.1 (p 958) Business Launch and Development Stages:

- *Pre-launch:* why people start in business; sources of new business ideas.

- *Launch:* the problems of designing the marketing mix and testing the product idea.
- *Survival:* factors leading to successful launch and survival: differential advantage; niche marketing; market entry strategy; key customers; competitor reaction; distribution; communication; flexibility.
- *Consolidation and growth:* importance of consolidation; influences on growth; product development; market development; positioning; professional marketing; sustaining growth.
- *Maturity and renewal:* strategic management of consolidation, further growth and diversification.
- Factors leading to small business failure.

Introduction to franchising (pp 969-975):
- Definition of franchising
- difference between a franchisor and a franchisee
- types of franchise relationship: distributorships; licensing; celebrity endorsement; trade marks; business format franchise.
- The emergence of the business format franchise as an important area
- types of business format franchise
- the importance of the contract
- degrees of franchise independence
- scope and growth of franchising.

Risks and benefits of franchising (pp 975-978):
- Benefits to the franchisor
- problems for the franchisor
- benefits to the franchisee
- problems for the franchisee
- general franchising problems.

Launching a franchised system (pp 978-984):
This section is based on OHP 96, figure 24.4 (p 980) Stages in Launching a New Franchised Business System:
- *Concept development:* ensuring that the idea will work as a franchise; designing the system.
- *Pilot operation:* refining the system through a live operation for at least a year.
- *Designing the blueprint:* (including pp 978-979); establishing the fine detail of every aspect of how the system will work and what the franchisee will contribute to it.
- *Prepare operating manual:* guidelines for day to day conduct of the business in very fine detail.
- *Marketing the franchise system to potential franchisees:* locating potential franchisees.
- *Selecting franchisees:* defining the criteria for an acceptable franchisee; the franchisee's problems in deciding whether to accept the franchise; agreeing contractual obligations.
- *Implement, maintain and develop the system:* ensuring the payment of fees etc; maintaining good relationships with franchisees; further developing and expanding the system.

Note: This chapter could easily be divided into two lectures, one on small business and one on franchising.

QUESTIONS FOR REVIEW

24.1   What are the qualitative differences between large and small businesses? (pp 953-957)

Small businesses tend to:
- Have a small share of the market
- be owned by an individual or small group who are closely involved with all facets of the business
- be independent of outside ownership and influence
- face a greater degree of uncertainty
- be innovative
- evolve quickly and change rapidly

- have to make the best of scarce resources.

24.2 How is a small business defined in terms of the number of employees? (p 957)

- *Micro-enterprise:* 0-9 employees
- *Small enterprise:* 10-99 employees
- *Medium enterprises:* 100-499 employees
- *Large enterprises:* over 500 employees.

24.3 What are the stages in small business development? (pp 957-969)

- Pre-launch
- business launch
- survival
- consolidation and growth
- maturity and renewal.

24.4 What factors might trigger the decision to start a small business? (pp 958-962)

- The entrepreneur's previous experience and career
- practical or managerial skills or ideas gained within another organisation
- knowledge that there is a gap in the market
- availability of capital
- unemployment
- craving for independence
- desire to take a risk.

24.5 Outline the factors that contribute to a successful small business launch. (pp 962-964)

- Developing a differentiated product that does fill a gap in the market
- targeting a viable segment or niche
- designing a marketing mix that is appropriate to the target market and can be implemented and managed within the abilities and resources of the small firm
- preparing for likely competitor reaction
- securing appropriate distribution channels
- investing in generating awareness and interest
- being flexible and responsive during the start up period.

24.6 What factors contribute to business growth? (pp 964-967)

- The entrepreneur's managerial and marketing skills
- intensity of desire for growth
- access to resources for expansion
- product development or adaptation
- expansion into new markets or segments
- consolidating and strengthening competitive position.

24.7 What are the five types of franchise relationship? (pp 970-973)

1. Distributorships
2. license to manufacture
3. celebrity endorsement
4. licensing trade marks
5. business format franchise.

24.8   What benefits does franchising offer (a) the franchisor and (b) the franchisee? (pp 975-977)

Benefits to the franchisor include:
- Allows rapid growth in coverage and penetration
- start-up investment risks shared with franchisee
- day to day management and risks borne by the franchisee
- achieving economies of scale
- the ability to concentrate more on strategic rather than operational issues.

Benefits to the franchisee include:
- Generally lower risk than an independent start-up
- access to established brand name and image, hence quicker establishment of business
- access to proven systems and procedures
- access to franchisor's additional management support and services
- access to and benefits from franchisor's marketing expertise
- sourcing through the franchisor and benefiting from their bulk buying power
- some territorial protection
- access to new products.

24.9   What are the stages involved in developing a new franchised system? (pp 979-984)

- Concept development
- pilot operation
- designing the franchise blueprint
- preparing the operating manual
- marketing the franchise system
- selecting franchisees
- implementing, maintaining and further refining the system.

24.10   What factors does a franchise agreement or contract usually cover? (pp 982-983)

- The nature and name of the franchise activity
- the territory covered
- the terms of the franchise
- fees and royalties
- the franchisor's responsibilities
- the franchisee's obligations
- conditions under which either party may terminate the contract
- conditions under which the business may be sold or re-assigned.

QUESTIONS FOR DISCUSSION

24.1   What kind of small business would you like to start? What problems do you think you would face in trying to turn that idea into reality?

This question encourages students to explore the commercial potential of their own interests, hobbies and experiences. It might also encourage them to discuss their own fears of entrepreneurship and their own 'suitability' for it. The problems of starting a business generally include:
- Sourcing capital
- developing the necessary range of management skills
- turning the idea into a marketable product
- fine-tuning the product or service design and production method or system
- researching the market's needs
- determining whether there is a sustainable market there

- ensuring differential advantage over direct and indirect competition
- writing the business plan
- developing the launch marketing plan
- generating enough cash flow in the short-term to keep the business afloat until regular custom is established
- sourcing and negotiating with suppliers
- recruiting staff
- finding suitable premises
- securing distribution channels.

24.2   What are the practical problems of designing and implementing a marketing mix in a small business compared with a large business?

A small business might:
- Not have access to as wide a range of management specialists and business planning expertise
- not have the skills or the resources to invest in extensive market research
- not have enough managerial time free to devote to a lengthy planning process
- not have a lot of pricing flexibility if it does not have a wide range of products that can be used to subsidise each other
- not have the skills or resources to invest in extensive promotional mix activities
- not have dedicated R&D staff to ensure a constant flow of new ideas or to design and develop product adaptations quickly
- not have the production capacity or flexibility to go for new products, new markets or increased market penetration
- not be able to gain access to major distribution channels
- find it harder to achieve the economies of scale that help to give marketing flexibility and access to mass markets.

24.3   What do you think are the advantages of a business remaining small? What kinds of pressures might push or pull an organisation into growth?

A business might remain small because:
- The owner does not know how to make it grow
- the owner prefers to give a small number of well-known clients personalised service
- the owner does not wish to invest in expanded production facilities
- the owner does not wish to expand the business' geographic boundaries
- generally, the barriers to growth (investment, facilities, marketing etc) are thought to be too high
- the owner wants to retain total control over all aspects of the business
- there is no further market potential, or growth would mean expanding out of a comfortable niche into a wider market
- competitive pressures make growth difficult.

Push factors encouraging growth include:
- Saturation of the current niche
- reaching the limits of current production capacity
- availability of investment funds
- current customers demanding higher volumes
- current customers demanding an expanded range of goods and services
- competitive pressures squeezing current market share or prices
- the need to establish a stronger, more defendable market position
- stress and strain on current personnel suggesting that the point has been reached where more staff are needed and perhaps specialist managers should be employed.

Pull factors encouraging growth include:
- The attraction of more lucrative segments
- the attraction of export markets

- the desire for economies of scale
- product development exercises offering new opportunities
- a desire to achieve more mass market penetration
- a desire to be a more aggressive competitor.

24.4   Develop a checklist of factors that a potential franchisee should consider before deciding to invest.

The checklist might include the following factors:
- How long the franchise has been established
- how many franchisees it has
- how well proven the system is
- how much the initial investment is
- what royalties or annual fees are due
- what financial support the franchisor might offer to help with start up costs
- average turnover expected
- average profits expected
- average number of weekly hours invested by a franchisee
- how much marketing support the franchisor puts behind the enterprise
- what the franchisor offers in terms of training (initial and ongoing) and general management support
- whether the franchisor is offering a starting list of potential customers
- whether the sales territory is exclusive
- the strength of the competition within a territory
- what the average lead time is between signing the contract and being able to start the business
- the number of years commitment specified in the contract
- whether existing franchisees are totally happy with their relationships with the franchisor.

24.5   Find out about a potential franchise opportunity. How much is the licence fee and what does it include? What benefits would the franchisee derive and what risks would they run if they decided to take up this opportunity?

This question is a means of getting students to explore the real world of franchising and to think about the costs and risks involved in a range of opportunities. Students can also be encouraged to compare packages offered by different franchisors in essentially the same market in terms of risks and benefits. Potential benefits that might generally be raised include:
- A reasonable degree of autonomy with a relatively low degree of risk
- buying into a proven product or service and marketing system
- help and support from the franchisee
- benefiting from the franchisor's economies of scale in sourcing equipment, materials, components or merchandise.

Potential risks that might generally be raised include:
- Being committed by contract for a number of years
- no guarantee of good performance or profit
- commitment to sourcing equipment, materials, components or merchandise from the franchisor
- the franchisor's abuse of power
- the franchisor's neglect of the franchisees' interests
- being directly affected by the franchisor's poor marketing decisions or management
- being locked into a poorly performing territory.

CASE STUDY 24.1 Styles Precision Components Ltd (p 986)

Teaching Objectives

1. To gain an insight into the kinds of problems that can make a serious impact on a small businesses;
2. to examine the factors that influence and constrain small business decision-making;
3. to evaluate the strategic choice taken by a small business and its future plans.

1   What factors led to the problems encountered in 1992? Could these have been avoided or otherwise dealt with?

The causes of the problems facing Styles in 1992 developed over many years:
- In a mature market, a lack of innovation, product and market development created a stable subcontract engineering business that did not develop far beyond the initial concept
- Gordon Styles had started to turn the business around but was unable to break out of the traditional sector before disaster struck
- over dependency on two major customers created additional problems when both pulled out, even though there was nothing intrinsically wrong with their relationships with Styles
- there was difficulty in creating a distinctive advantage in a subcontract sector.

A number of alternatives could have been pursued to avoid the problems or lessen their impact, but it is easy to be wise after the event:
- Closer personal relationships and more detailed market intelligence at account level to pick up proposed changes in sourcing policy earlier
- a wider spread of customers to reduce dependency
- developing Styles' own product or component (rather than just manufacturing to order to customer specifications) to help stabilise production and ensure regular business.

2   What factors do you think Gordon would have considered when deciding how best to turn the company around?

Factors considered by Gordon might have been:
- Careful analysis of the market to spot gaps
- the resources required to implement any change, as resource scarcity can be a major limiting factor in many small firms
- if internal resources are insufficient to fund a venture, where can they be sourced from and to what extent will this overstretch the business?
- The fit between any new proposed activity and the existing capabilities and expertise of workforce
- the fit between any new proposed activity and the established customer base and loyalty
- the owner's personal interests and objectives that dominate strategic development in a small firm
- tolerance of risk and vulnerability
- the sustainability of new opportunities and predicted short- and long-term competitor response
- ability and capability of building business from a new idea over an extended period.

3   Gordon eventually decided to go for a new product in a new market. What were the risks of doing this and do you think it was the right choice?

The risks revolved around the high cost of market entry. Gordon had to raise finance for the investment. If the company had failed to develop the market the business would have had to be liquidated. It is a very high risk decision. Particular areas of concern would have been:
- The company was not familiar with the product technology, but was familiar with the typical demands made by customers in a fast turnaround subcontract environment. Gordon regarded this as a key skill that provided the base for the successful adoption of the new product area.
- There were risks that as the market developed, new entrants would move in. There is some evidence of this already happening. If machine prices fall, buyers may produce their own prototypes rather than buying in the service.

- A further risk for Styles was the emphasis that would have to be placed on developing a customer base. This would mean developing a proactive stance to finding customers, undertaking a technical assessment of the application, managing the prototype production project and meeting the fast service standards required.
- Technical support staff and technical sales thus required a much higher priority than in the subcontract precision engineering business. This would impose further demands on limited resources with an increased emphasis on marketing and customer support.
- There were additional complications for management and staffing in the small business. Not only did there have to be considerable investment in staff training, but the management team also had to learn and adapt to new, sometimes unforeseen challenges as they entered a relatively unknown market.

It is difficult, however, to disagree with Gordon's decision, given the significant impact on the growth of the business. However, the risks outlined above would not suit many entrepreneurs seeking a more secure and less uncertain business climate.

4   Where does Gordon go from here? How can he minimise the threat from new entrants?

There is probably little that Gordon can do to stop new entrants. Even if the contract signed with the US company has some limitation clauses regarding the number of machines that would be sold in the UK, it might still not be enough to guarantee that Gordon can build a long term defence. The main short-term priority for Gordon should be to cement the relationships with existing customers through technical capability, guaranteed service and ensuring that they are provided with no reason to consider re-sourcing. Unless an organisation is producing a large number of prototypes, it would probably be more economic to buy-in services as needed rather than investing in in-house prototyping capability. Gordon will have to reinforce the financial and strategic advantages of outsourcing over the coming months.

Additional effort might also be needed to expand the customer base in order to make it more difficult for a new entrant to build their own base. This could be on a geographical as well as sector basis. The new lower cost machines might not be able to offer the same specification as the more sophisticated machinery. Again. Gordon will have to reinforce these points. While price might not be an issue with current customers and in market conditions, it still needs to be carefully watched. Too high a price, unsupported by perceived value, will enable new competitors to enter the market more quickly. There might be a need for further new product development, perhaps in some new areas where the business can again build upon its core competencies values. Gordon cannot rest on past successes. These new developments might not result in growth in sales or profit, but they will at least enable the existing level of activity to be retained through careful diversification.

CASE STUDY 24.2 Developing a New Franchise Proposal: Budget-priced Hostels (p 987)

Teaching Objectives

1. To examine the strengths of franchising as a method of business expansion for the franchisor;
2. to consider the concerns of a potential franchisee in assessing a franchise proposal;
3. to explore the stages in developing a franchise proposal from the initial idea to the point where successful franchises are operating.

1   Is franchising the best way forward for this business? What are its alternatives?

Franchising offers a number of advantages to the owners of Western Hostels, provided they can convince prospective franchisees of the benefits of entering a franchised system. The main advantages would be:

- *Financial:* they could expand more quickly and with a lot less risk through a franchising system than by direct ownership. They will be able to expand the number of locations in Ireland and the UK one by one without the need to borrow for each property, and without incurring the costs of starting up and operating at each location. They do not appear to have any plans to purchase the properties themselves and then to select franchisees to operate from the site. That route would, of course, have reduced the risks for the franchisees but would have increased the franchisor's own exposure to risk. A further financial advantage of the franchised route is the ongoing revenue flow that can be realised through royalties on the franchisees' sales or the sale of supplies to franchisees. Thus with a start-up licence fee charge and an ongoing revenue flow, Western Hostels can build a viable business more quickly as well as creating a critical mass of franchisees to enable group marketing.
- *Managerial:* within the service sector, staff commitment and participation can be crucial to the quality of the service experience as well as for chasing new business. Franchisee owned hostels may encourage more dynamic management at each location than could be found with a salaried manager.
- *Economies of scale:* the franchising route will generate economies of scale in some areas that could lower the total franchise system costs for the benefit of all parties. Such savings could be found in purchasing fixtures and fittings, operating supplies, access to cheaper capital funds, marketing and promotional costs. For a reservation system to work for the benefit of all parties, the number of alternative hostels must be sufficient for potential guests to consider it worthwhile to book ahead and to plan an itinerary.

Despite the benefits of adopting a franchised route, there are some potential disadvantages that Western Hostels would have to consider:
- It has to be sure that it can keep control of the franchisees to provide the necessary system compliance and commitment. If the franchise contract has to repeatedly quoted then the relationships are not that strong.
- Western Hostels will have to be sure that it has the ability to offer both an initial start-up package and proposition as well as being able to provide ongoing advice and support to franchisees in terms of consultancy, marketing training etc. This would be essential if it is to develop a flow of new franchisees and royalty payments.

The main alternative to franchising would be direct ownership at a steady rate of expansion. Although progress would be slower, Western Hostels would retain far more control over the business and avoid having to keep franchisees in line within a system that Western Hostels would have to design. Much would depend upon whether the owners wanted rapid expansion and the demands of building a franchised system.

2   **Is the product concept, as outlined in this case, a good candidate for franchising?**

A number of factors would have to be considered when deciding whether to franchise the concept:

Opportunity assessment:
- The importance of the 'right' location - what is right?
- Does a long term market exist?
- Is there a gap in provision beyond the local area?
- Is the market growing, static, or declining?
- What alternative provision could be regarded as competition?
- Will the occupancy be high enough to sustain a viable business, given the nature of the hostels?
- What returns can be expected under different trading conditions?
- Can a year round business be developed?
- Will franchisees pay for an eight month per year franchise?
Branding:

- If the full benefits of a franchised approach are to be gained, a clear branding strategy will be needed. This will include the nature of the brand identity, how it will be developed, maintained and extended to cover the expansion in locations.

System design:
- Can Western Hostels design a system that is attractive to both customers and potential franchisees?
- What real expertise can it offer in such areas as site selection; packaging the service; detailing the infrastructure needed; marketing; training; raising finance; providing advice and assistance?
- If Western Hostels is deficient in any of these critical areas it will find that the proposition is less attractive to franchisees. It will also have to embody many of these points into both an operating manual and franchise contract.

Franchisee recruitment:
- Western Hostels has no well-known name, reputation or market presence to make it more attractive to potential franchisees. This could reduce the attraction of the concept in the franchisee's mind.
- Can it find enough willing franchisees who would value a franchised rather than independent start-up?
- Does it have the skills to vet potential franchisees to ensure that it recruits the best?
- Are the financial profiles attractive, especially given the high capital cost of entering the market?

Overall the difficulty facing Western Hostels is one of timing. As it is just at the start of the venture, it can offer few benefits to prospective franchisees and only a limited track record. The concept is unproven beyond the pilot, so the owners may find it difficult to expand rapidly until there are some successful franchisees. The argument is, of course, circular: how do you attract franchisees without being able to demonstrate that there are successful franchisees? One major issue is likely to be the seasonal nature of the business and the effort that Western Hostels can put into extending the season. By extending by an extra month or so, a real difference could be made to profitability.

3   If you were one of the potential franchisees at the meeting, what questions would you be asking?

A potential franchisee wants to know whether taking the franchised route will reduce risks and provide a greater financial return than adopting an independent start-up would. Typical questions would include:

Success/failure prospects:
- Examples/models of existing franchisees
- detailed examination of Western Hostels' accounts
- margins and returns under different trading scenarios
- track record of owners
- overall market and financial viability.

The nature of the support that will be provided:
- Start-up assistance and marketing
- capital needs
- training
- manual guidelines
- quality and standards
- financial guidance
- expansion
- problem solving
- national/regional marketing plan
- reservation system.

Contractual issues:
- Royalty/licence fees payable
- special advertising royalty payable
- territorial protection
- territorial expansion
- rights and remedies for default

- sourcing of supplies
- local variations allowed

length of contract.

4   What are the next stages the owners will have to go through to create and implement a franchised system?

Western Hostels might not be ready to launch fully into a franchised system. It does not appear to have all the answers to the questions proposed in question 3 above. It needs a more co-ordinated approach to system development. The stages proposed in the text can be related to the case to assess the position of Western Hostels.

- *The need to refine the concept:* specifying the equipment, premises, presentation, and image etc has been completed. This stage would also involve defining broadly how the product concept would work as a franchise, in terms of what would be expected of both franchisor and franchisee.
- *Undertake a pilot operation:* the product concept has been tested on a directly owned basis, but the franchise package has not been piloted on real franchisees.
- *Prepare a franchise blueprint:* this appears to be well underway but might need some more detailing. Points covered include interior design, layout, staffing, marketing, management systems, the reservation system etc.
- *Assemble an operating manual:* further work is necessary in this area. The manual is essential for guiding the franchisee through the start-up and business establishment process, while the new systems are being learned. It covers such items as opening hours, pricing, service standards, staff requirements, book keeping, reporting systems etc.
- *Marketing to franchisees:* Western Hostels appears to be at this stage, although this may be somewhat premature given the comments made about Western Hostels' accomplishments in previous stages!
- *Develop criteria for franchisee selection:* there is no evidence that Western Hostels has given much consideration to this issue. Finding willing franchisees with capital is not enough.
- *Prepare the franchise contract:* this is a major omission in Western Hostels' preparation. The contract should be prepared to cover all the contractual issues, payments, responsibilities, termination conditions etc.

Marketing in Action A Reason to Celebrate (p 955)

Discussion question
What are the key factors that are likely to determine the success of the Celebrations concept?

The themed dining concept is proven in the USA, and the main question is whether it will transfer into the European context. There are different traditions in terms of eating out, what constitute a good night out, and not least, the range of alternatives available. Many pubs have moved into an entertainment market that can involve drinking, food and dancing. The pilot scheme appears to have been successful, but will it now develop through a franchised format? Issues for discussion should include:

- Is there a real service difference compared with current offerings?
- If not, how will established competitors react?
- Is the local market, in terms of parties sold, likely to be big enough on a sustained basis, by day, week and month etc?
- What methods should be used to launch the new business? with what investment?
- Is the franchising route the most appropriate for developing the business?

Marketing in Action Small Businesses Move into International Markets (p 968)

Discussion question
Why did AirRide start exporting much more quickly than Morellato?

- *Personal aims and strategies of the owners:* AirRide is a commercial company with entrepreneurial ambitions, unlike the inventor who was not interested in commercialisation. AirRide is far more opportunity driven and sees the product as a means to an end. It is thus happy to consider methods that will mean less control i.e. licensing. In contrast, Morellato is a family dominated business, protecting a dynasty, and thus might be a little more risk averse focusing on retaining control. This has also meant building a direct sales and distribution network to supply the retail sector. It is now hoping to replicate its success in other markets.
- *Market factors:* AirRide has a relatively small number of customers worldwide and many of them have international operations. It also has the advantage that it is operating within a high growth market. Morellato is operating in a fairly stable market with the need for new designs, but with a focus on evolution rather than revolution. Many retailers are national allowing country by country expansion.
- *Product technology and specification:* both companies are in relatively small niche markets but AirRide has a radically new innovation that will soon attract competition in the growth stage of its life cycle. Morellato operates within a niche that has been established over many years. It is a mature product based on differentiation.
- *Resource requirements:* AirRide avoided heavy R&D costs through royalty payments which are effectively a direct cost rather than an overhead. Morellato has developed incrementally without major market investment.

Marketing in Action La Compagnie des Petits (p 971)

Discussion question
What are the main benefits that to a franchisee in return for sacrificing an independent start up?
- Cost of adopting the franchise route: licence fee plus start-up fee; and percent royalty on turnover.
- Costs that would be incurred anyway under an independent start-up would be: Fr 290,000 opening stock; premises, shopfitting etc.
- Benefits to the franchisees:
  ⇒ Premises, fixtures and fittings service to reduce the chances of error
  ⇒ careful stock selection and merchandising service
  ⇒ good margins due to careful sourcing of stock
  ⇒ fewer start-up risks from buying into a proven concept over 20 shops
  ⇒ ongoing advice and support.

Marketing in Action Domino's Pizza Franchises (p 983)

Discussion question
What is the basis of the success of the Domino Pizza chain?

At the heart of Domino's success has been a consumer trend towards fast food in general and towards pizzas in particular. Its particular strengths include:
- Careful selection of sites to maximise coverage and local trade
- extensive support to franchisees to ensure their success
- relatively low entry cost for the franchisee, considering the proven nature of the package offered
- financing schemes and willingness to set up the site and equipment etc for the franchisee
- proven marketing support at launch and to expand the franchisee's sales
- centralised buying to keep material costs down
- careful selection of franchisees, with a focus on community knowledge and involvement
- extensive training and a comprehensive operating manual
- a hands-on approach id expected from the franchisees.

The comprehensive franchise package is designed to create a win-win relationship. The franchisee has both initial and ongoing support from Domino to maximise the chances of success while the franchisor has a better chance of successful franchisees who can generate both the revenue and the basis for future expansion.

- Questions for Discussion 24.2
- Questions for discussion 24.5 could be adapted as a group assignment thus: find out as much as possible about a potential franchise opportunity, including fees, royalties etc payable. Imagine that you have been asked to advise a potential franchisee on whether this is a good opportunity or not. Present your analysis of the benefits and risks to the potential franchisee of accepting this package and whether it should in fact be accepted or not. Make clear any assumptions you are making about the potential franchisee.

Chapter 25
INTERNATIONAL MARKETING

LECTURE PLAN

A lecture based on this chapter should help the student to:

1. Understand what international marketing is, and why it is so important to many organisations;
2. appreciate the problems of analysing international marketing environments and selecting markets to enter;
3. define the various available methods of international market entry, outlining their advantages and disadvantages within the context of the broad factors influencing the choice of market entry method;
4. develop an overview of the factors that encourage organisations to adapt their marketing offerings to suit specific international markets, and those that push them towards standardisation; and
5. appreciate the reasons why individual elements of the marketing mix might have to be treated differently in different international markets.

The key sections of this lecture should be:

Rationale for international marketing (pp 990-998):
- Definition of international marketing.
- Reasons why organisations internationalise, including OHP 97, figure 25.1 (p 996) Reasons for Internationalisation:
  ⇒ Define the scope of each of the factors
  ⇒ differentiate between push and pull factors
  ⇒ discuss the impact of the SEM on these factors
  ⇒ compare Europe with the rest of the world as international markets.

The international marketing environment (pp 999-1002):
- Relate to STEP factors of chapter 2.
- *Sociocultural factors:* language; social structures; business culture; values and attitudes.
- *Technological factors:* differences in technological sophistication in different markets; impact of technology on ability to reach remote international markets.
- *Economic and competitive factors:* economic information needed; impact of trade barriers and constraints; differing competitive profiles.
- *Political and legal factors:* impact on market stability; impact on trade; restraints on foreign operators or importers; varying trading laws and financial regulations; impact on marketing communications.

Selecting an international market (pp 1002-1004):
- Product fit
- market factors
- competitive factors
- entry factors
- resourcing factors
- trade restraints.

Market entry methods (pp 1004-1013):
This section is based on OHP 98, figure 25.5 (p 1005) Market Entry Methods:
- Trade in goods and services: direct export; indirect export.
- Trade in knowledge and expertise: licensing; franchising and contracting.
- Investment: types of investment (sales subsidiaries, manufacturing subsidiaries, joint ventures); factors affecting investment, including OHP 99, figure 25.6 (p 1010) Factors Influencing the Investment Decision:
  ⇒ Outline the nature and scope of each group of factors
  ⇒ differentiate between controllable and uncontrollable factors
  ⇒ importance of assessing risks fully
  ⇒ thus importance of understanding the foreign market fully before making an investment decision
  ⇒ emphasise the degree of commitment investment implies.
- Strategic alliances: definition; risks and rewards; good alliance management.

International marketing strategy (pp 1013-1020):
- Standardisation *vs.* adaptation, including OHP 100, figure 25.8 (p 1015) Factors Influencing the Adaptation or Standardisation Decision:
  ⇒ Outline range of factors
  ⇒ demonstrate how essentially external (STEP) factors affect decisions on the marketing mix
  ⇒ emphasise push - pull nature of these factors and tensions and conflicts between them
  ⇒ outline different degrees of standardisation and adaptation.
- The international marketing mix: product, price place, promotion; effects of adaptation; special international considerations.

QUESTIONS FOR REVIEW

25.1   Why is marketing in an international context more complex than in the domestic market? (pp 990-992)

International marketing involves:
- More complex analysis of potential markets
- choosing a market entry method
- determining the extent to which a product and its marketing mix should be standardised or adapted, and how
- dealing with different economic and pricing structures
- dealing with different types of intermediaries and distribution infrastructure
- understanding different cultures
- understanding different competitive situations
- understanding different trading customs and conventions
- understanding different legal and financial structures.

25.2   Define Lynch's five categories of international European organisation. (pp 992-994)

1. *Local-scale organisations:* operate within relatively narrowly defined geographic boundaries within their domestic market.

2. *National-scale organisations:* focus on their own national domestic market.
3. *Regional-scale organisations:* have some international links, but in specific regions or groups of countries within Europe, for example Benelux or Scandinavia.
4. *European-scale organisations:* operate extensively across the whole of Europe.
5. *World-scale organisations:* have a strong European base, but also operate within parts of the rest of the world.

25.3   Why do organisations internationalise? (pp 994-998)

- Because of small or saturated domestic markets
- under pressure to strengthen position against internationalised competitors
- to achieve economies of scale
- to benefit from cheaper production costs elsewhere
- to maintain relationships with internationalised customers in organisational markets
- to diversify.

25.4   For each STEP element of the marketing environment, outline three factors that might make the international market different from the domestic one. (pp 999-1002)

Sociocultural:
- Language
- social structures, customs and mores
- values and attitudes.

Technological
- Degree of penetration of technological sophistication
- impact of technology on distribution systems
- impact of technology on marketing communications.

Economic and competitive:
- Local economic conditions
- taxes, import duties and tariffs
- competitive structures.

Political and regulatory:
- Governmental attitudes and support
- laws and regulations affecting marketing, selling and production activities
- laws on foreign ownership, investment and/or joint ventures.

25.5   What six broad groups of factors should be taken into account when selecting a foreign market? (pp 1002-1004)

- Product fit
- market development stage
- competition
- market entry method feasibility
- resources
- trade restraint.

25.6   What factors influence the choice of market entry method? (pp 1004-1005)

- Speed of entry desired
- cost and resource implications
- flexibility desired
- risk
- payback period
- long-term profit objectives.

25.7 Differentiate between direct and indirect exporting. (pp 1005-1007)

Direct exporting means that the organisation produces the product at home and then sells directly to foreign customers without the aid of an intermediary. Indirect exporting means that an intermediary, a distributor or an agent, based either at home or in the foreign market, takes on the task of selling to foreign customers.

25.8 What are the main strengths of licensing as a market entry method? (pp 1007-1008)

- It can be used to reach very remote markets
- it can serve markets that are not worth direct investment
- it minimises the licensor's involvement in the market
- it can overcome import duties
- it effectively expands production capacity
- the market risk is borne by the licensee
- it might be more acceptable to foreign governments than some other market entry methods
- the licensor benefits from the licensee's local knowledge and contacts.

25.9 What are joint ventures and what are the risks associated with them? (pp 1011-1012)

A joint venture is formed when two or more companies come together and create a new, separate, jointly owned entity for a specific purpose. The risks include:
- The degree of commitment required
- conflict re objectives between the owners
- conflict re division of profits
- conflict re responsibilities
- incompatible cultures or ways of working.

25.10 Summarise the factors that might create pressure towards adapting the marketing mix for a foreign market. (pp 1015-1017)

- Different demographic profiles
- local tastes, needs and wants
- different packaging needs, both aesthetic and practical
- product formulation differences accounting for different tastes, climates or regulations
- different positioning to take account of different competitive structures
- regulatory pressures
- differences in distribution channel structures and abilities
- different marketing communications media and approaches.

QUESTIONS FOR DISCUSSION

25.1 To what extent do you think that internationalisation is essential for today's organisations?

Issues that might be raised in discussion include:
- Large *vs.* small organisations
- Europeanisation *vs* globalisation
- economies of scale
- changing competitive environments
- changing consumer tastes
- the existence of international segments
- customers in organisational markets going global
- the need for large markets to exploit investment in high technology
- saturated domestic markets

- internationalisation of media
- international distribution infrastructure
- international financial infrastructure.

25.2   Choose an fmcg product from your home market that has not yet become an international product. Decide which foreign market you would like to launch this product in and find out as much relevant information as you can about the marketing environment in that country. What recommendations would you make to the manufacturer of your chosen product about the launch?

This question could be used as a written assignment. Having chosen a product that is not yet international and a country in which to launch it, the student should systematically research the STEP factors to justify the choice of country. Recommendations for launch should not only take account of the local marketing environment, but should also be sympathetic towards the product's image and positioning and the organisation's skills and resources. Students may be asked to do a full marketing plan for the launch, or just to produce a broad rationale for proposed 4Ps strategies.

25.3   Discuss the problems that small businesses might face in internationalising and the feasibility of the various market entry methods for them.

Some of the problems facing small businesses when internationalising are:
- Lack of funds to research a foreign market
- lack of management or selling skills
- overstretching already limited production and management capabilities
- spending time and resources trying to adapt a product for another market
- finding and liaising with intermediaries, distributors or customers
- the costs of administering and distributing relatively small amounts of product over long distances
- *ad hoc*, non-strategic development i.e. internationalising because an unsolicited order has suddenly appeared from a foreign customer.

In terms of market entry methods, students might wish to debate the advantages and disadvantages of all available methods, but in general terms for a small company the most appropriate methods are likely to be:
- Direct export, particularly for organisational products which need a high degree of interaction between buyer and seller, or for mail order selling
- indirect export, using distributors or agents as a relatively low cost, low risk method of market entry that makes the most of the intermediary's expertise and contacts in the market.
- Other methods might involve too much commitment or too high a level of investment for a small company, although in certain circumstances, licensing, contracting or franchising might be possibilities.

25.4   Find an example of a successful joint venture in an international market. What benefits have the parties to the venture derived from it?

Likely benefits that might be raised include:
- Pooled financial resources
- complementary knowledge, skills and assets
- more powerful competitive force
- not having to compete against each other
- easier entry into a market if one of the partners is a company registered there
- learning from each other
- sales and profits
- shared risk

- taking calculated risk, in the sense that a joint venture involves setting up an entirely separate jointly owned company. Thus any losses are confined to whatever the parties have chosen to invest, rather than overtly jeopardising the entire assets of the parent companies.

25.5   Citing examples that you have found, discuss whether standardisation is possible or desirable in international markets.

Issues to be raised in the standardisation *vs* adaptation debate include:
- Variations in customer needs internationally and existence of cross-border segments
- cultural differences
- product complexity and degree of customisation
- product formulation for different tastes and climates
- practical packaging needs in different markets
- regulatory influences over products and marketing
- achieving economies of scale
- marketing communication issues
- the nature of distribution channels
- differing competitive pressures.

CASE STUDY 25.1 Martin Joinery (p 1023)

Teaching Objectives

1. To examine international market entry strategies from a small business perspective;
2. to consider the problems of undertaking market research in a foreign market;
3. to analyse the launch strategy adopted by a small business for a foreign market.

1   What kind of market entry strategy has Martin Joinery used for entering the UK market?

The decision to focus on the UK for an Irish company is a very typical first step into exporting. Although there are a number of factors to be considered before market entry, at least the sociocultural and economic differences are minimal between the two markets. Even from a technological perspective, Ireland has tended to follow UK standards and practice closely. However, any exporter immediately loses any home country competitive advantage. In this case, a group direct export entry option has been selected. The decision can be evaluated against the following criteria:
- *Speed*: the group direct export approach enables some control to be maintained and a more rapid entry to be achieved because of sharing resources and expertise.
- *Costs:* shared costs in research, cost of sales and marketing management.
- *Flexibility:* the group scheme is very flexible because if sales build more rapidly than expected, Martin can shift to a fully managed direct operation or some other method.
- *Risk:* the risks of market entry are reduced considerably through the shared approach and the commission structure which reduces the up-front working capital demands of the project. Should the project fail the sunk costs are not that great.
- *Payback:* the payback period will be quicker by adopting this route as the initial investment is much lower.
- *Long-term profit objectives:* the approach might not fit with long-term plans to build a more substantial presence in the UK.

Supplementary question
Why did Martin Joinery decide to move into international markets in the first place?

The main reasons were:
- Limited domestic market demand

- declining demand in recent years
- a desire to reduce dependency by expanding the customer base
- capacity expansion through continuous production created a need for regular demand of higher volumes to achieve economies of scale.

2   What are the potential advantages and disadvantages generally of participating in joint research into a foreign market?

Advantages:
- Shared cost of research
- better quality, professional research
- the scope of research can be wider, thus generating additional opportunities
- the research might highlight potential synergies that can be jointly exploited by the partners
- learning from each other's approach to problem definition.

Disadvantages:
- The information is not unique to one company
- the information might give one of the other partners ideas for diversification
- the research might become too general, not focused specifically on a narrow product sector
- it is more difficult to do in-depth interviewing, given the breadth of the product areas being researched
- the complexity of the research brief might increase the time taken to complete it.

3   Outline the marketing mix used by Martin Joinery to enter the UK market and assess its appropriateness.

A major decision made by Martin was to focus first on the standardised window framing and then to enter the special, adapted sector later. As a result of selecting that target, Martin had to work hard to create a unique marketing offering. A particular problem was building a distribution network. This was effectively dictated by the trade. The multiple builder's merchants would not import directly, as they had plenty of UK options to consider. To have any chance of exporting, Martin had to launch its own distribution centre to supply the UK trade. This requirement meant higher investment in warehousing and stock but was essential for servicing the market. The distribution centre also enabled faster turnaround on customer orders than would have been possible if all products had to shipped direct from Ireland to the customer. Customer service was also a major buying criterion that had to be met. House builders wanted direct delivery with fast turnaround.

Many of these distribution problems could have perhaps been avoided if Martin had decided to focus on the specialised window market where the ability to meet specifications and price levels was more important than fast delivery. By targeting the volume segment, Martin had to incur greater distribution and service costs than the specialist segment would have required.

The rest of the marketing mix was in part dictated by the requirements of the market, whether specifiers or intermediaries:
- Products were positioned as high quality, BSI tested and comparable with those of local suppliers
- price was set at a level similar to, or below those of competitors, despite the transport costs incurred with delivery from Ireland
- promotion consisted mainly of personal selling, brochures, trade journals and direct mail in order to generate awareness and interest. The costs of the sales representative were shared with the other small suppliers.

4   What would have been the likely risks and rewards of sticking with the original idea of seeking a joint venture in the UK market? Has Martin Joinery made the right choice?

Risks:

- Ability to find an appropriate partner in the first place
- Martin might not get on with the venture partner, if there is poor compatibility or commitment to the project
- power might not be equally balanced between the partners, thus creating a source of conflict
- there is less potential profit to either party once established
- joint decision making may result in less flexibility
- it makes it harder for Martin to get out of the market if performance is disappointing
- Martin would have had to have invested more.

Rewards:

- A more focused operation as both parties have to define what they want and what they can offer
- shared risks, which is especially important in the early stages of the venture
- complementary skills and assets adding value to the venture
- useful advice possible on local conditions
- established networks and relationships might be present
- there might be an established distribution system to speed up the entry process
- access to local marketing skills and established customer loyalty.

CASE STUDY 25.2 Vinprom-C (p 1025)

Teaching Objectives

1. To look at the problems of market entry for a foreign company trying to enter the UK market;
2. to consider how and why marketing strategies might have to change after a company has entered a foreign market;
3. to assess a company's future international expansion options and strategies.

1   What kind of market entry strategy did Vinprom-C use to get into the UK market?

The market entry strategy used was indirect export through a variety of export distributors based in the home country.

Supplementary question
Why were Bulgarian distributors used as intermediaries?

The Bulgarian distributor was used because:

- Vinprom-C essentially specialised in production rather than distribution or marketing
- Vinprom-C would not have the resources or expertise to start researching and developing foreign markets
- it minimises Vinprom-C's commitment to any one foreign market, and thus retains its flexibility
- the distributors had knowledge of foreign markets whereas Vinprom-C had access to very limited informal research
- the distributors had established contacts and customers in foreign markets
- the distributors know how to market Bulgarian wines
- the EU market in particular is very competitive and 'hostile' to non-EU producers and thus needs especially expert handling
- the distributor is better placed to anticipate and deal with instability or fluctuations in foreign markets
- by representing a number of companies like Vinprom-C, the distributor could exercise more bargaining power than Vinprom-C could on its own
- by representing a number of companies like Vinprom-C, the distributor could offer customers a wider range of complementary products than Vinprom-C could on its own
- distributors would be familiar with export/import regulations and procedures

- distributors would be experienced in shipping what is a relatively delicate product over long distances.

2 **After 10 years' experience in the UK market, is that same strategy still the best for distributing the company's products to the UK? Debate the issue, giving due consideration to alternative courses of action.**

In favour of continuing with indirect export through the Bulgarian distributor:
- The EU barriers to entry are still high and difficult to negotiate
- the UK market is even more competitive with the entry of other low priced new world, third world and emerging country wines
- the UK retail wine trade is dominated by a small number of extremely powerful multiples who drive very hard bargains with smaller suppliers, and thus there is good reason for concentrating selling power into the hands of a specialist Bulgarian distributor
- the UK retailers want a wide and flexible product range which again can be better provided by a centralised Bulgarian distributor than by any one producer
- given the distributor's 'secrecy' in protecting its information about foreign markets, Vinprom-C is still likely to be relatively ignorant about what is happening
- Vinprom-C is likely to have had to concentrate on streamlining its production, coping with phylloxera and quality problems, working on cutting costs and dealing with problems arising from Bulgaria's precarious economic situation, and thus is still unlikely to have developed the resources and management expertise to 'go it alone' into export markets.

Against continuing with indirect export through the Bulgarian distributor:
- The distributors handle a number of producers' products and thus might not be selling Vinprom-C's goods with as much enthusiasm as it could
- Vinprom-C cannot be sure that the knowledge and expertise that the distributor had ten years ago is still relevant and valid
- Vinprom-C cannot be sure that the distributor has the right contacts with the key retailers
- Vinprom-C might feel that it has developed enough confidence to try an alternative method
- Vinprom-C might feel that changes in the nature of the UK market point to a change in policy.

Alternative courses of action (see figure 25.5, p 1005):
- Transfer of expertise and ideas through franchising, licensing or contracting is inappropriate, as the product has to be produced in Bulgaria!
- Direct investment is similarly inappropriate, in terms of both production and distribution. Vinprom-C is unlikely to have the resources, skills or inclination to set up or buy into a UK-based wine distributor or retailer, especially given the concentration of distribution in the UK.
- Direct supply could be a feasible option if Vinprom-C could win one or two key customers. This would have the advantage of giving Vinprom-C more control over what happens to its own products, more direct knowledge of what is happening in the UK market and cuts out the Bulgarian distributor's margins. These benefits will only emerge, however, if Vinprom-C can:
  ⇒ Persuade at least one key customer of the benefits to them of sourcing direct from the producer rather than through a Bulgarian distributor
  ⇒ negotiate a realistic price at least as high as the Bulgarian distributor could achieve
  ⇒ provide the breadth of product range, volumes, quality and flexibility that the big customers demand
  ⇒ manage the legal and administrative complexities
  ⇒ develop stable, ongoing buyer - seller relationships.
- Strategic alliances might also be feasible. Vinprom-C could join forces with other producers to create a new Bulgarian distributor, but only if they feel that they could perform the same tasks as the existing distributors more efficiently and cost effectively. Given their likely state of inexperience, lack of knowledge of foreign markets and lack of established contacts in the UK, it is difficult to see how they could be successful unless there is perhaps one key customer who is dissatisfied with existing arrangements and is prepared to be part of an alliance.

3   **If Vinprom-C had to make a choice, do you think the company would be better off investing in further development of the UK market or in the eastern European market? Why?**

The advantages of further development of the UK market:
- Vinprom-C has proved over ten years that it has a product that appeals to the UK consumer
- Vinprom-C's distribution arrangements seem to be stable and working well
- the concentration of wine retailing into a few large organisations' hands ensure efficient geographic coverage of the UK market once the retailer accepts a product
- UK wine consumption is still growing.

The disadvantages of further development of the UK market:
- Import duties and quotas imposed by the EU might hinder Vinprom-C's further penetration
- aggressive competition from other major EU wine producers could hinder Vinprom-C's expansion
- cheap wine competition from non-EU producers could damage Vinprom-C's volumes and margins
- the power of the retailers could make Vinprom-C over-dependent and put Vinprom-C at risk if it could not accede to retail demands on price, quality, product range, delivery etc.

The advantages of further development of the eastern European market:
- Vinprom-C has some past experience of these markets
- they are closer to home and culturally perhaps more similar
- consumption is low, but could be increased
- high earning segments are starting to emerge
- the retail sector is likely to be less powerful than in the UK
- the retail sector is less likely to be aggressive in terms of price, quality, range, delivery.

The disadvantages of further development of the eastern European market:
- Uncertain political, economic and trading conditions
- uncertainty as to whether payment will ever be forthcoming; whether it will be in hard currency
- unpredictability of the market and its future development
- having to rebuild market contacts and distribution arrangements
- poorer distribution infrastructure might make it difficult and expensive to achieve geographic coverage of the market
- competition from low-priced, low-quality Italian and Spanish wines.

4   **One of the potential growth markets of the future was Japan. What do you think would be the problems of planning an entry into that market?**

Vinprom-C is likely to face many problems in entering the Japanese market. If the same kind of strategy as before is employed of using a Bulgarian distributor for indirect export, then the main problem would clearly be finding a Bulgarian distributor with relevant experience. If Vinprom-C wanted to go into direct export, however, its problems might be:
- Researching the market and its needs and preferences
- understanding the competitive environment
- ensuring that products conform to any legal requirements, e.g. labelling, hygiene, content etc
- ensuring that Vinprom-C understands the import regulations with which it must comply
- establishing a reliable logistics system for transporting the goods safely to Japan when required
- overcoming the cultural and language barriers for any labelling or promotional materials
- pricing the products appropriately within the market context
- making contacts with potential customers
- negotiating an acceptable deal for both parties
- establishing and maintaining good buyer - supplier relationships
- finding the resources and developing the necessary management skills to implement all this.

Marketing in Action Novo Nordisk (p 996)

Discussion question
What factors have led to Novo Nordisk's emergence as a major international company in the health care market?

The key factors are:
- A small domestic market
- the need to exploit new technology on a worldwide scale because of short life cycles
- the need to exploit worldwide demand for new innovation through a niche strategy
- the opportunity to penetrate otherwise difficult export markets such as Japan and the USA
- international production to exploit manufacturing economies of scale
- competing against similar world wide competitors.

Marketing in Action Eastern Europe Strikes Back (p 1003)

Discussion question
Identify some of the main issues facing eastern European companies when they are looking for new markets to enter and develop.
- *Product fit factors:* whether the specification, especially in terms of design and quality, meets customer expectations (CHKZ).
- *Market factors:* assessing whether the market is worthwhile in terms of potential and the likelihood of being paid.
- *Competitive factors:* ensuring that product niches entered give rise to a competitive advantage over local producers. This has meant the adoption of new lines (Graboplast and CHKZ).
- *Entry factors:* selecting the most appropriate methods. Graboplast sells through representatives but expects to directly produce in other eastern European markets.
- *Resourcing factors:* CHKZ had to invest in quality and productivity to compete with more efficient companies on equal terms.
- *Trade restraint factors:* both companies featured would have to understand EU or national regulations that might impact on the type of products and trading relationships possible.

Marketing in Action Barco - Projecting the Future (p 1010)

Discussion question
What has been the basis of the success at Barco since its change in strategic direction in 1985?

After the decision to focus on changing its product and market strategy, a number of supporting strategies have been necessary:
- A focus on niche markets for professionals on an international scale
- involvement in high growth areas across Europe i.e. media
- concern with innovation, R&D and exploitation of new products in worldwide markets
- involvement with a range of international markets to spread risk
- willingness to invest in manufacturing whether in Europe or beyond.

Marketing in Action British Airways and American Airlines Take Off (p 1014)

Discussion question
Should the British Airways - American Airlines strategic alliance be allowed to go ahead?

Arguments in favour:
- Other EU and US airlines have similar arrangements
- it would improve customer service and handling for a lot of transatlantic passengers

- it could open US markets for other EU carriers flying intercity, a right for US carriers in Europe
- more efficient and co-ordinated marketing could open up new segments or travel opportunities
- it could open up more intra-EU competition from US airlines and greater access to Heathrow.

Arguments against:
- Danger of distorting competition through transatlantic domination resulting in ...
- ... a major impact on small share airline such as Virgin
- ... higher fares unless regulatory bodies are prepared to intervene
- it might reduce customer choice of routes
- it would disadvantage some EU states' national carriers who do not have such strong alliances.

SUGGESTED ASSIGNMENTS

- Questions for Discussion 25.2
- Questions for Discussion 25.3.

ADDITIONAL CASE STUDIES

CONVATEC (UK): LEADERS IN STOMA CARE

ConvaTec (UK) is a leader in a specialised niche of the medical care market, concentrating on colostomy, ileostomy and urostomy bags. These are used by patients who have undergone major surgery to have parts of their bowel removed, often to prevent the spread of cancer. They are products that consumers have little or no awareness and understanding of, unless they themselves become stoma patients. Then, stoma bags become essential for the rest of the patient's life and patients have to learn rapidly about the technology and products used. The number of stoma patients in the UK is around 100,000. Around 350 specialist nurses play a major role in helping patients to adjust to the use of stoma products, and in advising them what to purchase, how frequently, and how to dispose of the bodily waste. The nurse, therefore, plays a key role in influencing the patient's usage and in directing customer loyalty towards particular brands. The market is a competitive one, with several players with ConvaTec for market leadership.

The patient might well be the end user of the product, but actually takes little part in the choice of a stoma case system. Stoma care starts in hospital, and the patient is advised as to the best system for them by the nurse working in conjunction with the surgeon. Initially, this prescription is dispensed by the hospital pharmacy, and once the patient has left hospital, assuming that there are no medical complications, their own GP simply gives repeat prescriptions for the same system. The stoma nurses can reinforce product loyalty, because they continue to maintain relationships with patients after they have gone home. The hospital is thus the key for the stoma system marketers. It is not just the surgeon and the nurse that influence the choice, but also the hospital pharmacist and to some extent the accountant. The accountant wants to control the hospital's drugs and appliances budget and the pharmacist wants to streamline the number of different product lines carried and dispensed. The hospitals negotiate prices for the bulk supply of drugs and appliances, and the suppliers often sell to them at a significant discount, effectively as loss leaders, in order to get that initial prescription. Once a patient on long-term medication has been started on a particular brand, they are unlikely to switch, and goods supplied on repeat prescriptions from GPs are charged at the full market price.

ConvaTec has developed a marketing strategy that has achieved a 50 per cent share of a domestic UK market valued at around £35m. Market research plays a major role in the formulation of strategy. Some of this research is *ad hoc*, designed to provide information and insights into specific marketing problems, and some is ongoing research to track changing patient attitudes and perceptions of the product. ConvaTec recognises that it needs a detailed understanding of two main segments: the patients as the users of the product, and the nurses who play such an important role in shaping patient usage decisions. A major survey of 5,000 patients in 1993 found four main buying criteria for stoma bags, in descending order:
- Security
- comfort
- ease of use
- discretion.

These findings reflect patients' concern over unwanted seepage of fluids or smells which could be embarrassing in social situations. Patients do not usually wish it to be known that they need or use stoma products. Further research into the nurses' views also has an influence on ConvaTec's marketing thinking. Annually, 50 specialist nurses are interviewed on a semi-structured basis. The findings reinforce the need to be concerned with product quality, innovation and aesthetics. It also confirms the continuing role of nurses in influencing patients' brand choice. Unless major problems emerge, once a brand has been recommended by the nurse, the GP tends to issue repeat prescriptions without question, and there is little incentive or reason for patients to consider or initiate brand switching. It is, therefore, essential that patients are exposed to ConvaTec products early on to build and retain market share. Other manufacturers are also aware of the importance of that first brand choice and the nurses' influence over it. Around 25 per cent of nurses are sponsored by other manufacturers, which might influence the recommendations they make to patients. This sponsorship also might help the hospital pharmacists and accountants to appreciate the cost effectiveness of stocking certain systems.

ConvaTec has chosen not to pursue the route of building their own nurse base through sponsorship. The marketing approach adopted by ConvaTec aims to build a direct relationship with the patient at the same time as helping the independent nurse to keep up to date with new methods and products in the stoma area. The programme with nurses includes regular symposiums where nurses are encouraged to give feedback on their experiences; provision of educational materials, sometimes linked with training; a quarterly journal Eurostoma to present information on current issues and research; and a resource centre is made available for stoma nurses to use. This approach is far less direct than that of other manufacturers as the nurses, although clearly being influenced by the various promotional methods, are encouraged to remain independent and indeed that is presented as being of benefit to both nurses and patients. Patients are also encouraged to make direct contact with ConvaTec should they be experiencing difficulties or if they have ideas for product improvement. A confidential advisory helpline has been installed and often between 2,000 to 4,000 calls per week are received. Sometimes, it is simply about reassuring the worried patient. About half the callers are seeking advice on the impact of travel or special diets. Others use it for requesting products or samples, while a small minority use it as a vehicle for making complaints. The important point is that a one-to-one relationship is being forged with the user. This all helps to foster product use satisfaction and to reinforce brand loyalty. All incoming calls are classified according to their content on criteria such as usage, complaints, and product ideas. The calls are all entered into a database for further analysis and tracking.

Patients and nurses are also used in the new product development process. Patient panels are used to test potential responses at different stages in the new product development process. This is supplemented by encouraging regular patient visits to the factory where again customer reaction to new ideas and problem areas can be gauged. This is vital in such a sensitive product area. ConvaTec has taken very seriously indeed the need for direct and meaningful customer relationships, and this has contributed to their marketing success. However, there is still the outstanding issue of whether ConvaTec should build its own nurse base if other manufacturers continue to expand their coverage beyond 25 per cent of the specialist nurse population.

Sources: Management Today, *September 1996 pp. 86-87; and with thanks to Dr Dick Foskett.*

Case Assignment Questions

1   **To what extent and why do you think ConvaTec (UK) is a market orientated company?**

2   **How do the buying criteria differ between the nurses, patients, GPs and hospital administrators?**

3   **What improvements, if any, could ConvaTec make in its use of market research and information gathering?**

4   **Should ConvaTec change its policy towards sponsoring nurses?**

A MARKET FULL OF BEANS

The market for Coffee has become extremely differentiated, reflecting taste differences across Europe and various market segments within national boundaries. Espresso, for example, dominates in Italy, ground coffee in Germany, and instant is more popular in the UK. Demand patterns are, however, slowly changing as consumers develop more sophisticated tastes and become more prepared to try new coffee types, even at premium prices. In the UK, instant coffee was estimated by Taylor Nelson as being worth £563.3m in 1996, with a 3.2 per cent growth in value and 1.2 per cent growth in volume over 1995. Liquid and ground coffee is worth around £64m with a 1.6 per cent growth in volume and value. The dominance of instant in the UK reflects patterns of drinking. Like tea, it is regarded as a quick, refreshing and relatively inexpensive drink. On average in the UK, 1.6 cups of coffee are drunk per day compared with 3.6 cups of tea. However, the rate of coffee consumption has been growing for a number of years.

The coffee market is dominated by manufacturer branded products, taking over 70 per cent of the market. The leading suppliers are Nestle and Kraft Jacobs Suchard (KJS) which markets Kenco and Maxwell House. Retailer own-label brands from Sainsbury's, Tesco and Asda make up the balance of the top five. Own-label has been growing at a more rapid rate in recent years, despite the fact that the manufacturer brands are heavily promoted. One of the most successful campaigns has perhaps been Nestle's Gold Blend series of ongoing soap opera campaigns. Manufacturers typically spend between 3 and 4 per cent of retail sales revenue on advertising. KJS recently launched Carte Noire to battle with Gold Blend in the UK market, but it is probably too early to assess what impact it has made on Nestle. Nevertheless, at the end of 1996, KJS was claiming that it had gained more than 20 per cent of the premium instant sector.

The ground coffee segment is dominated by retailer own-label brands, with Kenco and Douwe Egbert providing the main manufacturer brands. One of the problems for the UK consumer has been the ability to appreciate the likely differences in taste between different brands and coffee formats. While consumers are willing to experiment, the differences in strength, aroma and preparation method demand a level of knowledge that appears to make some consumers apprehensive. The supermarket multiple Safeway decided to tackle this problem by improving the amount of information available at the point of sale and encouraging the use of trial jars to make experimentation more cost effective and less risky. Most suppliers agree that the key to the future is attracting younger consumers and those susceptible to a youthful appeal. Education about the alternatives is an important part of that process. New formats have also been growing in popularity in recent years. This has in part been caused by the growth of quality coffee bars and restaurants specialising in unusual or minor yet premium coffee brands. The success of the espresso format has been attributed to this influence. While espresso is all powerful in Italy, it is only over the last five years that consumers in the UK have become more attracted to the format. Sales in the UK have grown year on year by over 20 per cent in a market dominated by Lavazza from Torino, Italy. The prices for espresso are often premium, varying from £1.99 to £3.39 per 250g vacuum pack and they have attracted an above average share of ABC1 consumer groups.

Lavazza is not able to match the large promotional expenditure of the main players in the coffee market such as Nestle. Instead, it concentrates on ensuring that restauranteurs, a more defined segment, use the best methods to prepare espresso to a defined standard. They also have their cafe bars in Brent Cross, London and the Lakeside shopping centre at Thurrock. By experiencing the best prepared espresso and cappuccino coffees in these settings, consumers might be more willing to try them at home. Again, it is important that consumers are aware of the potential of espresso. The manufactures want to get the point across that it can be brewed at home without too much fuss and even that it does not have to be drunk in small cups. To help in this process, some media advertising is also being undertaken by Lavazza. A campaign for 1997 will emphasise the Italian connection, the quality of the coffee and the sophisticated image. Another area that is small but growing is the development of niche products that appeal to the sophisticated consumer. Flavoured coffees such as raspberry, almond and chocolate are premium priced, and sometimes only available by mail order or through specialist coffee retailers. The differentiated nature of these products makes them almost a status symbol, to be tasted with due ceremony after dinner along with the mints.

The high level of activity in the UK market and the tendency towards premium prices makes an interesting contrast to the German market. In that market, ground coffee dominates and because it is a staple item, consumers appear to be more aware of the price differences between stores. Supermarkets have encouraged price sensitivity by often featuring coffee as a promotional loss leader. In Germany, the prices have been pushed down by the supermarkets to levels that raise questions about long term viability. The retail price in Aldi of some ground and roasted coffees is below the market prices for raw beans paid by some producers. In-store coffee preparation is now regarded as uneconomic by many retailers, and the Eduscho and Tchibo coffee shops in which coffee is roasted and prepared in front of the customer are certainly thought to be suffering from the low prices that dominate the sector. The pressure on price may be acceptable to supermarkets which can cross-subsidise, but the coffee producers and specialist retailers are being heavily squeezed.

Sources: Ensor, J. (1996), 'Eastern Europe - A Tough Nut to Crack' The Grocer, 16 November, p. 52; The Grocer (1996a), 'Boiling points', The Grocer, 16 November, pp. 45-46; The Grocer (1996b) 'Italy's Espresso Entry into the UK Via the Cafe Bar', The Grocer, 16 November, p. 51.

Case Assignment Questions

1   What are the main environmental influences that are shaping the coffee market?

2   Identify the main market segments within the coffee market.

3   What are the main factors to be considered in developing a consumer education programme such as that associated with coffee?

4   Given the aggressive pricing policies adopted in the German retail markets, what strategies might the coffee manufacturers pursue to retain viability?

SNCF SEEKS RELATIONSHIPS

SNCF, the French national railway organisation, has to buy a wide variety of products and services in order to handle passenger and freight demand and to ensure that the infrastructure is developed and maintained to high levels of safety and efficiency. SNCF spends Fr 30bn annually, so purchasing plays a vital part in the operation of the organisation. It also represents a considerable supply opportunity for a variety of organisations supplying everything from rolling stock to catering supplies, and from signalling systems to staff uniforms. The decision making units within SNCF vary according to the criticality and complexity of the purchase and the degree of experience. Commercial staff consider the impact of the purchase on the services SNCF can offer; technical and engineering staff focus on performance and operational matters such as reliability, running costs and maintenance; and finally purchasing staff control contracts and supplier selection. Some major investment decisions require the authorisation of national and regional governments, such as the decision to upgrade and build a new line from Paris to Strasbourg in order to cut journey times by 50 per cent.

The main, fairly general requirements that a supplier has to meet have been described by SNCF as being financially sound; commercially responsive; capable of responding to a range of product specifications; innovative yet maintaining continuity; responsive to the need for cost cutting productivity improvements; and maintaining high levels of quality assurance and delivery reliability. Many of these points seem to be obvious and appropriate for any supplier in any industry. It also hides the more fundamental trends that are changing the shape of purchasing within SNCF and influencing the development of buyer-seller relationships. The trends according to SNCF are:

- A move towards longer term, usually five year contracts. This is useful when purchasing rolling stock and infrastructure such as signalling systems and trackwork, as it encourages suppliers to promote specifications that will provide a longer service life and options for improved productivity in exchange for price concessions by SNCF.
- A more European focus. In line with European Union rules, contracting invitations are now sought around Europe and the expanded supplier base has become more European.
- The use of more functional specifications to open up a wider range of design and operational alternatives while still allowing scope for significant innovation. Specifications based on user analysis and wants allow suppliers greater design freedom than the previous practice of buyers preparing detailed technical specifications. New approaches can be developed and innovation is encouraged by suppliers having more freedom. It also can help to avoid situations where engineering staff are influenced by favoured suppliers, restricting the range of serious alternatives.
- More careful attention not only to purchase costs but also to life cycle maintenance costs for evaluating alternative suppliers' proposals. The trend in some parts of the industry is towards manufacturers playing a greater role in managing the maintenance and upkeep of the fleet.
- More complete systems purchasing rather than buying individual components and then incurring the cost of assembly and installation. This also reduces purchasing complexity.
- To seek more SNCF-wide or supplier-wide contracts by pooling activities to maximise the value of orders in order to improve the bargaining position.
- To seek continually to assess the role and responsibility of suppliers alongside SNCF in establishing areas that can be outsourced more cost effectively, for example catering, cleaning etc.
- To promote mutual co-operation with suppliers in technical and quality improvement.
- To broaden the role of IT for procurement and for information exchange with suppliers.

Although these trends are still working their way through to purchasing, they are starting to have an impact on practice. However, the process is far from complete. For example in the Europeanisation area, in line with many other national railway authorities just before 1992, a large number of advance orders were placed with national suppliers in order to avoid wider tendering. National suppliers still dominate purchasing and recently SNCF refused to support the European Commission's White Paper on "The Revitalisation of the Community's Railways" which aimed to bring transparency and openness to the rail sector across Europe by increasing competition.

Given the changes in its markets, SNCF is seeking to build a philosophy of strengthened supplier partnership for mutual long-term benefit. This is well demonstrated by the close working relationship that has been developed with France's leading locomotive producer, GEC Alsthom. This relationship has produced the well known French high speed train the TGV. Launched in 1981 it has revolutionised intercity traffic in France, has been adopted by Eurostar, and in Spain and South Korea, and has the potential to transform European travel even further. SNCF has worked closely with GEC Alsthom for many years on a number of projects. This has meant considerable dialogue between the respective engineering departments, especially where leading edge technology has been introduced. SNCF is able to buy better, higher performance products while GEC Alsthom has a steady stream of orders from a major buyer, which until recently, was not required to tender beyond France. Through continued close co-operation with GEC Alsthom, a number of new designs have been introduced to build upon the success of the TGV. The double-decker version, TGV Duplex, provides extra capacity on the heavily used Paris-Lyon route with a more economical design that saves 13 per cent on the cost per seat as well as increasing the number of seats by 50 per cent. GEC Alsthom has received an initial order for 30 trains with an option on 55 more as a result of its ability to meet SNCF needs. Another project is for a quadrivoltage TGV that can work on Paris-Brussels-Cologne-Amsterdam services, with four different overhead line voltages and seven different signalling systems. The prize for success is a firm order for 17 sets at Fr 125m with more possible.

Many of the programmes require considerable research and development before product prototypes are produced. The French Ministry of Transport, Industry and Research recently agreed to contribute Fr 36m to a total of Fr 170m agreed jointly between SNCF and GEC Alsthom to produce a tilting TGV which could work at high speeds on existing rather than new lines. For the 21st century SNCF and GEC Alsthom engineers are working on a TGV Nouvelle Generation that can travel 1000km in three hours. The development cost of this project to bring a prototype to test is around £200m and will take three years. Despite co-operative successes on the TGV, problems do emerge in the relationship. GEC Alsthom blamed SNCF when it had to cut 7 per cent of its workforce due to either cancellation or deferment of orders. SNCF did not agree, claiming that some alleged firm orders for new stock were not yet concluded and in other cases it was GEC Alsthom who had requested that firm orders should be delayed. To the unions at the Alsthom works, it was suggested that SNCF had been 'set up to take the flak for a workforce cleansing that was wholly company driven'. However, overall the extensive nature of the trust and understanding that has developed between the two parties makes it very difficult for outsiders to penetrate. In addition to the TGV, GEC Alsthom is involved with most other rolling stock projects being undertaken by SNCF.

Sources: *Abbot J (1996), 'SNCF Equips for the 21st Century'*, European Railway Review, *2 (3) Sept 1996, pp 25-27. Freeman Allen G (1994), 'GEC Alsthom Cuts More Than 600 jobs: Europeview'*, Modern Railways, *Jan, p 41. 'Community of European Railways'*, Modern Railways, *Jan 1997, p 38. 'More TGV Variants: Europeview'*, Modern Railways, *Jan 1997, p 37. Richard J-M (1996), 'SNCF Procurement in the Era of the Single Market Europe'*, European Railway Review, *2 (3), p 21-23.*

Case Assignment Questions

1   How might the purchasing trends identified have an impact on developing buyer-seller relationships?

2   What advantages does a domestic supplier have over other non-domestic suppliers, despite the SEM? What strategies could an outside supplier adopt to build a relationship with SNCF?

3   What advantages and disadvantages are to be found when buyer-seller relationships become as strong as the SNCF-GEC Alsthom case?

DIRECTORY PUBLISHING

Most organisations need access to directories to find information on suppliers, customers or experts. For many years, directories were printed by publishers and then offered for sale to commercial organisations, libraries and other interested parties. Kelly's, Dun and Bradstreet, and Yellow Pages are just a few of the well known brands that provided products for finding information about organisations. In the 1980s, expectations of the outputs of the electronic revolution suggested that a significant amount of print material would be replaced by electronic media, given the potential for space savings, ease of updating and the possibility of downloading for further processing and networking. By the mid 1990s, however, less than 10 per cent of spend on directories was on electronic media. Print had proved to be remarkably resilient in the face of challenges from alternative formats such as the Internet, CD-ROM and specialised on-line services such as Lexis-Nexis and MAID.

The electronic revolution that did not quite happen to plan or to expectations. One of the reasons often quoted is the failure of many electronic publishers to add real additional value beyond reproducing electronically what had previously been in print-based directories. The additional flexibility of on-line electronic media through downloading and re-working databases has often not been made available by publishers. CD-ROM, although it was the first electronic format to enter the directory market, suffered especially from this problem. Many CD-ROM disks offer little more than a print directory that can be read from a screen. There are few additional benefits on offer, other than speeding up the data search process. Another reason is simply customer inertia; old habits appear to die hard. Users seem to prefer information that they can touch, feel and take home with them, rather than just displayed on a screen. In direct mail operations, for example, some companies still buy labels with addresses printed on them rather than purchasing an electronic list. Some users are reluctant to switch to new methods. Others are not aware of the full potential offered by electronic systems, while a third group regard CD-ROM as a vehicle for home entertainment that may not be needed in the office. Additionally, a lot of smaller businesses either do not have access to the Internet or restrict its use on operational grounds.

Directory providers are also concerned about how to best make money out of setting up a web site. Although the technology exists for Internet access, publishers are not entirely convinced that they could recoup the costs of setting up a Web page or the costs of providing the full directory through usage charges. They are not even sure whether customers would be prepared to incur the telephone charges involved in on-line searching. Assessing what should be given free on-line and when charges should be introduced and at what rate is a critical decision. Providing restricted access to an on-line service for free can whet the customer's appetite for mainstream use of the directory, regardless of format, but giving too much away free would affect sales adversely.

In part, these uncertainties arose because many directory publishers did not spend enough time researching their users to assess their main requirements. Some research, for example, indicated that a key facility wanted by users was the ability to integrate a directory with a marketing application, such as direct mailing. Many directory publishers developed a mixed format approach. Yellow Pages, for example, offers an Internet site but also retains a large print portfolio. The Internet site is almost regarded as a complementary product to its print media. BRAD is a major directory for those wanting details of agencies, publications and schedules for a wide cross-section of the advertising media. BRAD has also introduced an on-line service for which a licence to download information can be purchased, and BRAD undertakes to update the directory on a regular basis through a special dialling system. The product, therefore, is kept right up to date compared with print and CD-ROM. The pace of introduction of new formats has also been influenced by the pricing strategy of directory publishers. In print form, publishers make money from display advertising and direct sales of the directories. Established operators such as Dun and Bradstreet have adopted a premium priced strategy by charging over ten times the price for CD-ROM versions compared with print. This means that some CD-ROM directories can cost £10,000. Some publishers are now introducing lower priced entry products such as the CD-ROM book at £300 and then they can encourage trading up. Pricing on the Internet is more complex. Advertising can be sold on a web site and the main directory can be sold either through subscription or by a direct charge using a credit card. As part of the price justification, publishers have had to commit to updating on a quarterly or even monthly basis. Soon it will be possible to update a CD-ROM through the Internet to add further value to the service. The market appears to be moving towards accepting one of two pricing alternatives, One approach adopted by some publishers has been to offer low priced disks with the need to purchase regular and expensive updates, while the alternative is to go for an expensive disk with low priced or free updates.

Sources: *White, M. (1996), 'Digital Dreams',* Marketing Week, *29 November, pp. 49-53.*
Witthaus, M. (1996), 'Technical Hitch', Marketing Week, *29 November, pp. 43-47.*

Case Assignment Questions

1   **What factors have influenced the shape of the product take up of electronic directory publishing?**

2   **What actions could electronic directory publishers take to improve the amount of usage of their CD-ROM and Internet sites?**

3   **Consider ways in which marketing research might be used to improve the understanding of market needs.**

PRICE VOLATILITY

Price setting poses a special problem for marketing managers in markets that either become unstable or unpredictable because of a combination of various circumstances. The carefully designed pricing models for price setting often become meaningless as the focus has to switch to predicting rapid changes in the slope of the demand curve, and then adjusting prices accordingly. Two industrial sectors, pulp and semiconductors experienced considerable price volatility during 1995-6, resulting in considerable problems for producers. This case examines some of the factors that have caused the volatility and looks at the responses of different manufacturers.

Pulp is the main raw material for paper production, whatever the quality or grade. It is mainly offered on the open market by paper mills which cannot consume all they produce in their own continuous paper production. It is a worldwide business but many of the mills are concentrated in Scandinavia, North America and Brazil. It has been estimated that about 80 per cent of all pulp is exported from the country in which it is produced and no single producer has more than 6 per cent share of the market. It is therefore a market ripe for tough competition. Demand for pulp is derived ultimately from the magazines, newspapers, packaging and blank paper we consume. If demand for those end products sags, as it did in 1995 in Asian markets, there is a subsequent impact on the stocks held by the pulp producers. Worldwide pulp stocks rose by 50 per cent to 3.1m tonnes in just three months at the end of 1995. This means that suppliers hold high stocks, cut capacity or lower prices. Most initially favoured the latter route. The benchmark product, northern bleached softwood kraft (NBSK), had reached a record high of $1,000 per tonne in September 1995 before prices started to decline sharply. Mills in all the main producing countries cut prices by between 15 and 20 per cent and worldwide pulp prices dropped to $725 a tonne by January 1996. The spot market price acts as a guide to the strength of demand in a market and this continued to fall in 1996 back towards the low reached for NBSK in 1993 of $400 per tonne.

The pulp market is thus very price volatile. After the spectacular rise in 1994, there was concern in the industry as to just how far prices would fall. The decline continued in the first half of 1996 as producers sought to maintain share and shift rising stocks. Stocks worldwide were estimated to have reached a high of over 4m tonnes and prices reached a low of around $500 a tonne. Given the volatility of the market, different suppliers started to consider alternatives to continuing to build stocks that could only be sold at uncertain and probably falling price levels. Although analysts were suggesting that the market would bottom out by the middle of the year, there was always a degree of uncertainty. Some of the Canadian mills announced temporary closures which stripped out 137,000 tonnes. Others in the US and Canada, however, were still producing at up to 90 per cent of their overall production capacity at a time when between 80 and 85 per cent was considered by many as the maximum level for bringing stability back into the market. The Finnish producers did cut back to the lower levels rather than build stocks but this still had an effect on overall profitability. The large Finnish producers UPM-Kymmene, Enso and Metsa-Serla cut capacity utilisation back to between 75 and 80 per cent, but as a consequence suffered a severe drop in profits. The cost structure in the industry, however, meant that even at the low prices, production costs could still be covered. The combination of production cuts and some improvement in demand as China resumed large scale imports and as demand for fine paper and paper board recovered, started to suggest some optimism for the second half of 1996. However, worldwide stocks remained high and some experts thought that North American and Scandinavian stocks would have to fall to around 1.5m tonnes before prices would stabilise and confidence return to the market. Some buyers were still delaying making significant orders in the expectation that prices would fall further. It did not make sense for pulp buyers to hold stocks in a volatile market. Ironically, during this period some producers actually introduced new capacity, planned during the more buoyant period the year before.

The price volatility of computer chips in the semiconductor industry has also been extreme over the past year. Again, it is a world market, but one that is dominated by a smaller number of producers than in the pulp market. In 1995, demand for chips was very high and shortages were feared. This was not just as a result of the Kobe earthquake in Japan which affected supply, but also reflected major increases in worldwide demand. New chip factories were being planned and the industry was upbeat. The price crisis in 1996 was caused by a combination of factors. Firstly, sales of computers in the US did not achieve expectations, especially in the consumer market, and new production techniques enabled more chips to be produced from each silicon wafer. Thus with weaker demand and a greater supply of chips, prices started to fall even before some of the new capacity came on stream. The price of the main memory chip for computers, the D-RAM (dynamic random access memory) dropped around 70 per cent in seven months. Prices normally fall year on year in this sector due to technological innovation and improved production efficiency, but the size of the fall in 1996 was well beyond expectations.

In an effort to protect volume and market share, the major players decided to implement progressive price cuts. A drop from $25 to $10 for a 16Mb D-RAM chip resulted in some manufacturers operating at below breakeven point. The three big Korean manufacturers, Samsung, Hyundai and LG Semicon, supplying around one-third of chip production, were highly dependent on D-RAMs rather than on the more advanced chips and microprocessors which had not experienced such severe price volatility. Most of them planned production cuts of between 15 and 22 per cent to bring supply closer in line with demand and to seek to stabilise prices. Other producers such as NEC, Hitachi and Fujitsu from Japan also cut production and delayed plans for new plant. The problem for the suppliers was assessing how far prices would fall in a market that was clearly destined to achieve long term growth with the wider acceptance of IT solutions. The reference used was the ratio of price to the cost of manufacturing, which indicated that there was less scope for further significant falls. Additionally, the prices that the Koreans were offering to the spot market indicated to the rest of the industry that the bottom of the spiral had been reached. However, the real long term test is going to be how quickly demand will recover. D-RAM prices will depend a lot on how quickly consumers switch to the higher specification 16Mb needed to run Windows 95. If the switch is slower than expected, growth may remain in single digits. The difficulty for manufacturers is to predict these changes in advance. Many use the ratio of sales to orders to predict the future strength of demand. This ratio compares the value of chips shipped over the previous month with the value of new orders. If orders are below sales, a downturn could be starting. Over-emphasis on this limited ratio has been criticised for creating instability in the market and prices.

Sources: Brown-Hulmes, C. (1996), 'Sharp Rise But Metsa Warns of Tough Year Ahead', Financial Times, 27 February, p. 22; Burton, J. et al (1996), 'A Low Point for High Tech.', Financial Times, 28 June, p. 21; Carnegy, H. (1996a), 'MoDo Damps Down Hopes of Rise in Pulp Prices', Financial Times, 15 May, p. 24; Carnegy, H. (1996b), 'Finnish Paper Group Hit by Lower Prices', Financial Times, 19 June, p. 30; Simon, B. and Brown-Hulmes, C. (1996), 'Pressing Down on the Pulp Matter', Financial Times, 8 February, p. 17.

Case Assignment Questions

1   What are the main causes of price volatility in a market? To what extent and how have these general causes applied in the pulp and semiconductor markets?

2   What actions (a) in the short-term and (b) in the long-term, can the manufacturers in the pulp industry take to minimise the effects of dramatic price volatility?

3   Is price volatility in the customer's interest?

CATEGORY MANAGEMENT

Category Management (CM) has made a major impact on product management strategies within the fmcg retail sector. Although primarily concerned with the retailer - consumer interface, the adoption of CM techniques has embraced the manufacturer and wholesaler as well as the retailer. A category is a group of products that serve similar needs, perceptions and buyer behaviours and are seen by shoppers as close substitutes. Examples of categories are soups, cooking ingredients and wines. Different categories of products can be managed at retail level both strategically and tactically. Strategically they can be grouped to achieve the desired market position for the co-operating organisations, while tactically they can be managed to build share for the category by increasing total category sales. For example, if the category is aimed at single-person households, the range of products offered, positioning, packs, and point of sale promotions would be designed accordingly. A category manager therefore acts as a type of strategic business unit manager responsible for the well being of that category within the retailer's portfolio.

There are two important implications when adopting the category management approach. Firstly there is the need to consider retailer, manufacturer and consumer objectives. This may involve some give and take between supplier and retailer. For example retailers see product categories as important vehicles for achieving their own objectives. The category might involve a mix of own-label and manufacturer brands. Manufacturers are naturally interested in their share of business but need to adapt their thinking to reflect a philosophy that aims to expand the performance of the whole category, not individual brands or products. This demands trust and a commitment to a long term trading relationship. It also demands that manufacturers change their attitudes. Rather than adopting strategies that encourage brand switching, the focus has to be on growth in total category sales and the degree of consumer loyalty to that category. Some suppliers however might become 'category captains', dominating the category, and if they invest resources they might well expect to receive a disproportionate return from the retailer in return for their efforts.

The second major aspect of CM is the need to better integrate the supply chain to offer improved products, lower stocks, better availability and lower total system costs. Efficient Consumer Response aims to improve product development, consumer and trade promotions, product range and assortment and not least improved product replenishment. Central to these achievements is the fast and comprehensive exchange of data and information, especially on consumer needs and shopping behaviour that can guide innovation, replenishment and merchandising. Therefore with CM, suppliers have to tailor their activities to suit the needs of their retail partners and then develop new joint activities that support both parties.

Heinz has over 50 per cent of the UK soup market with cream of tomato alone taking nearly 15 per cent by value. Because Heinz is the market leader, it is able to play an influential role in soup category management within supermarkets. However through careful information gathering Heinz has been able to develop new product segments. It identified standard soups as replacement items, chunky soups that can serve as a substantial working meal, dietary and low calorie soups for the health segment, premium soups for special occasions, and finally soups that are used as a cooking ingredient. This formed the basis of a category strategy that saw the elimination of some soups and new product introductions in some previously unserviced areas. Heinz worked closely with Safeway stores in building the total soup category which is a major part of its portfolio. Information was shared to cater for strong regional differences in pack sizes, flavours and brands. Careful attention was then paid to the total soup display in stores, the supply chain, using ECR principles, and the promotional activity needed to supplement the refocused ranges. The results benefited both retailer and supplier.

Birds Eye Walls, part of the Unilever group, has used category management for its frozen food and ice cream brands. Shopper research has been undertaken in conjunction with the major retailers using a variety of techniques such as accompanied shopping ,where a shopper's behaviour is observed and questions asked in store, hidden video cameras and eye scanning devices to record how shoppers look at displays, as well as more traditional questioning and purchasing information tracking. From all this information Birds Eye Walls was able to establish different pack conversion rates, those items that built traffic, and how to establish the ideal shelf layout for the category. As part of this process virtual reality (VR) store modelling was used to experiment before layouts were implemented in real stores. Colours, textures, shapes and displays can be changed with VR far more easily than in a real store. This eventually leads to new product concepts and quicker product development. By concentrating on what happens at the point of sale the manufacturer can now communicate with confidence to retailers the most effective ways of increasing total category sales.

Walkers Snack Foods, the Pepsico subsidiary, is a major player in the UK crisp market where 10b packs are sold each year. Year on year growth in 1996 was over 10 per cent. Pepsico favours the term 'Category Development' rather than category management to reflect the dynamic aspects of the process. Its approach is to understand how crisp purchasing as a snack differs. For example it has found differences between the Sainsbury shopper and those using the typical convenience store. In the latter group, crisps are purchased in single packs as a snack between home and work or as a distress purchase. In a supermarket environment, the large ten-pack sells well, as consumers tend to make planned bulk purchases. Using this and other consumer information, Walkers works with the retail stores for product development, improving store presentation and ensuring in the fun food sector that appropriate displays are introduced. In some cases it has found that despite range rationalisation, total category sales have increased between 5 and 15 per cent.

Source: *Category Management: Special Report,* The Grocer *1996: 'Whatever the Definition, It's Got the Consumer at its Core', pp. 4-6. 'Shopping for Soup in Sequence', p. 15. 'From Building Blocks to Virtual Reality', pp. 16-17. 'Walkers' Aim is More Space For Snacks', p. 17.*

Case Assignment Questions

1   **What advantages does the category management approach offer over traditional approaches to product management in the fmcg sector?**

2   **Outline how market research is used to implement a category management approach linking manufacturer and retailer.**

3   **Where a manufacturer is a category leader, to what extent is it worthwhile entertaining a CM approach?**

ROYAL MAIL BY RAIL

There has been for many years in the UK a close relationship between the Royal Mail and the Railway companies, before and after the railways' nationalisation in 1948 and more recently since railway privatisation in the 1990s. Most of the main stations had some mail handling capability, special rolling stock had been built for the mail, and special services operated to ensure timely delivery. From the Royal Mail's, perspective, rail was just one of several transportation alternatives used to ensure next day delivery to any UK destination, regardless of location. To the railway operators, the mail was a valuable source of revenue. In short, it was a typical, mutually beneficial buyer-seller relationship. However in recent years traffic has declined due to a shift to road. In 1988 British Rail operated 200 trains per day to move the mail, but by 1995 it had fallen to just 55. Delays caused by late trains often meant that a next day postal service was not possible. In 1990 only 75 per cent of mail trains arrived on time but since then operating standards have improved to over 90 per cent on time. It was in the interest of both parties to develop a system that provided greater reliability and higher service standards.

In the autumn of 1996, the Royal Mail introduced a new system that involved a £200m investment programme shared between themselves and the railways as part of a revamped Railnet service. The purpose of the Railnet system is to:
- Reduce mail journey times through a faster service with fewer stops
- remove mail handling facilities from congested rail termini in London and large provincial cities
- create fast, dedicated mail trains rather than as attaching them to scheduled passenger services
- improve the reliability of rail transport for mail through quality enhancement and performance assessment. This includes penalties and bonuses against target figures.

The Royal Mail is not without alternative modes of transport. Road transportation predominates. It has been estimated that the addressees of 45 per cent of all letters posted are within the same postal area or within a two hour drive of the sender. Road transport dominates in this sector in the collection, sorting and distribution process. Bulk mail business, accounting for a further 25 per cent of letters is also handled by road. The flexibility of local and direct transportation favours road over rail, for which transhipment would be necessary resulting in extra costs and delays. Air is widely used for international mailings. It is the final segment that is the area for which rail is considered a viable alternative to road. Around 30 per cent of all mail is long distance, with two-thirds of it going by rail and the balance evenly split between air and road. Although rail has the advantages of speed and reliability over road, this must be considered alongside increased time in transhipment to and from mail distribution points. It is not surprising, therefore, to learn that an important part of the £200m Railnet investment programme is to be spent on improving rail mail handling facilities.

The plan for mail distribution centres includes building eight centres that will handle 70 per cent of all rail-borne mail. These centres are strategically located near major urban areas so that there is not only easy access, but also so that certain main stations can be closed to mail traffic. The first three centres are already open, in Willesden (London), Newcastle upon Tyne, and Tonbridge (Kent). Further dedicated centres will be located in such places as Glasgow, Bristol, Doncaster and Warrington. Some passenger stations will continue to handle mail, but they will be adapted to use the containers that are replacing the traditional mail bag. Purpose built buildings have been chosen to enable the introduction of highly automated handling facilities of these containers. The Willesden centre is perhaps a good example. It has easy access to the North Circular road, London's inner ring road. The building's floor area is around 27,000 m2, and it can handle 37 trains and 500 road vehicles per day to enable easier transhipment of around 5,500 containers. This centre now handles 20 per cent of all letters posted in the UK. It is in two parts. The first is for road to road distribution, around 50 per cent of the volume handled, thus enabling some smaller handling facilities to be rationalised. Adjacent to this is the road - rail link area with specially raised platforms for the new mail containers, moveable bridging plates for loading and a large area for container storage. There is also a special conveyor system which delivers trays of letters to the correct loading areas. The total system must offer fast handling of mail is essential, if the performance target of a maximum of thirty minutes transfer time from road to rail or vice versa is to be met.

The second part of the investment programme is the upgrading and introduction of new rolling stock. Travelling Post Offices (TPOs) have long been a feature of the handling and sorting of mail on the railways. Over three hundred railway vans have been converted with roller shutter doors and improved lighting, new control vehicles and, not least, 16 new Class 325 electric multiple units have been introduced to provide a fast, reliable service on electrified lines. The top speed for mail trains is 100mph, although the planned introduction of some new locomotives could raise speeds to 125mph. This could start to give mail the commercial advantage over air on such routes as London to Scotland. All of these investments have been agreed as part of a ten year contract between the Royal Mail and the Rail Express System (RES) for creating the Railnet system. The Royal Mail has invested £150m in the Willesden depot and in buying the dedicated Class 325s, while RES has invested £30m in van and locomotive refurbishment along with special infrastructure just for this contract. The addition of new centres will be paid for by the Royal Mail while the new generation of locomotives will be supplied by RES. However the railway operators should not be complacent now that the contract has been agreed and Royal Mail have invested in large sums of specific use capital. The Dutch Post Office which provided the model to the Royal Mail, is in the process of shifting away from rail, despite setting up similar centres several years ago. After failing to agree on price, plans are now well advanced to shift to all road use in the Netherlands.

Sources: 'Railnet Opens on Time', Modern Railways, November 1996, pp. 705-707; Dasi-Sutton A (1996), 'NS Loses Postal Traffic', Modern Railways, November, p. 709; 'Finetuning the Postal Services' Modern Railways, April 1995, pp. 220-222.

Case Assignment Questions

1   **What factors influence the total cost of the alternative transportation modes for the Royal Mail?**

2   **Outline the main influences on the decision to use rail over road for long haul mail. Why has such a large investment in material handling been necessary?**

3   **Evaluate the decision by Royal Mail to enter into a ten year relationship with RES. What are the likely difficulties and benefits associated with a long term commitment?**

FINE FOODS DESERVE FINE MARKETING

The delicatessen and fine food sector in the UK has become very popular in recent years. In 1995 the market, excluding cheese, was worth £965m, a growth of 9.4 per cent over the previous year. The ethnic segment of that market experienced even higher growth as part of an increased preference for foreign food. Italian foods have particularly benefited from these trends, supported by health claims for Mediterranean food. Sun dried tomatoes from Italy, olives from Spain, charcuterie from Germany and cheese from France give a flavour of the European food sourcing policies of the deli sector. The cheese sector adds a further £1.6b to the deli sector with Cheddar and its variants dominating, with 60 per cent of the market. Given the importance of cheese, it tends to be at the heart of any deli counter, whether in a supermarket or independent retail outlet. The independent delicatessen retailer has traditionally been an important source of specialist and unusual foods, but since the supermarket multiples began to take an interest in delis in the 1980s, the number of independents has declined from 2,400 in 1987 to 1,500 by 1996. The prime role of the independent deli has been to introduce new food types to the market. Many foods such as yoghurt, speciality cheeses, charcuterie, olive oil and mineral water were launched through delis. The interaction between server and customer is important when introducing new products and the independents deliberately encourage customers to ask questions and to seek information. Even in supermarkets, such interaction is important although more limited because of the pressure of customer traffic.

Carluccio's in London is an example of a successful independent deli. The business has been built since 1991 by adapting the product range to suit a specialist niche. Carluccio's offers a wide range of home cooked food, cheeses, unusual cooked meats and bread. Specialist wines and pastas are also available. Other aspects of the retail format include tasting facilities, a clear store layout, the creation of an image of quality and cleanliness, attention to labelling and the provision of in-store education through recipes and information sheets. Carluccio's has also introduced a large range of own-label products. It deliberately sources from small manufacturers who work to traditional methods and recipes associated with their region of Italy. The next phase of its development is to go into wholesale with some of its own brands.

Nevertheless, supermarkets are now the dominant force in the deli and fine food sector. Supermarkets are a difficult market to develop for a small supplier with a new deli line. Specialists foods do not always attract the same attention from supermarket buyers as mainstream volume lines, and to be accepted, buyers have to be assured that a product will generate a mass market appeal. Sometimes dealing with the supermarkets, from a manufacturing perspective, will also have an effect on trade with the independents if they are not keen on stocking lines that are widely available in the multiples. Some manufacturers introduce some minor changes in packaging and display to emphasise differences between brands sold through supermarkets and the independents. The merchandising of fine foods in supermarkets has also developed in recent years. Originally, they were sold through special displays in supermarkets. Now, many fine foods can be found alongside regular brands and only a small selection are offered as special lines. This reflects the increased acceptance of deli and specialist foods as supermarkets increase the variety they offer. Increased press coverage in specialist and general media, along with the impact of television chefs and authors such as Delia Smith, in-store magazines, and speciality restaurants have all played their part in the market's growth and increasing acceptance of new and rediscovered food. Supermarkets capitalise on these interests by offering a carefully selected range of quality products with some personal service to create the sense of speciality and choice without the consumer having to pay excessive prices. The deli counter retains the personal touch in an otherwise impersonal retail environment.

Manufacturers have helped supermarkets in the growth process. Lazenby's quality sausages are sold loose on the deli counter or prepacked in the chilled section. The company recently launched a Deli 2000 deli display scheme where sausages are displayed under thin transparent plastic to keep them fresh and protected from strong supermarket lighting, while making them visible to the consumer. This builds upon the consumer perception that if a product is loose and on the deli counter it must be fresher, suiting those preferring a more traditional way of buying than pre-packed convenience. Edgmond Foods produce a range of baked quiche, savoury pies, real fruit pies and desserts, either chilled or frozen. The company offers a wide variety and is prepared to supply ready cut and packed foods, or even own-label products if wanted in order to service the main supermarkets. Visual appeal is again important with pies, and advice and information is given to the supermarkets to ensure freshness in display and knowledgeable assistants who can answer consumer queries about content. Edgmond has focused on flexibility in handling small orders alongside larger volume sales.

Overall, therefore, the independent deli sector has managed to survive alongside supermarkets due to high levels of customer service, unusual and new products along with in-store personalised advice. The range of products they offer tends to be wider than the supermarkets but the number of customers is much smaller. The supermarkets rely on their general customer pulling power and use the deli sector to build sales and to enhance overall perceived quality for the store. Manufacturers have to plot a distribution strategy to build a share in this growing market.

Sources: The Grocer (1995a), 'Doing the Continental', The Grocer, 28 October, pp. 55-56; The Grocer (1995b), 'Who Serves the Independents?', The Grocer, 28 October, pp 60; The Grocer (1996a), 'The Gourmet's Guide to Getting into the Multiples', The Grocer, 26 October, pp. 60-62; The Grocer (1996b), 'A Question of Taste', The Grocer, 26 October, pp. 49-52; The Grocer (1996c), 'Cashing in on the Latest Trends', The Grocer, 26 October, p. 66.

Case Assignment Questions

1   How have the independents managed to survive alongside the powerful retail multiples?

2   How and why does the role of personal selling for fine foods differ between the independents and the multiples?

3   What promotional strategies should a small supplier of deli foods adopt in order to increase sales through the retail multiples? Are the retail multiples the best outlets for small suppliers?

4   To what extent are suppliers able to create demand in the deli/fine food sector rather than just responding to existing tastes?

POWER GENERATION

The power engineering industry has become highly competitive in the 1990s as manufacturers have fought to retain share in a market with increasing spare capacity. A growth in capacity was fuelled in the 1990s by optimism that the market would continue to grow. The prospect of supplying new power stations in China, the new independent power producers in the west, and developing countries encouraged major new investment. The pace of new orders, while increasing, did not achieve the expectations of the six world-scale integrated manufacturers. They were forced into heavy competition and price wars in order to protect share. In the three years up to 1996 prices fell by 30 per cent in a market growing by between 2 and 4 per cent per annum. The power engineering business is an international business in demand and supply. The big six suppliers are Westinghouse (USA), General Electric (USA), Siemens (Germany), GEC Alsthom (UK-France), Mitsubishi (Japan), and ABB (Sweden-Switzerland). Smaller manufacturers and non-specialists tend to occupy narrow niches. Although manufacturing costs have been falling for all suppliers due to efficiency gains, job losses, rationalisation and closure have also taken place. The savings have largely been passed onto the customer in order to remain competitive. Steam turbine manufacturing capacity has remained at around 70,000MW per year, but gas turbines has been growing rapidly, with a 70 per cent increase in capacity between 1990 and 1994 to a level of 36,000MW per year. Unfortunately, despite growing sales, only 30,000MW of gas turbine capacity was sold. Nuclear plants offer very mixed prospects with no more plants planned at present in western Europe.

The future prospects for the industry will be determined in the next few years by the speed with which the developing countries invest in new power plant. Estimates have suggested that the installed power plant capacity will need to rise by 60 per cent by 2010, or 1,750,000MW of orders, with preliminary proposals already exceeding 1m MW from China, India, Indonesia and other developing countries. The difficulty for suppliers is spotting those proposals that will be frustrated through lack of funds and those that will be commissioned. There is a danger in cultivating the wrong potential customers.

With large scale projects, often purchased by governments or their agents, most suppliers chase the available business. Prices need to be very competitive and other conditions are sometimes imposed, such as with the Chinese insisting on associated technology transfer and some work being undertaken in China. The integrated suppliers have adopted different strategies over and above cost cutting to strengthen their international market position. Westinghouse has agreed a joint venture with the Shanghai Electric corporation, China's largest power plant manufacturer, as a means of developing a stronger base in China and the Far East. Other suppliers see the future in working more closely with customers. Siemens has invested in private power plants in order to gain business. It has been estimated that around 30 per cent of its orders include some kind of associated investment deal. The after sales market has also attracted increased attention as a means of compensating for squeezed margins on capital sales. Using computer technologies a number of power stations' turbines and equipment can be monitored simultaneously to assist preventative maintenance rather than waiting for breakdowns. . Serving and renovation now account for half of General Electric's sales compared with one-third a few years ago. At ABB the figure is 20 per cent but it is regarded as a major growth area. Although the large suppliers find greater competition from smaller, more flexible service companies concerned with power plant maintenance, the large suppliers have the advantage of technological know how and international experience. The after sales area also provides the opportunity to work more closely with plant operators which can then lead to future sales. The impact of ever-changing technology and demands by independent operators for raised service levels have all encouraged far more involvement by suppliers in plant management rather than just equipment supply.

Within the market environment context described above, ABB, the Swedish-Swiss engineering group has pursued a policy of active development in eastern Europe to build its competitive strength. Through a programme of acquisitions, it has over 60 companies in central Europe and the former Soviet Union. The main advantages have been the integration of low cost suppliers offering around 40 per cent cost savings on turbines and switch gear compared with the west. Standards are comparable through technology transfer in machine tools, computer programmes, technical drawings etc and the installation of new quality assurance systems. Training is a fundamental part of the development process. It has been very selective in its acquisitions to ensure a close fit with ABB interests. Zamech was Poland's only turbine maker and Dolmel the largest generator manufacturer. Similar purchases have been made elsewhere in central Europe, such as a power engineering complex in Brno in the Czech Republic and Ust' Kamenogorsk in Kazakhstan. Other operations in associated power engineering industries have been developed in Croatia, Bulgaria, Ukraine and Russia. One new company has been added each month in the former Soviet Union to the ABB portfolio.

The logic behind these acquisitions is the long term aim to have a strong position in power engineering in these countries where many power stations will need to be replaced over the next ten years. For the remainder of the 1990s, the priority will be refitting and upgrading of existing plant and completing projects that were mothballed due to a lack of funds. When western funds are being used for power station improvement to overcome ecological problems or as part of reconstruction aid, the central European governments are expected to use western suppliers capable of meeting exacting specifications. Orders from the region grew for ABB from $225m in 1990 to $1.65b in 1994 with expectations of achieving over $3bn by the year 2000, around 8 per cent of total group sales. At that stage over 20 per cent of output is expected to be exported from the region, but the rest will be for the central European and former Soviet Union markets. Interestingly, in a period when labour has been reduced by 16,000 in western Europe, it has increased in central Europe by 30,000 due to the acquisitions. The total cost of the acquisitions has been estimated as $300m, far lower than would be paid in the west. With the lower cost base, ABB has been able to gain international market share despite the tough competition and aggressive pricing.

There are risks in pursuing such an eastern European expansion strategy in the sometimes chaotic and unstable emerging economies. The infrastructure is poor in places, economic climate unstable and the level of workforce skill low in some areas. There is a premium on training managers and technicians along with new investment to replace outdated equipment. ABB insists on one group quality standard, regardless of source of production. Often marketing skills are found to be non-existent due to the previous over-reliance on planned orders from government rather than having to fight in the open market. Some mistakes have been made. One joint venture agreement in Moscow collapsed when ABB found that its new partner was involved in organised crime.

Sources: Wagstyl S (1996a), 'Woven into the Fabric', Financial Times, 10 Jan, p. 15. Wagstyl S (1996b), 'Under Pressure to Get Together', Financial Times, 3 Jun, p. 19. Robinson A (1996), 'Survey: Power Generating Equipment: Demand is Still Rising Rapidly', Financial Times, 26 Jun, p. 3. Wagstyl S (1996c), 'Power Generating Equipment: Intense Competition Squeezes Margins', Financial Times, 26 Jun, p. 8. Wagstyl S (1996d), 'Power Generating Equipment: Better Profits to be Made', Financial Times, 26 Jun p. 4.

Case Assignment Questions

1   **What competitive strategies are the power generating suppliers adopting and why?**

2   **Assess the impact of the main environmental forces affecting the industry.**

3   **Evaluate the strategic marketing decision and market entry strategy adopted by ABB in developing the central European market.**

4   **What are the typical problems that would face any supplier seeking to penetrate the emerging economies of central Europe?**

CHINA'S FLYING HIGH INTO THE FUTURE

Because of the Chinese government's efforts to improve China's industrial infrastructure to make it one of the leading economic forces in the world, the air transport sector has been given particular attention. Domestic air travel is increasing at one of the fastest rates in the world and further expansion is only limited by the capability of the air traffic control system to handle more flights, especially in the Beijing-Guangzhou-Shanghai regions. This growth, however, along with potential in the wider far eastern market has encouraged China to make a serious effort to enter the civil passenger jet market. Aircraft production in China is not new. From early beginnings in 1951 in Nanchang, it has been estimated that over 10,000 aircraft have been produced for military and commercial applications such as crop dusting. However, in the passenger jet market many of the well known manufacturers are represented in China Airlines' fleet, such as Boeing with its 737s and 747s.

It is now the intention of the Chinese government to enter the civil passenger jet market with a view to becoming a world class player during the 21st century. The route they have chosen is to seek a strategic alliance with an experienced western partner which would value a co-operative effort. This reflects the need to acquire expertise and know-how to implement the planned development programme seriously. In the past, the Ministry of Aerospace was responsible for aircraft production, but around 75 per cent of its output went to such diverse activities as buses and motorbikes. Most aerospace activities were focused on defence products.

A three part development programme is planned to transform the industry under a new state owned enterprise, Aviation Industries of China (AVIC). The stages are:
1. Production under licence of 20 McDonnell Douglas (MDC) MD 90-30 Trunk Liners.
2. Development of a 120 seat regional jet, the AE-100.
3. Development of a full range of planes in a number of sectors.

The first phase, which has already started, enables engineers to gain experience of manufacturing to strict international standards where quality is everything. Without such experience they could not hope to progress further. Another aspect of this co-operation is that it allows the Chinese to build a subcontract component sector that could encourage specialisation to the same exacting standards. MDC is happy to co-operate with this venture as it provides it with a platform for strengthening its position in the growing Chinese market.

The second phase is currently under negotiation and has interested a number of potential partners. The AE-100 is especially important to the Chinese as it means they can influence the design of the aircraft, rather than accepting another's design, as with the MD-90s. However they cannot do it alone in design, development and production. They must select partners from interested parties and learn from the partner's experience. The involvement in the total process will mean that in time an engineering capability and trained workforce will be make the Chinese better able to manage their own development in the third and final part of their programme. There are other reasons for joining with another company or consortium. The world market is dominated by the big three, MDC, Boeing and Airbus Industrie. It is easier to work with one than against all three!

However in the short term they must have the technical and commercial expertise of a major western partner. They are prepared to offer a significant minority stake in the venture around 40 per cent. The Chinese would take 45 per cent and the balance would go to a Singaporian company STAe for software development. Four players emerged as front runners: Daimler-Benz, with its interest in Fokker development; MDC with a similar proposal to the planned MD-95; Boeing, building on its expertise with 737s; AI (Asia). This is a consortium of European suppliers which includes Aerospatiale and BAe who are also members of Airbus Industrie. It thus offers a route into the Airbus family. A key factor in the selection decision was the commitment that the different players were thought to have to a genuinely new aircraft that could compete in world wide markets. This effectively eliminated Daimler-Benz because of the Fokker, MDC due to the MD-95 and finally Boeing. The Chinese did not want to become highly dependent on these companies in the long term for parts or patents. Instead, they wanted an alliance with a player who also wanted to develop its range in world markets in which it currently had no 100 seater plane. The AI (Asia) bid was accepted as a means of drawing on innovative European aerospace technology and more specifically to gain access, subject to the European partners' approval, to Airbus technology.

The Chinese were hopeful that by building an alliance with the European Airbus family, the AE-100 would fill a gap in Airbus' current product range, as Airbus' smallest plane is the A319, a 124 seater. Such a move could be critical for the next stages of Chinese development as it provides access to all the experience, marketing and after sales support that has accompanied the success of Airbus. Complex and high level negotiations are currently ongoing between all the partners. If an agreement is reached, China could build the wings and undertake final assembly, while Europe would concentrate on the fuselage and cockpit work and STAe would focus on the electrical, pneumatic and auxiliary power units' electronic integration. All sides would have to agree the final specification, thus providing useful exposure to new technological options for Chinese engineers. Part of the agreement was also planned to be a technology transfer and training package of $250m to enable local production to international standards in China.

There are, however, already problems within the potential alliance. There are major differences between AVIC and AI (Asia) over several design areas. China is keen to build the AE-100 in three variants, a 90-100 seater, a 115-120 seater, and finally a 135-140 seater, through different fuselage lengths. The latter category pitches the extended AE-100 right into the Airbus A319 market, creating the potential for cannibalisation and competition, rather than a complementary range. AVIC is arguing that it is targeting a different market and different seating configuration. The first planes are expected in 2002 with the 120 seater and 100 seater models. The stretched version, the subject of controversy, is planned for 2006, about the same time as Airbus might be considering replacing the A319. The stakes are high for all parties in a growing world market previously dominated by the American giants. With a world market predicted by AVIC of 3,000 aircraft similar to the AE-100 by 2015, and plans to capture one-third of that including 400 planned sales in China alone, the project, when finally agreed could be a powerful influence on future passenger jet market shares. Interestingly, Boeing has outsold MDC in China, despite the local licensing agreement, showing that local supply may not be the only factor influencing the buying decisions of national and independent airlines in China.

Sources: Lewis P (1996a), 'The Long March', Flight International, 6-12 November, pp. 29-30; Lewis P (1996b), 'Forging New Bonds', Flight International, 6-12 November, pp. 32-33; 'AVIC and AIA Discuss Extended-range AE-100', Flight International, 6-12 November 1996, p. 5.

Case Assignment Questions

1   Assess the benefits to both AVIC and AI (Asia) of the proposed alliance.

2   What, in general, are likely to be the management and marketing problems faced by such an alliance, and how might they be overcome?

3   MDC and Boeing both lost out in the battle to become AVIC's partner in phase 2, the development of the AE-100. How might this affect their future in the Chinese market?